POLITICAL CHANGE IN THE METROPOLIS

JOHN J. HARRIGAN
Hamline University

POLITICAL CHANGE IN THE METROPOLIS

LITTLE, BROWN AND COMPANY
Boston   Toronto

To
Louise and
Kevin, Patrick, and Timothy
For being there

JS
422
, H33

PREFACE

Three secular changes have occurred in the organization of political power in United States cities during the past century. First, beginning in the 1840s and extending to the 1930s, a new category of urban political elites was created, built around ethnic, sociological, and geographical bases of organizing power. These new elites did not necessarily replace the older, upper-class patrician elites; rather these diverse elites came to coexist side by side in the cities. Second, beginning in the 1930s effective urban political power was increasingly organized along functional lines rather than geographic and ethnic lines. This change was a consequence of other developments such as industrialization, the transformation of the economy from dominance by local firms to dominance by national corporations and institutions, the Great Depression, the New Deal, and unionization. Finally, since the middle 1960s the urban role of the federal government has undergone major alterations. Not only has the federal government massively expanded the amount of dollars spent, but there has also been increasing concern about coordinating the several hundred domestic programs under the guidance of a general framework which could be called a national urban policy. Such a policy has not yet been achieved.

As these secular changes occurred, they altered the *patterns of biases* inherent in the organization and operation of governments. By the term *bias* it is meant that governmental arrangements are not always neutral. Government actions benefit some people and injure the interests of other people. For example, although certain kinds of upward social mobility may have been possible under the ethnic and geographic organization of urban political power, they are no longer possible now that these bases for organizing power have diminished. And, conversely, certain kinds of social action that would have been fruitless during the era of ethnic and geographic organization of power are now potentially fruitful.

How changes can affect the biases of government is well exemplified by the financial crisis of New York City in 1975, a crisis that is likely to bring about subtle but important changes in New York politics and that has implications for cities throughout the country. New York City government was beleaguered by a complex of problems that included rapidly increasing costs to pay for heavily demanded public services and

v

programs, wage increases that would enable the hundreds of thousands of city employees to keep pace with or possibly stay in front of high inflation rates, and increasing interest payments needed to finance the city's rapidly growing debt. In the face of these increased costs, the city government's revenues and tax base were limited by the flight of businesses and middle-class families out of the city to the suburbs. For several years preceding the 1975 crisis, city government expenditures exceeded government revenues. And a series of mayors solved the problem of unbalanced budgets by taking out short-term loans. By mid-1975 the cumulative total of these short-term loans exceeded $3 billion.

The crisis developed when Mayor Abraham Beame presented the following year's $11 billion budget that was $640 million out of balance. A Municipal Assistance Corporation (called "Big Mac") was created to float long-term bonds that would replace the city's burdensome short-term debt. But the bankers were either unwilling or unable to sell the Big Mac bonds. As the city pared back its expenses by laying off fire, police, sanitation, and public school personnel, the public employees' unions balked. The fire fighters called sick-ins. Garbage went uncollected. Schools failed to open on time when the teachers struck. And the police association tried to circulate leaflets that labeled New York "Fear City." In order to make the Big Mac bonds saleable, the Municipal Assistance Corporation was given the power to review and limit the city's budget. The mayor was stripped of important budget-making powers. Large cutbacks were made in public services, especially those for poor and lower-middle-income persons. The loss of confidence in New York's financial competence may well impel the government to adopt a very cautious posture in providing future public services. But limiting the budgetary powers of the mayor and cutting back on services have not altered the fundamental problems which drove New York to the edge of bankruptcy in the first place.

New York's financial plight may be the most extreme in the nation and it may not be typical of most cities, but the fundamental political forces, changes, and biases behind New York's problem exist in cities throughout the nation. The main task of this book is to examine in detail the major changes which have occurred, which are occurring, and which are likely to occur over the next decade in the governance of metropolitan America, and to analyze the patterns of bias which accompany these changes.

The basic changes in the character of urban United States and the political implications of these changes are described in Chapter 2. This chapter provides the key definitions and descriptions of the urbanization process that are basic to understanding urban politics.

Chapters 3 and 4 focus on the rise and atrophy of ethnic-based political power, especially during the age of the political machines. A major factor in the decline of machine politics was the municipal progressive reform movement of the early twentieth century. The impact of this movement and the biases which it introduced into urban politics are presented near the close of Chapter 4.

Chapter 5 continues the examination of the bias implications of the reform movement. It examines the functional organization of power and its effects on the poor and the newer urban minorities. Finally, it examines community control as a proposal to counteract these bias implications.

Chapter 6 moves the focus of the book away from the central city as such to the broader political questions of the metropolis. First, some common beliefs about suburbia are examined for their accuracy. Then, the nature of suburban politics is described as leading to the emergence of a politically multi-centered metropolis. Finally, the consequences and biases of the multi-centered metropolis are examined.

Chapters 7 and 8 describe the strategic attempts to cope with the consequences of the multi-centered metropolis. These strategies are classified into two categories. The first category consists of strategies that seek to cope with the consequences of the multi-centered metropolis through a framework that would provide a limited form of governance in the metropolis without requiring a general-purpose metropolitan government as such. These strategies and their biases are examined in Chapter 7. The strategies in the second category, on the contrary, seek to scrap the whole existing system of governance in the multi-centered metropolis and create new, general-purpose governments at the metropolitan level. These strategies and their biases are discussed in Chapter 8. Most attempts to implement these latter strategies have failed, however, and the reasons for this failure are analyzed in Chapter 9.

Given the very limited scope of the kinds of governmental changes discussed in Chapter 7 and the unattainability of the more extensive governmental changes discussed in Chapter 8, proponents of metropolitan government are faced with a seemingly irresolvable dilemma. On the one hand, the changes they seek to attain (that is, the strategies to scrap the whole system) are too far-reaching to be acceptable. On the other hand, the changes that are acceptable (that is, piecemeal strategies that adapt to the consequences of the multi-centered metropolis) are not very far-reaching. The result of this dilemma has been a continuation of the kinds of evolutionary, incremental changes which have been characteristic of the American political system. These changes and their biases are analyzed in Chapter 10.

Chapter 11 analyzes the changing role of the federal government in urban politics. First, the inadequacies and biases of federal housing and highway programs are examined. Second, an investigation is made of how growing discontent with these and other programs has led toward demands for federal revenue sharing and the formulation of a national urban policy. The federal revenue-sharing proposals of the Nixon administration are evaluated for their implications and their biases.

Chapter 12 provides a comparative context for metropolitan policy making in the United States by analyzing the urban growth policies of England, France, and Brazil. Through presentation and evaluation of these policies, a broader perspective is created for the purpose of viewing the demands that the United States, too, establish a national urban growth policy.

Chapter 13 offers several speculations on the political changes that are likely to occur over the next two decades if present trends persist. Of greatest importance are the implications which present trends have for altering or not altering the current patterns of political bias in the American metropolis.

Finally, Chapter 14 presents a general summary of the major urban changes and the political biases related to them.

The main encouragement to organize this analysis around the bias of urban political structures and changes came primarily from Peter Eisinger of the University of Wisconsin. For this and for his copious criticisms of several drafts of the manuscript I am deeply indebted. I am also deeply indebted to Jeffrey L. Pressman of the Massachusetts Institute of Technology, who read several drafts of the manuscript and gave me the benefit of his insights. For reading and criticizing the entire manuscript and giving me the benefit of their suggestions, I am deeply grateful to Willis D. Hawley of Duke University, Jesse J. McCorry of Washington University, Francine F. Rabinovitz of the University of California-Los Angeles, Frederick M. Wirt of the University of Illinois, Allan P. Sindler of the University of California-Berkeley, and Milda Hedbloom of Augsburg College. The following persons read portions of the manuscript and graciously gave me their suggestions: James Lynskey, Leigh Kagan, and Walter Benjamin of Hamline University and Todd Lefko of the University of Minnesota. To all of these people I owe an enormous debt for alerting me to errors and misinterpretations that were in the text and for providing excellent bibliographic guidance. All viewpoints and any errors or misinterpretations which may exist in the book are my responsibility. Hamline University librarians Thomas Gaughan, Tinna Wu, Susan Job, and Patricia Tether were most graciously helpful. I would like to express gratitude to Rick Boyer of Little, Brown and Company for keeping faith in this project and for all the other help which he provided. My gratitude also goes to Madelon Cassavant for her typing assistance on the many drafts of the manuscript. The research for Chapter 12 was conducted in part with financial assistance from Hamline University and the Center for Latin America at the University of Wisconsin-Milwaukee.

Most importantly, I wish to express my appreciation to Louise Harrigan, my wife, for her encouragement throughout this long endeavor and to our children, Kevin, Patrick, and Timothy, for being there.

CONTENTS

PART III

COPING WITH THE CONSEQUENCES OF
THE MULTI-CENTERED METROPOLIS

PART 1

As background to Political Change in the Metropolis, it is necessary to introduce the basic concepts of change and bias as they are used in this book and to outline the major features of the metropolitanization process in the United States. This is accomplished in the following two introductory chapters.

Chapter 1 discusses the inherent bias of political organization and introduces the primary theme of this book: that changes in the organization of political power in American metropolises have had profound consequences on the groups and individuals that either benefit by or are hurt by the operations of urban governments. Three secular changes have occured in American urban politics. First, beginning in the 1840s the European immigrants, through ma-

METROPOLITANIZATION AND THE DEVELOPMENT OF URBAN POLITICS: AN INTRODUCTION

chine and ethnic-based politics, created a number of urban institutions which gave them influence and power in city politics. Second, beginning in the 1930s and continuing with growing momentum in the post–World War II period, the expansion of governmental services and activities led to the organization of political influence on a functional basis rather than on the ethnic and geographic bases which had predominated in the earlier era. Finally, beginning in the late 1960s with the rapid expansion of federal programs, the growing concern for coordinating and controlling these various functionally organized governmental programs, and the increasing concern for regulating future metropolitan growth, a third, contemporary secular change has been occurring in urban politics. This contemporary change is characterized by a stronger role of the federal government, an effort to coordinate various federal programs, and a concern for subordinating policy-making bodies to new, metropolitan-level institutions. Some of the implications of these changes are discussed in Chapter 1.

Chapter 2 defines some basic concepts of urbanization, explains why and how America urbanized, and examines the political biases which have accompanied urbanization and metropolitanization in the United States.

1

Chapter 1

Urban political structures and processes are not expected to be neutral. When changes are proposed in urban political structures and processes, some groups of people expect to benefit from the changes. Others expect to be harmed by them.

ITEM: When civil service reforms were introduced in municipal politics before the turn of the century, ethnic political leaders objected vigorously. Civil service would destroy their access to political jobs and political influence, they charged. According to George Washington

Bias and Change in Metropolitan Politics

Plunkitt, Tammany Hall's most articulate spokesman, civil service was the "Curse of the Nation."[1]

ITEM: More than half a century later, when proposals for metropolitan government were put forward in places such as Cleveland, Saint Louis, Indianapolis, and Miami, many black people objected vigorously. Metropolitan government would dilute the voting potential of blacks in central cities and diminish the access of black leaders to political decision makers, they charged.[2]*

ITEM: In the contemporary metropolis, there has been widespread resistance to attempts to equalize opportunities for housing by allowing decisions on zoning or site location of public housing to be made at levels of government higher than the local municipality or county. In

---

* In some other metropolises, such as Jacksonville, Florida, and Nashville, Tennessee, the proponents of metropolitan reform were able to secure black support by offering special concessions to black leaders and the black communities.

metropolis after metropolis, attempts to distribute federally sponsored low-income public housing evenly throughout the metropolitan areas have run into adamant opposition. By the mid-1970s, the over-whelming majority of all low-income public housing in metropolitan areas was still found in central cities.* In many metropolises, public housing and redevelopment authorities do not even have authority to operate in the suburbs.

ITEM: When attempts were made to equalize access to public educa-tion by bussing public school children across school attendance bound-aries for the purpose of achieving racial balance, these attempts were bitterly resisted. In Flint, Michigan, school buses were tipped over and burned to prevent desegregation. In South Boston, attempts to enforce federal-court-ordered bussing to achieve racial desegregation led to violent opposition.

These examples of urban politics span almost a century. In spite of the great time period they bridge, they illustrate and serve to introduce several common themes of American urban politics. First, in all in-stances, the political participants expected that a major change in gov-ernmental structure, boundaries, or decision-making process would produce policy changes that would be biased either for or against them. Second, the more recent examples involved not only the central cities but the suburbs, the metropolitan-level structures of government, and the federal government. Contemporary politics of the central city and the entire metropolis are intertwined, not separate. Third, in all in-stances the key issues at stake involved changes either in the channels through which people would have political access to key decision makers, or in their direct social access to important amenities of urban life such as quality housing and education. Fourth, the latter examples indicate that the federal government is emerging as a key participant in urban and metropolitan politics. It profoundly influences public deci-sions on matters such as housing and education which used to be thought of as exclusively local prerogatives. An understanding of these themes of bias and change in urban and metropolitan politics is essen-tial to understanding the metropolis itself, how it functions, and what its chances are of progressing beyond the contemporary stage of seem-ingly permanent crisis.

* Data for the entire United States are very sketchy. But in one representative metropoli-tan area (Minneapolis–Saint Paul), of 14,500 public housing units existing as of January 1973, over 90 percent were located in the central cities. [Metropolitan Council of the Twin Cities Area, *Metropolitan Development Guide: Housing; Policy, Plan, Program* (Saint Paul, Minn.: Metropolitan Council, June 1973), p. 16.]

THE BIAS OF POLITICAL ORGANIZATION

In all the examples of proposals for change cited earlier (civil service reforms, the introduction of metropolitan government, the making of housing and zoning decisions at levels above the local government, and the use of bussing to desegregate schools), the people involved in the changes which were about to occur fully expected that modification of the political structures and processes would either benefit them or hurt them. The governmental structures were not expected to be politically neutral; they were expected to be biased in terms of the interests and policy directions they would favor or disfavor. A major objective of this book is to examine whether these people were correct in their basic assumption that there is an inherent bias in the organization of political and governmental power in metropolitan America. The chapters that follow will investigate the hypothesis that such a bias does exist.

Political bias, as that term is used here, does not necessarily imply that the political actors are purposely and consciously biased for or against given groups of people. It does imply, as political scientist Harold Lasswell has argued, that the political process itself in some measure determines *who* gets *what* political or economic benefits, *when* they get them, and *how* they get them.[3] Political bias in metropolis, then, involves two questions. Who benefits from the ongoing political structure and process in the metropolis? And who pays the cost of those benefits? These political biases can occur either in the input into the political decision-making process or in the policy outcomes that result.[4]

In exploring the hypothesis of political bias, one must distinguish between the bias of specific actions on the one hand, and, on the other hand, the patterns of bias that underlie a series of actions. In practice, *any* specific *major* action of an urban government brings disproportionate benefits to some people and disproportionate costs to other people. In this sense all actions are biased. There is no absolutely fair way to apportion the costs and benefits of specific governmental actions. What is fair to one person may be unfair to another. For example, upgrading the pay levels of public school teachers has generally resulted in sharp increases in property taxes throughout the school districts of most metropolises. From the point of view of upper-middle-class parents, the increased quality of their children's schools may well have been worth the increased costs in property taxes. By contrast, many senior citizens, who may have neither children nor grandchildren living in those school districts, quite often deeply resent the increased property taxes. However, since all actions have some bias, the bias of *individual government actions* is not nearly so important as the *patterns of bias* that may or may not occur in many metropolises. Patterns of bias are indicated when some groups are systematically excluded from the governmental decision-making process and their interests systematically neglected by governmental policy outcomes. Are some groups or categories of people systematically disadvantaged or ignored or hurt by the nature of the urban political process? And conversely, do some other people systematically benefit from the same process?

The most obvious examples of persistent patterns of bias in both input and output are those of public housing and urban renewal.[5] Semi-autonomous urban renewal agencies (generically called local public agencies — LPAs) were created to carry out the objectives of federal housing acts that date back to 1937. The urban renewal provisions were initiated in the Federal Housing Act of 1949 and subsequent amendments, particularly those of 1954. The urban renewal program enabled an LPA to use federal funds to buy property in a blighted area, clear the land of existing buildings, and sell the cleared land at a reduced price to private redevelopers who, at a profit, constructed a mix of housing and commercial enterprises on the sites. This program was a compromise between conservative Republicans (such as Senator Robert Taft, who insisted that the program rely on private redevelopers) and liberal Democrats (such as Senator Robert Wagner, who insisted that a federal role be maintained in providing public housing).

Since the program came into effect, some of its persistent net effects in most cities have been to reduce the total amount of housing available to racial minorities, to reduce the number of independent small retail shop owners and to rebuild central business districts and other commercial areas of central cities. The poor and the minority groups suffered a decline in housing supply. Owners of small, marginal businesses were forced out of business. And middle-class payers of federal income taxes absorbed most of the costs without receiving many of the benefits. The beneficiaries were primarily the large construction and financial interests who profited from the redevelopment construction contracts and some of the larger commercial interests who saw some of their smaller competitors removed from the redevelopment neighborhood.

Not only has there been a persistent bias to the policy outputs, but there has also been a persistent bias in the inputs into the decision-making process. LPAs are structured and organized in ways which make it difficult for elected officials in most cities to exercise much control over them. Nor do either the middle-class taxpayers or the displaced poor have much influence on the urban renewal decisions. The most influence is exercised by bureaucrats in the federal agencies and the local LPAs and the major banking and real estate developers interested in bidding for the construction contracts. Thus, there has been a very obvious pattern to the bias not only of the urban renewal programs themselves, but of the governmental structures which organized power in such a way as to make the urban renewal programs so autonomous.

THE NATURE OF CHANGE IN METROPOLITAN POLITICS

Closely related to the bias of political structures and processes are the changes that occur in the ways of organizing power in the metropolis. As political change has occurred in the United States, one of its most marked features has been its evolutionary nature.[6] Some political analysts believe that changes in the American political system historically have been evolutionary, incremental, and marginal. That is, there has never been a revolutionary overthrow of the class structure of the society or a widespread disavowal of the sanctity of private ownership of the major economic institutions. One political scientist, Kenneth Dolbeare, argues that even the Civil War and the Reconstruction, which destroyed slavery and set the stage for the far-reaching Fourteenth Amendment to the Constitution, did not provoke fundamental political change in the United States.[7] In Dolbeare's view, all political change in this country has been marginal and has left intact the basic socioeconomic structure of the nation. Most political changes have also been interdependent with socioeconomic changes.[8] As the nation's population has become increasingly metropolitan, for example, and as the nation's economy has become dominated by nationally based corporations rather than locally based proprietorships, there have been political reactions to these changes. To cope with the increasingly metropolitan population, the amount of governance in metropolitan areas increased markedly.* And to cope with the transition from a regionally based to a

* One feature of metropolitanization has been a continuing proliferation in the number of governments in metropolitan areas. By 1972 there were a total of 22,185 governments in the 264 officially designated metropolitan areas (SMSAs) of the United States, an average of eighty-four governments to each metropolis. The proliferation of governments and its political implications are discussed in Chapters 6 and 7.

nationally based economy, the regulatory capacity of government, particularly of the federal government, increased markedly. Much of this change, however, in the view of political scientist Murray Edelman, has been *symbolic* rather than *substantive;* for example, the increase in regulatory capacity has been primarily a symbolic change that diverts popular attention away from making drastic, substantive changes in the distribution of power and wealth.[9] Political changes, in this view, normally focus on the symbols of power and seldom touch the substance of power.

These very perceptive insights have much applicability to metropolitan politics. In applying them, however, the student should be careful not to confuse change with instability. Some political systems can undergo rapid changes in the admission of new elites, such as following an election, and yet remain quite stable in terms of the class structure, the tenure of governments, and the widespread acceptance of common, underlying political and cultural values of the society.[10] This seems to have been the pattern in the United States. Some other political systems become quite unstable precisely because they are not able to tolerate political changes that would admit new elites into the political decision-making process.* Thus, it may well be that continuous, incremental, evolutionary change leads to political stability and forestalls the need for drastic revolutionary change. It may be that change which allows emerging sectors in the society to share symbolically and vicariously in the exercise of power also enables the elites of these emerging sectors to be co-opted into the decision-making elite structure and thus forestalls any need either to overthrow the structure or to bring about major redistribution of wealth.

In the American metropolises, political change has also occurred in an incremental, not a revolutionary, fashion. But this is change, nonetheless. For example, Tammany Hall was not destroyed overnight. But eventually, its tight control over New York City government, as it existed under Boss Tweed and some of his successors, was destroyed. And the destruction of this control helped make a significant difference in how New York City is governed and who benefits from this governance.[11]

---

* In many Latin American countries, for example, the lack of change in admitting new elites into the political decision-making process seems to have been one of the major causes of political instability. See Karl M. Schmitt and David D. Burks, *Evolution or Chaos: Dynamics of Latin American Government Politics* (New York: Praeger, 1963), chapter 6, "Political Dynamics"; Claudio Veliz, *Obstacles to Change in Latin America* (New York: Oxford University Press, 1969); and Seymour Martin Lipset and Aldo Solari, *Elites in Latin America* (New York: Oxford University Press, 1969).

The evolutionary nature of metropolitan political change can be seen in the historical development of political power in American cities. Three distinct evolutionary changes can be discerned. First, roughly coterminous with the age of political machines and extensive European immigration, there was an evolution of political power that was ethnically and geographically based. (This evolution is described in considerable detail in Chapter 3.) Prior to 1830, political power in many American cities was controlled by very small circles of economic elites that were labeled variously as patrician, Brahmin, Yankee, Bourbon, or (much later) WASP (White Anglo-Saxon Protestant).* The members of these elites typically belonged to the higher-status Protestant churches in their localities. They viewed with considerable distrust both the egalitarian principles of Jacksonian Democracy and the Catholic European immigrants who stood to benefit from these principles. From the 1830s until at least the end of the century, there was a steady evolution in the political influence of these European ethnic groups. Much of their political influence was founded on indigenous institutional power bases developed within the ethnic communities. The institutions that formed the base for their indigenous power remained the dominant urban political institutions up to the 1930s. The major institutions thus created were the political machines, the urban organization of the Catholic church dioceses, organized crime, certain labor unions, and certain sectors of business. In many instances, the institutions are still influential in today's metropolitan politics, although they are seldom dominant.

The second evolutionary change began with the progressive reform movement at the turn of the century and reached its zenith between the 1940s and the late 1960s. The evolutionary change during this period was the emergence of political organization *on a functional base* as distinguished from the ethnic and geographic base of the earlier period. Within given functional areas, public bureaucracies and private interests developed. In public education, for example, the top administrators in the school systems, the teachers' unions, the superintendents' offices, and the state departments of education came to dominate public education and diminish the effective control of the boards of education — the elected public officials.[12] In public safety a similar phenomenon occurred. The police bureaucracies, the policemen's associations, and conservative citizens' groups concerned with law and order served

---

* This was true particularly in the South and in New England. It was much less true in the newer cities of the Midwest and the West. See Peter H. Rossi and Alice S. Rossi, "An Historical Perspective on the Functions of Local Politics," in *Social Change and Urban Politics*, ed. Daniel N. Gordon (Englewood Cliffs, N.J.: Prentice-Hall, 1973), pp. 49–60.

to insulate the police from effective control by locally elected city councils and mayors.* But the most dramatic example of the emergence of functionally organized power occurred in the arena of public housing and urban renewal.[13] As noted above, the formulation of urban renewal policy soon got beyond the control of elected officials in most cities. Semiautonomous local public authorities were created in response to federal legislation, and they were largely financed by federal funds. In a sense, functional fiefdoms emerged in which the decision makers acted with considerable independence from control by elected public officials.

The functional organization of power enabled technicians and specialists to supersede elected politicians in making the most fundamental decisions about rebuilding the cities. Equally important, major decisions on metropolitan growth came to be made by specialized agencies called *special districts* rather than by general-purpose governments. Within each functional area the public bureaucracies, the special districts, and the related private interests acted in a fashion somewhat reminiscent of feudal fiefdoms in the Middle Ages when each fiefdom was virtually autonomous and its nobility was virtually answerable only to itself. In the 1950s and the 1960s in American metropolitan areas, an analogous situation occurred. Within many functional areas of public activity, the appropriate influential persons of the community were answerable virtually only to themselves. Highway, redevelopment, low-income public housing, public health, and public education

---

* The extent of police department insulation is difficult to measure, at best, and elected officials certainly affect the overall environment within which the police departments function. Nevertheless, evidence suggests that police law enforcement practices are more the product of a bureaucratic imperative than of legislative policy made by the city council in response to broad community demands. Jeffrey Pressman found that the mayor and city council in Oakland were unable to alter the police department's policies regulating handgun use by police officers [see p. 515 of Pressman's "The Preconditions for Mayoral Leadership," *The American Political Science Review* 66, no. 2 (June 1972): 511–524]. John A. Gardiner studied the enforcement of traffic laws in 697 communities throughout the United States and concluded that there was "almost no evidence to suggest that the police are carrying out *publicly* established enforcement policies" [p. 171 of Gardiner's "Police Enforcement of Traffic Laws: A Comparative Analysis," in *City Politics and Public Policy*, ed. James Q. Wilson (New York: Wiley, 1968), pp. 151–172]; input from council members and influential citizens almost always occurred on an *ad hoc* basis with little implication for overall policies (p. 167). And a study by James Q. Wilson of different approaches toward juvenile delinquency by a professionalized police department and a more traditionally, fraternally oriented police department found that the more bureaucratized and professionalized police force was much less sensitive to subtle community mores, was much less flexible in dealing with first offenders, and acted more in accord with the model of "an army of occupation" (p. 190 of James Q. Wilson, "The Police and the Delinquent in Two Cities," in Wilson, *City Politics and Public Policy*, pp. 173–195).

fiefdoms acted independently of each other. And little thought was given to coordinating their respective actions.

The third evolutionary change began in the middle 1960s and is still in a period of very early infancy. The chief characteristics of this change are a more massive role played by the federal government, an effort to coordinate the various functional fiefdoms, and a concern to subordinate them to policy-making bodies at the metropolitan levels. As in the second evolutionary change, the impetus for this third change has come largely from federal incentives. Significant national legislation has been passed since 1965 to curb the autonomy of special district governments, to promote comprehensive metropolitan planning, to encourage the formation of a new form of quasi-government at the metropolitan level (the council of governments, or COG), and to give the COGs significant authority to coordinate the purposes for which federal grants are spent in their respective metropolises. In addition, some influential persons are calling for the federal government to articulate a clearly defined national urban policy. Such a policy does not yet exist. Whether such a policy is desirable or even attainable is a subject of considerable debate.[14] (This subject is discussed in Chapters 10 and 11.)

The Johnson and Nixon administrations played special parts in this recent evolution of the federal role. Under Johnson, a massive increase occurred in the federal commitment to dealing with urban problems (see pp. 303–304 for details). During the Nixon administration, general revenue sharing and special revenue sharing were proposed as measures to reverse the trend toward increasing federal dominance over domestic policies and programs. General revenue sharing was enacted in 1972 and returned $6 billion per year to the state and local governments to use as they saw fit, with very few strings attached. Special revenue sharing attempted to replace over a hundred federal programs with six large block grants of money to the states and localities. Within each of the categories, the states and localities could determine for themselves what kinds of domestic and urban programs they wanted and how they wanted to spend the money. Only one of the six proposals was actually enacted into law before the end of the Nixon administration. Nixon's administration also took a major step toward decentralizing federal agencies as they operated in domestic affairs. And it was under the Nixon administration that guidelines were finally worked out for giving metropolitan planning agencies some input into the awarding of federal grants in their respective metropolitan areas[15] (see Chapter 10, p. 279).

Despite these attempts of the Nixon administration to reverse the trend toward national dominance of the federal relationship, the federal government's role has not diminished. At the end of Nixon's administration, the amount of federal aid to states and localities was over 60 percent higher than it had been at the beginning of his administration. If present trends continue into the foreseeable future, it seems inevitable that the federal role will continue to expand. Pressures to unify federal involvement under more clearly articulated federal metropolitan policies are likely to increase. In particular, metropolitan growth is becoming a prime target of attention for both the federal government and the state governments. If the physical expansion of American metropolises continues unabated for the next quarter-century at the same rate as during the previous quarter-century, one-sixth of the land mass of the forty-eight contiguous states will be covered by officially defined metropolitan areas (SMSAs).[16] Many people think this urban and suburban sprawl is undesirable, and they have pressed and are likely to continue pressing for federal intervention to prevent it from occurring.

To sum up, three broad evolutionary changes have been observed in the structure of political power in metropolis. The first change was the emergence of power that was organized on an ethnic and a ward, or geographic, base. Second was the emergence of power organized on a functional base. Third was a major transformation of the federal government's role in urban affairs and a persistent attempt to subordinate the functional power bases to metropolitan-level policy-making agencies and to facilitate the implementation of federal policies in urban and metropolitan areas.

These evolutionary changes are of more than simple historical interest. Each of these three ways of organizing power continues to exist. The first way of organizing power did not destroy the older, closed circles of urban elites of the early nineteenth century. But it did open up new channels of political access for groups in the metropolis that did not have access under the older form. The second political change did not destroy the ethnic organization of power.[17] But it did create new channels of political access beyond the control of the ethnic-dominated political machines. Nor has the third political change destroyed the functional fiefdoms. But, if it proves successful, it may make them more accountable to general policy-making bodies at the metropolitan level, and these policy-making bodies may become very sensitized to overall policy guidelines established in Congress and the White House. Whether it will make them more accountable to general-purpose governments and to local elected public officials is somewhat dubious. These considerations are examined in Chapter 11.

Political change in metropolis, then, does not mean that one form of political organization replaces a previous form. On the contrary, it means that several forms of political organization have evolved side by side. The net result has been the emergence of a patchwork, incredibly complex structure of political organization that is continually evolving in an incremental fashion. For those that know how to navigate them, there are numerous channels of political access to decision makers. Each channel has its own set of biases. And any one channel offers access to influencing decisions only within a very limited scope of activities. Even the largest, most extensive general-purpose government in the metropolis as it now exists — the central city government — has a very limited scope of action open to it. And in most instances, the evolution of a decision-making capacity at the metropolitan level is not very far advanced. What exists in most metropolises is a very open political situation. Anybody with the resources can do something of a limited scope (for example, construct an apartment building or delay the extension of a freeway through a residential neighborhood). But nobody has the capacity to do something of a comprehensive scope that covers several functional sectors at a metropolitan-wide level (for example, integrate highway construction with public transit planning with sewer construction with residential construction with prior metropolitan land use planning with equalizing social access to housing, education, and employment opportunities). One of the most distinctive features of the federal involvement in recent years has been to create incentives for the establishment of such a metropolitan-level capacity.

BIAS, CHANGE, AND POLITICAL POWER

To sum up the argument to this point, urban political structures change slowly in an incremental, evolutionary fashion. As these changes occur, they have the potential to alter the existing patterns of bias concerning the ways in which political power is organized in the metropolis.

In the presentation of this argument, the terms *politics* and *power* deliberately have been used in a very broad sense. *Politics* has referred to the struggle over public decisions that determine public policies and allocate values, goods, and services. Hence politics, as used in this book, refers not only to the election of government officials, but also to the making of public decisions and the results of public policy established by those decisions.[18]* It also refers to the broader social and economic processes that establish the constraints, needs, and capabilities that limit governmental action.

Public policies quite often result from pressure placed on government by groups and individuals that have interests which will be affected by those policies. To the extent that a given group or individual has influence on what a government does or does not do, that group or individual is said to possess political power.[19] To the extent that a given group or individual lacks influence on what a government does or does not do, that group or individual is said to lack political power. Some political scientists have suggested that the concept of power is so vague and susceptible to multiple interpretations that it ought to be avoided whenever possible.[20] However, to the extent that some persons, groups, or public officials have the capability to influence official government actions, it seems useful to have a term to represent that idea. And this book will use the term *political power* for this purpose. Thus, mayors, city councils, and a host of other governmental officials and agencies are politically powerful, because they have the capacity to take official action directly. Interest groups are powerful to the extent that they can influence what the governmental actors do.

Three aspects of political power are important to understanding how metropolises function. First, metropolitan political power is generally contextual; that is, a given group usually has power only in a given context. It has power in those areas of public interest in which it chooses or is able to assert itself.† Thus, for example, real estate developers usually exert considerable influence on zoning and land use

* Political power also involves what are referred to as *nondecisions*. Nondecisions are the potential issues which never get placed on the agenda for public decision making because they are beyond the pale of what is politically acceptable. The importance of nondecisions to the exercise of power is argued by Peter Bachrach and Morton S. Baratz in "The Two Faces of Power," *The American Political Science Review* 56, no. 4 (December 1962): 947–952. The significance of decisions and nondecisions in urban politics is discussed in Chapter 5, pp. 138–139.

† This has been a sharply debated issue in community power studies. At one extreme, Robert A. Dahl, in *Who Governs?* (New Haven, Conn.: Yale University Press, 1961), argues that power is so bound up in a given context that it exists primarily in the making of key decisions on given issues. In Dahl's view, the ability to influence key decisions in one area of issues does not lead to the ability to influence key decisions in other areas. Bachrach and Baratz, in "The Two Faces of Power," seem to argue that a broad reservoir of power exists independent of specific decisions. The most common viewpoint among political scientists, however, seems to be that taken by Gordon: "Political and civic life in American communities has become sufficiently complex that no one person or group of persons is likely to want or to be able to attain power in all areas of community life" (Gordon, *Social Change and Urban Politics*, p. 61). This book, in order to avoid entanglement in the methodological argument of this point, leans to the point of view that the exercise of power and the power holders will vary from one context to another.

practices, but they are seldom influential in questions of air pollution control.

A second important aspect of metropolitan political power is that it is structured:* there are patterns to the distribution of power in the metropolis, and some categories of people are more powerful than others. The participating electorate possesses power to the extent that it chooses many of the political leaders and sometimes acts as a restraint on what policy makers can accomplish. In Boston, for example, the election of neighborhood school advocates to the school committee in the middle 1960s hindered the cause of school desegregation in that city.[21] Farther down the power scale from this real, if somewhat limited, power of the participating electorate is the extremely limited political power of the unorganized people and those who do not participate. In particular, the unorganized, the poor, and the elderly typically exert very little influence in the making of public decisions.[22] In contrast to the limited power of the participating electorate and the extremely limited power of the unorganized, the poor, and the elderly, some highly organized groups consistently exert considerable influence on public decisions that affect them. Certain businessmen (especially those from the utilities, the major financial institutions, and the major local retailers) generally have a considerable voice in projects that promote their metropolitan area's economic expansion.[23] The political influence of other groups — groups such as labor unions, political parties, church organizations, or organized crime — varies from one metropolis to another. In Detroit, for example, labor unions are a very strong political force, whereas in Chicago they are much weaker. This seems to be related to the greater strength of the Democratic party in Chicago and the more diversified economic base of that city.[24] But the important point here is that there is always a structure to the organization of political influence in metropolises. This does not necessarily mean that a small elite controls events. It does mean that political decisions do not occur randomly.

Political power is not only contextual and structured; it is also inseparable from private power. The broad sense of the term *political* power, as it is currently used by political scientists, makes drawing fine distinctions between the private and public aspects of power increasingly difficult. To take just one example: For the purely private finan-

---

* The statement that power is structured is often taken to mean that a small clique at the top of a hierarchy controls politics in a given locale and that the clique is founded in the top levels of a hierarchy of business leaders. The statement does not necessarily mean this, however. It does mean that permanent relationships exist between the politically relevant institutions in the metropolis and the governmental policy outputs.

cial reasons of trying to maximize profit and minimize losses, mortgage banks refuse to make mortgage loans in large sections of American cities. This practice is known as *red lining*, because the bankers supposedly draw a red line around the areas not eligible for loans.[25] Although these decisions are made for private reasons and for private profits, they have vast public ramifications. The urban neighborhoods which are denied the mortgage loans begin to deteriorate. Governments become obliged to spend public funds on stepped-up police and fire protection, public welfare assistance, renewal, and other services to deal with the consequences of that deterioration. For these reasons, the banks' exercise of private power is equally an exercise of public power. Furthermore, if the cities' public authorities do not or cannot use their influence to induce lenders to make loans in red-lined areas, then for all practical purposes the public authorities have publicly acquiesced in and legitimized* these privately made decisions that determine which neighborhoods of the metropolis are going to deteriorate and which ones are going to prosper. It is very difficult to call decisions of such magnitude private decisions rather than public decisions, even though they might be made privately, by private businessmen, for private motives. In this sense, the distinction between private and public has become vague. Private decisions can be public decisions in the proper circumstances.

This reliance on private decision makers to decide on developments of extreme public importance has been characteristic of American urban history.[26] However, this, too, is changing. If one compares 1975 with 1875, one of the most marked political differences is the increased ability of governments to have some input on private decisions which have public ramifications. As this change occurs, it is anticipated that it will also affect the patterns of bias in urban growth. In the case of red lining, for example, urban government intervention would probably have the effect of mitigating the bankers' bias against the red-lined neighborhoods.

* Legitimacy has been defined as the "quality of being justified or willingly accepted by subordinates that converts the exercise of political power into 'rightful' authority" [Jack C. Plano and Robert E. Riggs, *Dictionary of Political Analysis* (Hinsdale, Ill.: The Dryden Press, 1973), p.45]. In this example, the acquiescence of the public authorities in the actions of the mortgage bankers enhances the likelihood of popular acceptance of the notion that bankers have a "rightful authority" to take actions which have such far-reaching consequences. According to Dolbeare, fundamental political change is first of all a process of "de-legitimizing" existing institutions and then "legitimizing" new political institutions [Dolbeare, *Political Change in the United States* (New York: McGraw-Hill, 1974), p. 8]. Thus, in this example, fundamental change would first of all involve de-legitimizing the existing right of mortgage bankers to decide which areas of a metropolis qualify for mortgage loans. The second step would be to give this right to a new institution.

SUMMARY

The nature of metropolitan politics clearly involves questions of change and bias. It is difficult to improve on the phrasing of political scientist Harold Lasswell, cited earlier, who defined politics as the process of determining who gets what, when, how. In the fast-changing world of the late 1970s, it might also be added that changes in urban and metropolitan political structures principally alter *how* benefits are allocated in the metropolitan political system. One of the major tasks of the chapters that follow is to ask if these changes in *how* politics are structured also cause changes in *who* gets *what* benefits.

Some Suggested Readings

Political Bias

E. E. Schattschneider, *The Semi-Sovereign People: A Realist's View of Democracy in America* (New York: Holt, Rinehart and Winston, 1960). Introduces the term *bias* and argues that federal government agencies are biased toward certain clientele groups and against unorganized citizens.

Edward S. Greenberg, *Serving the Few: Corporate Capitalism and the Bias of Government Policy* (New York: Wiley, 1974). Attempts to measure the distribution of benefits in several public policy areas.

Grant McConnell, *Private Power and American Democracy* (New York: Knopf, 1966). A thorough analysis of the patterns and consequences of private influence on public decision making.

Political Change

Most studies of political change focus on developing countries rather than on the United States. Some works indicated below either deal with American political change or are relevant to it.

Kenneth M. Dolbeare, *Political Change in the United States: A Framework for Analysis* (New York: McGraw-Hill, 1974). Views political change in the United States as a nonrevolutionary process, but a process that is independent of social and economic change.

Daniel N. Gordon, ed., *Social Change and Urban Politics: Readings* (Englewood Cliffs, N.J.: Prentice-Hall, 1973). An excellent collection of articles. Gordon's own article, "The Bases of Urban Political Change: A Brief History of Development and Trends," analyzes urban political change as the consequence of underlying social and economic changes in the society.

Chapter 2

This chapter seeks to answer several broad questions about the process through which contemporary metropolises emerged in the United States. How are the terms *urban* and *metropolitan* defined? What are the essential urban characteristics of the American population? Why do metropolises grow? How has the character of American urbanization changed as the cities grew into metropolises? What are the political implications of these changes? Do these changes involve any political bias? That is, have they diminished some people's access to the political decision makers and to the social amenities of the metrop-

The Emergence of Metropolitan America

olis such as good schools and employment opportunities? If so, *who* are the people whose political and social access has been diminished?

URBAN CHARACTERISTICS OF THE AMERICAN POPULATION

The classic definition of *urban* has three elements: volume, density, and heterogeneity of population. The first two elements are basically demographic and the third is sociological.[1] The key criteria for distinguishing urban from nonurban places thus become: How large must a population be to be called urban? How dense must it be? And how heterogeneous must it be?

The United States Census Bureau applies these criteria by classifying as urban any incorporated or unincorporated minor civil division of

2500 or more people.* Using this definition, the 1970 census found that there are more than 7000 urban places in the United States and that 73 percent of the population is urban.

Although these widely accepted figures are used to indicate how urbanized the American population is, the figures also illustrate a key defect in the definition. It does not distinguish between a small town in central Wyoming of 2500 and New York City with its population of 7 million; both are considered urban. Nor does this definition distinguish between central cities and suburbs.

To cope with these definitional defects, the Census Bureau utilizes the terms urbanized areas and metropolitan areas. The Standard Metropolitan Statistical Area (SMSA) was invented to define metropolitan areas. The SMSA is defined by the Office of Management and Budget (OMB) rather than the Census Bureau. SMSA is defined as any county containing a central city or two contiguous cities of 50,000 people plus all adjacent counties that are considered to be metropolitan in character and are economically and socially integrated with the central county. An adjacent county will meet the tests for integration with the central county if 75 percent of its labor force is engaged in nonagricultural work, at least half its population lives in densities higher than 150 persons per square mile, and either at least 15 percent of its population works in the central county or at least 15 percent of those working in the county live in the central county.[2] An urbanized area basically is any area within an SMSA that meets the Census Bureau's criteria for urban.

With these distinctions between nonurban, urban, urbanized area, and SMSA, a more accurate picture can be drawn of the urban status of the American population. As can be seen in Table 2-1, while the population is 73 percent urban, only 68 percent lives in metropolitan areas and only about 60 percent lives in the urbanized portions of metropolitan areas. Within the SMSAs, more people live outside the central cities than live within them. And about 21 million people who reside in SMSAs actually live in rural, not urban, places. As of 1974 there were 265 SMSAs.

These considerations point up one of the disadvantages of the SMSA definition of the term metropolitan. Not only does it include 21 million

* A minor civil division refers to the geographic territory below the county level that is the primary legal administrative subdivision according to state law. In the states where a subcounty-level minor civil division does not exist, the Census Bureau calculates a census county division for the purpose of identifying urban places. These states are found primarily in the South and the West. [United States Bureau of the Census, 1970 Census of Population; Volume I: Characteristics of the Population; Part A: Number of Inhabitants (Washington, D.C.: U.S. Government Printing Office, 1972), p. x.]

TABLE 2-1

SOME URBAN CHARACTERISTICS OF THE U.S. POPULATION: 1970

Population Category	Number	Percentage of U.S. Population
Total U.S. population	203,212,000	100
Urban	149,325,000	73.5
Rural	53,887,000	26.5
Nonmetropolitan population	63,798,000	31.4
Nonmetropolitan urban	30,878,000	15.2
Nonmetropolitan rural	32,947,000	16.2
Metropolitan population (i.e., in SMSAs)	139,387,000	68.6
In urbanized areas	118,447,000	58.3
In central cities	63,922,000	31.5
In suburbs in urbanized areas	54,525,000	26.8
In rural areas of SMSAs	20,940,000	10.3

Source: United States Department of Commerce, Bureau of the Census, *Statistical Abstract of the United States: 1971* (Washington, D.C.: U.S. Government Printing Office, 1971), p. 16.

rural people within metropolitan areas, but it also includes vast stretches of sparsely inhabited territory such as in eastern California or Nevada. Furthermore, using the relatively small central city population of 50,000 as the core of the SMSA makes it impossible to distinguish isolated SMSAs such as Billings, Montana, from the chains of SMSAs which together form a megalopolis.*

Because of these disadvantages, various urbanists have attempted to make more appropriate definitions of the term metropolitan. One approach has been to define as metropolitan any area with a population of at least 100,000 people that contains a central city or cities and has at least 65 percent of its economically active population in non-agricultural activities.[3] This is a fairly restrictive definition which excludes many areas considered metropolitan under the SMSA definition. A different approach to defining metropolitan areas has been to avoid putting precise political boundaries on what is considered metropolitan. This is done by defining an area not in terms of counties as the SMSA is defined, but in terms of commuting distance. One advocate of this approach is geographer John Friedmann, who

* Another problem with the SMSA definition is that the OMB finds it difficult to adhere to it completely in drawing up the SMSA designations. See Ira Rosenwaike, "A Critical Examination of the Designation of Standard Metropolitan Statistical Areas," *Social Forces* 48, no. 3 (March 1970): 322–333.

rejects the term *metropolitan area* and introduces *urban field*. He defines an urban field as a core area of 300,000 people plus all areas within a radius equivalent to a two-hour automobile drive.[4] Friedmann prefers such a definition — which would probably classify about 90 percent of the American population as urbanized — because, he asserts, most of the American people exhibit urban social traits regardless of where they live or what occupations they have. Whatever the relative advantages of these other approaches to defining metropolitan areas, the SMSA definition is the most widely accepted method of identifying American metropolises, and it is the definition according to which all federal statistical data are compiled.

In addition to urban places and SMSAs, another level of urbanization, called *megalopolis* by French geographer Jean Gottman,[5] is found along the North Atlantic seacoast where the metropolitan areas are growing into one another. This phenomenon cannot be accounted for by the single SMSA concept. While the New York SMSA has a total population of 11.5 million, its zone of influence spreads into neighboring SMSAs. The same thing is true of Chicago. Consequently, for New York and Chicago the concept of Standard Consolidated Area was invented to reflect their metropolitan impact more accurately.[6] The population of the Standard Consolidated Area of New York is 15.8 million and that of Chicago is 7.3 million. In contrast, the SMSA populations are 11.5 million and 6.9 million, respectively. But even the concept of Standard Consolidated Area does not describe the full impact of urbanization along the Northeast seacoast. The New York–New Jersey Standard Consolidated Area exists in the middle of a chain of forty-one SMSAs in nine states plus the District of Columbia that stretches from southern New Hampshire to Virginia and contains a population of more than 40 million people.[7]

The Eastern-seaboard megalopolis contains distinguishing features other than a continuous metropolitan strip. Covering some 50,000 square miles with an average density of 700 people per square mile in 1960, it is one of the largest dense areas in the world. It is the world's wealthiest concentration of people, with a higher per capita income than any other population of comparable size. It also contains one of the world's greatest concentrations of political and economic power and artistic and literary leadership. Although it contains the world's greatest manufacturing establishment, few of the ores, minerals, and chemicals processed in the megalopolis into capital and consumer goods are extracted from the megalopolis itself. On the contrary, the vast majority of these natural resources are extracted from other parts of the earth and fed into the megalopolis for processing or shipping.[8]

FIGURE 2-1   STANDARD METROPOLITAN STATISTICAL

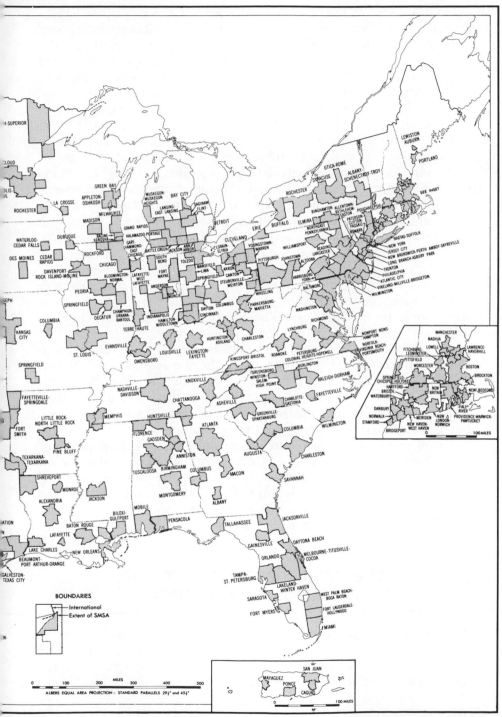

BOUNDARIES

International
Extent of SMSA

0   100   200   300   400   500
MILES
ALBERS EQUAL AREA PROJECTION – STANDARD PARALLELS 29½° and 45½°

Social and Economic Statistics Administration of the Bureau of the Census,
United States Department of Commerce

No other area of the country is comparable to the Northeast megalopolis on all these variables. However, metropolitan areas in three other regions are increasingly merging and growing together to the point that they, too, are commonly referred to as megalopolises. One of these regions is along the southern shore of the Great Lakes, particularly along Lake Michigan. Thirty SMSAs branch out contiguously from key lake ports at Milwaukee-Chicago, Detroit-Toledo, Cleveland, and Buffalo-Rochester. Seven others lie in the growth paths of these SMSAs or around isolated ports on the Great Lakes. This megalopolis contains about 25 million people in eight states, about 40 percent of them living along the Milwaukee-to-Chicago axis and another 40 percent living in the growth paths which branch from Cleveland toward Pittsburgh in one direction and toward Rochester in the other.

A third megalopolis is emerging on the southwest Pacific Coast from San Francisco to the Mexican border. Although great stretches of sparsely inhabited desert exist at places in these SMSAs, the area contains sixteen contiguous SMSAs and about 17 million people.

A fourth megalopolis is developing along the Florida peninsula from Jacksonville to Miami on the Atlantic Coast and spreading out from Tampa on the Gulf Coast. There are currently six SMSAs in Florida; together, they contain about 5 million people.

Although none of these last three megalopolises is really comparable to the Northeast megalopolis by most of the characteristics mentioned above, they do constitute the areas of the country where the population is increasingly concentrated. Together, the four megalopolises comprise a very small percentage of the land area of the United States, but they contain over 40 percent of the population.

Urban place, metropolis, and megalopolis are the three levels of urbanization that have developed thus far. A final stage of urbanization is predicted by the Greek planner C. A. Doxiadis. He foresees a continued growth and urbanization of the world population well into the twenty-first century to the point where the urban areas will form part of a worldwide urban network called ecumenopolis.[9]

THE BASIC DETERMINANTS OF METROPOLITAN GROWTH

Whether such a phenomenon as ecumenopolis will materialize is problematical at this point in history. But megalopolises exist on at least four continents, and giant metropolises exist on all continents but Antarctica. These developments have not happened by accident; they are shaped by basic economic, technological, and political forces. Only within the last one hundred years have these forces converged to create the great metropolises of several million people. The great cities of antiquity and the Middle Ages were relatively small. Babylon covered an area of no more than 3.2 square miles. Athens, at the height of its glory in the fifth century B.C., contained fewer than 200,000 people. Florence in the fourteenth century was a city of no more than 90,000 people, and Venice in the fifteenth century contained about 190,000. Of all the great premodern cities, only Rome approached a population of a million.[10]

There are three reasons why giant metropolises and megalopolises began to emerge only in the late nineteenth and early twentieth centuries. First, it was not until that time that a large enough agricultural surplus was produced to enable a majority of the population to live off the agricultural production of a dwindling minority of the population. The level of urbanization is directly proportionate to the number of farmers it takes to support one nonfarmer who lives in the city. While this may imply that the city dwellers are parasites living off the agricultural surplus, in fact city dwellers perform valuable services for the farmer. They transport his goods, finance his investments in crops, import or manufacture consumer goods he can purchase with the earnings from his crops, and administer the safety and well-being of the countryside. Without these services, the farmer would be reduced to living at a subsistence level. There is a vital ecological balance between the city and the surrounding farm region.*

In the contemporary era, this ecological balance has been altered by the second factor in the rise of the large metropolis — the innovations in transportation technology.[11] The contemporary metropolis requires a sophisticated transportation network in order to move the food and raw materials into the city and to move the city's production out to its markets. The availability of steamships, railroads, motor transport, and air transport makes it possible to supply increasingly larger populations over increasingly longer distances. These forms of transport are also much more energy intensive than the forms of transport which supplied any previous form of urbanization. Unless new forms of transport or new sources of energy are discovered before the existing supplies of petroleum are exhausted, contemporary metropolises and megalopolises will not remain viable.

* One long-standing dispute among urban theorists has been whether urbanization was dependent upon increased agricultural production. For the primacy of agriculture argument, see Kingsley Davis, "The Origin and Growth of Urbanization in the World," *The American Journal of Sociology* 60 (March 1955): 430–432. For the primacy of urbanization argument, see Jane Jacobs, *The Economy of Cities* (New York: Vintage Books, 1970), chapter 1.

In addition to the transportation network and the agricultural surplus made possible by modern technology, a third factor contributing to the growth of giant metropolises has been the increasing control over death rates. Until the nineteenth century, life in towns and cities was much more hazardous than life in rural areas. Sanitary conditions were so poor and death rates were so high that the growth of towns and cities was often very sporadic. Even as late as 1878 a two-month epidemic of yellow fever in the city of Memphis, Tennessee, killed 5,000 people, struck another 12,000, and caused 25,000 people to flee the city. In just two months, the city's population was reduced from about 50,000 people to fewer than 20,000.[12] Cities like Memphis could not grow into metropolises until people learned how to keep their excretion from polluting their drinking water, until they learned some elementary principles of hygiene, and until the practice of medicine began to eliminate the scourge of contagious diseases such as typhoid, typhus, cholera, and yellow fever. When these things occurred, the human population began to grow at an exponential rate and, in an economic sense, an excess population was created. Because of the ecological balance between the rural areas and the small rural towns, this excess population could not sustain itself in rural areas and had to migrate elsewhere. The problem became particularly acute during the nineteenth century in western Europe and England, where there was no more open land that could be colonized and cultivated. Much of the excess population therefore migrated to the first great cities of the Industrial Revolution — Liverpool, Birmingham, Sheffield, and London. And much of it migrated to the Western hemisphere, where it stimulated the urbanization of the United States.

HOW THE UNITED STATES URBANIZED: SMALL TOWN TO MEGALOPOLIS

The Urbanization of America: 1840–1920

The same three factors that permitted the development of large cities in general influenced the growth of cities in the United States. From 1730 to the end of the eighteenth century, the percentage of the population living in cities actually declined.[13] Large cities did not become commonplace until well into the nineteenth century. At the time of Independence the largest city, Philadelphia, contained only about 40,000 people.* The first city of 100,000 population did not emerge until al-

* Other large cities in 1790 were: New York, 33,131; Boston, 18,038; Charleston, 16,359; Baltimore, 13,503.

most 1820, and even as late as 1840 there were only three such cities. By 1850, that number had doubled.[14] The decade of the 1840s thus marks the beginning of intensive urbanization in the United States. The city-building phase of urbanization reached its peak by 1920, when for the first time a majority of the population lived in urban places. These eighty years of urbanization resulted from three historical forces.

The first of these forces was extensive immigration. Thirty-seven million Europeans migrated to the United States between 1841 and 1930. Politically, they were a very important force, for they created the basic institutions of urban politics which are influential in many of the central cities even today.

As can be seen in Table 2-2, the immigrants came in different stages. The period of heaviest Irish and German immigration came prior to the Civil War, with the Irish settling primarily in urban places in the Northeast and the Germans settling in both urban and rural places both in the Northeast and the Midwest. From the 1890s until the 1920s, immi-

TABLE 2-2

ORIGIN AND PLACE OF SETTLEMENT OF IMMIGRANTS

Immigrant Group	Era of Most Immigration[a]	Number of Immigrants: 1841–1930[b]	Regions of Settlement[c]	Estimated Degree of Settlement in Urban Places
Mainstream nationalities				
English	1845–1895	4,114,023	NE, ENC, South, West	Medium
Germans	1845–1885	5,747,710	NE, ENC, WNC, West	Medium
European ethnic minorities				
Irish	1845–1885	4,437,610	NE, ENC, WNC	High
Italians	1900–1914	4,648,503	NE, ENC, West	High
Catholic Poles	1900–1914		NE, ENC	High
Jews[d]	1900–1914	2,443,474	NE, ENC	Very high
Contemporary urban minorities				
Spanish speaking	1945–1970	3,419,590	SW, NE, SA	Low–medium

[a] Except for Spanish speaking, approximately two-thirds of all immigrants from 1841–1930 came during the period indicated. Over two-thirds of all Spanish-speaking immigrants came during the period indicated.
[b] Sources: United States Bureau of the Census, *Historical Statistics of the United States from Colonial Times to 1957* (Washington, D.C.: U.S. Government Printing Office, 1957), pp. 56–59. United States Bureau of the Census, *Statistical Abstract of the United States: 1971* (Washington, D.C.: U.S. Government Printing Office, 1971), p. 92. Spanish-speaking immigration is for the period 1840–1970; the figures here represent an understatement because of the large number of Mexicans who have crossed the border without going through customs. Jewish immigration is taken from *Encyclopaedia Judaica Jerusalem* (New York: Macmillan, 1971), vol. 16, pp. 1519–1524.
[c] ENC = East North Central; NE = Northeast; WNC = West North Central; SA = South Atlantic.
[d] Jewish immigrants prior to 1880 were mostly Germans. After 1880 they were mostly Russians and Poles.

grants came primarily from southern and eastern Europe and settled in both the Northeast and the Midwest cities. Through a survey conducted in 1972, the Census Bureau estimates that over 30 percent of the population of the United States traces its heritage to just six of these ethnic nationalities — German, Irish, Russian, Polish, Italian, and French.[15] Since the Irish, Russian, Polish, and Italian immigrants settled mainly in the metropolitan cities, they represent an even larger percentage of the metropolitan population. The urban political institutions created by these immigrants have had a disproportionate influence on the development of metropolitan America.

The combination of innovation in the technology of transport and the frontier movement to the West created a second force toward establishing American cities.[16] The discovery of gold in California, the existence of fertile farmland from the Appalachian Mountains almost to the Pacific coast, and the liberal subsidization of the railroads to expand westward spurred a continual westward migration of the population. Along these railroad lines there began to emerge "gateway" cities which functioned as transfer points for the exchange of goods between the railroads and the surrounding agricultural communities.[17]

In many instances the railroads created the cities. When southern Illinois towns refused to grant concessions which the Illinois Central Railroad desired in order to run its tracks through those towns, the Illinois Central ran its tracks through other locations and established its own gateway towns in competition with the existing cities. A typical practice was for the railroad to acquire title to empty land, survey it, parcel it out for city lots, and then sell the lots for a profit. At Kankakee, Illinois, for example, the railroad bought the land for $18,000, sold some of the subdivided lots for $50,000, and held the remainder, valued at $100,000, for future sales. When the Illinois Central was chartered in 1851, there were only ten towns along its route. Twenty years later there were eighty-one; and the total population of all these places, excluding Chicago, increased fourteenfold, from 12,000 to 172,000.[18] The creation of these western railroad towns opened up the western farmlands and turned the United States into the world's greatest agricultural producer. The agricultural surplus which began to emerge in the nineteenth century in turn became a further stimulus to the growth of American cities.

Growth within the cities was also conditioned by the technology of transportation. Sam Bass Warner, Jr., has shown how transit innovations affected the growth of Boston.[19] Until the 1850s, Boston was a pedestrian city with no transit system, and the outer boundaries of the residential areas were naturally limited to a radius of about two miles.

The introduction of horse-drawn railways extended the city's boundaries to perhaps two and a half miles by 1873 and to four miles by 1887. In the 1890s, electric streetcars were introduced and the city's boundaries were extended to a radius of six miles.

The streetcar had other important effects on city development. It facilitated a form of retail *strip* shopping areas along the streetcar routes where retail businessmen found it lucrative to establish their shops. Later, in the age of the automobile, these strip shopping areas would decline in most cities and the more successful retailers would move to the suburban shopping centers. The streetcars also enabled the first extensive suburbanization by connecting the central business district with newly urbanized places beyond the city proper. The streetcar outlined the physical growth of the Eastern central cities as we know them today.

The other major technological innovations in transportation were the elevated and subway railways. New York introduced the first steam elevated trains in the 1870s, but because of their dirtiness and their occasional tendency to spew hot ashes on pedestrians walking beneath the elevated structures, they were replaced with electric elevated and subway trains in the 1890s. Without these innovations, it is doubtful whether the population of Manhattan and Brooklyn could have grown from 1.5 million in 1870 to 3.5 million by the turn of the century.[20]

It is difficult to overestimate the importance of these technological changes to the prosperity of individual cities. Table 2-3 indicates how dependent most cities are on prevailing modes of transportation technology and how vulnerable they are to sudden innovations. Although budding nineteenth-century river cities such as Galena, Illinois, Wheeling, West Virginia, or Louisville, Kentucky, at one time seemed destined to grow into another Chicago, they found their growth stunted when transportation technology changed. They were bypassed because of other newer, more efficient means of transporting goods and people. The newer forms of transport are highly energy intensive, and contemporary cities which are dependent solely on them are very vulnerable to fluctuations in the availability of energy. If the petroleum crisis of 1973–74 should turn into a permanent petroleum shortage, then it is very likely that sharp declines will be suffered by cities such as Las Vegas which are exclusively dependent on air and motor transport. The same could occur in many suburbs and satellite cities in the megalopolises. On the other hand, if sufficient sources of electrical energy are found to sustain the increasingly widespread applications of electronic telecommunications technology, then settlement patterns within the megalopolises seem likely to continue dispersing and decentralizing.[21]

TABLE 2-3

TRANSPORTATION TECHNOLOGY AND THE GROWTH OF CITIES

Mode of Transport	Time Period of Most Importance	Source of Locomotion	Intensiveness			Representative City
			Capital	Labor	Energy	
Turnpike *Most important cargo: people, supplies for personal needs*	1800–1840	Animal and foot	Low	Very high	Very low	Cumberland, Md.
Canal *Most important cargo: grain from West to East*	1820–1850	Barge: first animal, then steam	Medium	High	Very low	Rome, N.Y.
River *Most important cargo: grain, agricultural products generally, people*	1840–1875	Steam, then diesel	Low	High	Very low	Galena, Ill.
Railroad *Most important cargo: agricultural products, coal, manufacturing goods, people*	1850–1920	Steam, then diesel	High	High	Medium	Vandalia, Ill.
Air/auto/motor *Most important cargo: people, manufactured products*	1920– ?	Gasoline engine, diesel and jet engines	Very high	Medium	Very high	Las Vegas, Nev.
Electronic communications *Most important cargo: information*	1965– ?	Telecommunications, computers, facsimile	Very high	Low	Very high	Suburb or satellite city of a metropolis

In addition to immigration and transportation technology, the third factor which led to the growth of the metropolis in the United States was the transformation of the economy from a small-enterprise base into a national corporate economy. Until late in the nineteenth century, most business enterprises in American cities were small-scale, family-owned companies that maintained few permanent employees.[22] After the Civil War, more and more business corporations set up national or regional headquarters in large cities such as New York, Chicago, and Boston. Not only did this concentration of business headquarters provide economic activity to make those regional cities grow. The modern business offices of those corporation headquarters also created millions of new and peculiarly urban jobs in fields such as advertising, marketing, financing, accounting, typing, office management, and general office work. The creation of these occupations in turn contributed to the demand for a growing urban labor force and population. Hence the corporate business office arose and provided another stimulus to the growth of large cities.[23]

The Westward Drift of Urbanization: 1920–1975

This urbanization process did not cease in 1920, but after that date it changed in two significant respects. First, there was a general westward drift of urbanization. A marked slowdown occurred in the growth of many places that had been urbanizing prior to 1920, namely, the central cities in the Northeast and the small towns that served rural areas, particularly those east of the Mississippi River.[24] As can be seen from Table 2-4, while the Northeast quadrant contained 60 percent of all cities that had grown to 100,000 population before 1930, 80 percent of cities reaching that size since 1930 are in either the Southeast or the Southwest quadrant. Politically this is important for several reasons. With few exceptions, such as San Francisco, the cities in these regions did not receive the millions of European immigrants that the cities of the Northeast had received, and consequently the style and ethnic base of their politics is different. The cities of the Southwest are also much more dependent on motor and air transport than they are upon water and rail transport, and this makes them more vulnerable to potential energy shortages in the future. These cities also tend to benefit more from the new sources of wealth — Texas oil, federal defense and aerospace expenditures, and the tourist and recreation boom — than do the cities of the Northeast and the Midwest. For all of these reasons the style and character of urban politics in these newer cities are likely to differ markedly from those of the older cities of the Northeast and Midwest.

TABLE 2-4

THE WESTWARD DRIFT OF URBANIZATION

Year	Location of Cities of 100,000 or More by Geographic Quadrant				Total Number of Cities
	Northeast	Southeast	Southwest	Northwest	
1850	5	1	0	0	6
1870	10	2	1	0	13
1900	27	3	2	2	34
1930	56	14	12	11	93
1940	50	14	12	13	89
1950	55	20	17	13	105
1960	58	27	29	15	129
1970	61	38	36	18	153

Northeast: Includes all cities east of or straddling the Mississippi River and north of the Ohio and Potomac rivers
Southeast: Includes all cities east of or straddling the Mississippi River and south of the Ohio and Potomac rivers
Southwest: Includes all cities west of the Mississippi River and south of the northern boundary of Oklahoma, plus all cities in the states of California and Nevada
Northwest: Includes all cities west of the Mississippi River and north of the Southwest quadrant.
Not included are the cities in Hawaii, Puerto Rico, and Alaska

Sources: Compiled from The World Almanac and Book of Facts for 1932, pp. 439, 440; Statistical Abstract of the United States: 1971, p. 21; and Twelfth Census of the United States: 1900; Vol. 1, Population; Part 1, pp. 430–433.

The Suburbanization of America: 1920–1975

The second significant change in the urbanization process since 1920 has been the shifting of urban growth away from the central cities and into the suburbs. The number of big central cities continued to grow, but, as shown in Table 2-5, the suburbs grew even faster. In 1920 almost two-thirds of the metropolitan population lived in central cities. By 1970 barely 45 percent of the metropolitan population lived in central cities.

Four factors have been responsible for the suburbanization of the United States: the automobile, the new technology in road and residential construction, the cultural deprecation of cities, and the invention of long-term, low-down-payment home mortgages.

The role of the automobile and road construction in stimulating suburbanization derived partly from the ease with which they extended

TABLE 2-5

THE DECLINE OF BIG-CITY POPULATION IN RELATION TO NATIONAL, URBAN, AND METROPOLITAN POPULATIONS

Year	Percentage of Population Living in:		
	Cities of 100,000 or More	Urban Places	Metropolitan* Areas
1920	26.0	51.2	43.7
1930	29.6	56.2	49.8
1940	28.8	56.5	51.1
1950	29.4	64.0	62.5
1960	28.0	69.9	66.7
1970	27.7	73.5	68.6

* For 1950, 1960, 1970, "metropolitan area" is the SMSA. For 1920, 1930, 1940, "metropolitan" is based on the criteria for the older concept of the Standard Metropolitan Area. Thus the large jump in metropolitan population between 1940 and 1950 does not reflect a population increase so much as a change in a definition of the term *metropolitan*.

Source: *Statistical Abstract of the United States: 1971* (Washington, D.C.: U.S. Government Printing Office, 1971), p. 17. Metropolitan area populations for 1920, 1930, and 1940 are calculated by Donald J. Bogue on the 1950 criteria used in establishing Standard Metropolitan Areas, in *Population Growth in Standard Metropolitan Areas: 1900–1950* (Washington, D.C.: Government Printing Office for the Housing and Home Finance Agency, 1953), p. 113.

the commuting distance for large numbers of people, and partly from the fact that they liberated real estate developers and retail business-people from having to build their residences and shops along the streetcar lines. The spread of the automobile was greatly facilitated by federal and state government highway and freeway construction. Particularly since the passage of the Federal Aid Highway Act of 1956, which earmarked the revenue from a gasoline tax for a highway trust fund to build and maintain the interstate highway system, freeway construction has stimulated the dispersion of the population throughout the suburbs. Where the roads were constructed, the population moved, and shopping facilities soon followed. The shopping centers in turn attracted more people to move into nearby areas. The first suburban shopping center appeared, fittingly, west of the Mississippi River in the country club district of suburban Kansas City.[25]

The introduction of the automobile and the freeway systems made suburbanization possible but not inevitable. To make suburbanization inevitable, several other things had to occur. For one thing, the mass of the population had to *want* to move to the suburbs. And in the United

States, historical-cultural developments worked in that direction. As far back as the writings of Thomas Jefferson, one common theme of American intellectual literature has been disparagement of city life.[26] The popular media have generally idealized the small town as the epitome of American civilization. And when survey researchers ask people where they would prefer to live if they had a choice, big cities are usually the least preferred place. The most preferred places are usually open country or small towns.* Since by the post–World War II era most people needed to live in the metropolis for economic reasons, the suburb represented the best compromise between access to jobs and being able to live where one wanted to.

People not only had to *want* to live in suburbia for the metropolis to become suburbanized. They had to *be able to afford* to live there. One device that helped satisfy this requisite was the invention of long-term, low-down-payment mortgage loans. These loans were pioneered by the Federal Housing Administration (FHA) and Veterans' Administration (VA). Their mortgage guarantees made it possible for any qualifying person to purchase a home with a small down payment or no down payment at all, with monthly payments spread over a thirty-year period, and with an interest rate slightly below the prevailing conventional mortgage interest rates. Once the government-guaranteed mortgages proved that long-term, low-down-payment mortgages were financially viable, mortgage banks began to use them in conventional mortgage loans. Because the cheapest large plots of land existed beyond the central city boundaries, that is where most of this new mortgage money was lent. For the first time in American history, home ownership was open to the majority of the urban population.

The government-backed mortgages were not without their critics. They were accused of being racist, because until 1962 FHA loans were restricted to caucasians. They also were accused of being biased against the lower-middle-income and lower-income strata of the society, since most of the mortgages went to upper-middle-class familes. And to observers concerned about the development of communities (as distinguished from the proliferation of housing projects), the government-

* One survey conducted in 1971 for the Commission on Population Growth and the American Future found that 34 percent of the respondents preferred to live in the open country, 30 percent in a small town or city, 22 percent in a medium-sized city or suburb, and only 14 percent in a larger city or suburb. When asked where they actually lived, the percentages respectively were 12, 33, 28, and 27. [The Commission on Population Growth and the American Future, *Population and the American Future: The Report of the Commission* (Washington, D. C.: U.S. Government Printing Office, 1972), p. 34.]

backed mortgages were accused of existing primarily as a government prop to the construction industry and the real estate developers.[27]

Thus the suburbanization of America after 1920 and especially after 1945 was virtually predetermined by a complex of factors which met at the same point in time: the intellectual disrepute of the city, the cultural value placed upon living in single-family homes in open spaces, the availability of cheap land beyond the city's boundaries, the unprecedented access to that land via new roadways, the massive use of the automobile, and the availability of long-term, low-down-payment mortgages.

It must be noted that this analysis of the causes of suburbanization places very little weight upon the cause most often cited — the flight of the white population away from the racial minorities that were moving into the central cities. Although there can be no doubt that much of the white population did move to the suburbs to avoid living with blacks, this fails as a sufficient explanation of suburbanization. For suburbanization occurred equally in metropolises with very small black populations (such as Seattle, Portland, Minneapolis) and in metropolises with very large black populations (such as Washington, Philadelphia, New York). The racial causes of suburbanization added only to the *want* factor of suburbanization. It did nothing to affect the technological factors, the availability of cheap land, and the revolution in mortgage lending practices.

Finally, it must also be noted that the rapid expansion of the urban population into suburbia does not necessarily represent an exercise of individual free choice. As indicated above, people migrated to suburbs because those were the places where acceptable housing was most likely to be found. That the acceptable housing occurred in the form of single-family homes in suburbs was not a consequence of individual choices. Rather it was a consequence of transit, housing, employment, and finance policies of the federal and state governments and the major mortgage banking institutions. In the early 1970s new single-family homes were no longer being purchased by very many working-class and lower-middle-class families.* But again, that was not a consequence of free choice or a change in tastes. Rather it was a consequence

* For a variety of reasons, forces since the late 1960s have placed the purchase price of new homes beyond the purchasing power of the average-income family. In 1974 the average price of a new home was $40,700 (*Wisconsin State Journal*, August 26, 1974, p. 3). Under normal circumstances this is beyond the purchasing power of families below the median family income. Furthermore, since the late 1960s, the majority of new housing construction has been in town houses and apartments rather than single-family homes.

of government credit policies and of the policies of real estate developers and financial institutions to produce more multi-family complexes and fewer single-family units. Where people live depends much more on the policies of these institutions than it does on their own preferences.

THE DUAL MIGRATION

The two points of racial discord and free choice are extremely important. Although suburbanization cannot be traced directly to racial prejudice or to individual choices, the fact of suburbanization has had profound consequences on race relations and the kinds of choices that are available on such social amenities as housing, jobs, and schools. Suburbanization was an integral part of the most far-reaching demographic trend of the post–World War II era: the dual migration of relatively poor, rural, and racial minority peoples into the large central cities and of more affluent, middle-class whites out to the suburbs.

Who Are the In-migrants?

The migration into the cities — the so-called "in-migration" — consisted in great measure of people from the South and the Appalachian Mountains who moved into the central cities of the Northeast and Midwest. Although a majority of these in-migrants were not members of racial minorities, substantial numbers of them were. For two decades after the end of World War II there was a steady migration north and west of Negro sharecroppers who were driven off Southern farms and plantations by policies of agricultural subsidies and by the mechanization of farm labor. Three migration routes developed along the principal railroad lines. From the Southeastern states there was a steady migration to Northeastern cities such as Washington, Newark, New York, and Philadelphia. From the more centrally located Southern states of Alabama, Mississippi, and Tennessee there was a migration to Midwestern cities such as Saint Louis, Chicago, and Detroit. From Arkansas, Louisiana, and Texas former sharecroppers drifted westward to the large Texas cities of Dallas, Fort Worth, and Houston, and to other cities as far west as Los Angeles.[28]

Whichever route the migration took, there was some terminal city beyond which the Southern blacks did not migrate in large numbers. On the East Coast it was New York. In the Midwest it was Chicago and

Detroit, and on the West Coast it was Oakland. Across the river from New York City, Newark was 56 percent black by 1970, and even Hartford, Connecticut, was 29 percent black. But beyond those cities, the black proportion of central city populations dropped off markedly. Albany was only 12 percent black, and Boston was only 14 percent black. The same thing occurred in the Midwest. Chicago was 34 percent black by 1970. Barely a hundred miles north of Chicago, however, Milwaukee was only 15 percent black, and the next large central cities, Minneapolis and Saint Paul, were only 6 percent black. The same phenomenon occurred on the West Coast, where the combined populations of San Francisco and Oakland were about 20 percent black (San Francisco was 13.4 percent, Oakland 34.5 percent) but the population of Portland was only 8 percent black. This phenomenon is very important to understand, for it indicates that there is a very broad range of variation in racial composition from one central city to another. The Negro migrations were conditioned by geographical factors as much as social and political factors. One must therefore speak cautiously when generalizing about the racial problems of central cities.

In addition to the black racial minority in the cities, there has also been an enormous influx of Spanish-speaking migrants. The magnitude of this migration is only beginning to be recognized. There are almost 11 million people of Spanish-speaking origin in the United States, making it the fifth or sixth largest Spanish-speaking country in the world.[29] Three-fourths of these people are Puerto Ricans, Mexicans (or Chicanos), and Cubans. About 1.5 million Puerto Ricans live in continental United States. They migrated principally to New York City, but large Puerto Rican settlements exist in other cities on the East Coast and as far west as Chicago. They are the most urbanized of the Spanish-speaking ethnic groups: 97 percent of Puerto Ricans live in SMSAs.

Mexican-Americans, with their population of 5.3 million, constitute one of the largest ethnic groups in the United States. Fully 87 percent of the Mexican-Americans live in just five states (Arizona, California, New Mexico, Colorado, Texas). But because so many Mexicans are migrant farm laborers, they have formed Chicano communities as far north as Minnesota and as far east as Ohio — over 15,000 Mexican-Americans live in Milwaukee, for example — and they are the least urbanized of the Spanish-speaking population. Only 79 percent live in metropolitan areas.

The Mexican-Americans are the largest group of immigrants into the United States during the 1970s. Of the 700,000 legal immigrants in

1973, 70,000 were Mexicans. In addition, an undetermined number of Mexicans (which may be as high as ten times that many) migrated illegally into the country.*

About 629,000 Cuban Americans live in the United States, principally in Miami. They differ from Puerto Ricans and Mexican-Americans in three respects. First, they came for mostly political rather than economic reasons. Second, since they arrived with little capital but many skills, they have tended to enter the mainstream of middle-class American life. Third, the Cubans, collectively, tend to be much more politically conservative than the Puerto Ricans or Chicanos.

There also has been a migration of Indians into the cities, although in much smaller numbers and usually localized to the urban areas close to reservations. In the substantial Indian communities found in Minneapolis and Los Angeles the native Americans exist in perhaps a greater state of poverty and disorganization than any other ethnic or racial group in those cities.

Since immigration statutes were changed in 1965 to remove the previous ceiling of 100 persons per Asian country per year, a small but steady migration of Chinese have come to the Chinatown communities of San Francisco and other cities. Another urban minority, although not a racial minority, are the people migrating into the cities from the depressed areas of the Appalachians, West Virginia, Kentucky, and Tennessee.

Dual Migration's Effects on the Cities

These migrations of relatively unaffluent people into the central cities constitute the first part of the dual migration. The second part consists of the migration of more affluent people out of the central cities. The large metropolitan areas have been compared to huge donuts with a hole in the middle. Since the suburbs become separate tax entities, the central cities do not share the increased tax revenue from more expensive homes, the increasing number of shopping centers, and the growing number of business establishments in the suburbs. Further, since the suburbs normally do not belong to the same school districts as the central cities, there is less and less mingling between the poor and the upper-middle-class children in the schools. Although it is not completely true that the suburbs became affluent while the central cities

---

* The United States Commissioner of Immigration, Leonard F. Chapman, Jr., is quoted as saying that 670,000 Mexicans were apprehended trying to enter the United States illegally in 1973. An equal number was estimated to have entered the United States illegally without being apprehended. (U. S. News and World Report, July 22, 1974, p. 27.)

became impoverished, it is true that the largest number of urban poor people settle in the central cities. And because suburbanization brought changes in the metropolitan political structure, the central cities found it more and more difficult to come up with the resources to handle the social problems which the poor brought with them.

The dual migration of the poorer people and the racial minorities into the central cities and of more affluent, upper-middle-class people out to the suburbs has deep historic roots. As the early Irish immigrants became affluent enough to move into the better neighborhoods, their slums were inherited by Italians, Jews, and Poles. As these ethnic minorities moved out of the slums, they in turn were followed by the post–World War II urban minorities. But what will happen if in-migration into the slums stops? This serious question has begun to plague large cities in the last few years. Black in-migration from the South has begun to taper off dramatically, and this has reduced the pressure on housing in lower- and working-class black neighborhoods. At the same time, open housing policies and a general rise in the incomes of middle-class, young black families have enabled unprecedented numbers of blacks to migrate out of the slums into more attractive central city neighborhoods. The net result has been a rapid deterioration in lower- and working-class black neighborhoods which are being abandoned to what one group of commentators called "a destructive residual under class."[30]

The Woodlawn neighborhood in Chicago illustrates this process. Located just south of the University of Chicago campus where it serves as a residential area for university personnel, the neighborhood changed in the 1950s from a predominantly white neighborhood to a predominantly black one. During the 1960s, Woodlawn also became the locale for the most highly organized and powerful of Chicago's teenage gangs, the Blackstone Rangers. Violence precipitated by the Rangers, along with the availability of nonsegregated housing elsewhere in the city, combined to drive out of the neighborhood most of the working-class and middle-class families who could afford to leave. At the same time, pressure on absentee landlords to bring their property up to the standards of the city's building codes put many landlords in the untenable situation where increased rents would not offset increased maintenance and repair costs. Many landlords responded by abandoning their buildings. The abandoned buildings then became prey to vandals, looters, and arsonists. The core of Woodlawn lost 41 percent of its population during the 1960s. In the last six years of the decade, over 400 Woodlawn buildings were demolished by the city.

Whether the experience of Chicago's Woodlawn section will be widely repeated in other large cities is not yet known. But the example of Woodlawn does suggest that simply ending the in-migration will not of itself end the growing deterioration of the core residential areas. The Presidential Commission on Population and the American Future argues that ending the in-migration may even contribute to the cities' deterioration. Metropolises grow in three ways — from in-migration, from expansion into previously nonmetropolitan areas, and from a natural increase through the excess of births over deaths. A metropolis that grows more rapidly through in-migration and expansion than through natural increase is in a more viable economic position. This is because most in-migrants are of working age and are able to contribute to the production of goods and services in the metropolis; but the babies that represent growth through natural increase constitute a large dependent population that typically will not do productive work for almost two decades. Historically, American metropolises experienced more growth through in-migration. During the 1960s, however, 74 percent of the growth within 1960 SMSA boundaries was accounted for by natural increase rather than in-migration. The Commission on Population Growth and the American Future expects this pattern to continue throughout the rest of the century.[31] Interestingly, in the context of the commission's thesis, the number of metropolitan residents who are receiving public welfare assistance has skyrocketed.[32]* If the Population Commission's theory is correct, then the dependent population of metropolises will continue to grow faster than the working population, and public welfare costs may continue increasing well into the 1980s in metropolitan America.

SOME POLITICAL IMPLICATIONS OF METROPOLITAN GROWTH

An underlying assumption of this chapter has been that demographic and technological forces have significant political implications. Three implications in particular stand out: (1) the nature of urban growth is shaped by political decisions; (2) urban growth inevitably leads to greater governmental activity and expenditures; and (3) urban growth

---

* There are other causes in addition to the increase in dependent population. For one, many action groups during the 1960s informed the poor of their rights to welfare. This alone would have increased the number of recipients even if the dependent population had not grown. See the discussion in Chapter 5, "Antidotes for Nonresponsiveness: Community Action and Model Cities Programs."

obliges governments to assume the role of arbiter between conflicting groups in the urban arena.

The effect of political decisions on urban growth can be seen by reviewing some of the items previously covered in this chapter. For example, political decisions shaped the technological innovations that caused urban growth. At every stage of new technological implementation indicated in Table 2-3, governments made significant public investments. At the earliest stage, government funds financed the construction of the canals. At the railroad stage, government lands were given to the railroads, and the railroads in turn sold these lands in order to construct their railroad cities. And in the automobile/motor transport stage, the federal government utilized the highway trust fund to provide a continual source of funding for the highways and the interstate road system. Not only have governmental decisions contributed directly to the application of new transportation technologies, but many governmental decisions have had profound impact on determining the locations where urbanization would occur. The rapid post–World War II urbanization of southern California was due in great measure to federal expenditures in aerospace and defense industries. The decisions in Nevada to legalize gambling contributed to the urbanization of Reno and Las Vegas. Finally, as indicated earlier, state and federal decisions on highway construction, home mortgage loan terms, and the subsidization of farmers to reduce acreage have contributed immensely to the dual migration that has characterized metropolitan United States since the 1920s.

A second political implication of metropolitan growth is that increasing levels of urbanization inevitably lead to increasing levels of governmental activity and governmental expenditure. The cholera epidemic in Memphis cited earlier indicates how important it is for urban governments to take the initiative in such matters as sewage disposal, water supply, and public health. At the metropolitan level, suburban growth has meant greater expenditures for streets, utilities, fire and police protection, and public education. This inevitable increase in governmental activity as urbanization proceeds conflicts sharply with the political value widely held in the United States that governments should engage in the least possible amount of activities.

A third political implication of metropolitan growth is that governments are increasingly obliged to satisfy demands put forward by emerging groups in the growing metropolis. Often these groups ask the government to redress grievances they have against other actors in the metropolis. Other times they ask the government to help them satisfy certain needs which they cannot satisfy themselves because they lack the economic resources to compete on an equal footing in the economic system. This has particularly been true in relation to the struggle of racial minority leaders and others to gain equal access to the social amenities of the metropolis — housing, jobs, and education. When they do not succeed in bargaining directly with institutions that control that access, they seek redress from the governments, and government officials are called upon to assist in the conflict.

Compared to the countryside, the urban ghetto is more conducive to militant political activity such as protesting, demonstrating, and rioting; it brings potential leaders into direct contact with many more potential followers; and it is more receptive to traditional forms of redressing grievances. In the city, lawsuits are brought before the courts. Lobbying is conducted before the legislatures and city councils. Candidates are run for public office. All this indicates that the more urbanized an area becomes, the more its governments will become involved in social conflicts.

POLITICAL BIAS IN THE CHANGES IN URBAN GROWTH

It may seem absurd to suggest that demographic movements might be biased politically, for demographic movements are neutral phenomena. Nevertheless, urban growth in contemporary America has certain patterns and consequences which favor certain groups of people rather than others. Three of these stand out.

First, a persistent motive force behind urban growth throughout United States history has been what Sam Bass Warner called *privatism*. Warner wrote: "The tradition of privatism is . . . the most important element of our culture for understanding the development of cities."[33] City growth was seldom promoted from a sense of community as much as it was promoted by private speculators and entrepreneurs who needed the growth to maximize their profit. Land, in particular, was seldom viewed as a public good. On the contrary, it was a private asset upon which the shrewd person not only could speculate wisely but also could build a city. The nineteenth-century masters in real estate speculation were the railroads. In the twentieth century they were the central city and suburban real estate developers. The provision of cultural facilities such as libraries and museums was left to philanthropists or to private subscription.[34] There was no concept of the public good for which the government could make such provisions. Even today in many cities, these facilities receive the leftovers of the municipal or county budgets.

As cities grow larger, the tradition of privatism conflicts sharply with the government's role as a provider of services and redresser of grievances. The extent to which governments at the metropolitan, state, and federal levels should try to guide the urban growth process is a hotly debated question. There are probably very few people who would any longer argue for leaving metropolitan growth totally to private initiative. But there is no general agreement on how much guidance government should provide or even which governments should provide it.[35]

A second bias of the contemporary metropolis is that it is probably more class segregated than it was before. When the cities were so small and densely populated that all classes were concentrated within a few miles of the central business district, the residential areas of the poor, the working class, the middle class, and the wealthy were necessarily located very close to each other. The contemporary metropolises are so much larger and less densely populated that this is probably no longer true. This question has not been systematically studied by social scientists, but some scattered supportive evidence exists. Census tracts in Milwaukee and Buffalo show a very high level of class segregation in both the cities and suburbs.[36] Also, studies show that suburban neighborhoods tend to specialize in the kinds of people who live in them.[37]

A third bias implication is that the changes over the past fifty or sixty years have made the contemporary metropolis less amenable to promoting the social mobility of the poor. The European immigrants lived within easy commuting distance from the urban growth areas where the greatest job and entrepreneurial opportunities existed. Today these opportunities have shifted to the suburban fringe. But the poor, urban in-migrant typically moves into an old residential neighborhood far removed from suburban job locations. In most metropolises, public transportation systems are not very efficient. The poor in-migrant's geographic distance from the growth area makes it much more difficult for him to partake in the metropolitan growth either as an employee or as a speculative entrepreneur than it was for the European immigrant who migrated into a still fast-growing city. Furthermore, the economic transformations in the past several decades have greatly reduced the number of unskilled and semiskilled jobs and have in large measure replaced small, owner-run retail stores with large retailing outlets and franchises. In summary, urban America in the days of European immigration was biased toward the entrepreneurial type who had the imagination and the capacity to profit from a growing situation. The urban America of the 1970s is much less conducive to the upward social mobility of the poor classes, particularly the poor classes within the racial minority communities.

These considerations of the potential bias of urban growth can be examined by comparing the politics of the central city during the immigrant phase with the politics of contemporary central cities. This will be done in the next three chapters.

Some Suggested Readings

General Works

Jane Jacobs, *The Economy of Cities* (New York: Vintage Books, 1970). A highly readable account of the reasons cities grow and some of the basic issues of urban economics. The scholarly use of this book is somewhat limited because the author footnotes none of her references.

Jean Gottman, *Megalopolis: The Urbanized Seaboard of the United States* (New York: The Twentieth Century Fund, 1961). Few students will want to read the entire book. But for an account of just how distinct the Northeast seacoast is, few works are better than the introductory pages of this book.

Histories

Blake McKelvey, *The Urbanization of America: 1860–1915* (New Brunswick, N.J.: Rutgers University Press, 1963) and *The Emergence of Metropolitan America: 1915–1966* (New Brunswick, N.J.: Rutgers University Press, 1968). A fairly encyclopedic treatment of American urban history.

Charles N. Glaab and A. Theodore Brown, *A History of Urban America* (New York: Macmillan, 1967). Much less comprehensive than the two works by McKelvey, but also much more readable.

Readers

Paul Kramer and Frederick L. Holborn, eds.,*The City in American Life: From Colonial Times to the Present* (New York: Capricorn Books, 1971). Containing mostly chapters excerpted from several classic urban studies, this reader introduces the student to some of the dominant themes of American urbanization.

Kenneth T. Jackson and Stanley K. Schultz, eds., *Cities in American History* (New York: Knopf, 1972). A varied collection of articles on American urban history.

Gino Germani, ed., *Modernization, Urbanization, and the Urban Crisis* (Boston: Little, Brown, 1973). Contains an original essay by Germani and articles that explore several theoretical aspects of urbanization.

Specific Urbanization Studies

Sam Bass Warner, *Streetcar Suburbs: The Process of Growth in Boston, 1870–1900* (Cambridge, Mass.: Harvard University Press, 1962). An important historical study of the impact of transit systems on the growth of a major metropolis.

Sam Bass Warner, *The Private City: Philadelphia in Three Periods of Its Growth* (Philadelphia: University of Pennsylvania Press, 1968). In this study Warner introduces his concept of *privatism*. The three periods are 1770–1780, 1830–1860, and 1920–1930.

Constance McLaughlin Green, *The Secret City: A History of Race Relations in the Nation's Capital* (Princeton, N.J.: Princeton University Press, 1967). Describes and interprets the life of the black community in Washington, D.C., since its founding.

Morton and Lucia White, *The Intellectual Versus the City: From Thomas Jefferson to Frank Lloyd Wright* (Cambridge, Mass.: Harvard University Press, 1962). An important treatment of the antiurban theme in American intellectual life.

Oscar Handlin, *Boston's Immigrants* (Cambridge, Mass.: The Belknap Press of Harvard University Press, 1959). A study of the impact of immigrants on the city and their adjustment to it.

PART II

The tone of contemporary urban politics in the United States has been greatly influenced by late nineteenth-century machine politics and the events which caused their decline. So much has this been so, that contemporary urban politics are virtually incomprehensible without some understanding of these historical forces. As the great industrial cities were born along the North Atlantic seacoast and the Great Lakes states, machine politics emerged. As governing devices, the machines were often deeply rooted in the social structures of the ethnic groups that inhabited these cities. The basic unit of political organization was a geographic unit, the ward or precinct. These developments are discussed in Chapters 3 and 4.

RISE, DECLINE, AND CONSEQUENCES OF MACHINE AND ETHNIC POLITICS

Because the political machines were often rooted in the social organization of certain ethnic communities, machine politics were biased toward and benefited those communities and certain businesspeople. In contrast, other groups, such as the racial minorities, benefited very little, for machine politics were effectively biased against them. However, there were very few cities with sizeable racial minority populations until the twentieth century.

The machine politics were also biased to the disadvantage of certain upper-middle-class, reform-minded citizens who wanted to upgrade the level of public morals in the city. To accomplish these objectives, the reformers promoted several devices to remove city government from the control of the political machines. They were aided in their antimachine efforts by the patterns of metropolitan growth and by some actions taken by the federal government. These developments are discussed in Chapter 4. The consequences of these developments for governance in the contemporary central cities are discussed in Chapter 5.

47

Chapter 3

Chapter 2 indicated that the first major change in patterns of urbanization in the United States took place between 1840 and 1930, when hundreds of medium-size and large cities were created in the Northeast and Midwest by the settlement there of most of thirty-seven million immigrants. Politically, this process gave birth to the organization of urban political power on geographic and ethnic bases. The present chapter will show how several powerful contemporary institutions in urban politics developed out of the indigenous community structures of four European ethnic minorities: the Irish, Italians, Jews, and Poles.

Institutionalizing Power in the Pre–World War II City

The choice of these four ethnic groups is not random. Irish, Italian, Jewish, and Polish peoples settled almost exclusively in urban centers and, as much as any other ethnic group, shaped the institutions which dominated urban politics prior to World War II. By 1970 the descendents of these four ethnic groups numbered thirty million, about a fourth of the urbanized metropolitan population in the country, and their ethnicity continues to be important in modern urban politics.

Some of the institutions surviving from the old, pre–World War II city, such as the parish organization of the Catholic church, were integral elements of the ethnic power base. Other institutions, such as organized labor, were not integral elements of the ethnic power base, but they disproportionately tended to be led by and to serve the descendents of the European immigrants. In both cases the institutions were created prior to World War II and have not adapted well to the needs of new urban minorities in the contemporary metropolis.

THE SIZE AND DISTRIBUTION OF ETHNIC SETTLEMENTS

Table 3-1 illustrates the distribution of major ethnic groups in the United States. The eight major urban ethnic groups can be divided into three general categories: (1) the mainstream nationalities that were assimilated the most thoroughly into the native white American population (especially English and Germans); (2) the European ethnic minorities that immigrated principally before World War I and still exhibit political characteristics of ethnic cohesion (especially the Irish, Italians, Slavs, and Jews); and (3) the newer racial and ethnic minorities that migrated into the cities primarily since World War II either from the American South or from abroad (especially blacks and Spanish-speaking minorities). As calculated in columns 3 and 4 of Table 3-1,

TABLE 3-1

ESTIMATED ETHNIC AND RACIAL COMPOSITION OF THE METROPOLITAN POPULATION

Nationality or Racial Group	(1) Approximate Number in United States[a]	(2) Percent Urban[b]	(3) Estimated Number in SMSAs[c]	(4) Percentage of Urbanized SMSA Population[d]
Mainstream nationalities				**35.0**
English	29,548,000	94	25,706,960	20.9
German	25,543,000	68	17,369,240	14.1
European ethnics				**26.5**
Irish	16,408,000	91	14,931,280	12.1
Italians	8,764,000	94	8,238,160	6.7
Catholic Poles	3,829,000	87	3,331,230	2.7
Jews	6,115,000	99	6,115,000	5.0
Contemporary urban minorities				**20.9**
Blacks	22,673,000	74	16,786,000	13.6
Spanish speaking	10,600,000	85	8,957,000	7.3

[a] United States Bureau of the Census, Current Population Reports, ser. P-20; no. 249, "Characteristics of the Population by Ethnic Origin: March 1972 and 1971" (Washington, D.C.: U.S. Government Printing Office, 1973); and Current Population Reports, ser. P-20; no. 264, "Persons of Spanish Origin in the United States: March, 1973" (Washington, D.C.: U.S. Government Printing Office, 1974). Alvin Chenkin, "Jewish Population in the United States," in American Jewish Yearbook (Philadelphia: Jewish Publication Society, 1973), vol. 74, pp. 308–309.
[b] Taken from a survey conducted among Catholic ethnics by the National Opinion Research Center. Harold J. Abramson, Ethnic Diversity in Catholic America (New York: Wiley, 1973), p. 34. The Jewish population as reported in the American Jewish Yearbook is entirely urban. Nonurban Jews were not included in its study.
[c] Estimated number = col. 1 × col. 2.
[d] Percentage = col. 3 ÷ 118,000,000 (i.e., the population of the urbanized areas).

the mainstream nationalities comprise about a third of the contemporary urbanized metropolitan population. The European ethnics comprise about a fourth, and the more recent in-migrants comprise about a fifth.

The population figures in column 3 of Table 3-1 indicate the importance of the European ethnic minorities to American urban development. At the end of the nineteenth century, when some of the most important urban political institutions were being formed, the European ethnics comprised an absolute majority of the population in almost three-fourths of all cities of 100,000 or more. In the Northeast, which contained two-thirds of all such cities at the time, European immigrants and their children constituted an absolute majority in all except four cities — Baltimore, Maryland; Columbus, Ohio; Indianapolis, Indiana; and Washington, D.C. In only five big cities in the entire country did American-born whites of American-born parents comprise an absolute majority of the population. And three of these five cities were west of the Mississippi River — Los Angeles, Kansas City, and Saint Joseph, Missouri.[1]

The immediate political implications of these statistics are two. First, the black, Spanish, and other urban minorities who in the 1970s are beginning to dominate many central city populations have found that the basic political institutions in these cities were established long before their arrival. Most of the leadership positions in these institutions are already occupied by people who are not eager to relinquish them. This has been and continues to be a serious source of friction as blacks, Puerto Ricans, and Chicanos seek greater representation in the public bureaucracies and in elective offices. Second, because the European ethnics dominated the populations of many Northeastern cities during their period of growth to their present size, these ethnics and their institutions had a disproportionate voice in setting the tone and style that still prevail in the politics of these places. For these reasons, the political institutions developed by these European ethnic minorities are important to the student of contemporary urban politics.

THE POLITICS OF DEVELOPING
INDIGENOUS POWER BASES

The Irish

The Irish were the first European ethnic group to migrate in massive numbers directly into the American city. Although some Irish were involved in urban politics as early as the 1820s, their influence remained relatively limited until the great waves of Irish immigrants began to inundate the Northeastern cities. Following the potato famine of the 1840s, Irish immigration reached a flood tide. Half a million Irish reportedly starved to death during the famine, and out of a total population of no more than 8 million, over a million people migrated to the United States in the seven years between 1847 and 1854. In the twenty years prior to 1861, over 1.7 million Irish migrated to the United States. Although these numbers may seem small in comparison to present-day populations, they represented almost 10 percent of the total American population of 1840. And since the immigrants were concentrated primarily in a few dozen cities on the East Coast and in the Midwest, their localized impact was very great. As early as 1850, 26 percent of New York City's population had been born in Ireland.[2]

As their numbers increased, the Irish were increasingly considered a threat by certain segments of the dominant society which could not appreciate their strange accent, their suspect religion, their high crime rates, and their lack of preparedness for anything but the lowliest forms of manual labor. A nativist movement arose to protest the integrity of American society from the supposed debilitating consequences of allowing the immigrants access to that society.[3] The Irish, like most later immigrants, found themselves in an alien and hostile environment. Periodically their churches and convents were burned and sacked by angry mobs. And an anti-Catholic book by Maria Monk, *Awful Disclosures*, was so well received in a populace apparently willing to believe the worst about the Irish and the Catholics that it went through twenty editions and sold 300,000 copies.

Politically, this nativist movement found expression in the Know Nothing party that was organized in the early 1850s. The Know Nothings hoped to restrict Irish immigration and to prevent the Irish from holding office. They enjoyed their greatest success in Massachusetts, where they won the governorship, all state offices, and huge majorities in both houses of the legislature. But they let their vigilance in weeding "popery" out of the government turn to excess. One Know Nothing legislative committee was organized to investigate convents. On a visit to inspect a particular convent, some committee members charged to the state not only their liquor bills but also the "expenses incurred in their off-duty relations with a lady 'answering to the name of Mrs. Patterson.' "[4] The revelation of these activities plus the fact that the legislature voted itself a pay increase did not endear the Know Nothings to the electorate. And when the national Know Nothing party, under the dominance of Southerners, endorsed both a proslavery platform and a proslavery candidate for the presidency in 1856, they lost their support among the Northern electorate, which was becoming increasingly abolitionist.[5] This demise of the Know Nothings as a formal political party marked the end of the last serious threat to place legislative restrictions on Irish immigration or the activities of the Catholic church.

THE AMERICAN RIVER GANGES.

The anti-Catholicism which plagued the Irish in the United States during much of the nineteenth century is illustrated in this cartoon by the great political cartoonist, Thomas Nast. Note the bishops portrayed as alligators attacking the public schools, the Bible, and the defenseless women and children, while Boss Tweed leans on his elbows and smiles at the assault. Tweed was not a Catholic, but many Tammany leaders were. Tammany Hall is placed side by side with "the political Roman Catholic schools"; furthermore, its center dome is capped with a cross, while the two smaller domes are capped by flags of the Catholic church and the Irish. (The significance of Tammany and the political bosses will be discussed later in this chapter.)

Source: J. Chal Vinson, *Thomas Nast: Political Cartoonist* (Athens, Ga.: University of Georgia Press, 1967), plate 48.

It is difficult to compare the relative hardships that different ethnic and racial groups faced. The Irish never suffered the direct oppression of slavery or segregation that the blacks endured. They never encountered discriminatory immigration or antimiscegenation laws as the Chinese did. And they never faced the lynchings which both blacks and Italians endured.[6] But historical accounts of living conditions in Irish ghettoes clearly indicate that life was brutish, oppressive, and surrounded by open hostility.

The Irish reacted to the hostilities they faced much in the way militant blacks began to react to whites during the middle 1960s. They took the most disparaged of their characteristics and began to stress that these were virtues rather than vices. First among these characteristics was their religion, Roman Catholicism — not only a minority religion but a generally disliked and untrusted religion.

Religion as Community Development

Largely because of this distrust, Catholicism made several important contributions to the development of the social structure of the Irish community. Its first contribution was to give the Irish a symbol for psychological identification and community unification. Just as blacks a century later were to derive a considerable psychological satisfaction from accentuating the very characteristics which had been the most scorned by the rest of society (skin color and type of hair),* Catholicism gave the Irish their own set of distinguishing characteristics that bound them together. The liturgy, ritual, and practice of the Catholic faith distinctly marked them as different. In particular, Irish Catholics were clearly distinguished from Protestants and virtually everybody else by several practices and beliefs — confession, Sunday Mass, meatless Friday, Lenten observance, the belief that the Catholic church is the only means of salvation, ashes on the forehead when Lent began and Easter palms when it ended, religious relics carefully placed on the walls of Irish homes, and the lack of a fundamentalist puritanism about liquor and gambling.

These ritualistic observances gave the Irish the symbols of identity which were to become very useful to aspiring civic leaders in the American cities. For once a group of people begins to think of themselves as different and unique, their sense of uniqueness can be exploited for purposes of political mobilization. Ethnic solidarity thus gave the professional politicians an effective way of building electoral coalitions that could cut across class lines.[7]

Whatever spiritual or religious salvation the church brought to the

* Malcolm X commented that Negroes degraded themselves when they attempted to straighten their hair. And he stressed that they must learn not only to accept but to be proud of their natural hair and their blackness. [*The Autobiography of Malcolm X* (New York: Grove Press, 1966), pp. 54–56.]

Irish, this symbolic identification cannot be overestimated, for it enabled Catholicism to make a second great contribution to the Irish. Very early in the period of Irish immigration, the Catholic hierarchy decided that the preservation of the Catholic faith in this Protestant land demanded the creation of parish churches and parish schools. This decision was later followed by admonitions to Catholic parents that they were bound under pain of sin to send their children to the parochial schools.[8]

These decisions had two significant results. First, by developing parishes, the Irish were bound together in *geographic* units. The Catholic churchgoer not only attended church in his neighborhood; he lived there, he educated his children there, and often he worked there. This would prove to be an enormous advantage in electoral politics which were also organized on the geographic units of wards and precincts or assembly districts.

A second result of the parish development was the stimulation of considerable construction activity that channeled business opportunities to Irish contractors and job opportunities to Irish laborers. Not only were churches and schools built, but so were rectories, convents, parish halls, cathedrals, chanceries, high schools, bishops' residences, homes for retired religious persons, and seminaries. Church historian John Tracy Ellis stated that the church's energies and attentions during this period were almost entirely absorbed "by the laborious task of building churches and establishing a school system such as no other Catholic, national community had ever attempted."[9] From 1850 to 1950 the number of Catholic churches in Illinois, for example, increased fifteenfold, from 59 to 977.[10] Similar increases occurred in other areas with growing Irish populations. Just before the Civil War, one Catholic weekly noted "that hardly a week passed without the laying of a cornerstone or the dedication of a new church."[11]

All of this construction activity generated a significant number of jobs and construction contracts. Quite naturally, the Irish Catholic bishops and pastors awarded these construction contracts to Irish businessmen or at least to businessmen who were willing to hire Irish laborers. The early decision to create parochial schools was a built-in guarantee that some Irish could build successful businesses in the construction trades, trucking, real estate, insurance, and related business enterprises.

The success of these early entrepreneurs was highly dependent upon the very limited base of the Irish community, and their hopes for continued success made it imperative for them to reinvest a portion of their profits into religious and social institutions of the Irish community. Operating almost exclusively at the community level as small contractors, tradesmen, grocery or saloon owners, retail tradesmen, lawyers, and physicians, they depended for their continued success upon adherence to what one commentator called two unwritten rules for the rising businessman or professional. "One was to live in the neighborhood . . . . The other requirement was a willingness to help the worst off in time of need . . . . No one who hoped to prosper or be well regarded in the community turned them down."[12] The very purposes behind the formation of the Knights of Columbus was in fact to institutionalize this kind of charity.

As a consequence of these unwritten rules and the ingrown nature of Irish Catholic social life, the Irish communities soon blossomed with insurance organizations, fraternal and service organizations, Catholic hospitals, high schools, Knights of Columbus centers, colleges, and even universities. An institutional framework was established to advance young men in society, to provide help for the less fortunate, and at the same time to bind the community together.

A third feature of Catholicism that contributed to Irish community development was the church's interpretation of the Third Commandment, to "keep holy the Sabbath." Whereas some orthodox Protestants interpreted this commandment as an instruction to keep stores closed on Sundays and prohibit drinking, card playing, gambling, and other pleasures, the Irish Catholics simply interpreted it to mean that they had to attend Mass each Sunday. To be sure, the Catholic was supposed to abstain from any unnecessary manual labor on Sunday, but all that he really had to do in order to fulfill his Sunday obligation was to show up at Mass, the focal point of the Catholic liturgy. And, of course, once he got to church, he was reminded that in addition to keeping the Lord's Third Commandment, canon law demanded that he contribute to the support of the church. Both of these commandments were binding under threat of eternal damnation. The net result was to turn the parish into an agency for mobilizing substantial financial and physical resources, many of which were reinvested into the development of the community, often into valuable real estate holdings.*

The key figure for guiding this development was the parish pastor. With the power to forgive sin as well as to mobilize resources, his sacral and worldly functions gave him an aura and power that kept the Roman Catholic community cohesive and unified. On occasions, the

* Nathan Glazer and Daniel Patrick Moynihan contend that this financial sacrifice to the church has prevented the formation of an Irish upper class in the United States. See their *Beyond the Melting Pot: The Negroes, Puerto Ricans, Jews, Italians, and Irish of New York* (Cambridge, Mass.: M.I.T. Press, 1963), p. 230.

Catholic's awe of the clergy was bizarre. Archbishop Ireland of Saint Paul, for example, was reported to placate his passionate hatred of liquor by making house-to-house tours of the Irish slums and sending "whiskey bottles flying out the doorways."[13] This intrusion into the private home was a remarkable demonstration of the lengths to which the Catholic clergy could go without provoking rebellion among their Irish faithful.

Because of both the nature of its ethical rules and its extensive construction activities, the immigrant church in America came to be a significant agency for building institutions that provided social mobility for the Irish. Through the parochial school and the Sunday collection plate, the parish and the diocese efficiently mobilized both human and financial resources to build the business, educational, and religious institutions through which individual Irishmen could live what they considered to be productive and dignified lives.

The church not only provided jobs and business opportunities; for a long time it also constituted the focal point of institutionalized Irish social life.[14] Indeed, during the early years of immigration the only locale that seriously competed with the parish as an Irish gathering place was the saloon, which served as an informal communications network in the Irish social structure.[15] Because of the saloon's social importance, the saloon proprietors were very important personages in the Irish communities, and they often assumed positions of lay leadership in the parish organizations and societies.[16] The importance of the saloon is illustrated in the rise of the Kennedy family in Boston. Some of the early successes of Joseph P. Kennedy were directly traced to the political and economic advantages which accrued to his father as a respected ward politician and saloon keeper.[17] During the early years, except for the saloon (and even *it* dwindled in importance as the Irish grew more affluent), the parish dominated the social organization of the Irish ghetto. Some bishops went so far as to discourage any Irish social contacts outside the confines of the church.

Politics as a Business Venture

These social institutions built through the church dovetailed neatly with urban political developments in the late nineteenth century. Already bound together symbolically, geographically, and economically by the church, the Irish developed into a cohesive voting bloc that eventually gained great influence over the Democratic party in city after city.

In the days of the long ballot, the spoils system, patronage, and other innovations of Jacksonian Democracy, control over the Democratic party and the elected city offices soon developed into the well-known phenomenon of machine politics. (Machine politics as such will be discussed later in the chapter. For now, the discussion concentrates on their implications for the Irish community.) For the Irish, the period of dominance in machine politics enabled them to secure two advantages which they still have not entirely relinquished. First, they were able to get patronage jobs in the bureaucracy. For example, the Irish in New Haven were disproportionately employed as public servants.[18] In Boston, the city government's employment practices were so heavily weighted against Italians that one Sicilian got hired only after he changed his name to Foley.[19] The pervasiveness of this patronage can be seen in the stereotype of the Irish policeman, which still contains a great deal of truth. As late as 1950 a majority of the members of New York City's police force were Irish. Almost two-thirds of all the police commissioners Chicago has had since the Civil War were Irish. And as late as 1964, forty-one of that city's seventy-two highest police department positions were staffed by Irish.[20]

A second advantage which control of the government conferred upon the Irish was that it multiplied greatly the success which the church had given them in construction, real estate, and related businesses.[21] No longer was it simply churches and parish halls whose construction provided employment for Irish laborers and contracts for Irish businessmen. Now it was the physical growth of the entire city. There were contracts and jobs for schools, hospitals, precinct stations, and power lines. By controlling the city government, Irish political leaders could make sure that a disproportionate share of the jobs and business contracts went to their fellow Irish political supporters. Although few Irish city bosses got wealthy, more than one retired a millionaire.* It is doubtful if Irish ethnic political contacts any longer count for much in the way of social mobility.† There can be no doubt,

---

* Richard Croker of New York's Tammany Hall amassed a fortune of $3 million, and Hoboken's Bernard McFeeley amassed at least $1 million. However, Harold Zink's study of political bosses suggests that the millionaires were very few. [*City Bosses in the United States* (Durham, N.C.: Duke University Press, 1930).]

† In his book on Mayor Richard J. Daley, Chicago columnist Mike Royko catalogues an impressive array of contracts that enriched Democratic supporters with Irish names such as Gill, Cullerton, Horan, and Dunne [*Boss: Richard J. Daley of Chicago* (New York: Signet Books, 1971), p. 71]. It is important to stress, however, that these men belong to the oldest generation of Irish politicians in Chicago, and their enrichment does not necessarily provide social mobility for younger Irish men and women. Daley himself has carefully nurtured the image that he is a man of modest means. But a report in 1974 estimated his worth at least at $200,000 — not a fortune by any means, but certainly a comfortable nest egg (*Minneapolis Tribune*, July 12, 1974, p. 4-A).

however, that at least until the Great Depression, the relationships between city growth and business contracts provided enormously productive channels for social mobility in the Irish community. In a sense, the
control over the Democratic party enabled politicians to reverse the
truism of American politics that political power results from great
wealth. In the case of some of the Irish, it was the political power which
enabled the wealth to be acquired, rather than vice versa.*

In summary, the elementary channels for social mobility created by
the Irish were based on the hierarchically organized church, the Democratic party, control over the city's elective offices, and the use of
that control to provide jobs and business opportunities. All of these
elements were mutually reinforcing, and they provided an indigenous
base of Irish political power. The Irish were symbolically bound together by a strong sense of ethnic and religious identification that in
city after city gave rise to the founding of chauvinistic fraternal and
social groups such as the Sons of Erin, the Society of the Friendly Sons
of Saint Patrick, or the Ancient Order of Hibernians. At its most extreme, Irish nationalism led to the Molly Maguires and the Fenian
movement invasion of Canada.

Irish ascendency in the urban political process probably reached its
peak at the turn of the century,† by which time the reformers' assault
on machine politics and the competition of other ethnic groups threatened the Irish hegemony in the city. But by the time that occurred, the
Irish were already well entrenched. Even where other semblances of
ethnicity have died among them, the Irish are still disproportionately
concentrated in the bureaucracies of many city governments and in the
organizations of the Catholic church. For the Irish, these institutions
formed the core of what sociologist Andrew Greeley calls an ethnic network of social mobility. But, as Greeley also recognizes, the ethnic
network forms a trap as well, because the person who relies on that
network as a channel of mobility often becomes entrapped in it and has
difficulty gaining recognition outside of it.[22] If indeed the Irish have
truly made it in America, the measure of their success is probably not

---

* This argument applies, obviously, not only to the Irish but to any politican who uses
his political influence as a vehicle for social mobility. See Raymond E. Wolfinger, *The
Politics of Progress* (Englewood Cliffs, N.J.: Prentice-Hall, 1974), pp. 80–81.

† Others might put the date at 1928 (when an Irish Catholic, Al Smith, was a presidential
candidate) or even at 1960 (when an Irish Catholic, John F. Kennedy, won the presidency). But actually Irish control of the urban political parties began to suffer inroads
from other ethnics as early as 1900. In Providence, the percentage of Irish ward committeemen in the Democratic party increased from the 1870s until it reached its peak of
73 percent in 1900. After that date it slowly but steadily declined. [Elmer E. Cornwell, Jr.,
"Party Absorption of Ethnic Groups: The Case of Providence, Rhode Island," *Social
Forces* 38 (March 1960): 205–211.]

so much their continued dominance of the ethnic networks as their ability to move out of them. The third and fourth generations of Irish have burgeoning numbers of college graduates, lawyers, business-people, and professionals who are making their own way in the world on their individual merits with very little reliance on the ethnic networks.

Finally, a normative judgment is often levied against this Irish eth-nic network of social mobility on two counts. First, as Daniel Patrick Moynihan and others have charged, the Irish network was extremely deficient in making any intellectual contributions to American life. Second, in the political machine's dedication to political pragmatism, it was entirely devoid of any ideological content. Historically there has been considerable merit to those charges. In some respects, however, they may be less true in the 1970s than they were previously. The number of Irish on university faculties has apparently increased.[23] And Moynihan himself is evidence of Irish who are making intellectual contributions. Concerning the ideological leanings of the Irish, survey data on racial attitudes (as shown in Table 3-2 on page 84) find most Irish to be fairly liberal, but a substantial core is highly segregationist. The South Boston school desegregation disorders of 1974–75 illustrate that this core can be moved to considerable violence.

The Italians

Italian ethnic networks of political influence and social mobility were similar to those of the Irish in some general respects. But they were very different in terms of the politically important institutions that the Italians created. Like the Irish, most Italian immigrants were unskilled laborers, and very few of them had experience as merchants or skilled tradesmen.* The greatest bulk of Italian immigrants after 1880 came from impoverished southern Italy. They settled mostly in Northeastern and Midwestern cities, where their initial economic function was to compete with the Irish for jobs in the general unskilled labor force.[24] Italians who migrated to California were mostly northern Italians who were a little less destitute than — and did not get along well with — the southern Italians.[25] They also had immigrated much earlier and were much less alienated from the surrounding society.

The southern Italian immigrants tended to settle in Eastern and Mid-

* One source estimates that three-fourths of the Italian immigrants were general laborers, one-seventh were skilled tradesmen, 6 percent were farmers, and about 5 percent were merchants and dealers [Rudolf Glanz, *Jews and Italians: Historic Group Relations and the New Immigration 1881–1924* (New York: Shulsinger Brothers, 1970), pp. 31–33].

western big-city neighborhoods called "Little Italies." Normally there were several Little Italies in a big city: Chicago had seventeen.[26] And usually, people from other ethnic backgrounds also lived in the Italian neighborhoods. People from the same district in Italy would settle in the same building or on the same block. Thus the buildings and sometimes the blocks were homogeneous, while the neighborhoods themselves were usually heterogeneous.[27]

Although the Italians started with an occupational base and a settlement pattern similar to those of the Irish, they created an entirely different network of social mobility. No doubt much of the difference was due to the fact that the Italians arrived later, when the channels of social advancement that earlier had been open to the Irish — that is, the church and the Democratic parties — were closed.

In the American Catholic church, Italians have not been able to penetrate the top leadership. There have been few Italian bishops. Almost 60 percent of *all* American bishops since 1785 have been Irish or of Irish descent,[28] and most of the rest were German. The care of Italian souls was therefore mostly left to the Irish.[29] These ethnic differences estranged many Italians both from the Irish clergy and from the institutional church, which was much more puritanical than the churches they had known in Italy.* Consequently, they demanded parishes with Italian priests and Italian-language services. The first Italian church in Chicago was built in 1881.[30] By 1920 there were more than a dozen. The Italians were also skeptical of the parish school and preferred to send their children to the public schools.[31]† This estrangement of the Italians from the Irish-dominated church institutions was termed the *Italian problem* by some of the clergy, and the American archbishops responded by encouraging more American seminarians to study in Italy and more Italian priests to migrate to the United States.[32] Nevertheless, even today there are few Italian names among the American hierarchy. The church has not performed economic and organizational services for the Italians to the same extent that it had performed them for the Irish.

* One scholar of Italian Americans writes that "they did not feel that they could speak intimately with priests in America as they had in the old country," and consequently they tried at first to sustain their religious contacts with the village priests in Italy [Lawrence Frank Pisani, *The Italian in America: A Social Study and History* (New York: Exposition Press, 1957), p. 165]. Another scholar argues that even in Italy the peasantry was alienated from the clergy [Joseph Lopreato, *Italian Americans* (New York: Random House, 1970), pp. 88–89]. In either interpretation, early Italian immigrants had difficulty in relating to the American Catholic church.
† As the Italians grew more affluent in the post–World War II era, this changed, and Italians became strong supporters of the parochial schools (Lopreato, *Italian Americans*, pp. 89–90).

Italians found the Democratic party less closed to their ambitions than the church, but it took many years for them to capitalize on its opportunities. Because the Democratic party was dominated by the Irish, politically ambitious Italians had three possible courses of action. In cities such as New Haven, where local Republicans welcomed them for the purposes of regaining control of city government, Italians tended to become Republican.[33] In cities such as Boston and Chicago, where the Republicans did not seek their support, the Italians became Democrats and fought running battles to break down Irish control over nominations and patronage in Italian neighborhoods.[34]* In Providence, the Italians were originally Republican, but many joined the Democrats when the Republicans failed to give them their share of the political spoils.[35] Eventually, they remained active in both parties.[36] In addition to local conditions, national political events also affected the party allegiance of Italians. Republicans gained many votes in Italian precincts during the late 1930s and early 1940s as a result of President Roosevelt's hostility to and eventual war with the Mussolini regime in Italy.[37]† But since the end of the war, the long-range trend of Italian voting has been in favor of the Democrats.[38]‡

Although heavy Italian immigration began as early as the 1880s, it was not until the 1930s and 1940s that Italians began to capture many important public offices. They elected a governor in Rhode Island and a mayor in New Haven in the 1940s. Perhaps the earliest prominent Italian mayors were Angelo Rossi in San Francisco (1933–1944) and Fiorello La Guardia in New York (1933–1945). La Guardia was elected on a fusion ticket of Republicans and anti–Tammany Hall reformers. Throughout his mayoralty he greatly diminished the control of Irish-dominated Tammany Hall over the major political appointments in the city.[39] In 1949 Carmine De Sapio became the first Italian to head Tammany Hall. For the next decade he tried to balance organization Demo-

---

* In Chicago, the running battle consisted of two patterns. One was a pattern of acquiescence in which the Italians let the Irish bosses dominate Italian wards as long as they got minor payoffs and jobs. The other pattern was one of overt resistance. But the Italians usually lost at this, at least until the 1920s. In one instance the cost of defeat was murder. See Humbert S. Nelli, *Italians in Chicago, 1880–1930: A Study of Ethnic Mobility* (New York: Oxford University Press, 1970), pp. 88–124.

† Italian communities in American cities were deeply split by Mussolini's ascension to power in Italy. See John P. Diggings, *Mussolini and Fascism: The View from America* (Princeton, N.J.: Princeton University Press, 1972), chapter 6, pp. 111–143. Also see his "Italo-Americans and Anti-Fascist Opposition," *Journal of American History* 54 (December 1967): 579–598.

‡ Survey Research Center data for the Northeast during the 1950s found that 57 percent of Italians identified themselves as Democrats, 13 percent as Independents, and 30 percent as Republicans. (Cited in Wolfinger, *The Politics of Progress*, p. 39.)

crats and reform Democrats who were competing for control over the party.[40] Although La Guardia and De Sapio were at opposite ends of the political spectrum, they symbolize the peak of Italian influence in New York City politics.

One reason the Italians took until the 1930s to gain political prominence involves the skill with which the deeply entrenched Irish politicians played elements of the Italian communities against each other and minimized the potential voting strength of Italians. In both New York and Chicago, the Irish political leaders gerrymandered council and legislative district lines through the Little Italies and thus divided the Italian vote into several districts.[41] In the Hull House neighborhood of Chicago, Irish ward boss Johnny Powers stayed in power until 1927, even though many years previously Irish voters had become just a small fraction of his ward. He maintained his power by giving patronage and minor political appointments to Italians who were willing to cooperate with him and intimidating those who might work against him. So secure was his position that for the last several years of his reign he did not even live in the ward. One historian writes that Italians could have ousted this absentee Irish boss many years earlier if only "the Hull House reformers and the Italian community had worked together to effect his defeat."[42]

Italians took many years to develop an indigenous power base capable of effectively challenging the Irish. When this indigenous power base finally did develop, three elements were of prime importance — the nature of the social structure of the Italian communities, Italian business, and organized crime.

Political Relevance of the Italian Community's Social Structure

One theme that pervades most of the commentary on Italian social structure is the tremendous importance of kinship and personal relations. Italians apparently preferred (and still prefer) to interact with relatives and other Italians than with nonrelatives and non-Italians. National Opinion Research Center (NORC) surveys conducted in the 1960s found that Italians were much more prone than other European ethnics to live in ethnic neighborhoods, to visit their relatives regularly, and to visit often with others of the same ethnicity. They also were much less prone than any other European ethnics except Jews to marry outside of their ethnic group.[43] These tendencies were much stronger among the immigrant generation than they are now. A study of marriage records of an Italian church in Chicago in 1906 found that only 3 percent of the marriages were with non-Italians, and a majority of the marriages occurred between persons born in the same province in Italy.[44]

The NORC survey discovered other characteristics about Italian preferences, as well: Italians are less trusting than any other European ethnics except Jews and Anglo-Saxon protestants and more authoritarian than any other ethnics except the Slavs.[45]

These data about Italian-Americans suggest an ethnic community that was bound together by a strong web of kinship and personal relationships. There was a high level of mistrust and suspicion about persons who fell outside the web (especially non-Italians), and there was a tendency toward authoritarian relationships in which roles were relatively stable, well defined, and well understood. Insiders were to be trusted insofar as they conformed to the well-defined role patterns for family members and friends. Outsiders were to be trusted only after they had established a stable personal relationship.

Several researchers have commented on the implications of these characteristics for the development of a community social structure. Historian Rudolph Vecoli suggested that in the Italian community in Chicago, trust seldom extended beyond the immediate nuclear family. "Only through the ritual kinship of comparaggio (godparenthood) could nonrelatives gain admittance to the family circle."[46] This emphasis on mistrust and this ethnocentricity were much stronger among immigrants from southern Italy than among newcomers from northern Italy. Edward Banfield, in researching a village in southern Italy, found the lack of trust between families to be so pervasive that the community was virtually immobilized and incapable of any cooperative action for community projects such as getting a hospital or improving schools.[47] William Foote Whyte studied an Italian slum in Boston in the 1930s and found that Italians participated in the political process principally through the device of establishing personal relationships based on mutual and reciprocal obligations. For example, they generally felt that it was preferable not to accept pay from a politician for working on his campaign, because that would allow the politician to discharge his reciprocal obligation very cheaply. They usually preferred to work voluntarily in order to have some claim once the politician was elected. Before engaging in a campaign, younger men would often wait for cues from the more dominant family members in order to avoid supporting a candidate who was disfavored by the family.[48]

This dual importance of the family in politics and of close personal relationships is most likely an outgrowth of the conditions under which Italians immigrated to and settled in the American cities. These conditions did little to make the Italians trust outsiders, and they virtually demanded that the immigrants learn cooperation in order to avoid perpetual exploitation.

The first exploiter the isolated immigrant was likely to encounter was the *padrone*. Immigrants were required to have the means to support themselves before they could enter the country. If there were no family to meet the immigrant at the port of entry and vouch for him, labor contractors called *padrones* would meet him, find him lodging, and offer him employment. For these services the padrone received a share of the immigrant's wages, and he dominated an exploitative relationship with his workers that not only included their work but often extended to other aspects of their life. The padrone system lasted from the 1880s until about 1910.[49]

About the same time, a violent form of extortion known as the black hand appeared. Black handers sent notes demanding payment of money under the threat of murder or bodily harm if the money were not paid. Until strong Italian community organizations were created, there was no one to whom the isolated Italians could turn for help when threatened. The police were very ineffective against black handers. Black hand activities flourished until about World War I, when they began to diminish for a variety of reasons.[50]

Not only did the immigrants face exploitation from within the Italian community; they faced open hostility from without. In the 1890s, eleven Italian prisoners in New Orleans were lynched after a jury had *not* found them guilty of murdering the city's police chief. Italian residents of an Illinois town were driven out of their homes and beaten, and their houses burned, in a fit of mob hysteria. And in Boston in the 1920s, two Italians were executed after being convicted of murder by a jury which included no Italians and which based its decision on evidence that appeared very circumstantial.[51] Even aside from the violence, Italian immigrants commonly were cheated by non-Italian merchants or lost their savings when bankers went bankrupt.

Political Ramifications of an Ethnic Business Class

Facing these circumstances, Italians perhaps naturally turned to relatives, friends, and fellow Italians when they sought to establish business enterprises. The earliest businesses were small newspapers and retail operations that catered to the particular needs and tastes of Italian communities. Every city with a sizeable Italian population soon had its Italian newspaper and was soon dotted with numerous small, autonomous family restaurants. Fruit peddlers, peanut sellers, and pushcart vendors soon plied their trade on the major commercial streets. Non-

Italians increasingly dined at Italian restaurants and purchased goods from Italian merchants. These Italian businessmen began to perform for the Italian community a capital mobilization function similar to that which the parish performed for the Irish.

Italian entrepreneurs and workmen had an enormous capacity to save. At the turn of the century, when the laborer's average wage was less than $2.00 per day, the Bureau of Labor estimated that 95 percent of Italian laborers saved from $25 to $30 of their wages each month. Among Italian immigrant families in New York, 35 percent took in roomers, even though the typical tenement apartment contained only three or four rooms.[52] Many of the tenants were young men who had traveled ahead without their families. And much of the savings, of course, was by these same men who wished to finance an eventual return to Italy or to bring their families to the New World.

Whatever the reason for this high level of saving, the net result was that the Italians aggregated capital to invest in their own community enterprises. Typically, these enterprises were restaurants, taverns, construction, trucking, the marketing of produce, roofing, and rock masonry.[53] Produce and fruit marketing in particular were lucrative for the Italians. By the turn of the century they reportedly controlled the fruit trade in Manhattan, and in Boston about a fourth of the Italian population was engaged in the fruit business.[54] Directing funerals, publishing newspapers, and developing real estate were other avenues of Italian business success.

In a community organized around strong family loyalties and personal relationships, it was perhaps inevitable that accumulated savings were deposited with Italian bankers rather than in non-Italian financial institutions. The Italian banker became an intermediary between the immigrant and the institutions of the outside world. He was a familiar figure in the Italian community, not, in the words of one historian, "an anonymous teller behind a cold steel wicket."[55]

The most successful of the Italian bankers was A. P. Giannini, who founded the Bank of America. He started his banking operations by making credit available to immigrant fishermen, fruit peddlers, small ranchers, and workmen who lacked the collateral or the credit standing to get loans from the already established banks. As his banking operations stabilized and he built up trust among the immigrants, he also attracted their savings deposits. Many of these people would not have put their money in a non-Italian's bank.

Not only did Giannini build a huge fortune; he also kept his bank relevant to the Italian communities that he served. According to historian Andrew Rolle, Giannini "saw to it that immigrant branch managers, cashiers, lesser as well as major personnel, were Italians."[56] Giannini was not alone in his preference for Italian workers. Many of the famous California vineyards such as Gallo and Italian Swiss Colony were begun by Italian families and employed primarily Italian workers.[57]

As the Italian business, professional, and middle classes developed, they maintained their preference for conducting their affairs with Italians rather than non-Italians. There developed strong ethnic networks: "The Italian doctor sees an Italian lawyer when he wants legal advice, both of them have their expensive suburban house built by an Italian contractor, and all of them vote for an Italian political leader to represent the interests of their community at city hall or the state house."[58]

Politically, the businessmen and professionals used their new wealth to advance Italian candidates and Italian causes. Bank of America's Giannini apparently did not hesitate to use his prestige and wealth to further certain political causes.[59] And Samuel Lubell describes how the growth of Italian political influence in Providence was directly related to the increasing number of Italian lawyers who passed the bar examinations during the 1920s and 1930s. The rise of John Pastore to the governorship of Rhode Island was heavily dependent upon a group of newly wealthy Italians who, although Republicans, contributed heavily to Pastore's gubernatorial campaign in 1946.[60]

The businessmen not only were helpful to politicians; they also helped form many Italian community organizations. Some of the organizations, such as the Sons of Italy, promoted general ethnic solidarity. Others, such as the Italian-American Labor Council or the Italian-American Chamber of Commerce, had a narrower functional base.

Italian businessmen thus performed at least three functions in the development of the Italian community. They mobilized capital that was reinvested to produce jobs and more businesses. They contributed financially to certain Italian politicians and Italian political causes. And they helped form civic organizations that in turn promoted solidarity and cohesion among Italians.

Organized Crime: Its Myth and Reality in Italian Community Development

Few aspects of Italian-American life are more controversial than its supposed relation to organized crime. It is now widely believed that *all* organized crime in the United States is subordinated to an exclusively Italian organization called the Mafia or La Cosa Nostra. This belief stems from two general sources — official government investigations[61] and popular exposé writings.[62] According to these reports, there is a national confederation now called La Cosa Nostra. It is composed of twenty-four regional groups or families located in many big cities of the Northeast, the Great Lakes states, the South, and the Southwest. Membership in these twenty-four families totals about 5000 men who are *all* Italians.[63] Their elder statesmen, who immigrated from Sicily when Mussolini cracked down on the Mafia in the 1920s,[64] form the directing group that "ratifies or rejects agreements with other non-Italian criminal organizations."[65] Through them this "Italian organization in fact controls all but an insignificant proportion of the organized crime activities in the United States,"[66] which may involve as many as 100,000 people. The net income of this organization in the mid-1960s was estimated at $6 billion to $7 billion per year.[67] The organization has infiltrated many legitimate businesses and bought off a wide range of public officials ranging from police officers to United States congressmen, and it is continually growing stronger. Its ultimate aim is to control all significant legitimate business activity in the United States and to control the United States government itself.[68]

This interpretation has come under severe criticism on several counts. Former Attorney General Ramsey Clark challenged the profit estimates of $6–7 billion as too high.[69] Other critics question whether an organization that employs so many people could exist without a corporate headquarters, but no Mafia corporate headquarters has been identified.[70] The lack of a corporate headquarters, the vagueness of the profit estimates, and the number of people involved all make the elementary problem of even defining organized crime most difficult. One critic complained that the definition offered by the Organized Crime Task Force was so vague that it was useless.[71] And this vagueness in turn prompted another critic to assert that we are "not dealing with an empirical phenomenon at all, but with an article of faith, transcending the contingent particularity of everyday experience and logically unassailable."[72]

Most criticized has been the supposed link between Italian-American organized crime and the historic Mafia in Sicily. One of the most perceptive scholars on Italian-American organized crime, Francis Ianni, argues that until the 1920s there was little reason for Sicilian Mafia leaders to migrate to the United States. They were *all* "men of some wealth, considerable power and prestige and hard-earned status and there was no reason for them to leave the island until Mussolini . . . began arresting and killing suspected Mafiosi in the 1920s."[73] But after the 1920s, Sicilian Mafia influence appears to have been slight. Italian criminals after that time modeled their operations "not [on] the old-country oriented Mafioso . . . but [on] the more sophisticated Irish and Jewish mobsters who had mastered the secrets of business organization."[74]

Rather than being a Sicilian import, Italian-American organized crime was probably created in the United States. This would be entirely consistent with the experiences of other ethnic groups; both Irish and Jewish slums were plagued by organized crime gangs.[75] And, in the 1970s, ghettoes in New York and elsewhere are beginning to see black and Puerto Rican gangs successfully challenge Italian crime families for control over the numbers racket and narcotics distribution.[76]

In organized crime, as in the political parties, there has been an ethnic succession.[77] As one ethnic group vacates the slums and is replaced there by another, it loses its recruitment base and becomes estranged from the new people in the slums. But the need for jobs, opportunities, and illicit economic services does not disappear, and new organized gangs arise among the new slum dwellers to provide them. The notorious Al Capone supposedly remarked about his illegal beer-running operations, "It's a shame that a working man can't have a glass of beer after a long day's work. All I'm doing is providing a service."

Italians in recent years have expressed considerable opposition to the prevailing idea of a Mafia-dominated national crime confederation, because it creates a stereotype that is difficult for many Italians to avoid. Joseph Alioto's chances of election to the governorship of California, for example, were probably hurt by a *Look* magazine article which linked him to the Mafia.[78] Most of the evidence was highly circumstantial, and there was no evidence that Alioto had been involved in any specific crimes that may have been committed. Alioto was unsuccessful in his suit; but in many other instances, Italians have successfully convinced government agencies and private organizations to stop using the words *Mafia* and *La Cosa Nostra*, which are felt to denigrate all Italians.*

Because of the widespread belief in a close relationship between the Italian community and the Mafia, students of urban politics should thoroughly understand both the widely held beliefs and the criticisms that have been raised against them. However, neither the beliefs nor the criticisms shed much light on the importance that organized crime had in the development of *some* Italian communities. It must be stressed

* The FBI has ceased using the terms Mafia and La Cosa Nostra. Film makers were persuaded to delete any use of these words from the movie *The Godfather*. The attorney general's office was persuaded not to allow Joseph Valachi's written manuscript to be published. Relying instead upon his extensive interviews with Valachi, Peter Maas wrote *The Valachi Papers* (New York: Putnam, 1968). Maas's dispute with the attorney general's office is described in the preface of that book.

that in many cities organized crime has had no political impact on Italian community development.[79] But in some cities it has.

Where organized crime has played a role in Italian community development, three features stand out. First, many of the criminal leaders are bound together by the "web of kinship." In a study of marriage ties among prominent crime figures, Francis Ianni found that the interactions of Italian criminals were not modeled on the highly rationalized organizational structure described by the President's Commission on Law Enforcement. Rather they were based on a kinship web. In one New York-based Italo-American syndicate, all of the fifteen leaders had marriage or blood relationship ties. In a major Midwestern city, the leaders of all the syndicate families were related through marriage. They also had marriage ties with criminal leaders in Buffalo, New York, and New Orleans. Ianni also examined the kinship ties of the identified participants at the famous Appalachian meeting of organized crime figures in 1957. Nearly "half were related by blood or marriage, and even more if godparenthood is included as a kin relationship."[80]

However, not all children of Italian crime figures married exclusively within the crime families. As some of them married out of crime families, the web was in some respects expanded to include the in-laws. In addition, personal friendship ties extended beyond the crime family to include people with whom crime figures had grown up or people they had dealt with in many Italian clubs or organizations. As these people began to achieve adulthood and middle-class status in the 1930s and 1940s, it was entirely consistent with the social structure of the Italian community that they would maintain ties.

> Now, the new judges, the new lawyers and prosecutors, councilmen and even police had grown up in the Little Italies along with the new leadership in organized crime. They had lived together as children and strong bonds had been established; still they kept the associations through friendship and marriage.
> Alliances of power, friendships and kin relationship all merged and today this presents a difficult if not impossible job of sorting out those which are corrupt or corrupting from those which merely express the strength of kinship relations among Southern Italians and their descendents.[81]

A second aspect of Italian organized crime is that it helped to finance some Italian businesses and some community organization. Since much, if not most, of the revenue generated by the organized gangs came from non-Italians who used the services of gang-controlled numbers games, alcohol, narcotics, and prostitutes, great sums of capital were brought into Italian hands. By mid-twentieth century, much of this money was being invested into legitimate enterprises, especially hotels, nightclubs, vending machines, real estate, and even stock markets. William F. Whyte observed that the racketeers provided investment capital to some Italians in Boston to start their own businesses.[82] Huey Long in Louisiana invited Frank Costello to set up slot machines in New Orleans, and Costello remitted some of the profits from this enterprise back to Manhattan for investment there.[83] How extensive this legitimate investment is and how important it was for the development of Italian business is impossible to determine. But it cannot be ignored. Nor can it be assumed that such investments were always made for nefarious purposes.* Whatever their purposes, to the extent that investments were made within the Italian community, they helped provide jobs for Italian workers and they helped businessmen get established.

A third way in which the Italian experience with organized crime affected Italian community development was through its use of political influence. Several cities present good examples.

When New York's reform mayor Fiorello La Guardia sought to deny the Democratic organization of Tammany Hall as much patronage as he could, the organization became desperate. With its traditional sources of funds (i.e., kickbacks from the patronage job holders) drying up because of La Guardia's opposition, the Tammany organization needed a new source of money. And one source was organized crime. Daniel Bell describes how Frank Costello and Joe Adonis gradually used their newly found wealth to get Italians appointed to judgeships and elected to other offices in New York City.[84] In Boston, as William F. Whyte describes, a process of "reciprocal obligations" was established, through which a loosely knit, interlocking organization worked through both political parties by paying off the appropriate political and bureaucratic leaders. The racketeers were virtually given a free hand in their business enterprises, and they were able to obtain favors for their constituents. In Chicago, a direct relationship was formed between Italian acquisition of political influence and the emergence of strong crime leaders. Humbert Nelli writes, "Italians did not move up the political ladder of success in Chicago — to appointive and elective office, patronage jobs, and exemptions from the law — until the 1920's.

---

* Former Attorney General Ramsey Clark argues that many legitimate investments by crime figures are not made for the purpose of control [Ramsey Clark, *Crime in America* (New York: Simon & Schuster, 1970), p. 73]. Others also note significant legitimate investment by organized crime figures but look on it much more suspiciously than Clark. See, for example, Richard D. Knudten, *Crime in a Complex Society* (Homewood, Ill.: Dorsey Press, 1970), p. 193.

Then, under the leadership and guidance of Johnny Torrio and Al Capone, Southerners found politics and its handmaiden, crime, to offer an increasingly important source of money as well as a means of social mobility."[85]

In Kansas City an aggressive Italian named Johnny Lazia became both a ward boss and a criminal boss. After serving a year in jail in 1917, Lazia organized a series of real estate, gambling, and bootlegging enterprises. He used his wealth to lend money to friends, to keep youngsters out of jail, to support local charities, and to help out many down-and-out Italians. Through these means Lazia built a strong following in Kansas City's North Side Italian community. In the 1928 elections, he challenged the existing Irish ward boss for political control of the Italian neighborhoods. Lazia conveyed the seriousness of his intentions by abducting several of his adversary's political aides. As he gained control over the North Side Democratic organization, Lazia entered an alliance with the city-wide machine boss, Thomas J. Pendergast. With his political power thus consolidated, Lazia was able to influence appointments to the Kansas City Police Department, obtain gambling and liquor concessions, and get police tolerance for his organized vice operations.[86]

It is impossible to know how important the criminal influence was in the achieving of political power. In New York, Boston, Chicago, and Kansas City, criminal power directly helped Italians attain political power. In many other places with substantial Italian populations, New Haven and Providence among them, Italian political power developed without any evidence of support from organized crime.[87]

What, then, is one to conclude about the emergence of ethnic-based political power among the Italians? Four conclusions seem apparent. First, by themselves the political parties and the Catholic parishes which had worked well for the Irish were of extremely limited utility to the Italians who sought political power. Second, Italian ethnic-based political power did not materialize until a distinctive social organization, built in great measure on a basis of kinship and personal loyalties, began to emerge in Italian communities. Third, Italian ethnic-based political power was dependent on large numbers of immigrants who vitally needed this kind of personalized social structure in order to survive in a very impersonalized and remote big city.

Last, the rise of Italian politicians was directly related to the rise of an Italian middle class which had developed the skills and the financial resources needed to sustain political campaigning. This middle class had a diverse economic base in business, the professions, and in some instances organized crime. As noted earlier, John Pastore's rise was helped immeasurably by sizeable financial contributions from a group of newly wealthy Republican Italians during Democrat Pastore's gubernatorial campaign in 1946.[88] Raymond Wolfinger takes the middle-class argument one step further and argues that in New Haven it was not until the Italians developed a middle class that they were able to elect a mayor and get their share of the patronage.[89] When all three of these developments (the kinship-based social structure, the large number of immigrants, the middle class to provide leadership) matured, as they did in many cities in the 1930s and 1940s, an indigenous base of political power was created.

The Socioeconomic Base of Jewish Political Influence

The political influence of the Irish and the Italians in the United States developed through what can be called traditional channels of urban politics. The urban experience of Jews in this country has been very different and probably much more successful. The differences emerge in four major respects.

First, whereas Irish and Italian involvement in urban politics has been marked by pragmatism rather than ideology, the Jewish involvement has had a strong ideological component, marked principally by liberalism, socialism and antimachine reformism.* There have been a few Jewish bosses, but not very many. In opinion surveys, Jews consistently outscore other whites on indexes of liberalism and racial tolerance.[90]

Second, whereas the Irish and Italians have been strong Democrats, the Jews have had a much more varied partisan background. Until the 1920s Jews were mostly Republican. This stemmed in part from what Lawrence Fuchs called "enormous gratitude toward the Republic which granted them refuge," in part from dislike of the Irish-controlled Democratic machines,[91] and in part from the Republican party's abolitionist and Reconstruction origins. Jewish influence was also strongly felt in the organization of socialist movements in the early twentieth century. Much of this support was dissipated by the administration of Franklin Roosevelt, who not only supported many economic measures proposed by the socialists but also appointed many liberal Jews to high national office.[92] As a result, Jews have consistently voted Democratic at the level of national politics in every election since 1932 except for the 1972 elections.

* Lawrence Fuchs comments that the early twentieth-century socialists won more votes with their denunciations of local corruption than they did with their socialist programs [The Political Behavior of American Jews (Glencoe, Ill.: The Free Press, 1956), p. 124].

On the local level, since 1932 Jewish political influence has been the greatest in the Northeast, where Jews are the most heavily concentrated (see Table 3-1). Particularly in New York, Jews have fluctuated between reformism within the Democratic party and support for reform candidates put forward by the Republican and Liberal parties. Reform mayors Fiorello La Guardia and John Lindsay received some of their strongest support in Jewish precincts.[93]

Third, the economic base of the Jewish middle class differed significantly from that of the Irish and Italian communities. In comparison to the Irish and Italian male immigrants, who were mostly unskilled laborers, only 14 percent of Jewish immigrants from 1899 to 1910 were unskilled laborers; two-thirds of the immigrants were skilled laborers, many of them tailors. In addition, the Jewish immigration contained a higher proportion of persons who had experience as merchants.[94] One of the most common enterprises among the early twentieth-century Jewish immigrants was to open "sweatshops." These were often begun in the entrepreneur's own apartment where he could set up sewing machines, employ many Jewish tailors to operate them, and bid for contracted work from the larger garment manufacturers in New York or Boston. If successful, he could eventually move the establishment from his apartment to an actual shop; and if he were very successful, he might even become a garment manufacturer. A majority of the sweatshops were Jewish owned, and about half of the workers were also Jewish. The working conditions in the sweatshops were deplorable, but the enterprises themselves were an agency of social mobility for the owners.[95]

In addition to the garment trades, Jewish merchants entered small retail trade delicatessens, restaurants, bakeries, and other small shops. Much of the capital accumulated through these Jewish enterprises was reinvested in the professional and graduate training of the immigrants' children. More than any other ethnic group, the Jews have placed a very high value on formal education and have produced a disproportionate percent of the country's doctors, dentists, scholars, intellectuals, and creative artists. Correspondingly, they have been less likely to become executives of large corporations.[96]

This economic base of the Jewish community has had politically important consequences. Fewer Jews than Irish or Italians became economically dependent upon political patronage jobs or upon benefits to be derived from allegiance with the political machines. Even where large numbers of Jews did work for local bureaucracies, they were usually in professions such as teaching or social work that were not under the direct control of the political machines. The conditions of their employment were structured by professional standards rather than political connections. Because of this, fewer Jewish leaders than Irish or Italian had to support the machine for reasons of economic dependence.

The fourth difference between the Jews and the Irish and Italians lies in the social structure of their communities. The Irish and Italians had left their countries largely for economic reasons and, consequently, a substantial number of these immigrants returned to their homeland once they had saved enough money. Jewish emigration, however, had been largely to escape political or religious persecution. From the eruption of the European revolution of 1848 until the American Civil War, approximately 100,000 German Jews immigrated to the United States. From 1880 to 1920, about two million Jews emigrated from Eastern Europe, principally from Russia and Poland. Unlike the Italian emigration, Jewish emigration was a one-way trip. Even if they became economically successful, Jews had nothing to return to in Europe except more persecution. For these reasons, Jews were often said to be more eager to integrate into the mainstream of American life.[97]

One of the pervading themes of Jewish community development has been that of reacting to anti-Semitism in the United States and elsewhere.[98] This was probably the most unifying element in what otherwise was a very heterogeneous people. Although all Jews nominally shared the same religion, there were strongly felt differences between those of reform, orthodox, or conservative persuasions and between the earlier German immigrants and the later Russian and Polish immigrants; and there were sharp class divisions between the upwardly mobile middle-class Jews and the poor. Even within the same economic arena — the garment industry, for example — there were sharp differences between the Jewish union leaders and the Jewish owners. In spite of all the differences, they became united because, as Jews, they were all endangered by outbreaks of anti-Semitism which have flared in the United States and elsewhere. Even when anti-Semitism was not rampant, Jews, regardless of wealth, faced discrimination and exclusion from the most prestigious clubs, schools, and residential areas. This led to the formation of a bond between many Jews which crossed class lines. The bonds were strengthened by the development of the Nazi regime in Germany, the horrors of World War II, and the establishment of the state of Israel. Perhaps the most obvious indicator of these bonds has been the very low rate of intermarriage between Jews and gentiles. But this is breaking down. Since 1965, almost a third of all Jewish marriages have been to non-Jews.[99]

The political consequences of these developments in the Jewish communities have been very important. As noted, the economic base of most Jews made them independent of the urban political machines. The social conditions of Jewish life and the oppression of anti-Semitism led them to support liberal causes such as civil rights and social welfare legislation that the political machines quite often opposed. Given these differences between Jews and the machines, it was probably inevitable that much of the anti–Tammany Hall reform leadership in New York's Democratic party came from the Jewish community.

In the 1960s the Jewish communities were brought into direct conflict with black communities. One commentator wrote that personal contacts between Jews and blacks have come in five areas: Jews have been retail merchants selling their goods to blacks, landlords of black tenants, social workers among black families, educators in black schools, and allies in the struggle for civil rights. Of these contacts, only the last facilitated friendly relations between blacks and Jews, and even that contact area declined in relevance as the civil rights objectives were largely achieved and black leaders in the middle 1960s turned their attention to separatism, political influence, and other goals. The contact between blacks and Jewish retail merchants and landlords has especially occurred in the context of ethnic succession. In the late 1960s Jews owned about 60 percent of all apparel stores and about 40 percent of all retail stores in central Harlem.[100] Only a miniscule percentage of these same merchants lived in Harlem, and this left them vulnerable to the criticism that they were siphoning money out of the black ghetto. Black militants demanded that Jewish and other white merchants abandon such retail establishments and leave them to be owned by blacks. In the riots of the 1960s, many nonblack stores were burned or looted.

These developments placed the Jewish leadership in a very uncomfortable position. Historically, no other ethnic group has consistently supported black demands for civil rights and social advancement as much as the Jews have. Even today there is probably as much, if not more, support for black advancement among Jews as among any other ethnic group. Although the Jewish leadership has been divided on many specific questions, Jews were among the most ardent supporters of black demands for decentralization of urban government.

Jewish organizations have not objected very much to the demands that white and Jewish store owners be excluded from the ghetto.[101] But the demand that Jewish professionals in the public schools and the welfare departments be replaced by black professionals caused a storm of protest. Partially this was because the teachers and welfare workers are more articulate than the shopowners and landlords. But, more im-

portant, it strikes at the very core of Jewish success in America —
professional competence. While Jews were excluded because of anti-
Semitism from some other areas of the economy (e.g., the diplomatic
service), they have prospered in professions with fewer barriers against
the exercise of individual competence. One Jewish observer wrote, "If
Negroness or Jewishness has something to do with being a teacher, the
Jew fears he may become an object of discrimination; equally important, he is not able to escape the condition of his Jewishness."[102] Consequently, the leaders of many Jewish organizations opposed the concept
of placing quotas on hiring. Jews have, however, strongly supported
affirmative action programs which require both public and private employers to make special efforts to hire minorities and women.

The Poles

The fourth largest European ethnic community in the United States is
that of the Poles.[103] Large-scale Polish immigration began in the 1870s
and continued until World War I. The motive force behind it was primarily economic. About a fourth of the Polish immigrants were Jewish
and entered the Jewish community; the other three-fourths were Catholic. Although some Catholic Poles turned to farming, the overwhelming majority entered the economy as unskilled laborers and settled in the great manufacturing cities such as Buffalo, Detroit, Cleveland, Pittsburgh, Milwaukee, New York, and Chicago. Many of them
found their economic base in the automobile industries, steel mills,
foundries, and other heavy industries.

Much of Polish community development resulted from the activities
of two large, national organizations which established local lodges in
each Polish community. The first was the Polish Roman Catholic Union
(PRCU), established in 1873. The PRCU was organized with a local in
each Polish Roman Catholic parish. It was dominated by the Polish
clergy, who sought to use the PRCU to establish a network of Polish
parishes and Polish parochial schools. The Polish clergy resented the
dominance of the Catholic church by the Irish, and they thought that if
they could establish a strong parish and school network, the Irish-
dominated church hierarchy would have to become open to the Poles
as well as to the Irish.

The larger organization is the Polish National Alliance (PNA). The
PNA was not restricted to Roman Catholics, and it was organized by
community rather than by parish. Founded in 1880, its major goal was
to achieve the liberation of Poland from its German, Austro-Hungarian,
and Russian conquerors. So divided was Poland by its conquerors that

many Poles acquired a consciousness of their national character only after they arrived in America and organizations like the PNA made them aware of it.[104] So successful was the PNA in attracting members through its goal of Polish liberation that the PRCU was also forced to adopt liberation as a major objective. Once that objective was accomplished in 1919, both organizations turned their attention toward maintaining the Polish heritage among the immigrants and their children. The PRCU discouraged participation in non-Polish institutions. Both organizations ran a variety of activities and enterprises which ranged from selling insurance to conducting English classes for the immigrants.

As a result of these and similar mutual-benefit organizations, a vibrant institutional life was created in Polish communities. By 1960 an estimated 830 Polish parishes and over 500 Polish elementary schools existed in the United States. Polish convents were established, a Polish college was established in Pennsylvania, and the PRCU subsidized a seminary that trained Polish priests. Polish-language newspapers abounded. Polish businessmen's organizations flourished. Like the Jews, the Poles made special efforts to provide higher education for their young. Both of the two major organizations and several others maintained scholarship programs.

In summary, a strong ethnic community developed. By the 1970s, however, the strains on this community are very strong. While fewer of the younger generation can speak Polish, more are beginning to marry into other nationality groups.* For many years the Polish community has resented the doctors, lawyers, dentists, and other professionals who increasingly have deserted the ethnic neighborhoods and migrated to the suburbs; frequently their professional training was received through special scholarships offered by the Polish ethnic organizations, and the doctors and lawyers often earned their income from their practices in the Polish neighborhoods. But these professionals have been accused of not supporting the Polish community organizations or being willing to live in the Polish neighborhoods. One critic noted that "the nationally minded Polish immigrants regarded their professional and intellectual class with reproach and disappointment."[105] As a consequence, the maintenance of the Polish community is left primarily to the clergy who want to maintain their Polish

---

* In the 1960s, National Opinion Research Center surveys found that 50 percent of their Polish respondents were married to non-Poles. The corresponding numbers for other ethnics were: Irish, 57 percent, Italians, 34 percent; Jews, 6 percent. [Andrew M. Greeley, *Why Can't They Be Like Us? America's White Ethnic Groups* (New York: E. P. Dutton, 1971), pp. 87, 92.]

parishes, the businessmen who want to maintain their economic base, and the politicians who want to maintain their Polish constituencies.

Despite these problems, the Poles have been able to acquire significant political representation. They have a strong tendency to vote for Poles rather than non-Poles.[106] Primarily Democrats,* their greatest success has probably been in Chicago, where in 1972 they held four of the city's nine congressional seats.

The major problem confronting the Polish communities in the 1970s involves maintaining the community social structure and expanding the opportunities for upward social mobility. Both of these objectives bring the Polish community leadership into conflict with the newer urban minorities who are also seeking social mobility and greater social access to employment and housing opportunities. As the most successful of the professionals abandon the old neighborhoods for the suburbs, Polish communities lose a potential liberalizing force. Local leadership is left in the hands of those who have the most to lose from contemporary social changes — the clergy and the businessmen. The politicians also have much to lose ultimately, because the rising influence of blacks and Puerto Ricans ultimately means less influence in city hall for the Poles. Consequently, many Polish politicians were among the most vociferous advocates of generally anti-black law-and-order slogans in the late 1960s.

Chicago presents a good illustration of this. The Irish- and German-dominated archdiocese has put pressure on the Polish parishes to reduce services conducted in the Polish language and to make financial contributions to programs designed to benefit Puerto Ricans, blacks, and the minorities. As more families move out to suburban, single-family residences or to large apartment and condominium complexes owned mostly by large, non-Polish real estate concerns, and as blacks and Puerto Ricans move into formerly Polish neighborhoods, thousands of Polish landlords of small, family-owned apartment buildings find their buildings becoming less attractive to middle-class renters. Polish-owned small businesses also find themselves at a disadvantage in competing with corporate discount stores which can practice economies of scale and which also are insensitive to the subtle nuances of the Polish community.

Politically, the Poles are still very influential in Chicago, but it is not likely that their influence will grow. As the Chicago population of

---

* National Opinion Research Center (NORC) surveys of 1961 college graduates found that Catholic Poles had a greater tendency to identify themselves as Democrats than any other group of college graduates except for blacks and Jews (Greeley, Why Can't They Be Like Us?, p. 206).

blacks and other minorities increases, the influence of the Poles is bound to decline. When a Pole, Roman Pucinski, gave up his seniority in the United States House of Representatives in 1972 to run against Charles Percy for the Senate, not all Poles interpreted Pucinski's ambitions as recognition for the Polish community. Some felt that Mayor Daley's machine needed to add a third black congressman to Chicago's delegation and could accomplish this with the least friction by getting Chicago's most prominent Polish congressman to enter an unwinnable contest for the United States Senate. Although a Pole may eventually be elected mayor of Chicago, the population growth of the racial minorities makes it unlikely that Polish dominance will last very long.

Consequently, in terms of politics and community development, the Chicago Poles find themselves in the unenviable position of having several forces converging to dilute their influence precisely at the time when they are beginning to acquire substantial power. It is not surprising that Polish leadership has been conservative and cool to demands for civil rights, open housing, and equal employment opportunities.

THE RELATIONSHIP OF ETHNIC POLITICS TO BROKERAGE AND MACHINE POLITICS

In reality, the politics of the ethnic groups were never as isolated as they appear on being analyzed one by one. Considerable interaction existed between members of the Polish, Jewish, Italian, Irish, and other ethnic groups. The political interactions of these groups were normally handled by *brokerage politics*. In a sense, to the extent that all politics involve bargaining and the exchange of favors, all politics are brokerage politics. But here the term refers to politics characterized by material incentives in bargaining for political favors, by the jockeying for relative political advantages among the representatives of various groups in the political system, and by the trade-off of votes or financial contributions for political favors. The political favors are always specific and material as distinguished from diffused and symbolic.[107] And brokerage politics tend to be nonideological.*

Closely related to brokerage politics is the concept of *machine pol-*

---

* Political scientist Murray Stedman argues that the political progressive reform style was also brokerage politics. He seems to perceive brokerage politics as any pluralist political system in which the government balances off competing contenders for political favors and in which political organizations adhere to the principles of concentrating on administrative problems and limited government. See his *Urban Politics* (Cambridge, Mass.: Winthrop Publishers, 1972), pp. 127–134.

itics. This term refers to a political process that is characterized by the presence within a political party of a political organization that endures for several years; by the rule of a "boss" who oversees the awarding of patronage jobs and the selection of party nominees; and by a reliance on patronage, awarding of government contracts, and other material incentives to secure campaign workers and campaign contributions. Machines are nonideological. They usually have a political base among the underprivileged sectors of the society, and they usually portray themselves as serving as intermediary between the government and these underprivileged peoples. Machine politics always involve brokerage politics, but the reverse is not necessarily true: it is possible to have brokerage politics without having a machine.

Closely associated with both of these concepts is the concept of *ethnic politics*. Although machine politics do not necessarily have to be linked to ethnic politics, in the cities of the Northeast they quite often occurred together.* The political machines fit into the ethnic networks of social mobility through which some members of the ethnic communities could prosper. At the same time, the ethnic base to politics facilitated symbolic payoffs to those people who did not participate in the tangible payoff from machine politics. For these people, ethnicity played a very important symbolic role. Nominating an Italian or a Pole to high office supposedly granted recognition to that ethnic group. And either because this recognition gave them vicarious pleasure or because they hoped that their own children might rise in a similar fashion, the members of the group remained loyal to the nominating party.

The oldest and most famous combination of ethnic and machine politics occurred in the Tammany Hall machine in Manhattan.[108] The Tammany Society was founded in 1789 primarily as a sociable fraternal organization. It slowly became politicized and, particularly under the Irish, served as the mechanism for controlling the activities of the neighborhood district clubs. The district clubs were the heart of the organization. They dispensed patronage and controlled nominations within their jurisdictions. But for city-wide nominations and patronage or for settling disputes between clubs, a city-wide organization was needed; and this was the role reserved for Tammany Hall. Tammany reached its greatest strength in the era that extended from the Civil War

* Raymond Wolfinger argues that machine politics and ethnic politics do not necessarily go together, and he indicates several examples of machine politics without a European ethnic base. See his *The Politics of Progress*, pp. 122–129. Elmer Cornwell argues that even where machine politics were not linked to ethnic politics, they were organized in reaction to either immigrant or black demands for inclusion in the political arena. See his "Bosses, Machines, and Ethnic Groups," *The Annals of the American Academy of Political and Social Science* 353 (May 1964), pp. 27–39.

until the early 1900s under the leadership of William Marcy "Boss" Tweed, Charles F. Murphy, and Richard Croker.

Boss Tweed was surely the most colorful of the bosses. He rose from a foreman in the fire department through the positions of alderman and congressman to the position of boss of Tammany Hall. As boss he controlled the dispensing of government contracts to the point where he was able to steal millions of dollars from the New York City treasury. Tweed was finally arrested and served a jail sentence for his crimes, but few other Tammany bosses ended their careers in prison

Despite their inefficiencies and high levels of graft, the machines, including Tammany Hall, did serve to integrate the competing demands of various ethnic groups for patronage jobs and representation in government. They also served as a link between the government and the impoverished immigrants (particularly for the Irish) and provided a channel through which the larger ethnic groups (particularly Italians and Poles) were able to demand concessions from city governments and to get a share of the representation and patronage. The fact that ethnic groups could be represented as such through the machines meant that machine politics offered a way of diffusing class divisiveness in the cities: aspiring ethnic politicians, in order to rise, had to mold a core of followers from all classes within the ethnic group.

The Tammany Hall model of deeply intertwined ethnic, brokerage, and machine politics was not, however, the only pattern which emerged. It predominated mostly in the Northeast, particularly in the North Atlantic and New England states.[109] In the South, brokerage politics had little ethnic content. In some Southern states, such as Virginia and Louisiana, relatively permanent political machines developed and endured for an entire generation. In some other states, permanent machines failed to develop, and the dominant brokerage pattern was what political scientist V. O. Key called "one party factionalism." In most of the South the machines and factions had a rural rather than an urban base.[110]

In the Midwest, politics had a high ethnic content, but it evolved in two mutually incompatible patterns.[111] In Ohio, Indiana, and Illinois, politics were *jobs oriented* and similar to the politics of the Northeast. The major motivation behind political activity was to control the substantial patronage that existed in those states. Strong machines developed in Cleveland, Toledo, Indianapolis, Gary, and especially in Chicago. In Michigan, Wisconsin, and Minnesota, by contrast, politics were *issue oriented*. Strong machines in places like Minneapolis and Saint Paul succumbed very early to the progressive reform movement. In Minnesota and Wisconsin, third parties developed (the Farmer-

Labor party and the Progressive party, respectively) after World War I. And when they captured control of their state and local governments, they used their new-found power not so much to provide patronage jobs for their supporters as to institute broad economic and social reforms through legislation. In this sense, the politics of these states were issue oriented rather than jobs oriented.

In the Far West, an entirely different pattern emerged. California, Oregon, and Washington all had strong progressive movements that weakened the political parties.[112] In San Francisco, a system of politics rose which was characterized by an extremely high ethnic content with very little reliance on political machines.[113]

In practice, then, the concepts of ethnic, brokerage, and machine politics are distinct, not synonymous, and a variety of practical arrangements has evolved. In some places, such as New Haven, New York, and Chicago, the three types of politics are virtually indistinguishable. In other places, political machines existed even though there were no European immigrant and ethnic groups; the most prominent example was the Byrd machine in Virginia. In other places — Mississippi, for one — a form of brokerage politics existed without either permanent political machines or an ethnic base. In still other places, principally in Wisconsin, Michigan, and Minnesota, politics had a high ethnic content combined with an issue-oriented political process. And finally, in San Francisco, a type of ethnic politics developed that was characterized by neither a political machine nor an issue orientation.

THE SIGNIFICANCE OF ETHNIC, BROKERAGE, AND MACHINE POLITICS TODAY

These patterns of ethnic, brokerage, and machine politics have more than simple historical interest. They continue to have relevance to contemporary political events. The persistence of ethnic-based politics and ethnic voting has been noted by several studies.[114] Ethnic considerations are most influential in nonpartisan elections; without the party label to provide guidance, voters look for ethnic labels. Ethnic considerations are also influential when a member of an ethnic group runs for a major office. In the early 1970s there was a resurgence of interest in and self-consciousness among various European ethnic groups.[115]

Assuming that this resurgence of self-consciousness among the ethnics will persist for several years, it is not clear what the political consequences will be. One possibility is a continuation of ethnic-based voting. Political scientist Raymond Wolfinger has argued that ethnic voting is most likely to occur in later generations when the ethnic group develops not only a sense of ethnic identity but the economic and political resources to back ethnic candidates. His evidence, however, refers to just one ethnic group (Italians) in only one city (New Haven).[116] And a reanalysis of the same data by another political scientist cast doubt on the usefulness of the concept of ethnic voting, even in New Haven.[117] Furthermore, the breakup of old ethnic neighborhoods, intermarriages, and the large-scale migration of ethnics to the suburbs make a continuation of ethnic voting very difficult in the 1970s and 1980s except in localities which still have cohesive ethnic neighborhoods.

A continued ethnic impact on politics seems much more likely to persist on the question of social issues than on support for candidates merely because of their ethnicity. Significant attitudinal differences still tend to exist among ethnic groups about major social issues. To take just one example: Table 3-2 shows the differences between ethnic groups found in a 1967 National Opinion Research Center (NORC) survey on three key questions of equalizing social access for blacks.

According to the NORC findings, only about one-fifth of the Irish supported the statement that blacks should attend separate schools. Yet when the issue shifted slightly from a theoretical question to the real issue of bussing Irish children to achieve desegregation of schools in

TABLE 3-2

ATTITUDES OF ETHNICS TOWARD SOCIAL ACCESS FOR BLACKS: 1967

Statement	Percentage Agreeing with Statement among:				
	Irish	Polish	Italian	Jewish	White Anglo-Saxon Protestant
Negro children should go to separate schools	20	38	17	30	64
Negroes should be on separate sections of streetcars and buses	5	21	14	8	22
Unfavorable to Negroes living in same block	25	46	36	30	41

From *Why Can't They Be Like Us?: America's White Ethnic Groups* by Andrew M. Greeley. Copyright © 1971, 1970 by Andrew M. Greeley. Reprinted by permission of the publishers, E. P. Dutton & Co., Inc.

South Boston in 1974–75, violent opposition arose in the Irish neighborhoods. The least receptive ethnics, according to NORC data, were the Catholic Poles, but even they were considerably more receptive to school integration than were the Anglo-Saxon Protestants. If desegregation occurred in Irish neighborhoods in Boston only after considerable violence, physical assault, and disruption of the school calendar, it is difficult to see how Polish neighborhoods or Polish schools could be peaceably integrated when almost twice as many Poles as Irish have antidesegregation attitudes. The ethnic differences in attitudes — probably more than the differences in voting — continue to have relevance to contemporary urban politics.

Ethnicity, then, continues to affect the process of urban politics in the 1970s. Can the same thing be said for the process of machine politics? In cities such as New Haven and Chicago, which have strong machines, the answer is clearly yes. Whether machine politics in these cities are typical will be examined in Chapter 4.

THE BIAS OF ETHNIC AND MACHINE POLITICS

Are any biases inherent to ethnic and machine politics? Three generalizations have been offered. First, some argue that both ethnic and brokerage politics have promoted a conservative bias. Except for the Jews, the immigrant generations consistently voted for conservative candidates.[118] When the Irish achieved political power, they seldom used their power to promote social programs.[119] Furthermore, the ascension to power of an ethnic group actually meant the ascension of only *the leadership* of that group; for the masses, the ascension was mostly symbolic and vicarious. The recognition accorded to a group by the appointment of one of its members to a major office was supposed to give the group enough vicarious pleasure that it would remain loyal to the appointing party. Raymond Wolfinger characterizes the ascension to power of an ethnic group as "monetary rewards for a few and symbolic gratification for the rest."[120] To the extent that this politics of recognition gave the ethnics a stake in the society by holding out the Horatio Alger promise that they too could rise to the top, it contributed greatly to stabilizing the political system in the United States.[121]

Because they divided the electorate along ethnic lines, ethnic politics had the additional conservative effect of muting class antagonisms. Within their ethnic group, political leaders had to appeal to all classes.

Finally, the inevitable social conflict between ethnic groups inherent to ethnic politics has facilitated incremental change in political relations.[122] Through the process of ethnic succession, newer ethnic groups were brought into the political arena. As newer groups became active, their leaders were given opportunities for personal advancement. As long as these opportunities were open to them, the ethnic populations had little incentive to join revolutionary movements.

In summary, the argument for conservative bias states that ethnic politics became a stabilizing force in the urban political system. By providing a channel for ethnic leaders to gain prominence, ethnic politics obviated any recourse to revolutionary social changes but did little to improve the living conditions of the masses of the ethnic populations. A Kennedy here or a Giannini there may have entered the upper class, but the class structure itself was preserved intact.

These arguments are valid, but ethnic and brokerage politics had an equally important liberalizing bias. Within limits, ethnic and brokerage politics *did* serve as channels of social mobility for lower-class immigrants. And the machine politicians *did* represent *some* of the interests of their constitutents. The ethnics *did* create institutional channels to represent their interests. It is doubtful that their living standards would have been any better had urban politics been class-based rather than ethnic-based. Nor were all the machines as devoid of social accomplishments as Tammany Hall. In Cincinnati, a Republican machine under Boss Cox muted racial and ethnic antagonisms, ameliorated conditions for the blacks, brought public improvements to the city, and ran the city government in a relatively honest and efficient fashion.[123] Furthermore, the propensity of the *antimachine, antiethnic* reform leadership to be drawn from the upper classes and the top business leadership in cities would suggest that the ethnics and their institutions *were perceived* by the upper classes as a liberalizing threat. As Melvin G. Holli has shown, when these upper-class reformers came to power in cities, their first moves were often to slash payrolls and reverse the decisions that were both opening up jobs for the lower-class ethnics and providing public services for their neighborhoods.[124]

A second bias of ethnic and brokerage politics has been against small and unorganized ethnic groups and racial minorities. The brokerage nature of the political machines was effective in ameliorating relations between groups that had their own indigenous power bases — groups such as the Irish, the Poles, and the Italians. With a few exceptions, the political machines have been notoriously unsuccessful in offering the Spanish-speaking and racial minorities a channel to political influence.[125] There are several reasons for this. Until the past decade these minorities were poorly organized politically and did not have an indigenous power base to confront the political machines. Even where blacks were well organized politically, as in the Dawson machine in Chicago,[126] the white political leaders very effectively minimized the patronage available to the blacks by successfully co-opting the black politicians. Some high-ranking members of Chicago's Democratic party have made statements and committed actions that indicate the most blatant of racist attitudes.*

The inability of Chicago's machine to cope with the needs of the blacks was more fundamental, however, than individual racist attitudes on the part of whites or the lack of an indigenous power base within the black community. Because Chicago as a city has been a polyglot of ethnic and racial minorities and because of the process of ethnic succession, the social and political systems themselves inherently made racial conflict inevitable. This is most obvious in the case of the Poles and the blacks. The pressures leading to disintegration of the Polish community in Chicago are heightened by the racial minorities' demands for social access. The oldest Polish neighborhoods along Milwaukee Avenue lie precisely in one expansion path of the black and Puerto Rican ghettoes. Following a familiar historical pattern, the more the neighborhoods and schools are integrated, the greater the number of Poles who abandon the old neighborhoods. And the greater the abandonment of the old neighborhoods, the less viable become the neighborhood-based businesses, the Polish parishes, and the Polish community organization. The national headquarters of the oldest Polish organization, the PRCU, now exist in the middle of a Hispanic ghetto in Chicago. Social access for blacks and Spanish in Chicago is interpreted by many Polish leaders as destructive of the Polish community. As long as Polish leadership is exercised by those Poles whose vested interests are likely to be damaged by black and Spanish expansion, social conflict between Poles and these minorities is inevitable. If this analysis is correct, then the greatest threat to black advancement is not individual racism, because all but the poorest of the racists can pack up and move farther out, away from the black frontier. The greatest threat to the new minorities lies in the very structure of ethnic and machine politics in Chicago. This situation is also very threatening to the Poles, for it inherently pits the vested interests of Polish leadership against the vested interests of black and Spanish leadership. Michael Novak has suggested that much of this conflict could be

---

* The most prominent example is former Cook County State's Attorney Edward Hanrahan, who led a police assault on a Black Panther headquarters in Chicago. A government inquiry into the incident found that the assault was unprovoked and the murdered Black Panthers had not fired on the police.

alleviated simply by a subsidy to the residents of racially integrated neighborhoods.[127] This would give the white ethnics an incentive to remain in the old neighborhoods, and, consequently, the in-migrating blacks and Puerto Ricans would not diminish the community base of support for the priests, politicians, businessmen, and other leaders within the Polish community. So far, Novak's suggestion has not received much support.

Finally, a third bias of ethnic and machine politics stems from their conservative and racial bias. Ethnic and machine politics are biased against systematic approaches to the great urban social issues of the 1970s — education, race relations, housing, welfare, and crime. Because the nature of the political machines lies in balancing off competing interests, machines of necessity approach social issues in the same manner. As Banfield and Meyerson have shown for Chicago, the machine does not deal with housing problems by positing housing goals and then carrying out a sequenced set of programs to meet those goals. Although such goals may exist on paper, the key issues on public housing, especially location, are resolved by balancing competing interests of bankers, realtors, neighborhood groups, construction unions, racial group leaders, housing experts in specialized agencies, and political leaders in the various neighborhoods of Cook County.[128] As will be indicated in Chapter 5, there are advantages to this method of dealing with social problems; at least the machine is tuned to political realities. But there are also disadvantages, the chief disadvantage being that dealing with social problems in a systematic way becomes impossible. And the tendency of machines to react to existing balances of power inherently makes it difficult for them to respond favorably to the needs of people without power. The machines' reliance on material incentives to attract contributions and to stay in power makes it difficult for machine politicians to place systematic policy considerations ahead of demands of the contributors and powerful groups.

THE TRANSITION FROM ETHNIC-BASED TO FUNCTION-BASED POLITICAL POWER

This chapter has indicated how political power developed out of ethnic social organization. Particularly crucial was the emergence of a substantial number of wealthy or upper-middle-class people whose interests or inclinations demanded that they invest their resources in the institutions of their own ethnic community. The creation of these institutions laid the foundation for ethnic political power, for the ethnic networks of social mobility, and for the symbolic unity of the ethnic peoples.[129] Initially, the financial stability of the upper middle class was heavily dependent on the growth of the ethnic community institutions. As time passed, the financial base of the ethnic leaders expanded beyond a single ethnic community. The ethnic institutions still had influence, but other, more functionally oriented urban institutions developed which were not the peculiar creation of any particular ethnic group. Nevertheless, they worked as channels of social mobility for European-American lower classes. Relevant examples of such institutions are found in organized labor and in the intellectual and artistic worlds.

Organized labor has been a very effective political voice for its members. Although unions are not principally ethnic institutions, in many ways they reinforce the influence of the more ethnically oriented institutions. The Catholic church has tended to support the economic objectives of labor, and labor has usually refrained from hostility toward the church. Numerous instances exist of close collaboration between unions and elements of organized crime. And labor influence in political parties, has generally but not always been supportive of the Democrats.

Noticeable in the intellectual and entertainment worlds is a heavy recurrence of Jewish names. More than any other ethnic group, the Jews have used the intellectual and artistic professions as channels for advancement. So important has been their influence that it is difficult to imagine contemporary American literary or artistic life without their contributions.

Perhaps more important than questions about which ethnic groups disproportionately influence which institutions is the observation that most of these institutions have become more concerned with the *functional sector* of the society in which they operate than the *geographic area* in which their members reside or with ethnic social advancement. The hierarachy of the Catholic church may be disproportionately staffed by Irish, but the social advancement of the Irish is no longer a prime concern of the hierarchy. The sphere of interest of the church has narrowed considerably to a much more religious focus. The sphere of interest of most institutions in contemporary society is normally focused on whatever function that institution performs. This makes it much more difficult today to create indigenous power bases in ethnic communities than it was two generations ago, when society was not so specialized. These considerations will be dealt with more fully in Chapters 4 and 5.

SUMMARY

Several important themes have emerged from this review of ethnic power. First, in all the communities, political power was ultimately based on social organization. Second, political power rested in part on a substantial number of middle-class people serving as clergymen, lawyers, politicians, racketeers, businessmen, or professionals who could give their money and talent to political causes that furthered the group's cohesion. Third, institutions such as the parish churches, local businesses, and in some instances crime organizations were created to mobilize money and manpower that would constitute a net investment in the community. Fourth, the political power that resulted from these ethnic groups was indigenous; it was not dependent on outside benevolence. Fifth, although ethnic organization was remarkably effective for mobilizing political power, it had biases that were inherently conservative, nonprogrammatic, and opposed to the interests of the black and Spanish-speaking minorities.

One of the key questions now facing urban America is whether the new urban minorities of Mexicans, Indians, Puerto Ricans, blacks, and Appalachian whites can develop institutional structures which will bring them the advancement that the European immigrants found through their own urban institutions. Two changes in the political organization of the metropolis have hindered such a development. First, the ethnic forms of political organization have been rendered much less effective by several decades of political reform movements. Second, the organization of effective power in the contemporary metropolis tends to be based much more on a functional basis than on an ethnic basis. These two changes and their implications are discussed in the next two chapters.

Some Suggested Readings

Ethnic Politics Generally

Edgar Litt, *Beyond Pluralism: Ethnic Politics in America* (Glenview, Ill.: Scott, Foresman, 1970). A short survey of the major themes of ethnic politics.

Harry A. Bailey, ed., *Ethnic Group Politics* (Columbus, Ohio: Merrill, 1969). A broad collection of articles on a wide range of aspects of ethnic politics.

Brett W. Hawkins and Robert A. Lorinskas, eds., *The Ethnic Factor in American Politics* (Columbus, Ohio: Merrill, 1970). An excellent collection of mostly empirical articles which attempt to analyze the relation of ethnicity to public policy and to governmental forms.

Mark R. Levy and Michael S. Kramer, *The Ethnic Factor: How America's Minorities Decide Elections* (New York: Simon & Schuster, 1972). Journalistic in approach but a readable and useful treatment of the subject.

Michael Novak, *The Rise of the Unmeltable Ethnics: Politics and Culture in the Seventies* (New York: Macmillan, 1971). Novak is a prominent spokesman for the new ethnicity. Focusing mostly on Slavic and East European peoples, he describes some of their life conditions and their grievances.

Andrew M. Greeley, *Why Can't They Be Like Us? America's White Ethnic Groups* (New York: E. P. Dutton, 1971). Greeley makes liberal use of National Opinion Research Center survey data to explain why the Irish, Poles, Italians, and Jews are distinct and how they differ one from the other.

Specific Treatments of Ethnic Politics

Nathan Glazer and Daniel Patrick Moynihan, *Beyond the Melting Pot: The Negroes, Puerto Ricans, Jews, Italians, and Irish of New York* (Cambridge, Mass.: M.I.T. Press, 1963). This is probably the first serious attempt to make a scholarly assessment of different ethnic groups and their interaction in a city.

John M. Allswang, *A House for All Peoples: Ethnic Politics in Chicago, 1890–1936* (Lexington: The University Press of Kentucky, 1971). Assesses the role of nine ethnic groups in the evolution of Chicago's Democratic party into a political machine. A highly sophisticated empirical, historical study.

Charles Wollenberg, ed., *Ethnic Conflict in California History* (Los Angeles: Tinnon-Brown, 1970). A collection of nine articles on Indians, Chinese, Chicanos, and blacks in California.

Machine Politics

Raymond E. Wolfinger, *The Politics of Progress* (Englewood Cliffs, N.J.: Prentice-Hall, 1974). Chapters 3 and 4 present Wolfinger's theses on ethnic and machine politics. The remainder of the book deals with the policy-making process in New Haven, Connecticut.

Mike Royko, *Boss: Richard J. Daley of Chicago* (New York: E. P. Dutton, 1971). Royko has written a fascinating polemic against the Daley machine in Chicago. Because of Royko's unrestrained hostility to Daley and his loose presentation of evidence to support many of his viewpoints, he must be read cautiously.

Edward C. Banfield, *Political Influence* (New York: The Free Press, 1961). Banfield examines several issue areas in Chicago politics and arrives at the conclusion that Daley is much less a dominating force in public policy making in Chicago than he is a reacting force to initiatives taken by others. This view of Daley contrasts markedly with that presented by Royko.

Zane L. Miller, *Boss Cox's Cincinnati* (New York: Oxford University Press, 1968). An excellent treatment of a Republican machine. Miller concludes with a favorable impression of Cox's machine.

Harold F. Gosnell, *Machine Politics: Chicago Model* (Chicago: University of Chicago Press, 1937; 2nd ed., 1968). This classic study is still a readable and useful book for students of urban politics. The 1968 edition contains an introduction by Theodore Lowi which contrasts the Chicago machine to what Lowi calls the new political machines.

Harold Zink, *City Bosses in the United States* (Durham, N.C.: Duke University Press, 1930). This classic study of the operations of several bosses and their machines is still one of the best comparative studies of the phenomenon of machine politics.

The Annals of the American Academy of Political and Social Science 353 (May 1964). This issue is devoted to machine politics.

Chapter 4

The purpose of this chapter is threefold. First, it defines machine politics and examines the widespread belief that machine politics have passed away. The argument advanced here is that machine politics have not disappeared, but they have ceased to be the dominant form of political organization in most metropolises. They have declined in importance and, in most metropolises, have been bypassed by other forms of political organization. Second, this chapter describes the forces which led to these changes in the fortunes of machine politics. Three forces have been paramount in these urban political changes: (1)

Urban Reform and the Decline of Machine Politics

the progressive reform movement of the early twentieth century, (2) the changing role of the federal government, and (3) the demographic changes discussed in Chapter 2. Finally, this chapter analyzes the bias that resulted from these changes in urban political organization.

HAVE MACHINE POLITICS REALLY DISAPPEARED?

The years immediately before and after World War II stand as a symbolic period in urban political history. One after another, several famed central city machines lost their holds on their electorates. James Curley, the boss-mayor of Boston, was sent to prison,* as was Thomas Pendergast, the head of the political machine in Kansas City. The Hague machine in Jersey City was defeated in 1949, as was the Crump machine in

* Even while in prison Curley managed to get himself reelected.

Memphis. In an attempt to defuse complaints about the corrupt practices of the incumbent Kelly-Nash machine in Chicago, the Chicago Democrats dumped mayor-boss Ed Kelly in 1947 in favor of a reform candidate businessman, Martin Kennelly. They hoped that Kennelly would draw the support of the good-government reformers. Through their astuteness, the Chicagoans were able to maintain their power for at least another generation. But a general feeling persisted that the day of the boss was past, that urban political machines were on their way out. Novelist Edwin O'Connor portrayed the decline of the urban political boss in his novel *The Last Hurrah,* a story well worth reading by any student of urban politics.[1]*

So widespread has been this view that political machines have disappeared that it has become part of the conventional wisdom about American urban politics.[2] Yet the persistence of Democratic machines in Chicago, New Haven, Philadelphia, and upstate New York, and even the perseverance of the Tammany organization in New York City, suggest that machine politics are not entirely dead[3] — at least not in the northeast quadrant of the country. In a sense, the conventional wisdom seems at odds with the reality of the perseverance of certain machines.

One reason for this discrepancy lies in the fact that there is no commonly accepted definition of what constitutes machine politics. What perseveres may be defined as machine politics by some observers but not by others. For example, Raymond Wolfinger asserts that machine politics have not withered away, while his fellow political scientist Fred I. Greenstein asserts that they are passing away. Part of the reason for their different interpretations lies in their different definitions of machine politics. Wolfinger appears to define a political machine as any organization that controls a significant number of patronage jobs and other material incentives and is more concerned with the routine operations of staffing government positions than it is with implementing ideologies or substantive policies.† Greenstein, in contrast, pre-

---

* O'Connor's novel is important, because its romanticization of machine politics was so popular and widely read. Most of the early twentieth-century literature presented very unfavorable treatments of machine politics. Afterward, a reaction set in and machine politics were treated much more favorably.

† Wolfinger writes of the two major Democratic party leaders of New Haven that they were "seldom present at meetings where decisions about municipal policy were made, nor did they play an active part in these matters. On strictly party topics like nominations they were, with Mayor Lee, a triumvirate. Appointments, contracts, and the like were negotiated among the three, with Lee delegating a good deal of routine patronage administration to Barbieri. But substantive city affairs were another matter; here the organization leaders were neither interested [in] nor consulted on the outlines of policy" [*The Politics of Progress* (Englewood Cliffs, N.J.: Prentice-Hall, 1974), p. 104]. Wolfinger's rationale for his definition of a political machine is explained in considerable detail in

sents a much more restricted definition. He suggests that machine politics entail four elements in addition to patronage:

1. There is a disciplined party hierarchy led by a single executive or a unified board of directors.
2. The party exercises effective control over nomination to public office, and through this, it controls the public officials of the municipality.
3. The party leadership — which quite often is of lower-class social origins — usually does not hold public office and sometimes does not even hold formal party office. At any rate, official position is not the primary source of the leadership's strength.
4. Rather, a cadre of loyal party officials and workers, as well as a core of voters, is maintained by a mixture of material rewards and non-ideological psychic rewards — such as personal and ethnic recognition, camaraderie, and the like.[4]

Since both of these definitions are phrased in terms of *elements* of an ideal type of political machine, the important questions become: Which *elements* of machine politics have passed away? Which elements have declined in use? And which have not? When observed from this perspective, the problem becomes easier to handle. Four changes can be seen to have occurred in the practice of machine politics in American cities. First, in reference to Greenstein's criteria that machine politics demand a party hierarchy, very few such hierarchies remain operating city-wide across many functional areas. The Democratic party in Chicago is one of the few remaining cases of such a hierarchy. In other cities, party control is much less pervasive. In his study of mayoral appointments in New York City, Theodore Lowi noted four entirely separate functional arenas. Each functional arena had its own separate set of criteria for appointments and its own separate set of organizations that made the appointment nominations.[5] Furthermore, party organization in New York traditionally operated on a borough-wide, not a city-wide, basis. In recent years, Tammany Hall, the most famous of the nation's machines, has found its patronage restricted primarily to the Manhattan courts and to a few agencies under the mayor's office.* In the cities beyond the Northeast, the declining fortunes of party hierarchies are even more marked. Cities such as Miami,

---

"Why Political Machines Have Not Withered Away and Other Revisionist Thoughts," *Journal of Politics* 34 (May 1972): 365–398, and in *The Politics of Progress*, pp. 101–106.
* Tammany's restriction to patronage in the courts developed during the 1930s when Mayor Fiorello La Guardia denied Tammany as much patronage as possible. See Wallace S. Sayre and Herbert Kaufman, *Governing New York City* (New York: Russell Sage Foundation, 1960), pp. 140–141; and Martin Tolchin and Susan Tolchin, *To the Victor: Political Patronage from the Clubhouse to the White House* (New York: Vintage Books, 1972), p. 152.

Atlanta, Los Angeles, Seattle, and San Francisco have no rigid party hierarchy.[6]

A second change in the fortunes of machine politics concerns the role of political patronage. One of the common beliefs among political scientists has been that patronage is declining both in attractiveness to the parties and in use by them.[7] Patronage is considered unattractive because it is so difficult to administer without losing more supporters than are gained:[8] since there are always more applicants than patronage positions available, most applicants end up disappointed. In addition, civil service reforms have decreased the number of patronage jobs at the same time that the welfare system and increasing general affluence have made low-paying government jobs unappealing to many people.[9]

There can be no doubt that patronage is very difficult to administer, particularly in light of civil service, the welfare system, and a long period of increasing affluence from about 1940 to 1970. But there is evidence to indicate that patronage is still important in some regions at the state, county, and urban levels of government. It is especially important in parts of the East and in portions of the Midwest — especially Ohio, Indiana, and Illinois.[10] In short, the disappearance of patronage is not a universal phenomenon.

More marked than the disappearance of patronage has been the proliferation of different forms of incentives — both material and symbolic. Consider the proliferation of urban programs in the late 1960s and the increased use of outside consultants to conduct studies or to carry out government projects.[11] These forms of incentives differed from traditional patronage in two major respects. First, many of the jobs created through the urban programs and through the use of outside consultants went to middle-class people rather than to working-class or lower-class people. Second, in most instances, the awarding of these newly created forms of material incentives was not controlled by political party machines. In this sense non–civil service material incentives did not necessarily decline. What declined was the centralized political party control over the awarding of these incentives.[12]

A third change in the process of machine politics has occurred in their role of providing a channel of social mobility for the urban dependent populations. Historically, the machines received their electoral support from the immigrant dependent populations.[13] In turn, the machines provided certain welfare services on a sporadic basis to the poor. Furthermore, they existed as a channel for social mobility for some immigrants who were aggressive and ambitious. As these few were nominated for high office, their ethnic supporters received symbolic recognition. As immigration was curtailed in the late 1920s, the immigrant dependent population was replaced by a new mass of urban immigrants that consisted mainly of racial minorities, Spanish-speaking minorities, and poor whites. These new urban minorities have voted overwhelmingly Democratic. But the machines have not provided them with the same resources they provided the European immigrants. Nomination of a few blacks to high office has not been symbolically rewarding to black militants who fail to get such nominations. And Theodore Lowi's study of the class origins of high public officials in New York City over a sixty-year period found that the Democratic party in that city "is no longer the clear channel of social mobility."[14] In this sense the party has declined in its ability to provide benefits for the racial minorities, the Spanish-speaking minorities, and the poor whites who constitute the dependent populations of the 1970s. This does not suggest that parties are useless to the new minorities. For, to the extent that parties control nomination for electoral office, they can be very useful.[15] But the parties do not fit into networks of social mobility for the new urban minorities as they once did for the Irish, Italians, and Poles.

A fourth change in machine politics is that new organizations have been created to meet many of the needs that the political machines once met. Machines originally evolved in part because they filled certain needs of urban society in the late nineteenth century. In addition to meeting some of the welfare needs of the immigrant dependent populations, they filled at least two other needs. First, because of the rapid growth of cities in the late nineteenth century, city governments were faced with overwhelming demands to provide services such as streets, sewers, water supply, lights, transportation, public safety, and health inspections. But city governments were organized to perform very few of these functions. Even elementary functions such as police and fire protection were provided on a voluntary basis well into the nineteenth century. The machine offered a mechanism of getting the services provided. Second, the machines filled a need of the cities' businessmen. The business sector needed appropriate responses from the city governments in the form of licenses and franchises to operate streetcar lines, install natural gas, or provide electric power. By allowing themselves to be bought, machine politicians provided the appropriate responses to the businessmen.[16]

Actually none of these needs has ceased to exist, but new institutions have been created to meet them. Welfare is highly institutionalized. And the most dynamic growth in public services occurs in the suburbs, which are usually controlled by county governments or suburban municipalities that are very independent of the central city machines.

In summary, it is not very useful to talk in terms of the *dis-*

appearance of the political machine, because so many cities (at least in the northeast quadrant) still retain some elements of machine politics — especially patronage and the availability of other material incentives. However, the changes which have taken place in machine politics clearly indicate that *the machines have declined* in their abilities to meet many of the needs which they traditionally were supposed to have met. For meeting these needs, the machines have been bypassed by other, usually newer, public and private institutions.

If the practice of machine politics has declined but not disappeared and the machines have been bypassed in the performance of many functions that they used to perform, then two obvious questions are: (1) how did this come about? and (2) what difference does it make in terms of who benefits and who is hurt by the changes? The second question will be examined at the end of this chapter. In response to the first question, three developments have been most often cited for the decline of machine politics: the political reform movement, changes in the role of the federal government, and changes in the demography and locale of urban growth.

REFORMING THE MACHINES OUT OF BUSINESS

Reformers and Bosses

Tammany Hall leader George Washington Plunkitt once referred to the political reformers as "morning glories" who bloomed at election time but lacked the staying power to combat the machine on a long-term basis.[17] For many years the history of Tammany Hall bore out Plunkitt's observation. Reformers ousted Boss Tweed only to have the Tammany Society reinstated in city hall a few years later. Despite occasional defeats, the Tammany Hall machine ran New York virtually as it pleased from the 1870s until well into the twentieth century. But in the long run, Plunkitt was wrong. The reformers lost most of the battles for control of city governments, but they did succeed in restructuring the city government in ways that made it very difficult for the machines to govern.

To understand the reform movement, it is necessary to understand that its conflict with the political machines was in great measure a conflict between cultures. The machine leaders rose from the working and lower classes in the immigrant communities. In contrast, the reformers were primarily upper-class and upper-middle-class business-people, lawyers, professionals, and university people. There were some

sharp ideological differences within the ranks of the reformist movement; but, in contrast to the machine politicians, the reformers shared
many traits. Rather than being immigrants or first-generation Americans, the reformers came from families that had lived in America for
generations. They were Protestant rather than Catholic, and very often
they had graduated from colleges and professional schools rather than
being poorly educated. Rather than conducting their occupational affairs through personal and old-fashioned, informal methods as did the
political machine leaders, the reformers came from occupations in
which they had mastered modern, rational, and quasi-scientific
methods of organization. Intellectually, they came from an antiurban
heritage that placed considerable value on individual initiative, agricultural life, and a town meeting form of democracy. Somewhat at odds
with their belief in democracy was their elitist belief that government
should be conducted by the best-educated and best-qualified people in
the society.

Coming from such backgrounds, the reformers could never reconcile
themselves to the fact that city government was dominated by the kind
of people on whom the machines relied for their leadership. One group
of reformers investigated the backgrounds of the delegates to the 1896
Cook County Democratic Convention and revealed an intriguing cross
section of Chicago's Democratic leadership.

> A Cook County convention of 1896 — held, it may be well to remember,
> before the Illinois legislature had undertaken mandatory reform — indicates
> the appalling degradation that might be observed occasionally in the poli-
> tics of the period. Among the 723 delegates 17 had been tried for homicide,
> 46 had served terms in the penitentiary for homicide or other felonies, 84
> were identified by detectives as having criminal records. Considerably over
> a third of the delegates were saloon-keepers; two kept houses of ill fame;
> several kept gambling resorts. There were eleven former pugilists and
> fifteen former policemen. [18]*

Historian Richard Hofstadter has described the conflict between the
reformers and the machine leaders in terms of two incompatible percep-
tions of the very *raison d'etre* of politics. The immigrant politician
viewed politics in personal terms. Government "was the actions of
particular powers. Political relations were not governed by abstract
principles; they were profoundly personal."[19] The payoffs from political involvement also were highly specific — a job for a relative, a government contract, perhaps, or advance information on a proposed government land purchase that could enable one to make a quick profit by

---

* The author commented, "The policemen of Chicago at that period were not highly
regarded."

buying it beforehand and reselling it later to the government. Even those who were not close enough to the bosses to make money from their political involvement often received special payoffs — the proverbial bucket of coal or Christmas turkey, the intercession of the ward leader with the police in certain circumstances, or even just the friendship of the precinct captains and the ward leaders.[20] In contrast to this highly personal view of politics held by the immigrant, the upper-middle-class reformers looked upon politics as "the arena for the realization of moral principles of broad applications — and even, as in the case of temperance and vice crusades — for the correction of private habits."[21] The reformers were convinced that the immigrants and machine politics were detrimental to their concepts of a democracy in which the business of the town was to be conducted directly, and in a businesslike fashion, by the best-qualified citizens.

THE TAMMANY TIGER LOOSE — "What are you going to do about it?"

In this cartoon Thomas Nast illustrates some of the themes which irked the nineteenth-century progressive reformers. As the Tammany tiger devours the feminine figure of the Republic, the ballot box lies smashed, the law is torn to shreds, and Boss Tweed, with staff in hand, sits satisfied in the grandstand, surrounded by the Tammany spoils. In a deliberate goad to the progressive reformers, Nast reported the rhetorical question that Tweed himself so often put to his critics: "What are you going to do about it?"

Source: J. Chal Vinson, *Thomas Nast: Political Cartoonist* (Athens, Ga.: University of Georgia Press, 1967), plate 52.

In two very influential writings, political scientists James Q. Wilson and Edward C. Banfield attempted to apply the Hofstadter thesis to the general urban population.[22] Through a study of voting on bond referendums for hospitals and public buildings, they concluded that the urban population was divided into two mutually incompatible outlooks on government activity. They called each of these outlooks an ethos. The first ethos was called *public regarding*. It was found mostly among Negroes, Jews, and the residents of upper-class neighborhoods who voted in a "public-regarding fashion" of seeking government expenditures for the common good of the city even if it cost them more in property taxes. In contrast, a *private-regarding* ethos was discovered among the non-Jewish European ethnics who voted against such expenditures. This thesis has enjoyed widespread acceptance. The obvious implication to be drawn from it, in the words of one textbook, was that "machine-type politics thrives in a lower-class milieu, while reform-type politics flourished in a middle-class environment."[23]

The difficulty with this thesis is that it is hard to verify empirically. It came under sharp criticism for several conceptual and methodological weaknesses.* In order to meet these criticisms Wilson and Banfield reconducted their study later in the 1960s and used more sophisticated survey research techniques to identify the existence of the ethos in a carefully constructed sample of Boston residents. But when they found that barely a fifth of the population held attitudes that could properly fit into the two ethos categories, they argued that the outlooks they had identified earlier were much more important historically than they are at present.[24]

---

* One of the major conceptual weaknesses was the lack of definition of several key terms by Banfield and Wilson, especially terms such as *public interest, middle class,* and *Anglo-Saxon.* Nor was it clear if the difference between the public-regarding group and the private-regarding group was an ethnic difference, a class difference, or some combination of the two. There were two major deficiencies with Wilson and Banfield's methodology of testing the theory. By using referendum votes to draw inferences about individual attitudes, Wilson and Banfield committed the *ecological fallacy.* This is the attempt to draw conclusions about individual attitudes on the basis of aggregate election returns from precincts or wards. Second, the choice of bond referendums as the test of public regardingness is a very restricted test that touches the economic interests of most lower-income homeowners much more sharply than it touches the economic interests of upper-income persons. No matter how the upper-class precincts voted, they could not be labeled as private regarding, because they were not going to receive many of the direct benefits from the bond issues. At the same time, as Timothy M. Hennessey puts it [see his "Problems in Concept Formation: The Ethos Theory and the Comparative Study of Urban Politics," *Midwest Journal of Political Science* 14, no. 4 (November 1970): 537–564], the middle- and low-income renters are "precluded from behaving in a 'public regarding' manner" (pp. 544–545). Consequently, since both groups of voters are not subjected to the same testing criteria regarding the costs of the referendums, the tests are invalid. Hennessy's article as a whole is a perceptive analysis of the conceptual and methodological difficulties of the ethos theory.

Despite its deficiencies, the Banfield and Wilson thesis continues to be important, for the images of public and private regardingness exist even if few people are totally polarized into one outlook or the other. In relation to the conflict between the political bosses and the reformers, the reformers were able to create a public-regarding *image* of themselves and they were able to attach a singularly private-regarding *image* to the bosses. As will be seen later, the objectives and programs of the reformers could be made to seem very public regarding. And any opposition to them could make the bosses seem venal and private regarding. If, as Wilson and Banfield's latest data suggest, very, very few people have a private-regarding attitude, the reformers obtained a certain advantage over the bosses by manipulating these two images.

The above characterizations of the reformers are not meant to imply that they constituted a cohesive, monolithic bloc. They were in fact sharply divided in their outlook on the capitalistic system and its relation to government. Many reformers had complete faith in the ultimate rightness and efficacy of the system. They, after all, had benefited from it. These reformers tended to concentrate on reforms in governmental structure that would make city government more efficient and less costly to the corporate and business taxpayers. For this reason they can be called *structural reformers*. Many other reformers were critical of the capitalistic system. They were appalled by the degrading living conditions of the urban lower classes, the social irresponsibility of many industrial corporations, and the open graft that seemed to characterize the relations between the business leaders and the big-city political machines. They tended to concentrate more on social reforms than on structural reforms.[25] They can be called *social reformers*.

The ideological differences between these two kinds of reformers were reflected in their practical activities. The social reformers were most apparent in three kinds of activities. First was the muckraking and reform journalism exemplified by the work of observers like Lincoln Steffens and Jacob Riis.[26] A second channel of social reform activity was social work, particularly the settlement house movement. A prominent social worker was Jane Addams, who founded the Hull House settlement house in Chicago to facilitate the assimilation of the immigrants and to influence government activities in a progressive direction.[27]

The third tactic of social reform activity was to take over the government and use it to implement progressive policies. Many social reformers sought election to public office and a few became mayors in major cities. Some of the more prominent were Tom Johnson of Cleveland (1901–1909), Samuel "Golden Rule" Jones (1897–1903) and Brand Whitlock (1906–1913) of Toledo, and Hazen Pingree of Detroit (1890–1897). Hazen Pingree was elected mayor of Detroit just before the depression of 1893. Through his efforts at regulating the public utilities, he succeeded in getting the public lower rates on electricity, gas, and telephone service. When faced with an intransigent, privately owned transit company that refused to lower streetcar fares, he put the city in the transit business and promoted a competing streetcar line. In addition to these kinds of objectives, the social reform mayors also sought free swimming pools, park expansion, school construction, and public relief for the unemployed.[28]

In contrast to the social reform mayors who were willing to spend public money to improve social conditions for the lower classes, most of the reform mayors were structural reformers who were most interested in honesty, efficiency, and cost cutting. Prominent examples were Seth Low and John Purroy Mitchell in New York, Grover Cleveland in Buffalo, and James Phelan in San Francisco. Rather than increase expenditures on services to the poor, these mayors cut payrolls, reneged on contracts to pave streets, and cut back on school expenditures. There is little argument that the structural reformers made a more honest accounting of their tax revenues than did the political bosses, but there is also little argument that the costs of their honest accounting were paid mostly by the poor and by the residents of poor neighborhoods.[29]

Not only did the structural reformers concentrate most heavily on efficiency and economy in government, but they supported a series of reforms (to be described shortly) that would institutionalize such business practices.* Historian Samuel P. Hays carefully examined several reform movements and concluded that the major initiators of the structural reforms came primarily from the cities' top business leadership and upper-class elite. According to Hays, the movement to reform governmental structures "constituted an attempt by upper class, advanced professional, and large business groups to take formal political power from the previously dominant lower and middle class elements so that they might advance their own conception of desirable public policy."[30] Among the many reform movements that Hays examined, he found none in which small businessmen, white collar workers, or artisans were represented.

The reformers focused their programs on destroying the root causes

---

* The social reformer and structural reformer are not mutually exclusive categories: many of the social reformers also supported some of the structural reforms. Even though these categories are not completely mutually exclusive, they are still useful because they typify two contrasting viewpoints, and most reformers leaned toward one or the other.

of corruption in the conduct of municipal government. Governmental corruption was believed to grow out of the fact that the city governments were controlled by political parties which in turn were controlled by political party bosses whose control in turn depended on (1) an untutored immigrant electorate and (2) businessmen who were willing to partake in the "honest graft" which the machines offered them. If this chain of control could be broken, then higher-quality persons, not dominated by the machine, could be elected to city office. City administrations could then be conducted according to accepted practices of efficiency and administrative honesty. In this way, not only would city government be more efficient and honest; it might even be less expensive. These beliefs in the inherent goodness of efficiency and honesty underlay the programs of the structural reformers.

The Programs of Structural Reform

The devices for accomplishing these strategic aims were quite simple, although it took several years for them to evolve. The heart of the problem was the party bosses. Since the bosses were very difficult to eliminate, the key to the solution lay in making them ineffective. And this was largely accomplished through two broad movements: (1) breaking the control of the party bosses over the electoral process and (2) administering the city government according to the designs that would make it efficient and honest. This demanded a restructuring of city government.

Breaking the Bosses' Control over the Electoral Machinery

Under the existing rules of the game in the process of competing electorally with the bosses, the reformers often turned out to be, in Plunkitt's felicitous phrase, morning glories. If the reformers were to be effective in the long run, the only recourse open to them was to change those rules. The devices for doing this were relatively simple. If the party bosses controlled the nomination process through control of the party nominating conventions, then conventions had to be replaced with direct primaries in which the people would nominate their own candidates without the interference of corrupt political middlemen. If another source of the bosses' strength lay in the geographic or ward organizations through which they could channel limited welfare benefits to the needy in exchange for their votes, the logical solution was to eliminate wards and hold city elections at large, with every candidate for a particular city office running against every other candidate. If the long ballot meant that fifty or a hundred offices had to be voted on at local elections — numbers so large that voters relied heavily upon machine endorsements to distinguish friendly from unfriendly candidates — then the logical solution was to eliminate this reliance by having a short ballot in which people would have to learn about the candidates for only a limited number of offices. If the machine's strength depended on its ability to control party nominations, the machine might be permanently crippled by holding nonpartisan elections in which partisan nominations were banned. And if the machines controlled the margin of votes in close elections by their dishonest election practices such as repeating, voting for persons who had died or moved out, buying votes, substituting premarked ballots for unmarked ballots, or simply having the election judges add up the tallies incorrectly, then the final *coup de grace* might be given to the machine simply by making such practices illegal and clamping down on election law violations.

The standard mechanisms for breaking the control of the party bosses, then, were the direct primary, at-large elections, nonpartisan elections, the short ballot, fair campaign laws, and the separation of local elections from national elections. In addition to these standard mechanisms for breaking down the party bosses, other devices were used in many places. Proportional representation guaranteed a minimal representation of minority factions on city councils and thus weakened party control. But proportional representation never became a permanently popular device in the United States as it has in some European countries. Referendum, recall, and initiative devices were instituted in some cities. By *initiative*, a group of citizens could draft a bill by petition. By *referendum*, the petition-drafted bill had to be submitted directly to the voters for approval. The party-influenced councils and legislatures could be entirely bypassed through the use of initiative and referendum. *Recall* was first adopted in 1903 in Los Angeles. It enabled the premature removal from office of elected officials who had subsequently displeased the voters. When a required percentage of voters requested the recall via a petition, a special election was held and the official could be removed.

The machines' power was further broken down by more stringent fair campaign laws. The most notorious voting frauds were virtually eliminated. Repeating was a common fraud which, when handled with a certain amount of delicacy, could be greatly effective. A party worker would get up early in the morning, go to different polling places, and vote in other citizens' names before those people showed up. So common was repeating that even William Foote Whyte engaged in the practice while conducting his research as a participant observer in Boston for his book, *Street Corner Society*.[31] Unless it were handled carefully, however, repeating could embarrass the machine. Plunkitt tells the story of the repeater who entered a polling place and requested a ballot under the name of Doane. "You ain't Bishop Doane," challenged the poll judge. "The hell I ain't," responded the repeater, betraying himself.[32] In addition to repeating, some other fraudulent electioneering devices were premarking the ballots, buying votes, accompanying the voters into the voting booth so they could be pressured into voting as the precinct workers wanted them to, and voting in the name of citizens who had died or moved out of the precinct. This last device was used so indiscriminately that the results were sometimes ludicrous. In 1844, for example, a New York City election had a voter turnout of 55,000 people — even though there were only 41,000 qualified voters in the city.[33] Because of these kinds of abuses, stricter controls were enacted on voter registration and on campaign practices.

To complete the assault on boss-controlled politics, many states permitted open primaries in which voters did not have to prove their party affiliation in order to vote in a party's primary election. Through cross filing, California even went to the extreme of permitting candidates to run in the primary elections of both parties.

It was easier to get the reforms instituted in places like California where the progressive movements had been able to gain temporary control over the state government. Thus, states with strong progressive movements — states like Minnesota, Oregon, Wisconsin, and California — became the leaders in the reform movements to get the political machines out of politics. Where reforms were put into effect, political machines often found themselves severely contained and in some instances completely put out of business. Studies of the effect of cross filing and open primary elections in California concluded that these devices did indeed weaken if not destroy the control of the party bosses.[34]

It is important to stress that the reform movements did not eliminate graft between politicians and special interests; graft is still rampant at all levels of American politics. What the reformers did accomplish was, in most cities and metropolises, to remove the old party machine from its highly influential brokerage position right in the middle of the exchanges between the politicians and special interests. The effects of this can clearly be seen when the politics of reformed cities are contrasted with those of unreformed cities. Wherever the reform movements went into effect, the *modus operandi* of party politics became completely different.

James Q. Wilson and Edward Banfield contrast a highly reformed city, Los Angeles, with a city in which few of these reforms took hold, Chicago. In Los Angeles, one finds nonpartisan primaries, the absence of party endorsements, a high ideological or issue content in the election campaigns, and the almost complete absence of machine politics. Races become wide-open contests which anyone can enter, and the quality of media advertisement is normally the key to victory. In Chicago, elections are based on wards. Although elections for city offices are nominally nonpartisan, each party in fact promotes its slate of candidates. In the dominant Democratic party, the key step in the nomination process occurs in the preprimary convocation of the Cook County Democratic Central Committee in one of the downtown hotels, where the party leaders choose the Democratic slate for the primary.[35] This slate seldom loses in the primary elections. Defeats of the committee's hand-picked candidates occur only occasionally, such as in 1972, when the machine candidates for governor and state's attorney were defeated in the primary election. Until the present, Chicago politics have been tightly controlled by the Democratic organization. Wide-open races for major public offices with large numbers of contenders, as occur in California, are a rarity in Chicago. Throughout the entire twentieth century, there has never been a three-way contest for mayor in Chicago. The ground rules of Chicago elections make such a possibility completely out of the question.* And the election campaigns are seldom conducted with any ideological or issue content,† except for the issue of scandals in the administration, which increased in frequency over the later years of Daley's administration.

Restructuring City Government

At the same time that reformers sought to break the control of the bosses over the election process, they also sought to have the city itself administered competently on a politically neutral basis.[36] Specifically, they wanted to eliminate patronage as a basis for employing city government workers, and they wanted to eliminate partisan favoritism from the delivery of public services. They rejected the notion that gar-

---

* The rules governing the number of petition signatures makes a third-party candidacy impossible. See Mike Royko, *Boss: Richard J. Daley of Chicago* (New York: Signet Books, 1971), p. 76.
† There are some advantages to issueless election campaigns. For one thing, "Chicago was not governed . . . by the pull and haul of a few irresponsible pressure groups which get the voters' ear at election time." [Martin Meyerson and Edward C. Banfield, *Politics, Planning and the Public Interest: The Case of Public Housing in Chicago* (Glencoe, Ill.: The Free Press, 1955), p. 291.]

bage collection, or any other public service, could be performed any better by Democrats than by Republicans. If it were only garbage collectors who held patronage jobs, the reformers might not have worried much, for very few reformers wanted to become garbagemen anyway. But they did want good schools for their children, and they resented any partisan interference in school administration or in the awarding of contracts to construct new schools. They were concerned about the connections between police departments and vice in the cities. They wanted parks and open spaces. They wanted honest systems of bidding for government contracts, and they wanted efficiency in general in city administration. In fact, they had a decided tendency to conceive of city government as a problem in administration that could be solved through improved organizational techniques rather than as a problem in politics that involved the balancing of competing interests. They assumed that administrative solutions could prevail in political situations. In the logic of the reformers, it thus defied rationality that garbage collection should be considered a political problem rather than an administrative problem. Theoretically, what mattered was that garbage be picked up and eliminated in the fastest, cheapest, and least inconvenient way possible.

These general features of the reformers' mentality and the faith in the superiority of administration over politics have become such generally accepted conventional wisdoms about the way city government ought to be administered that it is often difficult to imagine why anybody could have opposed them. But from the point of view of the machine politicians, patronage and political favoritism in the administration of public services were essential. Without patronage there would be very little reason for the party followers to do the party's campaign work. George Washington Plunkitt reserved his most bitter scorn for attempts to eliminate patronage. Civil service was "the curse of the nation," wrote Plunkitt. "Parties can't hold together if their workers don't get the offices when they win."[37] Nor, if patronage were eliminated, could the party bosses have enough control over the bureaucrats to ensure that the services got delivered where the bosses wanted them delivered — namely, in the neighborhoods of the party followers.[38] Political favoritism in the delivery of services thus was essential to provide rewards for the neighborhoods that supported the machines. Political favoritism was also essential as a means of raising campaign funds. For Mayor Bernard McFeely in Hoboken, New Jersey, to have removed politics from garbage collection would have been political idiocy. Garbage collection was a means of granting the city garbage collection monopoly to a trash firm he himself had organized just shortly after his election in 1925. It was also a means of getting kickbacks to finance his party's coffers. That McFeely was not adverse to feathering his own nest is demonstrated by the fact that although his salary never exceeded $5000, he accumulated a fortune of $3 million by the time he was finally ousted from office in 1947.[39]

For McFeely and Plunkitt and the machines they represented, patronage and political favoritism were essential. In vain the political bosses argued that the reformers were themselves politically biased and that in their efforts to get control over the city government they would only rob lower-class people of the jobs and welfare benefits which the machines gave them in exchange for their votes.* These were very private-regarding arguments, however, and in comparison to the public-regarding posture that could be adopted by the reformers, the political bosses made themselves look very venal and petty.

The programs of the reformers were articulated and promoted by several national and regional organizations. To work for the elimination of party-controlled patronage at all levels of government, a National Civil Service Reform League was established in 1877. A Municipal Voters' League was organized in Chicago in 1896 and a Bureau of Municipal Research was organized in New York in 1906. Similar organizations were established in dozens of other large cities across the country. These organizations drew their membership and financial support from reform-minded local businessmen.[40] A major development was the formation of the National Municipal League in 1894. The League drafted a model city charter in 1900 and disseminated a considerable amount of books, pamphlets, and reformist literature to local groups which were seeking ways to reform their own city governments. A major organ for expressing the league's reformist views was its journal, *National Civic Review*, which is still published.[41]

Strong and Weak Mayor Forms of Government   A key target for the reformers was the weak mayor form of city government, which was thought to be more susceptible to machine dominance than was a strong mayor form. Most machine-dominated cities had weak mayors.

---

* George Washington Plunkitt argued that the civil service was a device to deny jobs to the Irish who were not as likely to have been educated and capable of answering the questions on the examinations [*Plunkitt of Tammany Hall*, recorded by William L. Riordan (New York: E. P. Dutton, 1963), pp. 11–16]. Mayor Daley of Chicago once explained his devotion to the Democratic machine by stating simply, "The party permits ordinary people to get ahead . . . . Without the party, only the rich would be elected to office" (Royko, *Boss*, p. 84).

Even today, the most renowned surviving machine, that in Chicago, operates under a weak mayor form of government.

The weak mayor form of government derived from the traditional American distrust of executive authority. Powers over the bureaucracy and budget were typically divided into several offices, many of which were elective and most of which had considerable patronage to dispense. This division of budget-making and policy-making powers into many hands made it extremely difficult for citizens to know which officers were responsible for what policies.[42] It also inhibited any coordinated policy control over city government services. But as long as there was no strongly felt need in cities for governments to perform many public services, the weak mayor form of government functioned well.

As the city populations grew large, however, city governments came under considerable pressure to install water lines and sewers, grant franchises for power companies and transit lines, initiate public health inspections, and perform a variety of new services. In cities with political machines, the large number of elective offices fell under machine control, since the machine dominated the nomination and election machinery. But machine dominance did not necessarily lead to improved public policy, for the machines were normally much more interested in controlling the patronage and government contracts at the offices' disposal than they were in coordinating the policies of the offices.

The weak mayor form of government thus came under attack from several points of view. It hindered public accountability. It fostered the dominance of city government by machines. And it proved incapable of coordinating all public policies in the city. One proposed solution to these defects was to create a strong mayor who would not be subordinated to a political boss and who would be able to coordinate all the policies of city government departments.

The differences between the strong and weak mayor forms of government are illustrated in Figure 4-1. Under the strong mayor form, the mayor actually assumes authority over the administration of the city government, leaving to the council the responsibility for legislative functions. Since department heads are appointed by the mayor, they become more accountable to him. Through him they are (theoretically, at least) accountable to the voters. The strong mayor form does not eliminate politics from city administration, but it does in theory limit the government fragmentation that was felt to be conducive to machine dominance.

FIGURE 4-1

STRONG AND WEAK MAYOR FORMS OF GOVERNMENT

Weak Mayor Government

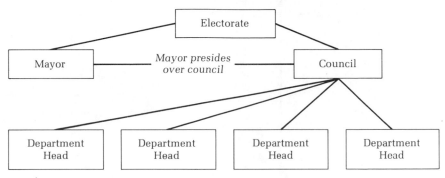

Strong Mayor Government

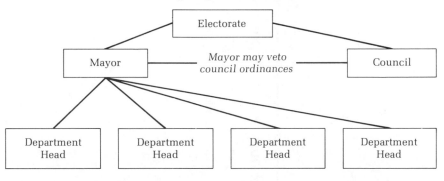

The Council-Manager Plan of Government   The city manager plan of government was an attempt both to obtain unified control over the city administration and at the same time to isolate city administration even further from political influence. All policy was to be established by the city council. Day-to-day operations were turned over to the city manager, who took care of the administrative details and stayed out of political questions.[43]

The city manager plan of government quickly became the most popular form of city government in the United States. As noted in Table 4-1,

TABLE 4-1

FREQUENCY OF CITY GOVERNMENT FORMS

Population Group	All Cities	Form of Government (Number and Percent)				Type of City (Number and Percent)		
		Mayor-Council	Council-Manager	Commission	Town Meeting[a]	Central	Suburb	Independent
Over 1,000,000	6	6 (100)	—	—	—	6 (100)	—	—
500,000 to 1,000,000	20	15 (75)	5 (25)	—	—	20 (100)	—	—
250,000 to 499,999	30	13 (43)	14 (47)	3 (10)	—	30 (100)	—	—
100,000 to 249,999	98	38 (39)	51 (52)	9 (9)	—	80 (82)	18 (18)	—
50,000 to 99,999	256	93 (36)	145 (57)	13 (5)	5 (2)	124 (48)	132 (52)	—
25,000 to 49,999	520	170 (33)	293 (56)	39 (8)	18 (3)	80 (15)	297 (57)	143 (28)
10,000 to 24,999	1,360	585 (43)	620 (46)	55 (4)	100 (7)	21 (1)	854 (63)	485 (36)
5,000 to 9,999	1,550	881 (57)	530 (34)	43 (3)	96 (6)	—	841 (54)	709 (46)
2,500 to 4,999	2,090	1,451 (69)	451 (22)	54 (3)	134 (6)	—	909 (43)	1,181 (57)
Total, all cities over 2,500	5,930	3,252 (54)	2,109 (36)	216 (4)	353 (6)	361 (6)	3,051 (51)	2,518 (43)

[a] Includes representative town meeting.

Source: International City Management Association, The Municipal Yearbook: 1975 (Washington, D.C.: 1975), table 3, p. xiii.

it was adopted by a majority of all cities in the 25,000-to-250,000 population range. The incidence of city manager government drops off sharply in cities below 25,000 because the cost of hiring a manager becomes prohibitive for very small communities. It begins dropping off in cities above 250,000 because the sheer size of such cities increases the number of conflicting interest groups concerned about city administration. City managers have been found to function best in cities where there exists a broad consensus on local politics. As cities become larger, a broad consensus is difficult to achieve, because the number of interest groups tends to grow very large. Large cities also tend to have more heterogeneous populations, which put conflicting demands on city government. However, in middle-sized cities and in cities where the ethnic and political composition of the population is relatively homogeneous, such as in many suburban cities, the city manager form of government is very popular.[44]

Political scientists have asked whether or not the city manager form of government lived up to the claims of its supporters that it would remove politics from city government. If politics are defined as active participation in party affairs, one would have to answer, "Yes, city managers are nonpolitical" in this limited sense. They are highly professionalized and even have their own International City Managers' Association which scrupulously advises them to avoid getting entangled in partisan affairs.

If, however, the term "political activity" is more broadly defined as involvement in the process of making public policy, the city manager is very politicized. Gladys Kammerer studied city managers and their activities in Florida and concluded that they exercise political leadership in three ways.[45] First, although the council is theoretically supposed to initiate policy and leave the manager to carry it out, in fact the city manager is more often than not the one who initiates policy proposals to the council. Second, the council members and the citizens perceive the city manager as a political leader. He is well known among the leaders of the civic organizations, chambers of commerce, and service organizations among his city, and it is as much to him as to the members of city council that these civic leaders look when they want a policy initiated or stopped. Third, successful city managers usually find it necessary to align themselves with the dominant factions on the city councils which they serve. A study of city managers in California found that some of them were so aligned with factions of their councils that some managers even urged candidates to run for city council and participated discreetly in their campaigns.[46]

Because he is appointed by the council, the manager serves only as long as a majority of the council supports him. If he aligns himself with a faction that is in control only temporarily or if he tries to be too innovative an administrator, the manager often risks sudden dismissal. But dismissal or short tenure in office is not necessarily harmful to the manager's career. As a professional administrator, he is expected to lead the council in the direction of adopting innovative techniques of city governance. Aggressive leadership may bring about short tenure and he may well rise to prominence among the corps of city managers by moving in a series of short-term assignments to the more sought-after manager cities.[47]

Because the manager career is highly professionalized, it serves as a mechanism for introducing cosmopolitan professionals into positions of local leadership. This had tended to break down the resistance of parochially oriented local governments to planning and to standarized administrative procedures. In the large cities, which (as shown in Table 4-1) tend not to have council-manager governments, many mayors have tried to avail themselves of the administrative expertise of the manager by hiring chief administrative officers (CAOs) or deputy administrators.

The Commission Form of Government   Another reform-style city government is the commission form. It was first developed in 1901 in Galveston, Texas, after a tidal wave inundated the city and killed 6000 people. Because the disaster was too great to permit a politics-as-usual conduct of government, a commission of three leading businessmen was established to run the city during the crisis. Their administration proved so popular that, after the crisis was over, Galveston adopted the commission form of government permanently. The number of cities adopting commission government spread rapidly in the next twenty years to about 500.[48]

A commission form of government uses the council members as administrators as well as legislators. As shown in Figure 4-2, each councilman (commissioner) is elected directly by the voters, usually in an at-large election. In addition to being a legislator, he is also the head of a particular department of government.

Although the commission form of government was widely adopted at the beginning of the century, it has not endured. The largest city with a modified commission form of government, Washington, D.C., dropped it in 1967. Of the three cities in the 250,000 to 500,000 population range with commission forms of government, Saint Paul, Minnesota, dropped it in 1972. It has proven ineffective either for running the government efficiently or for managing political conflict. Since the councilmen are also department heads, budget sessions frequently turn

FIGURE 4-2

MANAGER AND COMMISSION FORMS OF GOVERNMENT

Commission Government

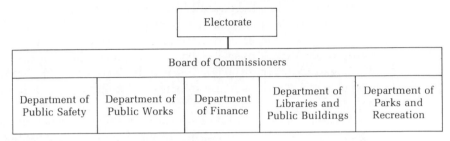

Council-Manager Government

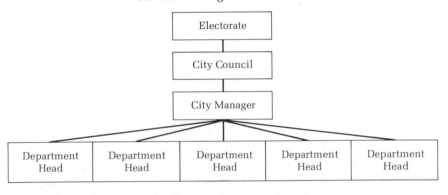

---

into logrolling sessions in which no overall capacity exists to budget for the city government as a whole. Coalitions form, as is normal on city councils, but councilmen who are left out of the coalitions find their departments left with smaller appropriations.

THE FEDERAL GOVERNMENT AND THE DECLINE OF MACHINE-STYLE POLITICS

The federal government became involved in urban politics as a consequence of the Great Depression and the resulting demands for federal action on economic problems. By the winter of 1932–33, 25 percent of the national work force was unemployed. Traditional forms of charity proved unable to cope with the immediate needs of the families of these workers. The urban political machines found themselves unable to cope with the problem, either. The magnitude of the economic depression had sharply reduced the revenues of municipal governments, and there were no surplus payroll funds which the machines could use to maintain their former high levels of patronage.* The machines no longer had the resources to donate food, clothing, or coal buckets on anything other than a piecemeal basis. When the federal government finally began to act in an extensive way to cope with the depression, two aspects of its actions had a detrimental effect on the political machines.

First, the New Deal instituted a form of public assistance to individuals that bypassed the political machines. For workers who were dismissed from their jobs, unemployment compensation was instituted. For workers who were injured on the job, workmen's compensation was begun. For mothers who were widowed or who had been deserted by their husbands, Aid for Dependent Children programs were established. As a supplement to pension plans, the Social Security Act was passed. Other welfare programs were established for the blind, the aged, and the disabled.

Two key features of all these programs made the recipients independent of the political machines. First, the recipients had a *legal right* to their assistance. They did not in effect have to buy the assistance by voting for the machine's candidates or by doing precinct work during the campaigns. Second, the assistance came directly to the recipients, usually through the mail in the form of a check. There was nothing that the ward leaders could do to increase the value of the checks being sent to supporters of the party or to decrease the value of the checks being sent to supporters of the opposition.† One net effect of the Great Depression and the New Deal, then, was to diminish the welfare functions which the political machines had previously performed. This deprived the party bosses of some of the material incentives they needed in order to maintain party discipline.

* This affected some machines more than others. In Chicago, the declining public revenues had very little detrimental effect on the machine's viability [Harold F. Gosnell, *Machine Politics: Chicago Model*, 2nd ed. (Chicago: University of Chicago Press, 1967), pp. 2–8.]

† The ward leaders were not left completely without influence, however. They could still give advice to welfare recipients on their welfare rights and benefits. And they could still try to intercede for the recipient with the welfare agencies. [William F. Whyte, *Street Corner Society* (Chicago: University of Chicago Press: 1970), pp. 196–197.]

A second general effect of the New Deal came from the rapidly expanding role of the federal government in urban areas. To support bankrupt cities, the federal government began making grants and loans directly to cities in order to finance public improvements such as water supply systems, sewerage systems, hospitals, and other public works. Increasingly, however, federal programs were carried out not by city governments but by agencies especially created to handle particular services. The Federal Housing Act of 1937, for example, enabled federal housing projects to be administered not through city governments but through quasi-public corporations called *housing authorities*.

Political scientist Morton Grodzins has identified several separate channels through which federal aid was directed to urban areas. In addition to the aid channeled directly to city governments, some aid went directly to individuals (e.g., Old Age and Survivor's Insurance). Some aid was channeled through the states (e.g., highway programs). And a considerable amount of federal aid was channeled through specially created local governments called special districts which were relatively independent of state or city governments. Much aid for conservation programs was of this type.[49] Because a substantial portion of federal aid was channeled into urban areas through special districts and quasi-public corporations, the federal government compounded the historic tendency in American government to fragment governmental authority.[50]

The impact of these proliferating government programs was to create new systems of material incentives which were increasingly beyond the control of the old-style machine. As the most dynamic functions of urban government came under the control of new agencies, the expansion of the machines was severely limited. Among the central cities of the West, machines are very seldom found. The functions traditionally associated with them are now performed by other agencies and there is no need for new machines to be created.

IMPACT OF METROPOLITAN GROWTH ON THE POLITICAL MACHINES

In addition to the political reform movements and the proliferation of federal programs, the decline of machine politics was also hastened by the basic demographic and technological forces which had transformed the historic city into the contemporary metropolis. The dual migration, the westward drift of the population, the decline in dominance of the Northeast, the encirclement of the central city by suburbs, and the shift of urban growth from the central city portion of the metropolis to suburban areas all made it impossible for the political machines to expand their influence.

The dual migration movements were detrimental to machine politics because the political machines never succeeded in absorbing the new urban immigrants as they had the European immigrants. In fact, the new minorities were often perceived as threats to the perquisites of persons who had worked their way up in the party. Even where the minorities were brought into the machine's operations, as in the case of the Dawson sub-machine in Chicago, the machine was powerless to promote the social reforms so desperately needed in the black wards.[51] Instead, it promoted highly visible construction activity in freeways, rapid transit, airports, convention halls, a university campus, and downtown office buildings that would give the city a progressive image, please the business sector, provide jobs for white construction workers, and open up enormous sources of graft to fill the party's coffers. This was an imaginative response to the fact that the city had reached its geographic limits and was completely encircled by water or suburbs, thus ending its physical growth. Daley's tremendous stroke of genius was to use the machine's political power to destroy large tracts of the city and subsequently to enhance the machine's control by rebuilding what it had just torn down. These actions created wealth.

However, very little of the wealth created in this fashion went to improve the collective status of the black, Chicano, or Puerto Rican minority populations in Chicago. A strange aspect of this is that the blacks so consistently and for so long kept giving overwhelming majorities to the Democratic machine's candidates. Equally strange is the fact that the Republicans never made any serious attempt to woo black voters away from allegiance to the Daley machine. And, of course, the fact that Daley could so successfully and for so many years keep the blacks loyal and prevent any substantial Republican opposition in the black wards was an eloquent testimony to his tactical genius. But if the blacks, Puerto Ricans, and other urban minorities become a majority in the city while the traditional ethnic majorities become a minority, then there will obviously have to be some drastic realignments in Chicago's machine.

The westward drift of the population and the rise of urban centers in the West are also relevant to the decline of machine politics. For in the Southwest, the most dynamic area of urban growth today, the elements which had facilitated machine politics were much less strong than they had been in the Northeast and the Midwest. The machines' reinforcing social institutions, in particular, were much weaker. Labor unions were not traditionally strong in the Southwest. Although ethnic communities developed in the West,[52] they seldom dominated local politics. Furthermore, many Western cities developed their basic political form after the antimachine reform movements had begun to take effect. The major exception to this is San Francisco. In that city the ethnic base of politics has remained very strong, but the political machine has disappeared.[53]* Particularly important in the Southwest and in California was the fact that for communicating campaign slogans newspapers and television became much more important media than the political parties. Finally, since the populace in the West and Southwest was one of the most affluent of the nation, and since these areas had jobs in abundance, the patronage jobs and piecemeal welfare assistance which the machines might have offered were much less attractive than they were in the Northeast and Midwest cities. For all of these reasons, the general westward drift of urbanization out of the northeast quadrant meant that the old machine politics would not be able to expand in the vanguard of urbanization. It would become a sectional phenomenon limited for the most part to the central cities of the older metropolitan areas.

Even within the Northeast, the demographic and technological forces were detrimental to the survival of the machine as an adequate governing force. Metropolitanization had brought a monumental increase in scale in the urbanization process,[54] turning the Northeast seacoast into a megalopolis of 40 million people. Most of the population increase occurred in the suburbs, which were not controlled by the central city machines. Even within the central cities there was an increasing tendency to bypass the parties as much as possible when it came to accomplishing concrete objectives such as urban renewal.

THE IMPACT AND BIAS OF THE MACHINES' DECLINE

The above-mentioned developments themselves did not necessarily destroy the old political machines. Machines in Jersey City and Chicago, for example, continued to thrive despite the existence of a formally nonpartisan ballot. And the McFeely machine in Hoboken was

* It is conceivable that ethnic-based political activity will increase in other Southwestern cities as Chicano political participation increases.

able to thrive under the commission form of government. Furthermore, where ethnically based politics were deeply ingrained, the passage of antimachine reforms did not necessarily change voting behavior. With party labels removed, the ethnic identification of candidates assumed even greater importance.[55]

If individual political reforms did not necessarily destroy the old machines or the ethnic basis to politics, then what difference did they make? Did the reform movement make any difference at all in urban politics? There has been considerable empirical research on various aspects of these questions, and the conclusions on the reform movement tend to fall into five general lines of thought. (1) Reform movements prospered more in certain kinds of cities than in others. (2) Individual reforms have a class bias and a partisan bias. (3) In cities where all the reforms occurred, their sum total has weakened the machines. (4) The reforms have led to an increased rather than a diminished fragmentation in city government. (5) The reforms have resulted in a lessened accountability of political leaders to the electorate.

Reform-style Governments: Their Success in Certain Kinds of Cities

If one distinguishes between a reform-style government and a non-reform-style government, some clear differences can be discovered between the kinds of cities which have and the kinds which do not have reform-style government. A city government may be considered reform style to the extent that it has adopted the major structural innovations of the political reform movement — nonpartisanship, at-large elections, and council-manager form of government. Such governments are least likely to be found in cities with heavy concentrations of European ethnics. Political scientist John H. Kessel found that the fewer foreign-born residents a city had, the more likely it was to have a city manager form of government.[56] Other demographic relationships were found. The faster the growth rate of a city, the more likely it was to have a city manager form of government. The more highly educated its population, the more likely it was to have reform-style government. When cities were ranked in terms of their major economic functions, there was an increasing reliance on the city manager form as cities' economic bases became less dependent on the manufacturing, transportation, and economic bases associated with the old, historic, industrial city. The fewer Catholics a city had, the more likely it was to have reform-style government. And, finally, another study found that reform-style governments were more prevalent in the West than they were in the East.[57] From this one can conclude that nonreform-style city government is most likely to be found in central cities, in the East, in cities with high percentages of ethnic concentrations, in slowly growing cities, and in older, industrial cities. Conversely, reform-style city government is most likely to be found in suburban cities, in the West, in cities with low percentages of ethnic concentrations, in fast-growing cities, and in newer, nonindustrially based cities.

The Class Bias of Political Reforms

There is some empirical evidence that nonpartisan and at-large elections are biased to the disadvantage of lower-income people.[58] A study in Des Moines concluded that nonpartisanship in that city reduced voter turnout among lower-income people and thus gave "upper-income groups relatively greater power in the local community."[59] Some other, less obviously class-oriented consequences have been identified with nonpartisanship. Nonpartisanship gives advantages to incumbents rather than to challengers in local elections,[60] reduces voting turnout among Democrats more than among Republicans, and usually favors Republican candidates rather than Democratic candidates in local elections, although in some places nonpartisanship favored the Democratic candidates.[61]*

A class bias is also found in the at-large system of local elections. Boston is a partisan city that used an at-large system from 1909 to 1924, switched to a district system from 1924 to 1949, and then switched back to an at-large system in 1949. In support of the expectations of the reformers, Banfield and Wilson found that the council members elected at large "do in fact take a larger view of city affairs than did the ward-based ones." But the ward system gave racial "minority interests better representation" in city government than did the at-large system.[62] In Saint Paul, at-large elections and a commission form of government combined in 1970 to produce a city council in which five of the six members lived within a few minutes' drive of each other in an area that comprised about a sixth of the city's land area and contained about a seventh of its population. The sections of the city where the five councilmen lived were the more affluent sections. In Detroit, the combination of an at-large system with nonpartisan elections had the effect for several years not only of keeping down the representation of blacks

---

* Some of the earlier studies had found evidence that in heavily Republican areas nonpartisanship sometimes helped Democratic candidates. The net bias, however, has been to the advantage of Republicans. In eighty-eight San Francisco area cities, Willis Hawley found that nonpartisanship favored Republicans twice as often as it favored Democrats [Hawley, *Non-partisan Elections and the Case for Party Politics* (New York: Wiley, 1973), pp. 31–33].

on the city council but also of limiting black councilmen to those who could get votes in the white, middle-class areas.[63] In one Midwestern city the representation system was deliberately altered from a ward system to an arrangement in which two nominations were made by each ward but only one of the nominees was elected by a city-wide electorate. The net effect of the change was to bring about the defeat of a militant black city councilman.[64] In Oakland a combination of at-large elections with several other reforms served to inhibit political participation by the unorganized lower classes of the city.[65]

There is also some evidence that the separation of local elections from national elections is biased against people of lower social status. A study in Toledo, Ohio, found that voter turnout was lower for the local election than for the national election and that it was primarily the people of a lower socioeconomic status who did not turn out. The net result was to give the middle and upper classes a greater electoral voice in city affairs than they would have if local elections were held at the same time as national elections.[66]

The above studies indicate that reform governments have a class bias on the *input side* of the political system, in that reform governments underrepresent the lower classes in city government. The studies do not, however, address themselves to the question of whether the *policy outcomes* of reform governments are equally biased against the lower classes. The most sophisticated attempt to answer that question has probably been the analysis of 200 cities of 50,000 or more population by Robert L. Lineberry and Edmund P. Fowler.[67] They found that reformed cities spend less and tax less than do unreformed cities. The reformed cities are also less responsive to sharp racial, ethnic, and socioeconomic divisions in the electorate. These are important findings, for they confirm some of the expectations of both the early reformers and the political bosses. Recall that many political reforms had been supported by businesspeople who hoped that the reformed governments would hold down both expenditures and taxes. In contrast, the bosses had opposed the reforms because they would diminish the political voice of the lower classes.

Lineberry and Fowler do not assert that political reformism is the only variable affecting policy outcomes in cities. Rather they conclude that policy outcomes are a consequence of three interrelated sets of variables: socioeconomic cleavages (e.g., ethnic or racial differences), political variables (party registration, levels of voter turnout, etc.), and political institutions (form of government, type of elections, and types of constituencies).

These conclusions of Lineberry and Fowler are partially supported by Terry N. Clark's study of fifty-one cities of between 50,000 and 750,000 population.[68] Clark found that general government expenditures on noncontroversial issues were likely to be higher in cities with decentralized decision-making structures and nonreform-style government. On controversial issues, such as the initial stages of urban renewal, the more centralized and reformed governments had the higher expenditures. The strongest correlation with high government expenditures, however, was not a political variable. Rather it was the size of the city's Catholic population. The higher the percentage of Catholics, the higher the level of expenditures.[69]

Machine Politics Weakened by Reforms

Although there is no evidence to indicate that the enactment of any one specific reform drove any particular machine out of business, when all or most of the reforms were put into effect at once, the political machines found it very difficult to operate. Even when machine politicians did get elected, they found it very difficult to govern. As more city jobs came under civil service protection, fewer workers felt compelled to make campaign contributions or to become precinct workers. Improved auditing procedures and a muckraking press made the "honest graft" of George Washington Plunkitt exceedingly more difficult to manipulate. Changes in government policies toward organized labor also increased the problems of the machines. The federal protection given to labor unions after the passage of the Wagner Act in 1935 created a new force that had to be taken into account in the calculus of urban political leaders. The emergence of militant public employees' unions in the 1960s, and the increase in the number of teachers, policemen, garbage collectors, and other civil servants who were willing to paralyze the city's operations through strikes if need be in order to make their demands heard, made the old-style, face-to-face, intimate-exchange politics extremely difficult to keep up. By midcentury, New York had 50,000 organized school employees, 26,000 policemen, and 13,000 firemen.[70] The size and magnitude of city bureaucracies, freed by civil service from dependence on the machines for jobs and organized by the public employees' unions to seek their own group interests, make the old-style personal politics impossible.

Fragmentation Increased by Reform

Reform-style government tended to increase rather than decrease the fragmentation of urban political power. The 1930s, 1940s, 1950s, and

1960s were years of almost unremitting expansion of governmental services in urban areas. Welfare services were greatly expanded. Increasing numbers of public hospitals were built. More and more urban areas began purchasing private transit systems and operating them publicly. Public employment offices were established. Airports had to be built to handle the rapid growth of airlines and then rebuilt to accommodate the jetliners. With the passage of the United States Housing Act in 1949, cities were able to tear down dilapidated buildings in blighted neighborhoods and try to replace them with housing and redevelopment projects.

One extremely important fact is that very few of these newly created services were turned over to the traditional city governments. Expanded welfare and hospital services became the province of the county governments. When privately owned transit systems were sold to the public, the general pattern was to create a metropolitan district to operate them. Airports also tended to be operated by metropolitan districts. Public employment offices were usually run by the states or the federal government. Housing authorites which administered the urban renewal programs often were appointed by the city councils, but they operated under very rigid federal guidelines, and in few cities did they serve as an arm of the city government. Central business district redevelopment plans were usually initiated by businesspeople who had a stake in the survival of the downtown business district. Funds for redevelopment usually came from federal urban renewal programs or from private investors, and the major actions required of city councils were often limited to making the appropriate zoning changes and setting up bond referendums when they were needed.

One of the most popular agencies for performing new governmental functions has been the special district. A special district is an autonomous government created to perform a specific service. The number of special districts in metropolitan areas has increased regularly since the 1930s. Because special districts are autonomous and relatively free from control by central city governments, their proliferation has necessarily increased the fragmentation of governing authority in urban areas.[71]

Public Accountability Decreased by Reform

A last consequence of the political reform movements was to reduce the accountability of the public officials to the electorate. Again, as in the fragmentation of local government authority, this was a result that the reformers had not counted on: the reformers had not intended to reduce government accountability, but a decrease in accountability did result from the reform measures.

Charles Adrian has asserted that nonpartisan elections prevent the groups that control the government from being held collectively accountable to the voters.[72] And Robert Wood has argued that nonpartisanship is based upon some very faulty assumptions about the ability of individuals to determine who in the government is responsible for what policies: "Inescapably, there is a belief that the individual can and should arrive at his political convictions untutored and unled; an expectation that in the formal process of election and decision-making a consensus will emerge through the process of right reason and by the higher call to the common good."[73]

Furthermore, as more and more authority shifted from the hands of the elected officials into the hands of the large public bureaucracies, it became exceedingly difficult for the elected officials to control the bureaucrats. The doctrine that policy making should be separated from policy implementation further served to insulate the bureaucracies from accountability to elected officials. On controversial actions on which bureaucrats did not want to suffer the interference of elected officials, they could demand that the actions dealt with policy implementation rather than policy making and consequently were not subject to scrutiny by the elected officials.[74] As the public bureaucracies became more and more insulated, they began to develop into functional fiefdoms. The implications of this will be discussed in Chapter 5.

Some Suggested Readings

Have Machine Politics Declined?

Edwin O'Connor, *The Last Hurrah* (Boston: Little, Brown, 1956). Romanticizes the big-city boss and machine politics. Details the last days of protagonist boss-mayor Frank Skeffington, who is supposedly modeled on Boston's James Curley.

Plunkitt of Tammany Hall, recorded by William L. Riordan (New York: E. P. Dutton, 1963). This reproduction of speeches and commentaries by a turn-of-the-century Tammany district leader, George Washington Plunkitt, captures better than anything else in print the spirit of old-style machine politics.

Raymond E. Wolfinger, "Why Political Machines Have Not Withered Away and Other Revisionist Thoughts," *Journal of Politics* 34 (May 1972): 365–398. This articulate argument that machine politics are still very much alive should probably be read in conjunction with an article expressing the opposite argument. Two likely candidates are Fred I. Greenstein, "The Changing Pattern of Urban Party Politics," *The Annals of the American Academy of Political and Social Science* 353 (May 1964): 1–13; and Joseph L. Bernd, "Comments on Wolfinger's 'Why Political Machines Have Not Withered Away,' " *Journal of Politics* 35, no. 1 (February 1973): 204–207.

Fred J. Cook, *American Political Bosses and Machines* (New York: Franklin Watts, 1973). Chapters on Tammany Hall, Boss Tweed, and Abe Rueff.

Martin Tolchin and Susan Tolchin, *To the Victor: Political Patronage From the Clubhouse to the White House* (New York: Vintage Books, 1972). Although their analysis of urban political patronage is drawn primarily from New York and Chicago and hence is not of general applicability, the authors demonstrate quite clearly that at least in those two cities patronage has not declined.

Urban Reform and Reform Government

Melvin G. Holli, *Reform in Detroit: Hazen S. Pingree and Urban Politics* (New York: Oxford University Press, 1969). In addition to presenting an interesting account of Pingree, Holli makes an important distinction between social reformers and structural reformers and demonstrates how differently they acted when they achieved power. Pingree is clearly described as a social reformer.

Samuel P. Hays, "The Politics of Reform in Municipal Government in the Progressive Era," *Pacific Northwest Quarterly* 55 (October 1964): 157–166. Demonstrates the link between the urban political reformers and the business community.

Eugene C. Lee, *The Politics of Nonpartisanship* (Berkeley: University of California Press, 1960). A study of nonpartisan government in California.

Ronald O. Loveridge, *City Managers in Legislative Politics* (Indianapolis: Bobbs-Merrill, 1971). A study of city managers in the San Francisco area.

Brett W. Hawkins, *Politics and Urban Policies* (Indianapolis: Bobbs-Merrill, 1971). This is probably the most complete review to date of empirical studies on the relationship between socioeconomic environment, political structure, and policy output in cities.

Chapter 5

The twentieth-century movements discussed in the previous chapter — the political reform movement, the transformation of the city into the metropolis, and the increasing federal role — reinforced some other important changes that were occurring in urban America. Together they have had important consequences for the conduct of urban politics in the 1970s and for the general beliefs which exist about the nature of the urban political process. Two sets of general beliefs have been sufficiently important to merit examination here. First is the belief that the central cities are becoming impoverished, that the contemporary

Contemporary City Politics: The Dominance of Functional Fiefdoms

metropolis in the United States is universally bifurcated into a growing, successful, affluent, white, Republican suburbia and a stagnant, unsuccessful, impoverished, nonwhite, Democratic central city.*

A second set of beliefs has centered around the question, "Who really runs American cities?" Some people respond that cities are run by an elite power structure. Others say that they are run through the interaction of various interest groups and power centers. These two responses have been termed, respectively, the *elitist* and *pluralist* models of community power. These models will be examined later in this chapter.

* One of the nation's most eminent political scientists, Norton Long, has argued that the movement of affluent people and holders of high-status jobs to the suburbs has turned the central city into a repository for all the unwanted urban problems. The city in his view is becoming a "reservation for the poor, the deviant, the unwanted, and for those who make a business or career of managing them for the rest of society." See Long, "The City as Reservation," *The Public Interest* 25 (Fall 1971): 33.

In addition to seeing the emergence of these sets of beliefs about central cities, the past few decades have also witnessed important changes in central city governance. One of the most important of these changes has been the emergence of functionally organized governmental power to complement and in some instances supersede the ethnically organized political power of the era of machine politics. The core of functionally based governmental power is found in the government bureaucracies.

As urban political power became increasingly organized on a functional basis, two other consequences occurred that have particular importance for the 1970s. First, the development of autonomous, functionally based governmental organizations seemed to inhibit the exercise of strong executive leadership. This led to demands in the 1960s and 1970s for structural and political antidotes that would strengthen the mayor's capacity to provide leadership. Second, the growing autonomy of the functionally based organization of power has been accused of making urban government unresponsive to the citizenry. As an antidote, various proposals for community control have been advanced.

These considerations are the subject of this chapter. The discussion will be based on the following questions. First, how accurate is the belief of central city impoverishment? Second, are the central cities dominated by a stratified power structure? Third, what is meant by the emergence of functionally based governmental power? and why is the strong mayor proposed as an antidote for it? Fourth, what is the nature of the charge that contemporary urban government is unresponsive to the citizenry? and why is community control proposed as an antidote for this alleged unresponsiveness? Last, does the organization of governmental power in the contemporary metropolis lead to consistent patterns of bias?

ARE CENTRAL CITIES IMPOVERISHED?

The term *central city impoverishment* refers to a complex of factors that include population decline, the flight of affluent people to the suburbs, a concentration of disadvantaged people and minorities in the central city, a deterioration of physical facilities, and the inability to attract new business enterprises and jobs, which also locate mostly in the suburbs. Examples of this supposed central city impoverishment are most often drawn from the older metropolises of the Northeast. Over the past two generations, the politics of the Northeast central cities changed from that of growth and dynamism to that of consolida-

The plight of the older central cities is illustrated in this 1966 cartoon by Herblock of the *Washington Post*. Herblock has drawn several cartoons that show the central city overwhelmed by its problems. This one is particularly distinctive for its portrayal of the isolation of the central city and its forlorn cry for help that obviously cannot be heard above the tall buildings.

From *The Herblock Gallery* (Simon & Schuster, 1968)

tion and holding the line. The housing supply deteriorated and even declined in some cities, despite the fact that many central city populations were declining. As the population migrations discussed in Chapter 2 began to reach their peak during the 1950s and 1960s, these central cities increasingly found themselves with inadequate resources to deal with their mounting problems of racial segregation, unemployment, underemployment, education, housing, and public assistance. Public discontent among the new urban minorities reached a peak in the civil disorders of the middle 1960s. In the years since the civil disorders, the pace of out-migration has increased, thus widening the gap between relatively affluent suburbs and relatively impoverished central city residents.*

Central city impoverishment, however, is not universal. The accuracy of the picture varies with the size of the metropolis, its age, and the region of the country in which it is located. The picture is most accurate in describing the large, older metropolises of the Northeast. In other sections of the country, where the central cities are newer, the contrast between an impoverished central city and a dynamic suburbia is not nearly as marked. In a 1963 study, sociologist Leo Schnore carefully analyzed city/suburban differences in affluence and discovered that the discrepancies were not nearly as pronounced in newer metropolises as they were in older ones.[1] At the time of Schnore's analysis, *all* of the suburbs of old central cities (those formed before 1880) had higher median incomes than their respective central cities, whereas barely a majority of the suburbs of newer central cities (those founded since 1950) had higher incomes.

The same pattern was found in other measures of affluence. *All* of the suburban areas of the older metropolises had a higher percentage of high school graduates and a higher percentage of white collar workers than did their respective central cities. But in the newer metropolises, less than a majority of the suburbs had a higher percentage of high school graduates and only a small minority had a higher percentage of white collar workers than did their corresponding central cities. In other words, in the newest metropolises, the central city residents on the average are at least as affluent as their suburban neighbors. In these metropolises, the picture of central city impoverishment is more mythical than accurate. In the older metropolises, however, the picture of central city impoverishment is not a myth. A sharp dichotomy exists

---

* The Census Bureau reported that in the three years from March 1970 to March 1973, the central cities suffered a net migration loss of 4 million persons, while the suburbs sustained a net gain of 3 million persons. The other million migrated past the suburbs into small towns in the exurbia zone. [*St. Paul Pioneer Press*, November 23, 1973, p. 21.]

TABLE 5-1

CITY / SUBURBAN DIFFERENCES BY AGE OF SMSA: 1970

Period Established	Number Established in Decade	Number of SMSAs in Which the Suburbs Are More Affluent than the Central Cities in:		
		Median Family Income	Percentage of Adult Population Who Are High School Graduates	Percentage of Population below Poverty Level
1800–1860	16	16 (100%)	16 (100%)	16 (100%)
1870–1880	17	17 (100%)	17 (100%)	17 (100%)
1890–1900	37	32 (87%)	34 (92%)	34 (92%)
1910–1920	55	42 (76%)	40 (73%)	46 (84%)
1930–1940	31	19 (61%)	21 (68%)	25 (81%)
1950–1960	62	30 (48%)	29 (47%)	36 (58%)
1970	24	11 (46%)	10 (42%)	14 (58%)

Source: United States Department of Commerce, Bureau of the Census, 1970 Census of Population; General Social and Economic Characteristics (Washington, D.C.: U.S. Government Printing Office, 1972), tables 83, 89, 90 for each state.

between affluent suburbs and impoverished central cities, as Table 5-1 illustrates.

In his analysis of city/suburban discrepancies, Schnore also found that the size of central cities significantly affected the discrepancies in affluence. The largest metropolitan areas had the most severe discrepancies between central city poverty and suburban affluence. In the smallest metropolitan areas, the central city residents were at least as affluent as the suburban residents. This is shown in Table 5-2.

Not only are newer and smaller central cities more affluent than older and larger cities in comparison with their suburbs, but cities in the western and southern parts of the country are better off as well.[2] This is undoubtedly related to the fact that most of the Southwest metropolises are newer and smaller than the metropolises of the East.

What all this means is that one must be very careful in accepting blanket generalizations about the impoverishment of urban areas. It is quite accurate to speak of urban impoverishment in terms of declining populations, lower growth rates in job opportunities, numbers of people receiving public assistance, and loss of business to the outlying suburbs in a great many of the older central cities of the Northeast and the Midwest. Pittsburgh, for example, lost a fourth of its population between 1950 and 1970. In these same terms, however, central cities

TABLE 5-2

CITY / SUBURBAN DIFFERENCES BY SIZE OF SMSA: 1970

Size	Number	Number of SMSAs in Which the Suburbs Are More Affluent than the Central Cities in:		
		Median Family Income	Percentage of Adult Population Who Are High School Graduates	Percentage of Population below Poverty Level
Greater than 500,000	65	56 (86%)	57 (88%)	62 (95%)
100,000 to 499,999	152	99 (65%)	101 (66%)	115 (76%)
50,000 to 99,999	25	12 (48%)	9 (36%)	11 (44%)

Source: United States Department of Commerce, Bureau of the Census, 1970 Census of Population: General Social and Economic Characteristics (Washington, D.C.: U.S. Government Printing Office, 1972), tables 83, 89, 90 for each state.

such as Lubbock, Texas; Tucson, Arizona; Las Vegas, Nevada; and Santa Barbara, California are not declining. On the contrary, they are dynamic and growing cities.

ARE CENTRAL CITIES DOMINATED BY STRATIFIED POWER STRUCTURES?

A second question about contemporary cities in the United States is, "Who runs American cities?" Are they controlled by a unified, upper-status elite that usually operates behind the scenes and is capable of subordinating to its own interests the formal governmental apparatus of the city? In other words, is community power in city governance *elitist*? Or is control over the city divided among several competing groups and power centers? Is it *pluralist*? For over two decades the elitists and the pluralists have debated basic methods of research, basic assumptions about the exercise of power, and basic conclusions about its dispersion.

The Elitist Model of Community Power

Although several sociological and anthropological community studies have commented on local politics,[3] the first community study that devoted itself exclusively to the exercise of power was Floyd Hunter's *Community Power Structure*.[4] His book is worth examining in some detail, because it establishes one major strand of basic research methodology and substantive conclusions that have influenced community studies since its publication in 1953. Hunter, a sociologist, set for himself the task of answering the question, "Who runs Regional City?" (For *Regional City*, read *Atlanta, Georgia*.) To identify the leadership of Regional City, Hunter compiled lists of prominent civic leaders, government leaders, business leaders, and status leaders. He then selected a panel of six knowledgeable people to examine the lists and identify the most influential individuals on each list and the most influential organizations. From these selections, Hunter identified forty individuals at the apex of the power structure in Regional City. Most of these forty served on the boards of directors of the same corporations and belonged to the same social clubs. Beneath the top leadership was a cadre of what Hunter called "understructure personnel" who carried out the will and the instructions of the top power structure.

Not only did Hunter identify a top power structure in Regional City; he also contended that this power structure initiated most of the major developments that occurred in Regional City and that it successfully vetoed projects it disliked. Enterprising newspaper or journal writers lost their jobs when they disagreed with the power structure. Social welfare professionals were carefully constrained not to raise issues such as public housing which might violate the interests of the power structure. On certain key issues, such as limiting the supply of public housing, Hunter pictured the governor, the United States senators, the key state legislators, the party leaders, and other officials with very few exceptions as subordinated to the top power structure. Power, in Hunter's view, was cumulative. That is, power in one area of activity gave a person power in other areas as well.*

* The following is an example of how things were done in Regional City. Hunter's scenario shows the power structure establishing an international trade council.

    We decide to have a meeting at the Grandview Club with select members of other crowds.
    When we meet at the Club at dinner with the other crowds, Mr. Homer makes a brief talk; again, he does not need to talk long. He ends his talk by saying he believes in his proposition enough that he is willing to put $10,000 of his own money into it for the first year. . . . The Growers Bank crowd, not to be outdone, offers a like amount plus a guarantee that they will go along with the project for three years. Others throw in $5,000 to $10,000 until — I'd say within thirty or forty minutes — we have pledges of the money we need. In three hours the whole thing is settled, including the time for eating.
    We went into that meeting with a board of directors picked. The constitution was all written, and the man who was to head the council as executive was named . . . a third-stringer, a fellow who will take advice.
    The public doesn't know anything about the project until it reaches the stage I've been talking about. After the matter is financially sound, then we go to the newspapers and say there is a proposal for consideration. Of course, it is not news to a lot of people by then, but the Chamber committees and other civic organizations are brought in on the idea. They all think it's a good idea. They help to get the Council located and established. That's about all there is to it.

From Floyd Hunter, *Community Power Structure* (Chapel Hill, N.C.: The University of North Carolina Press, 1953), pp. 173–174.

Early Critiques of the Elitist Model

In summary, Hunter described Atlanta as dominated by a very small and conservative business elite that acted for its own rather than the public benefit. Public officials were subordinated to this power structure, and power was cumulative. Because of this dominance of the city by a nongovernmental elite, Hunter's thesis is referred to as an elitist or stratificationist theory of community power. When the book appeared, it provoked a furor in the academic community, particularly among political scientists, for, in a sense, Hunter's downgrading of the governmental structures as totally subservient to the economic structures made the traditional political scientists' concern over forms of city government seem very irrelevant. If true power was to be found outside of the governmental structure, what difference did it make if the city government was organized under a strong mayor, a city manager, or a commission? Consequently, the appearance of Hunter's book precipitated a new rush of inquiry into the study of local government.[5]*

The political scientists generally disagreed with Hunter's conclusions, but since no political scientist had conducted empirical studies that could refute Hunter's thesis, their strongest criticisms attacked his research methods.[6] Perhaps the major critics of the stratificationist view were Robert Dahl, Nelson Polsby, Raymond Wolfinger, Herbert Kaufman, and Victor Jones.[7]

Of the several valid methodological objections to Hunter's approach that were raised, two stood out. The major objection dealt with his methods of trying to measure power. In using the panel technique, the critics claimed, Hunter had not measured power at all; he had really measured the *reputation* for power. To measure actual power, a researcher would have to do more than simply ask a panel of judges who they thought was powerful; he would have to examine the very *decisions* through which power was exercised. The second major criticism concerned Hunter's assumptions about power. Since Hunter was a so-

---

* The study or urban politics might roughly be divided into four stages. Prior to the appearance of Hunter's book in 1953, the dominant themes of the study of urban politics were highly normative, nonempirical, and devoted more to public administration than to political processes. Typical studies dealt with the relative administrative advantages of the city manager form of government vis-à-vis commissioner forms and weak mayor forms. From 1953 to the middle 1960s, urban political studies were dominated by questions of community power. A third stage emerged in the early 1960s and continues to dominate the study of urban politics today. This stage has been characterized by highly sophisticated empirical studies of the determinants of public policies in urban areas. A fourth stage seems to be emerging in an increasing number of studies that are branching away from strictly local policy analysis toward comparative national growth policies.

ciologist who perceived many other social relations as structured in a stratified form, it was perhaps inevitable that he would assume that relations of power were also stratified. Consequently, his first question was, "Who runs Regional City?" Such a question obviously assumes that somebody runs Regional City, and leaves to Hunter simply the task of finding out who it was. However, claimed his critics, Hunter should not have assumed anything at all about the structural relationships of power holders. Instead of asking "Who runs Regional City?" he should have asked instead, "Does anybody run Regional City?"[8]

The Pluralist Model of Community Power

The first major empirical work that used the decision-making approach to measure power rather than Hunter's reputational approach was the study of New Haven by Robert Dahl in Who Governs?[9] Dahl deliberately set out to test the hypothesis that New Haven is governed by the kind of economic and social elite that Hunter had discovered in Atlanta. He isolated thirty-four important decisions in the three functional areas of urban renewal, education, and the selection of party nominees for mayor over a period of time that extended from 1941 to 1959. He established rigid criteria for defining the economic and social notables of New Haven. Contrary to Hunter's findings, Dahl discovered that in New Haven there was no significant overlap between the economic and social elites, that these elites had almost no influence on the decisions he studied, and that power in New Haven was noncumulative (that is, power in one functional area did not lead to power in other functional areas).

In the three issue areas that concerned him, Dahl conducted extended interviews with forty-six top decision makers. He found very few instances in which an individual person was involved in more than one major decision, let alone more than one issue area. The major exception to this was the mayor of New Haven, Richard C. Lee. Lee was a supreme political tactician at bargaining with the leaders of all the major functional fiefdoms in New Haven plus some others in federal and state agencies that had programs in New Haven. Through his bargaining skill, he was able to initiate and carry out the kinds of programs he envisioned for the growth and prosperity of the city. Dahl perceived Mayor Lee as occupying the critical position in what Dahl referred to as an "executive centered coalition" of a plurality of interest groups in New Haven. Because this view sees power as noncumulative and dispersed among several power centers, Dahl's theories about community power are called pluralist theories.

Refinements of the Two Models of Community Power

Following the publication of the initial studies by Hunter and Dahl, an extensive body of empirical literature emerged that reported the results of increasingly sophisticated research methods which examined every conceivable subtlety of these two models. Comparative studies were conducted of community power in more than one city,[10] and in some studies, reputational methods of analysis were combined with decision-making methods.[11] A survey of almost three dozen community power studies found that sociologists had an overwhelming tendency to use the reputational method, whereas political scientists were much more likely to use the decision-making method of analysis. Political scientists were also much less likely to come to stratificationist conclusions than were sociologists.[12] Two aspects of this large body of research are most relevant to the politics of the postmachine central city — the role of businessmen and the importance of nondecisions.

The Role of Businessmen

Subsequent research has tended to dispel the picture of top businessmen operating as a cohesive clique and dominating city public affairs, the picture that Hunter presented of the businessmen in Atlanta. However, it is conceivable that Hunter's observations of Atlanta were accurate for that time period, and that businessmen did indeed dominate the city's politics during the early 1950s.* Hunter's finding of businessman dominance is consistent with the overwhelming majority of early anthropological and sociological community studies, which asserted the same kind of businessman dominance over their cities that Hunter found in Atlanta. Particularly dominant were the owners of key businesses in one-industry towns. The classic example was the dominance of Muncie, Indiana, by the Ball family, referred to as Middletown and the X family, respectively, by Robert and Helen Lynd in their monumental works *Middletown* and *Middletown in Transition*.[13] In one famous passage, the Lynds quote a Middletown man's comments on the pervasive influence of the X family over all aspects of life in Middletown.

> If I'm out of work I go to the X plant; if I need money I go to the X bank, and if they don't like me I don't get it; my children go to the X college; when I get

* Edward C. Banfield argues that businessmen may have dominated Atlanta in the early 1950s, but by the middle 1960s they were only one of two important blocs in the city. See his *Big City Politics* (New York: Random House, 1965), pp. 18–36. Also see M. Kent Jennings, *Community Influentials: The Elites of Atlanta* (New York: The Free Press, 1964).

sick I go to the X hospital; I buy a building lot or house in an X subdivision; my wife goes downtown to buy clothes at the X department store; if my dog stays away he is put in the X pound; I buy X milk; I drink X beer, vote for X political parties, and get help from X charities; my boy goes to the X Y.M.C.A. and my girl to their Y.W.C.A.; I listen to the word of God in X-subsidized churches; if I'm a Mason I go to the X Masonic Temple; I read the news from the X morning newspaper; and, if I am rich enough, I travel via the X airport.[14]

Despite the protestations of the pluralists that stratificationists such as Hunter and the Lynds were exaggerating the business dominance of local politics,* many other cities in addition to Muncie and Atlanta seem to have had a particular business elite which dominated local affairs. United States Steel Corporation planned and built Gary, Indiana, and exercised considerable influence over its government. The Mellon family had disporportionate influence in Pittsburgh. One-company mining towns often stayed under the control of their patrons for decades. And even today the Anaconda Corporation exerts extensive power over Butte, Montana.

In more normal situations, however, where central cities are not dominated by one locally owned industry, the patterns of business involvement in city politics are much more complicated. Most sectors of the economy are now dominated by national corporations rather than local companies. Some corporations are not very concerned about local issues. In towns dominated by national corporations, business leadership is often bifurcated between a local elite of retailers who are very much interested in local affairs, and the managers of the national corporations whose careers and interests impel them to pay more attention to the internal affairs of their corporation than to local politics.[15] Unless the corporation has a significant business reason to be interested in the local affairs of a community, the corporation executives often limit their involvement in local affairs to activities designed to do little more than maintain a positive corporate image. However, in cities where local affairs *do* affect the economic interests of national corporations, their managers are much more likely to become involved locally.[16]

Not only is the business sector divided between the owners of local businesses and the managers of national corporations; it is also divided into several functional categories. Few businesspeople exhibit much interest in civic affairs which lie beyond their functional sphere. Thus,

* Polsby in particular argues that the stratificationist conclusions of the elitists not only were inaccurate but also were inconsistent with much of the data that the authors recorded. See his *Community Power and Political Theory* (New Haven, Conn.: Yale University Press, 1963), pp. 14–68.

urban renewal agencies routinely seek out the advice and collaboration of real estate brokers and the financial community, while other kinds of businessmen — such as retail merchants, automobile dealers, or shopping center owners — are often quite uninterested. Utilities seek to promote a city's population, income, and employment, while railroads often display little interest in city politics.[17] Because of this divergence of interests, the business community is not nearly as cohesive in its approach to local politics as Hunter's portrayal suggests. It is highly competitive. And the resources with which businessmen can influence public affairs depend on the functional area involved, the issue, the interests of the businessmen, and the homogeneity with which they can act.

Another study of businessmen in local city politics discovered that they do indeed play a very significant role, although an anticipatory role rather than the manipulative role described by Hunter.[18] Political leaders anticipated the needs and desires of businessmen before taking any actions which might affect them. Businessmen seldom initiated or vetoed public policies; however, their acquiescence in certain projects was often crucial for the project's success due to the considerable prestige that they enjoy. When businessmen fail to support a public project, this fact is noted by the people in the community who respect the key figures of the business sector and take cues from them. If the projects require any private investments, the cooperation of the businessmen is deemed especially essential, for they are the ones who will have to raise the private funds.

The Importance of Nondecisions

If subsequent research on the role of businesspeople in city politics has tended to dispel the stratificationist notion that they manipulate public affairs as one cohesive, well-organized bloc, it has also found flaws in the decision-making approach to analyzing community power. Political scientists Peter Bachrach and Morton S. Baratz have charged that the concentration on actual decisions ignores "the fact that power may be, and often is, exercised by confining the scope of decision-making to relatively 'safe' issues."

> Of course power is exercised when A participates in the making of decisions that affect B. But power is also exercised when A devotes his energies to creating or reinforcing social and political values and institutional practices that limit the scope of the political process to public consideration of only those issues which are comparatively innocuous to A. To the extent that A

succeeds in doing this, B is prevented, for all practical purposes, from bringing to the fore any issues that might in their resolution be seriously detrimental to A's set of preferences.[19]

Such an exercise of power is referred to as coming to "non-decisions." Nondecisions are much more difficult to identify and measure than are actual decisons. The key area where nondecisions predominate is in preserving the dominant values, myths, and established political procedures of a community. Only certain kinds of questions are put on the agendas of the decision-making agencies. Other kinds of questions are never put on those agendas and hence never reach the point where decisions about them can be made. Although the methodology of researching nondecisions is only beginning to be worked out, pertinent examples have been cited in the literature on local politics.[20] In his study of New Haven, for example, Robert Dahl paid very little attention to the black community because it did not figure in the major decisions he analyzed. Even the urban renewal decisions, which deeply touched the lives of large numbers of New Haven blacks, were made without much input from the local black community. When a riot broke out in New Haven in 1967, some persons began to ask why decisions had not been made on questions which the blacks themselves apparently considered important.[21] The answer seems to be that the blacks did not constitute a strong enough interest group to have their demands placed on the decision-making agenda. The needs and demands of people who do not have the backing of strong interest groups and powerful civic leaders are likely to remain in the realm of nondecisions.

THE EMERGENCE OF FUNCTIONAL FIEFDOMS

Although this book cannot resolve the differences between the pluralist and elitist models of community power, it can at least present two important conclusions which tend to be supported by the research findings from both approaches. First, whichever approach one uses to examine community power, the number of important decision makers discovered is relatively small.* Second, the political influence of the important political participants derives from their positions of insti-

---

* In his review of Who Governs?, Floyd Hunter noted that despite Dahl's rejection of the elitist model, the actual number of participants in the large number of decisions studied in New Haven never added up to more than 0.5 percent of the city's population. See his review of Who Governs? in Administrative Science Quarterly 6 (1961–62): 517–518.

tutional leadership. The important participants are business leaders, labor leaders, party leaders, government leaders, or leaders of some other institutions which have interests at stake in the governmental process of their cities.

One of the most striking institutional changes that has occurred in the governmental process over the past two generations has been the growing importance of functionally organized political power. The traditional general-purpose governmental structures (the city council and the mayor) have been bypassed to a considerable degree. Especially created governmental agencies have been given substantial authority to operate specific, key governmental functions. Each agency acquires governmental authority in its determined functional sector. It develops a professional bureaucracy that soon identifies its own set of vested interests. It is nominally run by a board of appointed officials who are often eager to demonstrate their independence from politics and to set new milestones in the functional area. In addition, outside of the government structure there are labor unions, church spokesmen, downtown business interests, racial organizations, highway lobbyists, construction contractors, teachers' organizations, professional organizations, and a host of other special-interest groups that establish ties with the agencies that operate the functions of most concern to them.

Political scientist Theodore Lowi coined the term *functional feudalities* to describe these ties between the professional bureaucracies and their related interest groups.[22] The feudal analogy is very appropriate. Just as the elite nobility in the Middle Ages enjoyed relative autonomy in the conduct of affairs within their fiefdoms, so for the past forty years the elite bureaucratic officals have traditionally enjoyed considerable autonomy from effective outside interference by citizens and political parties (but not from members of Congress) in the conduct of their specialized operations. Just as the feudal nobility was not elected to its position of dominance but was maintained in it through a complex system of secular and ecclesiastical laws, the bureaucratic elite of the contemporary United States city is not elected to office but enjoys tenure through an equally complex system of laws and administrative rules. In Lowi's terms, the various functional feudalities constitute a "bureaucratic city-state."[23] The major inapplicability of the feudal analogy is that the fiefdoms of the Middle Ages were geographic in scope, whereas the fiefdoms of the contemporary bureaucracies are primarily functional in scope.

At the core of the functional fiefdoms are the administrative bureaucracies — what Lowi calls the new political machines. These new machines arose to perform service functions which the old political party machines were supposed to have performed. They also arose to perform new service functions (urban renewal, for example) which require more formalized administrative procedures than the old machines could provide.

In several respects the new machines, the functional fiefdoms, exhibit many of the characteristics of the old party machines. They pursue rational organizational goals, and each bureaucracy develops its own set of loyalties that must be protected by all members. In some instances, an ethnic base has been found to the new bureaucratic machines. This is most pronounced in New York City, where the Irish are disproportionately employed in the police and fire departments, the Italians in the sanitation department, the Jews in the public school system and the welfare department, and the blacks and Puerto Ricans in public hospital and health care services.[24] The public employees' unions associated with the new bureaucratic machines are influential in negotiating employment contracts with the city governments. In recent years they have exercised a strong voice in the legislative arena as well.* The main differences betwen the old party machines and the new bureaucratic machines are that the bureaucracies are functional in scope rather than geographic. They are more numerous and diverse than the old party machines. They rely for their legitimacy on the authority of law rather than on popular acquiescence. And in the conduct of their affairs they are probably less prone to graft than were the old-time party machines.[25]

Lowi's concepts of functional feudalities and the new bureaucractic machines are drawn primarily from his study of patronage in New York City, but the fragmentation of political influence and the emergence of functional fiefdoms can be found in other cities as well. A similar fragmentation was found in Cleveland.[26] In Oakland, California, the critical agencies dealing with housing (Redevelopment Agency and Housing Authority), port development (Board of Port Commissioners), and poverty (Economic Development Council, Inc.) all operated independently of one another and of city hall.[27]

The operation of a functional fiefdom can be illustrated by the decision-making process on urban renewal in many (but not all) cities.† In

---

* In their study of state legislatures, John C. Wahlke and his colleagues found that legislators in all four states they analyzed ranked their respective state education associations among the most influential interest groups of their states. See John C. Wahlke, et al., *The Legislative System* (New York: Wiley, 1962), pp. 318–319.
† In New Haven and Chicago, elected political leaders, principally the mayors, were in firm control of urban renewal and redevelopment plans. In Newark and New York,

Newark, New Jersey, for example, the most important actors involved in deciding the sites and terms for urban renewal were the professional staff of the Newark Housing Authority, the Federal Urban Renewal Administration, the Federal Housing Administration, and the private redevelopers who constructed the new buildings. Elected political leaders seemed to have played no major role. Their chief contribution was to provide a favorable local environment for urban renewal.[28]

Functional fiefdoms are found in public arenas besides urban renewal. The construction of urban freeways as part of the interstate highway system has largely occurred beyond the control of elected local officials. A federal highway trust fund was established in 1956 to earmark the revenue from federal gasoline taxes for the construction and maintenance of the interstate highway system. Many states, in addition, established their own highway trust funds. Both state and federal trust funds operated through state highway departments which, because of the automatic availability of the earmarked trust fund revenues, were able to become very independent of the policy preferences of mayors, governors, and state legislatures. Urban freeway planning was conducted by specialized technicians who showed very little regard for communities that might be broken up or displaced. Although freeways, bus service, and rapid rail service are all interrelated components of urban transit systems, the highway planners were soon reinforced by highway construction lobbies. Together they were able to establish highway construction as the highest transit priority at the federal, state, and local levels. Given the rapid growth of automobile usage in the United States, this was not unreasonable. But the consequences for public transit were disastrous. In Los Angeles a subsidiary of General Motors and Standard Oil of California purchased the city's transit system and were accused of tearing up its rail service.[29] And in city after city, public transit ridership peaked in the late 1940s and declined throughout the 1950s and 1960s.* Only in the 1970s have cities begun to fight successfully to gain some control over the location and condition of freeways through their cities.[30]

Another arena in which functional fiefdoms have developed is that

---

however, the urban renewal agencies operated with very little central control from city hall. See Jewell Bellush and Murray Hausknecht, "Entrepreneurs and Urban Renewal: The New Men of Power," *Journal of the American Institute of Planners* 32, no. 5 (September 1966): 289–297.

* In the early 1970s public transit ridership once again began to increase. In the first half of 1974, public transit ridership nationally gained 6.5 percent over the previous year [Twin Cities Area Metropolitan Transit Commission, *Transit News* 5, no. 2 (Saint Paul: Metropolitan Transit Commission, September 1974)].

of public education. Studies of decision making in the New York school system demonstrate this.[31] Both professional educators and middle-class parents distrusted the interference of politicians in the school system. Complaints about political interference on the part of every city administration since the 1940s inevitably led to increased delegation of responsibility to the Board of Education. The board in turn delegated increasing responsibilities to the professional corps of administrators. Political scientist Marilyn Gittell commented:

> As the school system has grown larger and more complex and policies demand more specialized knowledge, the Board has had to withdraw from an effective policy role. The Bureaucracy and special interest groups have gained power by means of their expertise, while the Board, lacking expertise, has lost power.
>   . . . in the last two decades, education in New York City has become . . . insulated from public controls.[32]

Through the dissipation of the authority of the elected political officials and the increasing strength of the public bureaucracy, New York's public education system has been transformed into a functional fiefdom. Quite conceivably most people would prefer to have public education insulated from partisan politics for fear that public education would be turned into a political football. But separation from partisan politics did not eliminate politics from the administration of public education.[33] The decentralization controversy of 1968–1969 demonstrated that politics is inherent to the administration of public education. The political issues were not over partisan control, but they proved to be just as disruptive as partisan issues. These issues were: decentralization, integration, appointment of school staff, and a contest of wills between the teachers' federations and organized groups of local parents.

The Fiefdoms' Effects on City Government

Two major consequences have resulted from the proliferation of functional fiefdoms in American cities. First, this proliferation has inhibited, but not necessarily prevented, the exercise of unified political leadership in tackling urban problems. Second (as will be seen later in the chapter), functional fiefdoms have compounded the problem of making urban government responsive to the citizenry.

The first consequence is apparent in two respects. First, political authority is so fragmented among competing agencies that the establishment of a clear-cut policy often becomes almost impossible. There often is no consensus among bureaucratic chiefs and public employees' unions on how programs should be run or even whether they should be run. This has particularly been the case in New York City, where, as political scientist David Rogers charges, "the centers of power . . . if indeed there are any, are in its municipal employees' unions and associations . . . [which] . . . veto innovative social development programs almost as a reflex reaction.[34] In this kind of situation, it takes an extremely adept mayor to exercise unified leadership. The second reason that the functional fiefdoms inhibit unified leadership follows upon the development of close ties between city bureaucratic chiefs and their federal counterparts, who have the same professional backgrounds and operate in the same program areas.[35] In setting up new programs, bureaucrats in federal agencies have tended to bypass the general-purpose local governments. Instead, they have put new programs into the hands of their colleagues in specialized lower-level agencies. In Oakland, California, for example, only about one percent of all federal spending in that city was administered through city hall.[36] For better or for worse, this insulates the programs from centralized policy direction by city hall.

The overall impact on city governance of this proliferation of functional fiefdoms has been to create a highly complex mechanism of city government that operates efficiently enough but is not very susceptible to unified policy guidance by the city council or the mayor. Nor have the major decisons normally been made by the city council and the mayor.

Saint Paul, Minnesota, presents an extreme but pertinent example of the impact of fragmentation through a proliferation of functional fiefdoms. The mayor-council city government structure is only one of many governments which make political decisions inside the geographic boundaries of the city. Some of the most important decisons within the city are made by other governments. Ramsey County makes the decisions on welfare and the city's public hospital. The Board of Education makes the major decisions on education. The Port Authority makes the decisions on commercial development along the Mississippi River. The Civic Center Authority constructed and operates a $19 million sports and exhibition arena. The complex of highway planners decided on the location of the freeways which slice through the city from three directions. The Metropolitan Transit Commission operates the buses in Saint Paul. A Metropolitan Airports Commission operates all the airports in and around the city. A Metropolitan Waste Control Commission operates all of the city's sewerage services. A Metropolitan Health

Board has a veto power over decisions concerning the construction of public or private medical facilities in the city. The Capitol Center Commission planned and executed reconstruction around the site of the state capitol in Saint Paul. A Housing and Redevelopment Authority directs most urban renewal efforts in the city. And, finally, a Metropolitan Council has a veto power over Saint Paul city development plans if it determines that those plans have metropolitan significance.*

Within the past fifteen years the downtown of Saint Paul, like that of most large cities, has virtually been rebuilt. New hotels and major department stores were attracted into the central business district. Also constructed were a civic center, seven public ice arenas around the city, and a new, modern public hospital. The entire area surrounding the state capitol was redesigned and beautified. Several public housing projects were initiated. And hundreds of homes were torn down to make way for the new freeways. But in none of these major projects did the traditional city government of Saint Paul act as the initiator.[37] The city council and the mayor do have representation on and input into many of these other governments in the city. But *as the government*, the mayor and city council have largely been passive bystanders who react to initiatives taken by others by occasionally, when called upon, giving zoning approval or bonding authority for the major projects initiated by and carried out by other agencies, governments, or organizations.

Saint Paul may offer an extreme example of a city government that is weak because of the fragmentation of its government authority. But the very extreme nature of the example illustrates the devices through which city governments generally have been kept weak. City government in the United States has traditionally been weak. Although it is the most visible of urban governing institutions and the one institution which people hold responsible for solving urban ills, its authority to cope with those ills is sharply circumscribed not only by the existence of other powerful, competing institutions but also by law and by constitutions. A long-standing principle of municipal law holds that municipal governments can exercise only those powers specifically granted them by state legislatures or those powers indispensable for carrying out the responsibilities that the legislatures have assigned them. This

---

* Although formal authority in these functional areas lies primarily in the agencies indicated, the city government does have input into the decisions of these agencies. There are many informal contacts between council members and agency officials. In some instances, council members appoint officials to the governing board. And in some instances, the city enters into formal agreements on the provision of agency services.

principle is called *Dillon's rule*, after Judge John F. Dillon, who formulated it. Dillon stated that "Any fair, reasonable, substantial doubt concerning the existence of power is resolved by the courts against the [city government], and the power is denied."[38]

For the past several decades there has been a movement away from applying Dillon's rule and toward increasing the powers of city governments. This so-called *home rule movement* seeks to secure for a city a home rule charter, which would give the city the authority to redraw its own charter and reorganize its structure of government without requiring the permission of the state legislature. The limits of home rule charters can be seen again in the example of Saint Paul. In 1972, Saint Paul voters approved a new charter which abolished the outmoded commission form of government and substituted in its place a strong mayor-council form. But the new charter neither changed nor legally could have changed the basic relationships between the city government and most of the competing governments and agencies cited above. The new charter may well have made the new city government more efficient, but it did not increase in the slightest the total governmental authority allocated to the city government itself. Whether Saint Paul's new city government can become an organ for decisive political leadership over the city's diverse functional fiefdoms will depend much more on the quality of the leadership personnel than it will on the charter revisions.*

ANTIDOTES FOR FUNCTIONAL FIEFDOMS: STRONG PARTIES AND STRONG MAYORS

As ways to develop political leadership to overcome the fragmentation of governmental authority into functional fiefdoms, two courses of action are normally advanced. The first is to revive the political party organization as a potent force in city politics. One of the most prominent advocates of this course has been political scientist Theodore

---

* To date, the Saint Paul experience has not been very encouraging. A liberal mayor, Larry Cohen, was elected in 1972 with substantial backing from environmentalists, professionals, and liberal elements within the Democratic Farmer Labor party. However, Cohen has had limited success in overcoming the claims of existing interest groups that they should have representation on the various boards and commissions which constitute the key contact point in the functional fiefdoms between the public bureaucracies and their related interest groups. Cohen has had more success in centralizing control over the city bureaucracy and in getting the city government to assert itself in questions of urban renewal and development.

Lowi. His prescription is aimed primarily at New York, but presumably he means for it to apply elsewhere as well.

> The City has little to fear and very much to gain from restoration of the machine. If parties do not reclaim primacy in policy-making and implementation, the chief executive will continue to be faced with the *ad hoc* adjustment of claims. Particularism will continue to spread, and the 'ordeal of the executive' will remain unresolved. Executive discretion — and therefore elective responsibility — will continue in its secondary role to a kind of functional representation.[39]

Many proponents of revitalizing the political party's role in city politics point to the model of Chicago. Despite some highly publicized deficiencies of its system of government, Chicago's system has enabled an extreme amount of formal fragmentation of government to be overcome through the informal centralizing tendencies of the political machine.* Because of the machine's influence, Chicago received a disproportionate share of antipoverty program funds and received them quicker than most cities, such as New York and Los Angeles.[40] Organized labor does not dominate the city's politics as happens in some other cities.[41] Interest groups generally are forced to work through the party.[42] And the mediating influence of the machine has lessened the ability of potential demagogues to take office by inflaming the electorate.[43]

The second model for political leadership is the strong mayor. In the view of strong mayor advocates, the fragmentation of government authority is not so much a cause of mayoral weakness as it is an opportunity for skillful mayors to pyramid their power by bargaining with the various power centers, particularly with the technical specialists in the bureaucracies and with the downtown business leaders.[44] In this view, leadership is seen more as a personal quality of the individual mayor than as a consequence of governmental structure arrangements.

How would such a strong mayor leader be characterized? Ideally, such a mayor would have four characteristics.[45] He would have *clearly defined goals* that would come to grips realistically with the social and economic problems of his city. He would exercise *effective influence*

---

* The major deficiencies of the Chicago system are that it is unresponsive to the demands of poorly organized groups and the minority communities and that it is conducive to extensive graft. On the question of unresponsiveness, see Edward C. Banfield and James Q. Wilson, *City Politics* (New York: Random House, 1965), pp. 124–125. For charges of graft and a generally polemic indictment of the Daley machine, see Mike Royko, *Boss: Richard J. Daley of Chicago* (New York: E. P. Dutton, 1971). For a discussion of the centralizing influence of the machine, see Banfield and Wilson, *City Politics*, pp. 101–111.

on the activities of politically relevant groups in his city. These groups would extend from the public bureaucracies and their functional fiefdoms to private businesspeople looking for places to locate their enterprises. He would make effective use of political party nominations, election of candidates, and public relations to *develop a base of support for his policies.* Finally he would make effective use of available financial, jurisdictional, staff, public relations, and other re-sources at his disposal.

In practice, the model of this ideal mayor would probably be Richard C. Lee of New Haven (1953–1969).[46] Lee's success illustrates that, in practice, divorcing strong mayoral leadership from strong political parties may be impossible. This can be seen most notably in his long, sixteen-year tenure in office. Mayors with only a few years in office are not able to see their projects carried to completion. A mayor with long tenure, on the other hand, has sufficient time to make sure that his projects are carried out. Bureaucratic officials who might oppose mayoral projects have to be more attentive to the demands of a long-term mayor than a short-term mayor for the simple reason that they will not be able to anticipate losing him as an antagonist at the next election. Without a strong party to ensure his renomination and to provide effective campaign resources, most mayors are likely to find long tenure a very elusive goal.[47]

Lee's success as mayor was not solely dependent on his party backing, however. His own leadership capacities were very important. When he became mayor in 1953 he moved swiftly and dramatically to gain control over the city bureaucracies,[48] and he quickly established urban renewal as his top administrative priority. As a consequence, urban renewal in New Haven was not insulated from the mayor's input and direction as it was in some other cities such as Newark and New York.[49] He was also very successful at taking the initiative in getting businesspeople, university people, union leaders, and other leaders of power centers in New Haven to support and work for the success of goals that he defined.[50]

In summary, the possibilities for strong mayoral leadership depend partly on the personal qualities of individual mayors and partly on the political environment in which mayors operate. Political scientist Jeffrey Pressman has identified seven elements of the political environment which enhance the possibilities of getting strong mayoral leadership. These are:

1. Sufficient financial resources with which a mayor can launch innovative social programs.

2. City jurisdiction in the vital program areas of education, housing, redevelopment, and job training.
3. Mayoral jurisdiction within the city government in those policy areas.
4. A salary sufficiently high that the mayor can work full time at his office.
5. Sufficient staff support for the mayor, such as policy planning, speech writing, intergovernmental relations, political work.
6. Ready vehicles for publicity, such as friendly newspapers and television stations.
7. Politically oriented groups, including a political party, which the mayor can mobilize to help him achieve particular goals.[51]

Not all of these seven elements can be legislated. In particular, if the attitudes of principal media are opposed to social welfare programs and if the politically oriented groups and the parties are threatened enough by such programs to oppose them adamantly, then the possibilities of achieving strong mayoral leadership behind social programs are very limited. The first five elements *can* be accomplished through state and city legislation, however. A good test of a city's willingness to cope with social problems might well be the extent to which the mayor's office is provided with these resources.

THE RESPONSIVENESS OF CITY GOVERNMENT TO UNORGANIZED CITIZENS

In addition to coping with the demands and interests of powerful functional fiefdoms, city governments must also cope with the demands and needs of unorganized citizens, of smaller and less powerful groups, and of newly emerging power centers. When the urban political process is viewed from the perspective of these actors, it is often portrayed as something beyond the influence or even the understanding of ordinary citizens. Michael Parenti studied three unsuccessful attempts of the Newark Community Union Project (NCUP) to obtain major gains for the residents of a poor, black neighborhood in Newark during the middle 1960s.[52] NCUP was organized by local black militants and white members of Students for a Democratic Society. Over a three-year period, NCUP attempted to get the city government to enforce the city's building codes and to install a traffic light at a particularly dangerous intersection. When these attempts failed, NCUP tried to elect new black candidates to the city council and the state legislature. But this attempt failed, too. Throughout these efforts, the tactics employed by NCUP ranged from traditional voter registration and electioneering to protest activity and agitation that involved rent strikes, sit-ins, and blocking traffic at the intersection where the traffic light was desired. Although NCUP held together and persisted in its efforts for three years, none of its three major projects were successful.

Drawing on his observations of these unsuccessful experiences, Parenti describes the urban political process as seen from below. First, "there exists the world of the rulers and the world of the ruled." Second, one of the crucial elements of power is the capacity to set the agenda of the struggle, to determine that certain questions will not come up for consideration by government agencies. These are the so-called nondecisions. "Much of the behavior of Newark's officials can be seen as a kind of 'politics of prevention' . . . designed to limit the area of issue conflict." Third, Parenti rejects the pluralist concept of "latent power" which, in this case, would imply that the ghetto dwellers possess a latent or "potential power that would prevail should they choose to use it."[53] On the contrary, the resources of the poor are infinitesimal in comparison to the resources of the interest groups. In contrast to Robert Dahl, who states that power is noncumulative, Parenti maintains that the *lack of power is cumulative.* Ghetto dwellers exist in a state of *cumulative inequalities* in which their unequal status in education, income, jobs, and discrimination all cumulate to reduce their potential collective political efficacy. Because of their cumulative inequalities, they are unable to translate their needs into effective demands. Since politicians respond to *demands* more readily than they respond to citizens' needs, the cumulative inequalities of the poor increase their difficulty in getting the government to meet their needs. Furthermore, politicians who do respond to ghetto dwellers' demands on certain kinds of issues such as building code enforcement "might incur the wrath of high political leaders or powerful economic interests." For this reason, "party regulars have little inclination to entertain the kinds of issues" pushed by organizations such as NCUP, and "they also try to discredit and defeat those reformers who seek confrontations on such issues."[54] As was seen above, the Daley machine in Chicago encountered the same problem in meeting the demands of militant blacks on social issues.

Not all studies of attempts to mobilize the poor have been as totally pessimistic as Parenti's study, but a remarkable consensus exists on the extreme difficulties of organizing the poor to articulate their demands in ways that will oblige government agencies to respond positively. One of the most common political tactics of the poor has been protest activity. But a study of rent strikes and protest activity in New York found that protest as a tactic has severe limitations, particularly over the medium and long range.[55] Protest groups are inherently unstable and difficult to keep together. In order to get the attention of the mass media, protest leaders tend to overstate their strength and their accomplishments, only to lose credibility with reporters when they are unable to produce on the statements and claims they make. In order for protests to be successful, the leaders have to capture the sympathy and oftentimes the financial support of third parties, particularly white liberals. This often involves moderating their position or making compromises which lose them support from other members of the protesting groups. In the Harlem rent strikes of 1963 and 1964, government officials and slum landlords were able to use delaying tactics and wait for the indignation aroused by reportage of slum housing conditions to wane. When public interest declined, the rent strike coalition collapsed.[56]

The limitations of protest as a political tactic probably exist in other cities as well as New York. The only comparative research on protest activity studied protests in forty-three cities over a six-month period in 1968. During that period, 120 protest actions were taken, but only in 18 cases were concessions made by the government to meet the demands of the protesters.[57]

The limitations of protest activity also are a reflection of the generally low state of power resources available to the unorganized, the poor, and the racial minorities. In Toledo, Ohio, young black leaders criticized the city's urban renewal programs for not consulting black leadership: "Even in urban conservation programs in largely Negro areas, there is no consultation."[58] In Chicago, a study that identified blacks who hold key decision-making positions in the city government and in private business found that despite a strong black component in the Democratic party, blacks were systematically underrepresented in every area of public and economic life. The key positions they did hold were more often than not especially created to serve a predominantly black clientele. The study concluded: "it is clear that, at this time, Negroes in the Chicago area lack the power to make changes in the areas of housing, jobs, and education."[59] In Oakland, blacks were not found to exercise much influence on the city government except for its antipoverty program, despite the fact that the city's population was a third black.[60] In Brooklyn, an experiment in decentralized control of public schools was ended after a local governing board of blacks and Puerto Ricans attempted to transfer teachers out of the ghetto schools and usurp authority held by the New York City Board of Education.[61]

Although these studies stress the powerlessness of the poor and the racial minorities, their powerlessness is not total and the power relations are not static. They do change. Changes have been most obvious in the arena of electoral politics. Astute use of political resources can maximize the voting potential of blacks and overcome reluctance of whites to vote for blacks.[62] In Atlanta, the position of blacks improved to the point where they were able to elect both a congressman and a mayor. In Baltimore, after several years of struggle, black leaders succeeded in breaking down the pattern of nondecisions which had kept race relations and poverty issues off the public agenda. Even with this success, however, sharp divisions within the community of black leaders fractionalized the voting potential of Baltimore's large Negro population and cost them the opportunity in 1970 to elect the city's first black mayor.[63] Despite the marked success of Baltimore's black leaders in recent years, two perceptive observers of the city commented that "the blacks' newly won access will not immediately produce sweeping changes in the size or character of anti-poverty and race relations policy."[64] Even in the many cities where black mayors have been elected in recent years, they have experienced very limited success in using their offices to improve the economic situations of their black and minority constituents.

The preceding arguments could be called the "powerlessness of the poor" point of view. This perspective offers two conclusions. First, the model of ethnic succession has not yet worked for the new racial and urban minorities in the cities. Second, the strong political influence of the functional fiefdoms casts serious doubt on the notion that contemporary urban government is responsive to individual citizens, regardless of race, whose demands are not consistent with the interests of large and powerful interest groups.

The conclusion of the inapplicability of the ethnic succession model seems warranted by the inability of the new urban minorites to achieve prominence in the traditional, ethnically based institutions described in Chapter 4. This inability can be attributed partly to the lack of unity and lack of a secure middle class within the minority communities[65] and partly to widespread discriminatory attitudes and practices among the white population. And a great part of it must be attributed to outright resistance on the part of many existing institutions to responding favorably to the demands of the minorities and the poor. This factor probably more than any other led to the popularity of the "internal colonialism" argument among many blacks. According to this argument, the black ghettoes are being exploited by outside forces and institutions just as overseas colonies were exploited by outside European powers during the nineteenth and early twentieth centuries.[66] Whatever the reason, the traditional institutions of influence and social mobility in the cities have not to date been very responsive to the racial and Spanish-speaking minorities.

The conclusion that the city does not respond to individual residents regardless of race is not supported directly by the above discussion. Most students of governmental responsiveness have focused on the racial minorities. But commentaries on certain white ethnic groups, poor white communities, and many big-city residents interviewed sporadically indicated that many whites feel they are nearly as powerless in city politics as are the blacks and the new urban minorities.[67] This white powerlessness may not be limited to just the poor; there may well be a middle-class powerlessness as well. Even within the functional fiefdoms, a person has influence only to the extent that he or she promotes the interests of his or her institution. In this sense the urban institutions have taken on a life of their own. One of the consequences of the emergence of functional fiefdoms has been to make individual people *politically* important only in the context of institutions they represent or other groups of people they speak for.

It must be stressed that the "powerlessness of the poor" viewpoint is not the only perspective on the question of how responsive urban government is to the needs of the poor and the minorities. In one of the most widely read urban commentaries in recent years, Edward C. Banfield has argued that the conditions of the urban poor are in fact getting better and that the so-called urban crisis is in great measure a consequence of unrealistic expectations about the capacities of governments to deal with social problems.[68] Banfield seems firmly convinced that the next thirty years will bring continued economic progress which will do much more to eliminate poverty than the massive urban programs instituted in the 1960s.

ANTIDOTES FOR NONRESPONSIVENESS I: COMMUNITY ACTION AND MODEL CITIES PROGRAMS

Despite Banfield's contention that the conditions of the poor were getting better, by the middle 1960s a substantial number of scholars and political activists believed that the conditions of the poor were not good enough. As a consequence, a massive number of ideas were put into law for dealing with the twin problems of economic deprivation and political powerlessness. Two ideas in particular aimed at dealing with the question of political powerlessness. The first sought to use the community action and model cities programs to create in effect a new functional fiefdom which would give the poor their own power base in urban politics. The second idea was to decentralize city government itself to the neighborhood level where individual citizens could have some impact on its operations. Both ideas held considerable potential for diminishing the power of existing functional fiefdoms over urban governments.

The community action programs (CAPs) were created by the Economic Opportunity Act of 1964 to attain three basic objectives in poor communities: (1) to provide and improve public services for the poor, (2) to mobilize both public and private resources to cope with the problems of poverty, and (3) to engage the maximum feasible participation of the poor in carrying out the antipoverty programs. Community action agencies (CAAs) were created to implement the community action programs. The CAAs were originally made independent of the city government, and neighborhood representatives dominated their boards of directors. Because of complaints of recurring clashes between community action agencies and city governments, Congress in 1967 passed the Green amendment to the Economic Opportunity Act (after Congresswoman Green), which limited the authority of the CAAs and guaranteed the city governments one-third representation on the CAA boards of directors. One consequence of this was that after 1967 the CAAs became much more oriented toward improving the delivery of services than toward mobilizing citizen participation. Finally, under the Nixon administration, the parent funding agency for the CAAs, the Office of Economic Opportunity (OEO), was eliminated and most of the antipoverty programs were turned over to other federal agencies. Because of this withdrawal of federal support, after 1974 individual CAAs became highly dependent on local city halls for their survival.

Despite the demise of the community action program as a national effort and its failure to eradicate poverty, it did have some important positive effects on poor communities. Under OEO sponsorship over a thousand CAAs were created which in turn stimulated the creation of thousands of citizens' organizations that might not have been created in the absence of a community action program. The programs also provided leadership training for thousands of people, especially in the black communities. Also, an entirely new and different type of neighborhood institution was created — the community corporation with legal powers to raise funds and engage in neighborhood community development.[69] The CAAs also brought to poor neighborhoods a new

series of federal services which had previously not existed there —
Head Start, neighborhood legal services, day care centers, job training,
and others. Finally, the community organizations which were created
as a result of the community action programs pressured existing public
and private social service agencies into providing improved services
for the poor.[70] This was particularly significant in the sector of public
welfare services where CAAs and welfare rights organizations taught
potential welfare recipients how to organize to obtain the welfare
benefits to which they were legally entitled but which the welfare
departments did not publicize widely. These activities by CAAs and
welfare rights organizations are undoubtedly one of the factors which
have caused the rapid increase in public welfare expenditures during
the late 1960s and early 1970s.

The second major federal effort to improve the status of the urban
poor and the racial minorities was the model cities program created in
1966.* It differed from the community action program in four respects.
First, in contrast to the community action program, which operated at a
county-wide or city-wide level in 1000 different communities, the
model cities program operated only in clearly delineated slum areas in
about 150 cities. Second, whereas the community action programs
quickly focused on improving the delivery of services to the poor, the
main objective of the model cities program was to coordinate all federal
urban programs and to concentrate them in a comprehensive effort to
rejuvenate the selected model city neighborhoods. Third, while the
community action programs aimed at immediate action and immediate
impact, the model cities program involved long-range planning for
comprehensive community development. Fourth, while the community action agencies received funding directly from the OEO and quite
often disagreed with city halls on how the CAA programs should be
carried out, the funding of model cities programs was intimately tied
in with the city halls in the hope of giving the city governments a stake
in the success of the programs. The special status of the model cities
programs as coordinators of federal urban activities for comprehensive
community development was ended with the Housing Act of 1974.
This act consolidated the funds of the model cities programs, along
with those of nine other federal programs, into a large, block grant of
community development funds. Cities are now able to use these federal
funds for a wide variety of purposes as they see fit. Many specific model

* The model cities program should also be viewed as an example of and evaluated in
relation to the capacities of the federal government to create and implement urban programs. See Chapter 11, pp. 304–307.

cities projects continue to operate, but the comprehensive coordinating, planning, and developmental functions originally envisioned in the model cities effort have been effectively terminated.

ANTIDOTES FOR NONRESPONSIVENESS II: COMMUNITY CONTROL

A second prescription for making urban governments more responsive to the citizenry has been that of sharing control over governmental services between centralized bureaucracies and community residents who receive the services. A wide variety of control-sharing schemes have been advanced under a bewildering array of labels as diverse as community control, consumer representation, decentralization, mini city halls, neighborhood councils, and neighborhood corporations. Each of them is based upon different assumptions about the nature of urban government, and each would have different results in dealing with the problem of bureaucratic unresponsiveness. One way of viewing these plans in order to distinguish the important differences between them is to categorize them along two dimensions of decentralization: whether they decentralize *political control* to the community level, or whether they simply decentralize the *delivery of services*.[71]

Figure 5-1 illustrates four different types of control-sharing models which can be differentiated — the *status quo* model, the *representational* model, the *bureaucratic* model, and the *neighborhood government* model. Where both the delivery of services and political control are highly centralized, there obviously is no decentralization. That is the *status quo* model. In public education, for example, the status quo model has administrative decisions being made centrally (in the superintendent's office). It also centralizes the groups and forces which influence major school policies such as desegregation, building site locations, employment of personnel, grading systems, and alternative educational programs. Such forces would most likely be the teachers' association, employees' unions, the school board, the professional staff, and city hall. In the *representational model* administrative decisions and their implementation continue to be centralized, but parents and residents of different neighborhoods of the city are guaranteed representation on the body making these decisions. In the *bureaucratic model* the political forces remain highly centralized, but many routine administrative decisions are delegated to individual schools or clusters of schools. Decisions on employment of teachers or desegregation, for example, remain at the city-wide level, while the

FIGURE 5-1

CATEGORIES OF CITIZEN CONTROL AND DECENTRALIZATION

Decentralization of Political Control →

Decentralization of Delivery of Services ↓

Status Quo Model *Examples:* Autonomous bureaucracies Functional fiefdoms Little city halls	**Representational Model** *Examples:* Client representation Little city halls
Bureaucratic Model *Examples:* Decentralized schools in New York since 1969; Detroit since 1970 Little city halls	**Neighborhood Government Model** *Examples:* Neighborhood corporations Community action agencies Model city councils Demonstration school districts in New York 1967–69

Adapted from *Decentralizing the City: A Study of Boston's Little City Halls* by Eric Nordlinger by permission of the M.I.T. Press, Cambridge, Mass.

principals and staff of individual schools can be given great flexibility in adapting school programs and policies to peculiar conditions of peculiar neighborhoods. Finally, complete decentralization along both the political control dimension and the delivery of services dimension constitutes the *neighborhood government* model. There are no examples of complete decentralization in the United States. But neighborhood corporations and New York's 1967–1969 experiment with demonstration school districts come closer to it than most other models.

There have been many instances of practical attempts to achieve decentralization of political control and/or delivery of services. Four of these have evoked the most interest among observers: (1) client representation, (2) decentralization of education, (3) decentralization of city hall and public services, and (4) modified forms of neighborhood government.

Client Representation

Client representation, which corresponds most closely to the representation model, does not necessarily imply any geographic decentralization.[72] Rather it is a plan to give citizens direct representation on the boards which govern public agencies. Low-income tenants might be given a position on a public housing authority or welfare recipients given a position on public welfare boards. The most volatile form of client representation has been the creation of citizen review boards to investigate complaints of police brutality. These devices attempted to allow the poor some voice in the functional fiefdoms. In contrast to decentralizing political control, which poses a threat to the integrity of the functional fiefdom, client representation simply means expanding the number of interests in the city that have input into the fiefdom. Consequently, there is less opposition to client representation as a means of sharing control over urban government than there is to geographic decentralization of political control. Another advantage of client representation is that it can also be applied to private corporations, such as public utilities, whose services and prices directly affect the lives of urban residents. Consumer representatives on the board of an electric utility will presumably be a voice for minimizing rate increases.

Decentralization of Public Education

In central cities with large numbers of poor children or racial minorities, the public school systems have been resoundingly criticized as being unresponsive to children's needs.[73] Because of residential segregation, big-city schools have traditionally been racially segregated in fact, even though there may have been no laws demanding their segregation. Schools for the racial minorities were also commonly the oldest, shabbiest, and poorest supplied with facilities. Teachers with enough seniority to have a choice tried to avoid teaching in the minority neighborhoods.

Black leaders attacked these problems for many years by seeking more school integration, but in few cities were they successful. Consequently, when the concept of decentralizing control over schools was advanced in the middle 1960s, it quickly won acceptance from those blacks who despaired of ever getting truly integrated schools and at the same time deplored the inferior quality of the black schools. Local control of schools was also consistent with the then growing philosophy of black separatism. Two of the most noteworthy experiments in decentralized control of schools occurred in New York City and Detroit.

In three of the most impoverished neighborhoods in New York City, the Board of Education established locally controlled demonstration districts to experiment with locally controlled schools. A local governing board was created in each district, and the members were chosen by popular election by residents of the district. The elected governing board members were remarkably representative of the economic and racial composition of their districts. Sixty-one percent were nonwhite (as compared to 56 percent of the pupil population), and only 16 percent were employed in middle-class professional, technical, or managerial positions.[74]

In the Ocean Hill–Brownsville district an explosive controversy soon developed between the local governing board, which acted in accord with the neighborhood government model of decentralization, and the school bureaucracy and teachers' federation, which acted in accord with the delivery of service model of decentralization. Apparently believing that they had the full governing authority of a board of education, the members of the local governing board hired an administrator, principals, and paraprofessional teachers' aides from the local black and Puerto Rican communities and from outside the traditional teachers' and administrators' associations within the city's school system. When the governing board attempted to transfer some teachers out of the district and replace them with others, it ran into the solid opposition of the United Federation of Teachers (UFT). Since some of the teachers to be transferred out were Jewish, the local blacks were accused of anti-Semitism, even though, it must be noted, most of the retained teachers were also Jewish. A long, drawn-out struggle ensued in which the schools were closed by a teachers' strike and the police had to be brought in to protect the peace. There was little popular support for the demonstration district's side of the strike outside the black community, and even among blacks barely a majority supported it.*

The strike proved so unpopular and divisive that the demonstration district experiment was brought to an end by the New York legislature in 1969. In its stead, thirty-one local school boards were created whose authority was clearly established along the lines of the delivery of services model rather than the neighborhood government model of decentralization. The key indication of this was the new local school boards' lack of effective authority over budget, personnel, and pro-

---

* Louis Harris conducted a survey of New Yorkers in April and May, 1969. On a question of whether the teachers' federation was more right or the demonstration district governing board was more right, the percentage favoring the teachers versus the percentage favoring the governing board was 63 to 8 among Jews, 48 to 9 among Catholics, 35 to 20 among white Protestants, 21 to 12 among Puerto Ricans, and 14 to 50 among blacks [Louis Harris and Bert E. Swanson, *Black-Jewish Relations in New York City* (New York: Praeger, 1970), p. 132].

grams.[75] Members of these new local school boards were popularly elected, but the results of the elections held so far indicate that they are not representative of the poor and the racial minorities. Whereas the demonstration district governing boards had had a high percentage of nonwhite and non-middle-class members, the new local school boards were only 17 percent nonwhite (compared to a pupil population that was 34.4 percent nonwhite); and almost two-thirds of the board members were employed in middle-class professional, technical, or managerial positions.[76]

In Detroit, the attempt to decentralize public schools also developed into an explosive controversy.[77] In 1969 the Michigan legislature passed a bill which created new local school boards that would be subordinate to the city-wide board. The city-wide board was dominated by liberals who were determined that decentralization would not be allowed to impede their plans for school integration. Consequently, they drafted a plan for local school boards in which about 9000 pupils would be bussed across local boundary lines in order to accomplish integration.

The public reaction was swift. Behind the leadership of a conservative board member who opposed the integration, protests and demonstrations erupted. Under local pressure, the state legislature quickly revoked its 1969 law and passed a new law that outlawed such bussing of students and mandated the decentralized school boards to be organized on the basis of neighborhood schools. That obviously meant that the schools would not be integrated. In addition, the new law gave each of the eight local school boards one representative on the previously at-large, city-wide Board of Education. A recall petition was filed in June 1970 and, in a special recall election, all of the liberal members of the city-wide Board of Education were removed from office and replaced with conservatives. The former conservative member who had led the anti-integration demonstrations was elected board president. The new board started its tenure of office by cutting $12 million from the budget in the first six weeks, cutting programs, and dismissing almost 200 noncontract teachers. In addition, the local neighborhood boards were given extensive sway to establish policies as they saw fit. In a black district, a principal was removed. In another district, the local board was permitted to refuse to administer a state-wide achievement test to students. And a district in a white region was allowed not to implement voluntary segregation guidelines which had been established.

The decentralized schools in Detroit seem to come much closer to the neighborhood government model of decentralization than do those in New York. Their net impact, however, has been to impede integration in Detroit, inflame latent racial tensions, and cut back educational programs. They have also failed to increase the representation of the poor or the minorities in school policy making. As in New York, almost two-thirds of Detroit's local school board members came from middle-class professional, technical, and managerial positions. And only 30 percent are nonwhite (compared to 63 percent of the pupil population).[78] Although local control was originally advanced by blacks in New York, it has not worked out to the advantage of blacks in either New York or Detroit.

In addition to Detroit and New York, proposals have been put forward for administrative decentralization in several other large city school systems. Decentralization of education will probably continue in coming years. But it is most likely to be patterned after the delivery of service model than after the neighborhood government model. The explosive controversies in Detroit and New York are likely to deter all but the most stout-hearted from delegating full policy-making authority to the local level.

Little City Halls

A third approach to decentralization has been to establish neighborhood city halls throughout the city. A neighborhood city hall is simply a mayoral branch office that seeks to expedite the provision of city services in neighborhoods and to improve ties with neighborhood residents. Little city halls were strongly recommended by the National Advisory Commission on Civil Disorders[79] as one means of lessening citizen alienation from the government. In terms of the three models of decentralization, little city halls contain elements of the status quo, the representational, and the bureaucratic models. They do not contain elements of the neighborhood government model, because they are basically a branch of the mayor's office.

Some form of decentralized delivery of services has been found in at least seventy-five cities, and at least twenty-five of them are significant enough to be called little city halls.[80] The most advanced program is the one in Boston, where fourteen little city halls were established and given a total staff of 155 persons to carry out their operations.[81] The neighborhood offices are coordinated through an office of program services located in the mayor's office. They engage in a variety of activities which include directly providing and managing services to citizens, performing as an ombudsman and complaint referral center, and acting as a catalyst in organizing community action activities. In their ombudsman role, they have handled about ten complaints for every one complaint dealt with by members of city council. At one point, they came under criticism from the council, for some council members felt the little city halls constituted a source of patronage for the mayor and a recruiting mechanism for campaign workers. Since most of the little city halls' staff worked on the mayor's subsequent gubernatorial campaign, the allegations had some truth. Nonetheless, through their various activities, the little city halls in Boston have made an impact on the existing city departments and their relations to neighborhood residents.

Little city halls in other cities apparently have been less successful than the ones in Boston. Under Mayor John Lindsay, New York established five little city halls and forty-five urban task forces throughout the city in 1967. However, most of them were not very visible and did not have much impact on their neighborhoods. They mostly followed the bureaucratic model of administrative decentralization and did not provide for input from neighborhood residents.[82]

Neighborhood Government

The most advanced form of decentralization is that of establishing neighborhood governments to make policy decisions at the neighborhood level. The major advocate of neighborhood government is Milton Kotler, who looks upon the neighborhood as the natural geographic unit on which urban government should be organized if the lower classes are to gain effective control over their immediate surroundings.[83] The ideal form of neighborhood government would subdivide the city into many neighborhood development corporations that would be chartered by the city or the state to perform governmental functions within their geographic boundaries. No city has yet established neighborhood government on the model which Kotler proposes. But several prototypes contain elements of neighborhood control. In Columbus, Ohio, the East Central Citizens Organization operates several services, including credit unions, legal and medical services, business establishments, and day care centers. The Bedford Stuyvesant Corporation in Brooklyn operates several urban and neighborhood development programs. Another prototype of neighborhood government can be found in the model cities programs and the community action programs previously discussed.

Another approach to neighborhood government has been tried by Indianapolis. In 1972 the Indiana Legislature authorized the establishment of community councils in neighborhoods throughout the consolidated Marion County–Indianapolis region. Each council was to serve a neighborhood of about 6000 to 7000 people. Although the councils would be considered "the political subdivisions of the city," they were restricted in power to receiving notice of and commenting on zoning or planning actions that might affect them.[84]

Is Community Control Desirable?

There is considerable disagreement over the desirability of community control over city government,[85] but much of the disagreement is caused by the tendency not to distinguish between the various models or types of community control. If one considers just the neighborhood government model — the most advanced proposal for control sharing — the major argument in its favor is that it would reestablish a sense of community between the ordinary citizen and his neighborhood. By transferring substantial decision-making authority from the city level to the neighborhood level, community control would also serve to break down the functional fiefdoms which dominate city government. It would also enable the residents of poor neighborhoods to have an indigenous power base. The major arguments against community control center around an interrelated complex of fears that it would allow neighborhoods to fall under the control of a minority of militants, it would be expensive, and it would Balkanize city government so much that no control could be exercised over area-wide functions.

Whether the concept of neighborhood control enjoys extensive popular support is also debatable. A survey conducted in New York City in the spring of 1969 found that outside of the black population, there was very little support for decentralized control of schools.* In the hundreds of elections for model cities planning council boards and community action agency neighborhood advisory boards that have been held in the past ten years, the voting turnouts have been pitifully small. In the elections to the local school boards in New York in 1970, the voter turnout was less than 15 percent.[86]

A last question about control sharing concerns whether it will really improve the living conditions of urban residents. This is the key to its

---

* Attitudes favoring versus attitudes opposing school decentralization were 27 versus 33 among Jews, 27 versus 31 among white Catholics, 36 versus 29 among white Protestants, 21 versus 20 among Puerto Ricans, and 6 versus 12 among blacks (Harris and Swanson, *Black-Jewish Relations in New York City*, p. 142).

becoming popular.[87] If it does lead to improved living conditions, one can fairly confidently predict that more and more cities will conduct more and bolder experiments. If such improvements in fact occur, they are most likely to come in three respects.[88] First, community control may improve the administration of urban services. Some services, such as health care and corrections, for example, might well be improved through decentralization of their delivery to a community-based level. Client representation on school boards and citizen militancy are already having the effect in many cities of expanding the alternative styles of education available to children. Some of these alternatives, it is true, have been formulated simply as devices to avoid school integration. But many of them are true alternative styles which enrich the educational offerings of city school districts. Second, community control may increase government responsiveness. The example of Boston's little city halls suggests that government agencies can be more responsive to citizen demands and needs. Finally, community control has the potential to reduce citizen alienation from government. The neighborhood government model would seem to have the most potential in this respect. It would not only have a governing board indigenous to the neighborhood community; but, as a development corporation, it could have the financial resources to undertake development projects on the neighborhood level. There are no neighborhood development corporations with the extensive powers that Kotler envisions, so there is no empirical base from which to judge whether they would reduce alienation. To the extent that the model cities programs and the community action programs have been prototypes of neighborhood government, however, there is little or no evidence that they reduced alienation.

In conclusion, the concept of control sharing was one of the most creative concepts to come out of the turbulent decade of the sixties. As experiments initiated during the early 1970s in New York, Detroit, Indianapolis, Boston, and other cities come to fruition, we will have a better idea of the effectiveness of the concept.

THE BIAS IN CONTEMPORARY URBAN GOVERNMENT

Several themes about contemporary urban government are dominant in the foregoing discussions. First, the myth of central city impoverishment does not apply to all metropolises. It most accurately describes large, older metropolises of the Northeast and the Midwest. Second, a feature of central city governance that is fairly common, if not universal, is the semi-autonomy of the functional fiefdoms. A functional fiefdom consists of an urban agency operating in some general arena of public affairs, its bureaucracy, its professional staff, its public employees' union, its board or commission of directors, its counterpart agencies in the state and federal government, and, finally, the private businesses, labor organizations, and interest groups which serve as a clientele for the agency. Third, the functional fiefdoms pose enormous problems for the exercise of decisive political leadership in large cities. Fourth, the existing structure and organization of power in urban areas, be it pluralist or stratified, is biased against people who are unorganized. This bias is felt most heavily by the poor and the racial minorities. Last, two entirely different remedies have been prescribed by social scientists and others as antidotes for the deficiencies of functional fiefdoms. For the weakness of inhibiting political leadership, the antidotes most often prescribed have been a simultaneous strengthening of the political parties and the big-city mayor. For the antipoor bias of the functional fiefdoms, the prescription has been some form of shared control with, or community control over, urban government.

The two antidotes appear to be antipathetic: it is not clear how a geographic decentralization of government can be consistent with strong mayoral leadership. But the two antidotes may not necessarily be inconsistent. As was indicated, decentralization and control sharing can take many forms. In Boston the little city halls were useful for a variety of mayoral purposes that ranged from prodding the bureaucracies to be more responsive to improving the lines of communication between the mayor and neighborhood residents. Client representation on the governing boards of public agencies and private organizations could also conceivably strengthen the mayor's hand in bargaining with these institutions. The most difficulties for strong mayoral leadership are likely to be posed by the model of neighborhood government. If the model cities programs and the community action programs are truly prototypes of neighborhood government, then the outlook does not seem favorable for strengthening the mayor's hand in public affairs. In most cities the history of model cities and the community action programs were rife with conflict with city hall. But it need not necessarily work that way.

The problem with assessing the impact of control sharing on strong mayoral leadership is that little empirical evidence is available to use as a basis for exercising judgment. Mostly there is speculation and educated guessing.

Clearly, however, the controversy over community control has exposed the biases of the status quo. The advocates of community control are demanding it not because they think that the bureaucracies are simply doing a bad job of helping the poor and the racial minorities. If that were the case, the problem could be remedied through the application of modern techniques of public administration and program analysis. Rather, in the writings of the advocates of community control, the functional fiefdoms are *inherently* biased against the interests of the disorganized, the poor, and the racial minorities. This is a direct result of the peculiar form of representative democracy that has developed in the United States. Legislatures and bureaucracies are most responsive to constituent and client groups and to citizens who participate in the political process. For a variety of reasons, the poor and the disorganized do not participate very well in these groups, in electoral activity, in campaigning activity, or in lobbying activity. The major institutional reason for their lack of participation is that there is no institutional mechanism which can mobilize them into action.[89] The closest thing to such a mechanism has been the affiliation of organized labor to the New Deal coalition within the Democratic party. The labor unions can mobilize their members to vote and can pressure the government for legislation that will benefit their members. But no institution in American society has mobilized the poor and the disorganized in the same fashion.

In this view, then, the key failure of the bureaucratic state is that no institutional mechanism exists for representing the interests of the disorganized and the poor. And, in this respect, community control is championed as the new institutional creation for accomplishing this representation directly in the administrative bureaucracy.

In concept, then, community control is truly revolutionary in scope. In practice, it has been applied very timidly. Bureaucratic decentralization has been accomplished without decentralizing control over policy; steps have been taken to place token client representatives on the boards of public agencies without cutting into the autonomy of the bureaucracies involved; and, despite the experiments with model cities and community action programs, no true neighborhood governments have been established. If the pattern established thus far prevails, community control will be applied in a fairly piecemeal and incremental fashion. In the words of political scientist Victor Jones, "Unless we have a revolution in the old-fashioned sense of the word, institutional changes will occur slowly."[90]

Some Suggested Readings

Central City Government, Functional Fiefdoms, and Executive Leadership

Theodore J. Lowi, *At the Pleasure of the Mayor* (New York: The Free Press, 1964). Analyzes mayoral appointments in New York City from 1897 to 1957 and introduces the concept of functional feudalities.

Jeffrey Pressman, "Preconditions for Mayoral Leadership," *The American Political Science Review* 66, no. 2 (June 1972): 514. Using Oakland as his point of departure, Pressman establishes some guidelines for maximizing the possibility for strong mayoral leadership in a city.

Henry W. Maier, *Challenge to the Cities: An Approach to a Theory of Urban Leadership* (New York: Random House, 1966). As mayor of Milwaukee, Maier has presented an interesting analysis of mayoral leadership.

Theodore J. Lowi, "Machine Politics — Old and New," *The Public Interest* 9 (Fall 1967): 83–92. Establishes the proposition that the contemporary public bureaucracies exhibit many of the characteristics of the old-style machine — rational goal seeking and personal loyalty — and that they have now become an inescapably important factor in local elections.

Leonard I. Ruchelman, ed. *Big City Mayors: The Crisis in Urban Politics* (Bloomington: Indiana University Press, 1969). A collection of articles on various mayors and their problems.

Community Power and Specific City Studies

Nelson Polsby, *Community Power and Political Theory* (New Haven, Conn.: Yale University Press, 1963). Although this book is somewhat dated in the fast-changing field of community power studies, it remains one of the most articulate and concise critiques of the early stratificationist and reputational community power literature.

Peter Bachrach and Morton S. Baratz, *Power and Poverty: Theory and Practice* (New York: Oxford University Press, 1970). Begins with the authors' thesis on the importance of nondecisions and proceeds to an analysis of the politics of poverty in Baltimore, Maryland.

Jean L. Stinchcombe, *Reform and Reaction: City Politics in Toledo* (Belmont, Calif.: Wadsworth, 1968). A short community power analysis.

Edward C. Hayes, *Power Structure and Urban Policy: Who Rules in Oakland?* (New York: McGraw-Hill, 1972). A short community power analysis.

Michael Lipsky, *Protest in City Politics: Rent Strikes, Housing and the Power of the Poor* (Chicago: Rand McNally, 1970). Based on Lipsky's study of New York City rent strikes, this is probably the most detailed work to date on the powerlessness of the poor and the inefficacy of political protest as a political tactic of the poor.

Todd Gitlin and Nanci Hollander, *Uptown: Poor Whites in Chicago* (New York: Harper & Row, 1970). A description of life styles of poor Appalachians in the city.

Edward C. Banfield, *Big City Politics* (New York: Random House, 1965). Short descriptions of city government and politics in Atlanta, Boston, Detroit, El Paso, Los Angeles, Miami, Philadelphia, Saint Louis, and Seattle.

David Rogers, *The Management of Big Cities: Interest Groups and Social Change Strategies* (Beverly Hills, Calif.: SAGE Publications, 1971). Makes an interesting comparison of New York, Philadelphia, and Cleveland.

Control Sharing

Mario Fantini and Marilyn Gittell, *Decentralization: Achieving Reform* (New York: Praeger, 1973). A clear, articulate defense of decentralization by two prominent scholars. Strong critiques of decentralization in the area of public education.

Joseph F. Zimmerman, *The Federated City: Community Control in Large Cities* (New York: St. Martin's Press, 1972). A clear, articulate argument against community control by a prominent author. This is probably the best organized and easiest to read outline of control-sharing approaches now in print.

Alan Altshuler, *Community Control: The Black Demand for Participation in Large American Cities* (New York: Pegasus, 1970). A theoretical discussion of the pros and cons of community control.

PART III

With the transformation of the city into a metropolis, new political structures emerged to deal with area-wide and localized problems in the suburbs. Suburban forms of government represented an attempt to re-create small-town government in the metropolis. This led to a proliferation of municipalities and single-purpose governments that fragmented governmental authority in the metropolis. This fragmentation, together with several other consequences of suburbanization, has made it difficult to alleviate social cleavages and deal with growth problems in the metropolis. Chapter 6 discusses these developments and their biases.

In trying to cope with these problems, governments at the suburban, central

COPING WITH THE CONSEQUENCES OF THE MULTI-CENTERED METROPOLIS

city, and metropolitan levels have experimented with a variety of approaches. The most commonly used approaches have tried to achieve metropolitan governance without creating a metropolitan government. This has been done by creating agencies which led to the growth of functional fiefdoms in the major developmental sectors of housing, transit, highways, water supply, and sewerage. These approaches are discussed in Chapter 7.

An alternative set of approaches for coping with metropolitan problems and biases involves creating a new geographic basis to political power that would give metropolitan elected officials the authority to control the functional fiefdoms and the suburbs and would entail the creation of a new metropolitan government. These approaches are discussed in Chapter 8.

The politics of campaigning for these metropolitan reorganizations are analyzed in Chapter 9. And Chapter 10 describes the changes in metropolitan governance which have followed the unsuccessful attempts to create new, geographically based metropolitan governments.

Chapter 6

Just as it was necessary to begin the discussion of contemporary central city politics by dispelling some prevalent myths about them, it is necessary to begin a discussion of suburbia by dispelling certain myths about it. Over the past generation an extensive body of sociological and popular literature has portrayed suburbia as a large dormitory that houses a homogeneous collection of white, upper-middle-class, conservative Republicans who universally ignore the country's social needs while they quietly pursue the acquisition of private wealth.[1] This is an extremely misleading picture, as Chapter 6 points out.

Suburbia and the Emergence of the Multi-centered Metropolis

This chapter also tackles one of the myths about suburban politics — their consistent conservatism — and investigates some of the political realities that divide suburban communities. It goes on to suggest that if the communities of the suburbs in any way present a united front, it is in their desire for political autonomy from central cities. Hence, the development of metropolitan areas with many political centers — the multi-centered metropolis.

THE HETEROGENEITY OF SUBURBIA

The suburbs of United States cities are as heterogeneous as the neighborhoods of the cities they surround. Just as there are different types of city neighborhoods, there are different types of suburbs.

One of the ways in which suburbs differ from one another is in the basic functions they perform. Some suburbs, called *residential* or *dormitory suburbs*, primarily perform the function of housing people; they provide little industrial or commercial activity. Others called *employing suburbs*, function primarily as the location for industries and employment centers. Sociologist Leo Schnore examined three hundred suburbs in the twenty-five largest metropolitan areas and discovered a third type as well, a *mixed suburb* which provided both residential and employment functions. Schnore's analysis clearly demonstrated that only a small minority of these suburbs (about a third) were the stereotyped dormitory suburbs. The other two-thirds were almost evenly divided between mixed suburbs and employment suburbs.[2]

Other studies have shown some suburbs to be even further specialized by the functions they perform. Some suburbs exist primarily as territorial enclaves to give large property tax advantages to industries or utilities plants.[3] Others exist primarily as locations for racetracks. Racetracks require considerable space, and since they do not make congenial neighbors in residential areas, they usually are built in suburban regions that are poorly populated.[4] And still other suburbs exist primarily as enclaves for honkytonk bars, nightclubs, gambling, prostitution, and narcotics traffic.[5] Examples can be found within easy commuting distance of many major cities.[6]

Just as the myth of suburbia as a dormitory does not withstand close analysis, neither does the myth about upper-middle-class homogeneity in suburbia. Particularly among the smaller and newer metropolises, the residents of a city's suburbs are no more affluent than the residents of the central city itself. In many areas they are less affluent.[7] Even between the suburbs of any given metropolitan region, there are wide variations in the average affluence. One study of working-class suburbs found that the simple act of moving out to the suburbs did not change basic working-class behavior patterns: auto workers retained such un-middle-class behavior as carrying lunch buckets, having no or few organizational memberships, shunning church attendance, and continuing to vote Democratic.[8]*

Suburbs range all along the scale of social class. Some are exclusive enclaves for the wealthy, others are predominantly upper middle class, and others are working class. Residents of a distant and wealthy suburb

* There may be important regional variations in working-class behavior patterns, however. One study of a very small sample of blue collar families in the Minneapolis–Saint Paul SMSA found that the suburban blue collar men were more status conscious than the central city blue collar men, were more concerned with upward mobility, and were both less liberal and less inclined to the Democratic party. See Irving Tallman and Ramonn Morgner, "Life Style Differences Among Urban and Suburban Blue-Collar Families," *Social Forces* 48 (May 1970): 324–348.

might refer to themselves as exurbanites and live in stately homes on large lots far removed from the center city. The government of upper-class suburbs is usually very nonprofessional and small, and most of the employees do not even live in the suburb.[9]

The middle-class suburb, in contrast, is much more likely to have a professional city manager and to have local residents engaged in controversies over local policies. The issues which arouse citizen concern will most likely be schools, zoning regulations, public improvements such as sewers or street paving, and public services such as recreation or garbage collection.[10] It is this middle-class suburb which has served as the focal point for so much sociological research and popular literature on the supposedly homogeneous, conformist suburbia.

The working-class suburb has become an increasingly common phenomenon. A survey of AFL-CIO membership found that about half of the members live in the suburbs rather than in the central cities; among the younger union members, as many as three-fourths live in suburbia.[11] The working-class suburb differs in several respects from the middle-class suburb.

> The working-class suburb is quite likely to be unincorporated. It is cheaper that way, and the residents must look for ways to save money so as to preserve their status as homeowners in time of economic difficulties — and in order to spend money on luxuries in imitation of the middle class. If the county or township administers the area, part of the cost of governmental protection and services, may, through the property tax, be transferred to residents in wealthier areas, and costly services are less likely to be demanded of a more distant government than one's own municipal organization. If the area is incorporated as a separate municipality, less participation in government is likely than is the case in the middle-class suburb. . . . Services will be few: Septic tanks are preferred to sewage disposal systems, state parks to municipal parks, inexpensive gravel to hard-surfaced roads, open ditches to curbs and gutters, building codes will place few limitations on the builder and will probably in any case not be rigidly enforced.[12]

Other social classifications of suburbs exist as well. An increasing phenomenon is the predominantly black suburb. Three distinct types of black suburbs have been identified. First are the old black neighborhoods that often predated the post–World War II black migration to central cities. These suburbs typically contain very cheap homes and often lack access to public water and sewer facilities. Second are the densely populated black settlements that have arisen near major employment centers, particularly in the North. Finally, during the 1960s new suburban residential areas were developed predominantly and sometimes exclusively for blacks. Most of the recent black suburbanization has occurred in this third type of suburb, and their residents are more affluent than blacks in the other two types of suburbs or in the central city.

Prior to the late 1960s, suburban blacks were less affluent than central city blacks. This pattern has now been reversed.* The average black suburbanite is now slightly more affluent than the average black central city resident.[13] Also important is the fact that black suburbanization has not meant a decrease in separated residential patterns. Increasing numbers of blacks are living in integrated suburban neighborhoods, but the majority of suburban blacks still live in census tracts that are a majority Negro.[14]† And in the dozen largest SMSAs the percentage of blacks who live in the suburbs increased during the 1960s by only 1 or 2 percent.[15]

In addition to differences in economic function and in kinds of residents, one of the most important variations between suburbs is their difference in spatial arrangement. Some scholars see the metropolis as developing in a series of concentric rings which radiate from the downtown central business district. Immediately adjacent to the central business district are the warehouse zones and the heavy industry zones, followed by the poorest residential neighborhoods, the working-class neighborhoods, the middle-class neighborhoods, and finally, on the fringes of the metropolis, the residential areas of the upper middle class and the wealthy.[16] Other scholars see the metropolis as developing in a pattern of sectors. Certain subareas of the city or the metropolis become specialized for serving as centers of certain activities and especially for serving as the residential neighborhoods of given classes.[17] The sectors do not exist in the form of concentric rings. Rather they emerge along the major transportation arteries. A third theory views the metropolis as developing a pattern of multiple and interrelating nuclei.[18] These three arrangements are schematized in Figure 6-1.

* Using data gathered prior to the 1970 census, Donald Canty found a higher percentage of black families living at poverty level in the suburbs than in the central city. [See his "Where the people, the Power and the Problems are Moving: A Profile of Suburban America," City 5, no. 1 (January–February 1971): 13.] But by 1972, the Census Bureau was reporting that 27 percent of central city black families had incomes below the low-income level. the comparable figure for suburban blacks was only 20 percent. [United States Bureau of the Census, Current Population Reports, ser. P.-23, no. 48, "The Social and Economic Status of the Black Population in the United States: 1973" (Washington, D.C.: U.S. Government Printing Office, 1974) table 22, p. 35.]

† A study of black suburbs outside of Philadelphia also concluded that segregation patterns continue to exist in the suburbs as they do in the central cities. But the black suburbanites there exhibited middle-class values. [Leonard Blumberg and Michael Lalli, "Little Ghettoes: A Study of Negroes in the Suburbs," Phylon 27 (Summer 1966): 117–131.] Present-day growth patterns suggest that there will be an increasing tendency for more integrated neighborhoods to appear in the suburbs. [Norman M. Bradburn, Seymour Sudman, and Gulen G. Gockel, Racial Integration in American Neighborhoods: A Comparative Survey (Chicago: National Opinion Research Center, 1970), p. 76.]

FIGURE 6-1

SCHEMAS OF THREE SPATIAL DEVELOPMENT THEORIES

Concentric Ring Theory

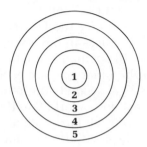

1   Central business district

2   Zone in transition

3   Working-class zone

4   Middle-class residential zone

5   Commuters' zone

Sector Theory

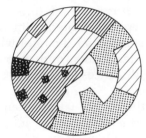

☐   Cheap housing

▦   Next cheapest housing

▨   Medium-cost housing

▨   More expensive housing

■   Most expensive housing

Multiple Nuclei Theory

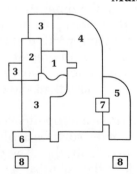

1   Central business district

2   Light manufacturing

3   Low-class residential

4   Medium-class residential

5   High-class residential

6   Heavy manufacturing

7   Outlying business district

8   Industrial suburb

Adapted from Raymond E. Murphy, *The American City: An Urban Geography*
(New York: McGraw-Hill, 1966), pp. 208–215.

These three theories are not mutually exclusive as they apply to suburbia. Elements of the concentric zone theory have general relevance because many central cities are surrounded by several tiers or rings of suburbs. Immediately adjacent to the central city lie the inner ring suburbs, often incorporated during the interwar years. These suburbs tend to have relatively high densities. Their residential character is indicated by apartment buildings lining the freeways that radiate from the central cities and by small houses in older neighborhoods of single-family homes. They are more likely than not to be working-class suburbs, but scattered throughout the inner ring are pockets of upper- and lower-income neighborhoods.[19] A second ring of suburbs exists beyond the inner ring where the great post–World War II housing boom promoted the sprawling subdivisions of fairly standardized, small houses. As the original residents of these suburbs became more affluent and moved further out, their place has been taken by lower-income persons. In many of the older tract developments, signs of neighborhood deterioration are already appearing, causing some observers to predict that these will become the slums of the future.[20] Beyond these second-tier suburbs exists a third ring inhabited primarily by professional and business people with substantial incomes who are able to afford living in large homes, on large lots, and who trade off the inconvenience of long commuting distances for their more comfortable surroundings.

Although the concentric zone theory of metropolitan development seems to explain well the growth of several tiers of suburbs surrounding the central city, other elements of suburban growth seem more readily explained by the sector and the multiple nuclei theories. In none of the rings of suburbs are the populations really homogeneous. Some of the wealthiest suburbs can be found in the inner ring and some of the poorest in the outer rings. Also, in most metropolitan areas, the central business district shares an ever decreasing portion of the commerical life, the social life, and the cultural life of the region. Particularly in areas such as Los Angeles, the multiple nuclei theory of metropolitan growth seems to be much more appropriate than the concentric ring theory.

Finally, the very fact that none of these metropolitan growth theories can adequately explain the diversity of the suburbs is additional reason for rejecting the homogeneous model of suburbia. The serious student of urban affairs can no longer look at the suburbs in such simplistic terms. The suburbs simply must be seen as diverse and heterogeneous places.

THE POLITICS OF SUBURBIA

Partisanship and Policy Bias in Suburbia

If the myth of a homogeneous, affluent, upper-middle-class, white suburbia does not withstand empirical analysis, neither does the myth that all of suburbia is Republican and conservative. This myth arose because the suburbs on balance have tended to vote Republican. In particular, during the 1950s some suburbs voted heavily Republican for Dwight Eisenhower for president. Shortly after Eisenhower's victory in 1952, Senator Robert A. Taft predicted that the Republicans would continue to dominate suburbia and, through suburbia, the White House.

Two hypotheses were offered to explain these early Republican successes in the suburbs. The first was the theory of *conversion,* which stated that central city Democrats who move out to the Republican-dominated suburbs convert to Republicanism in order to minimize partisan cross pressures. Furthermore, becoming property owners for the first time, these ex-city dwellers then become more conscious of the property tax effect of government expenditures.[21] In other words, they are influenced by their new status and new neighbors to vote Republican and conservative.

In contrast to the conversion theory was the *transplantation* theory, which had two versions.[22] The first version stated that it was primarily Republicans who moved out of the central city to the suburbs. Suburbanites were not converted Democrats; they were simply transplanted Republicans. The second version said that it was upwardly mobile Democrats who were moving to suburbia from the central city. Being upwardly mobile, they were ripe for a transformation from a Democratic to a Republican allegiance. However, the transformation occurred before rather than after the migration, so they, too, were transplanted Republicans rather than converted Democrats.

The problem with both the conversion and the transplantation theories is that they are based on the assumption that the suburbs are overwhelmingly Republican. As Table 6-1 shows, this was true in the presidential elections of 1952 and 1956, when the Republican candidate, Eisenhower, was an extraordinarily respected American. When 1952 and 1956 are put into the broader perspective of a series of postwar elections, the Republican dominance of the suburbs is not nearly so overwhelming. As the table shows, only in 1952 and 1956 did the Republicans gain more than 55 percent of the vote in both presidential and lesser elections in 400 suburbs in eighteen states. In all but one of

TABLE 6-1

REPUBLICAN PERCENTAGES OF SUBURBAN VOTE: 1948–1964

Year	Presidential Elections	Lesser Elections
1948	54.5%	54.3%
1950	—	54.5
1952	58.8	57.7
1954	—	51.6
1956	62.5	58.4
1958	—	49.0
1960	50.2	55.4
1962	—	54.1
1964	36.2	50.7

Reprinted by permission of the publisher, from On the City's Rim: Politics and Policy in Suburbia by Frederick M. Wirt, Benjamin Walter, Francine F. Rabinovitz, and Deborah R. Hensler (Lexington, Mass.: Lexington Books, D. C. Heath and Company, 1972), p. 85.

the other elections, party control over the suburban vote was highly competitive, although the Republicans hold a slim majority. These conclusions were confirmed by an analysis of congressional and presidential voting from 1952 to 1964 in the fifty-one suburban congressional districts; suburban voting patterns were found to follow national trends.[23]*

Democratic presidential candidates can capture the suburban vote under favorable circumstances (1964) or they can lose it heavily under unfavorable circumstances (1972). Under other circumstances (1960, for example), a popular Democratic candidate can offset and limit whatever advantages the Republicans have in the suburbs.† In one of the most sophisticated studies of elections to date, The American Voter, Campbell, et al. rejects the notion that moving to suburbia changes partisan allegiance. The "absence of a really unique change in political allegiance among ex-urbanites . . . further indicates that movement out of the metropolitan centers cannot stand as the factor responsible for changes in partisan loyalties that cut across non-movers as well."[24]

* Frederick Wirt's analysis of electoral returns in 154 suburbs suggests that this is true in the case of presidential elections. It seems to be less true in congressional and local elections. See Wirt, "The Political Sociology of American Suburbia: A Reinterpretation," The Journal of Politics 27, no. 3 (August 1965): 647–666.
† The 1960 and 1964 suburban presidential voting results can be seen in Table 6-1. In 1972, the Republican candidate, Richard M. Nixon, received 66 percent of the suburban vote. See Frederick M. Wirt, "Suburbs and Politics in America," Publius 5, no. 1 (Winter 1975): 122.

When voting trends are broken down by individual suburbs, the assumption of Republican dominance appears even more dubious. Benjamin Walter and Frederick M. Wirt analyzed presidential voting in 407 suburbs in 1956, 1960, and 1964 and, as shown in Table 6-2, found that *a slim majority of the suburbs leaned Democratic* rather than Republican.[25]

Table 6-2 also shows a very strong relationship between a suburb's affluence and its tendency to vote Republican. The Republican suburbs exhibit a much wider range of affluence than do the Democratic suburbs. And there is also considerable overlap in the categories, with some Democratic suburbs being more affluent than some Republican suburbs. But the overall pattern is quite clear. The most Democratic suburbs are clustered at the lower end of the affluence index. And the most affluent suburbs tend to be Republican.

Perhaps a more relevant question than the partisanship of the vote is the question of whether the supposed conservatism of suburbanites impels their policy makers to act more conservatively. Because not

TABLE 6-2

PARTY COMPETITION AND SOCIOECONOMIC STATUS IN SUBURBIA

Majority Party in Presidential Elections of 1956, 1960, 1964[a]	Number of Suburbs (and Percentage)	Score on Affluence Index[b]	
		Mean	Range of Scores
Democratic	70 (17.2)	−0.8	−1.5 to −0.1
Leaning Democratic	141 (34.6)	−0.4	−1.0 to +0.3
Leaning Republican	160 (39.3)	+0.3	−0.5 to +1.2
Republican	36 (8.9)	+1.3	+0.3 to +2.3
Total	407 (100.0)	0.0	−1.5 to +1.3

[a] Although there were eight possible combinations of patterns to the vote, the only combinations that actually occurred are the ones shown in this table.
[b] This index is composed of affluence factor scores which Walter and Wirt computed from a factor analysis of 11 separate education, income, and occupation variables in the 407 suburbs. The scores range from the least affluent suburb (−1.5) to the most affluent suburb (+2.3). The mean score of all suburbs is 0.0, and the scores are in a normal distribution around that mean. Each score represents its standard deviation from the mean. Thus, the affluence index for the 70 Democratic suburbs, for example, indicates that the mean of the 70 Democratic suburbs is 0.8 standard deviation below the mean for all 407 suburbs and that the affluence scores for the 70 Democratic suburbs range from 1.5 standard deviations below the mean for all 407 suburbs to 0.1 standard deviation below the mean for all 407 suburbs.

Source: Adapted from Benjamin Walter and Frederick M. Wirt, "The Political Consequences of Suburban Variety," *Social Science Quarterly* 52, no. 3 (December 1971): 750–753.

many rigorous empirical analyses of this question have been made, it is difficult to answer with finality. Nevertheless, the available data suggest that central city/suburban differences on policy preferences are not nearly as significant as other differences.

First, although some differences can be found between central city and suburban attitudes generally, labeling them as liberal or conservative is difficult. A study of suburbanites and city dwellers in the Dayton metropolitan area found that suburbanites tended to be more dissatisfied with their available public services than were the central city residents.[26] But this is hardly a liberal/conservative issue; and the Dayton suburbs may have been notably deficient in providing the services in question. A study in five metropolitan areas of Wisconsin found that although suburbanites preferred spending more money on public education than did city dwellers, they were not as willing to spend as much on other municipal services. The suburbanites preferred to scrimp on municipal services such as central water supply or sewerage. Through the use of wells and septic tanks, these services could be shifted to private expenditures and sometimes the central cities could be induced to provide the services for the entire urbanized area.[27] Another study of city and suburban attitudes and political activities, based on Survey Research Center national samples, found "that there is little or no difference between some urban and suburban attitude and activity patterns and that the nationwide urban-suburban division is the *least* rather than the most influential of the forces used to explain" urban and suburban differences.[28]

The sharpest differences in policy preferences are found not between the suburbanites as a whole and central city dwellers as a whole, but between persons of different socioeconomic statuses. In a study of Philadelphia suburbs, four political scientists asked both residents and public officials about their policy preferences toward keeping the tax rate down, acquiring business and industry, and keeping undesirable people out of the suburb. They discovered sharp differences in policy preference between suburbs of a lower social rank, those of a middle social rank, and those of the upper social rank. Even within suburbs of the same social rank, there were sharp differences from one suburb to another. The only issue which failed to provoke a direct breakdown along social class lines was that of keeping undesirables out.[29] On this question overwhelming agreement existed, and the middle-class suburbs were the most adamant. The racial overtones to the question are obvious. Race is the one question on which suburbanites demonstrate an implacable, united front in their attitudes. It is doubtful, however, that white suburbanites are any more implacable on the question than white central city residents; public opinion surveys find that central city residents respond much more liberally than suburbanites on racial questions largely because the central city samples simply have more nonwhites than do the suburban samples.

Whether residents' different attitudes affect actual decisions can be measured by contrasting the roll call votes of urban and suburban representatives. An analysis of congressional voting records during the Johnson administration failed to find significant differences between the voting records of central city congressmen and those of suburban congressmen. Where differences were discovered, they were traceable primarily to partisan differences.[30]

Cleavages and Issues in Suburban Politics

Since from one suburb to another there are very sharp differences in partisanship, policy preferences, and functions the suburb performs, two key questions about suburban politics become: In matters of local politics what characteristics divide suburbanites; and what are the main subjects about which suburbanites differ? These two questions involve the notions of *cleavages* and *issues*, respectively.

One of the most important cleavages is that which occurs between the old-timers and the newcomers who follow the subdivision tract developers. Robert Wood maintains that when newcomers arrive in suburbia, they intend to transplant their urban life styles. But they are slowly assimilated into the traditional pattern of doing things, and eventually the old-timers predominate.[31] Other conflicts exist betwen the commuters and the stay-at-homes. For those who work elsewhere, the suburb is truly a dormitory. The commuters are usually willing to pay the taxes necessary to supply the services they want for their families and their new neighborhoods. The stay-at-homes are found among the local business and real estate people and the old political leaders who not only live in the suburb but derive their livelihood there. They are often eager to keep the tax base down. Although the commuters may be many in number, they seldom predominate over the stay-at-homes.[32]

The classic struggle in suburbia, then, pits the old-timers and the stay-at-homes on the one hand against the newcomers and the commuters on the other hand in a struggle over the basic life-style values of the locale. One problem with this supposed cleavage is that although it undoubtedly applies to newly formed suburbs, the overwhelming majority of suburbs at any given moment are already formed and relatively mature. In the 1970s, the majority of suburbs may well be approaching their second generation of inhabitants. If the average American family moves once every five years, and if suburbanites are among the most mobile of Americans, then it seems likely that few suburbs still possess their first complete generation of newcomers. The conflict between newcomers and old-timers is not very applicable to the mature suburbs.

In Frederick Wirt's study of over 400 suburbs, he found that these cleavages of newcomer versus old-timer and stay-at-home versus commuter really served to mask very basic conflicts in values, life styles, and social class.

> This broad sequence of social change can be sensed in old hamlets and rural townships, once isolated on the far reaches of the central city. They have been assaulted by migrants. The white clapboard school house has been replaced by a school complex, outfitted with the latest educational technology. The suburban village has been tied into the life of the entire region by the freeways that have pierced the slumbering countryside. Blue — or white collar migrants — all "city folk" to the rural old guard no matter what distinctions the Census Bureau finds — spill all over the rural corners whose major source of excitement used to be the annual county fair.[33]

As the newcomers eventually achieve numerical superiority over the old-timers, the very nature of the locale changes from that of a small town to that of a suburb.

With this basic cleavage between life styles, the issues which dominate local suburban politics tend to be issues which reflect those life styles. Almost universally in suburbs, the most controversial issues have to do with schools, taxes, and zoning changes. The issue of taxes inevitably rises whenever the suburb is undergoing rapid development. Numerous, expensive services must be provided, ranging from schools to police protection to sewers and water. The revenues to provide these services have disproportionately been derived from the local property tax. By the late 1960s, property taxes accounted for over 85 percent of all locally raised revenue.[34] Unlike the central cities, in which the property tax burden is spread across the entire city, the property tax burden of suburbia is not spread across all of suburbia. Except for state and federal aid, each suburban jurisdiction has to raise its own revenue from taxes on property within its boundaries. Consequently, suburbs are very sensitive to the politics of attracting industry which pays more than its share of property taxes and to manipulating zoning laws to keep out people who will add more costs to the services than they will add revenue to the tax base. During a suburb's most rapid period of growth, conflicts over these issues become very intense, and the suburban municipal councils become divided into permanent factions which reflect the divisions within the suburb's populace over life-style differences. After the suburb's growth ceases, or in suburbs which do not undergo population growth, political conflict on these issues diminishes and a politics of consensus often sets in.[35]

The politics surrounding suburban schools became increasingly important over the past generation as the central city school systems were increasingly criticized for delinquency, segregation, racial unrest, and poor education.[36] Indeed, one of the most often cited reasons for which city dwellers, especially upper-middle-class professionals, are believed to move into the suburbs is to have decent schools where their children can be well educated and safe.* Suburbanites, like central city dwellers, feel that public education is much too important to become bound up with party politics.† Yet several mutually contradictory themes flourish in suburban school board politics. On the one hand, a complex of factors impel the suburbs to provide the best facilities possible for their schools. Not only do parents want the best for their children, but businesspeople and real estate dealers think that few things will attract more upper-middle-income professionals into their suburbs than the reputation for good schools. On the other hand, good schools are expensive, and in most suburbs bitter battles recur periodically over school expenditures. Tax-conscious citizens charge that their money is being wasted on superfluous frills. As teachers became more militant during the 1960s, much of the tax-conscious animosity was directed at the teachers, whose salary levels were unjustifiable to the fiscal conservatives.

Finally, for the same reasons underlying the tax and school issues, zoning disputes always have the potential to disrupt the peace in the suburbs. Suburbs inevitably go through a phase of rapid growth. During this phase, subdividers and real estate developers construct and sell large numbers of houses. To service the new population, shopping centers and other service facilities are built. This situation is always conducive to charges such as conflict of interest, graft, sellouts to big

---

* In Levittown, however, hardly anybody cited this as a reason for moving to the suburb. The most recurring reason given was the need for a bigger house and more space. [Herbert J. Gans, The Levittowners: Ways of Life and Politics in a New Suburban Community (New York: Vintage Books, 1967), pp. 32–33.] In a study of six Eastern and Midwestern metropolises, housing and neighborhood conditions were the reasons most often given for moving to the suburbs. [Basil G. Zimmer, The Metropolitan Community: Its People and Government (Beverly Hills, Calif.: SAGE Publications, 1970), p. 32.]

† Roscoe Martin stressed, "Any contact between urban politics and the schools is held to be destructive of sound educational practice" [Martin, Government and the Suburban School (Syracuse, N.Y.: Syracuse University Press, 1962), p. 58].

developers, absence of planning, and absence of public concern. The conditions under which the developers are allowed to operate, and the zoning restrictions that are put on the kinds of housing they can build are significant battles at this stage in the suburb's growth.

Suburbs against Cities

These cleavages and issues aside, there still remains one feature that characterizes all of the politics of suburbia. This is the myth that suburban government is small enough and close enough to home that the average citizen can have a personal impact on it.

This in particular is the thesis of political scientist Robert Wood, who argues that suburbia is essentially an attempt to re-create Jeffersonian democracy on the fringes of the cities.[37]* The outward growth of population and business *could have* occurred without the establishment of a ring of municipal governments surrounding the central city. Central cities *could have* continued to grow by annexing the newly settled areas. The fact that this did not occur reflects the strength of the political motivation to keep the new settlements separate from the old central cities.[38] The great political machines and the large public bureaucracies of the central cities had grown to the point where few citizens had any influence over them. Many people hoped that a proliferation of small, politically autonomous communities would enable their residents to have the best of two worlds — the intimacy of small-town government and the advantages of the metropolitan facilities. Accordingly, one of the key themes that has pervaded many specific issues of suburban politics has been that of defending local autonomy from encroachment by big-city or metropolitan government.

This motivation behind suburbanization is similar in some respects to the motivation behind the demand for community control in central cities.[39] But community control and the proliferation of suburban governments are very different in other respects. Even the most ardent advocates of neighborhood government within cities favor retention of an overall city-wide government. The staunchest advocates of suburban government, however, have opposed an overall, metropolitan-wide government. Politically, then, suburbia is distinct in that there is no overall suburban or metropolitan government; there are many governments. Governmentally and politically, the metropolis has become multi-centered.

* Daniel Elazar also asserts that the desire to maintain the small community is one of the primary motive forces behind suburbanization. See his "Are We a Nation of Cities?" *The Public Interest* 4 (Summer 1966): 42–58.

THE POLITICAL CONSEQUENCES OF THE MULTI-CENTERED METROPOLIS

Because of the long-term housing boom from the end of World War II until the 1960s, the almost universal adaptation of the automobile as the basic means of mass transportation, the proliferating incorporation of suburban governments, and the decentralization not only of retail shopping but of many kinds of employment opportunties, the central business district lost its dominance over the metropolis. More and more the metropolitan areas became multi-centered rather than centered on a single central business district. Los Angeles rather than New York became the model for the city of the future.

Politically, the multi-centered metropolis is characterized by a series of geographic fiefdoms which feud with one another over commercial facilities and tax bases and which exercise almost unfettered control over zoning decisions. Individually, if a suburb is well located it can maximize both high services and low taxes for its residents by behaving as a geographic fiefdom and yielding few concessions to its less fortunate neighbors. As Robert Wood points out, all suburbs have hoped to emulate this model.[40] From the vantage point of the metropolis as a whole, however, this geographic fiefdomization has several negative political consequences. Since these consequences are described in considerable detail in the following chapters, they will simply be outlined here.

Separation of Public Needs from Available Resources

Because local governments rely excessively on locally imposed property taxes for their local revenue, the division of the metropolis into hundreds of relatively small taxing units tends to separate the public needs from the available resources. The property tax revenue generated by an electric power plant or a factory or a shopping center goes only to the local governments which operate in that locality. As Table 6-3 indicates, most of the property tax goes to finance the local school district. If the school district area is very large — covering an entire central city or an entire county — it has schools located in affluent neighborhoods as well as in poor neighborhoods. It also has several large payers of property taxes within its boundaries. The residential areas of the city, including the poor neighborhoods, share in the property tax revenue generated by the factories, the central business district, and the commerical establishments. School districts are thus able to pool all of the available tax resources and redistribute them according

TABLE 6-3

WHERE PROPERTY TAXES GO: CITY AND SUBURB

Net Taxes on a $20,000 Home in the Central City
and a Suburb in Ramsey County, Minnesota

Saint Paul (central city) $465.10		Maplewood (suburb) $530.84	
Schools	38.97%	Schools	70.53%
County	19.24%	County	16.86%
City	38.81%	Village	10.97%
Other	2.98%	Other	1.64%
	100.00%		100.00%

Source: *Ramsey County Services and Taxes: 1970,* compiled by Thomas J. Kelley, County Auditor, Saint Paul, Minnesota.

---

to their priorities and their estimations of the public needs. If poor neighborhoods fail to get their fair share of these resources, the fault lies not in the lack of local resources but in the inequities of the established priorities.[41]

In most suburbs, however, the opposite situation prevails. There is no mechanism for sharing property tax resources. This fiscal imbalance has led to what the Advisory Commission on Intergovernmental Relations calls "the rise of lopsided communities."[42] The suburban school district with expensive homes, light industry, and elegant shopping centers will of necessity enjoy tremendous advantages over a neighboring school district that has lower-status homes, no industry, and no shopping centers. Table 6-4 illustrates this very graphically by showing the property tax disparities for municipalities and school districts in one Minnesota central city county. In this one county the range in actual tax payments on a house with a taxable assessed value of $10,000 (the equivalent of about a $30,000 house) varied from a minimum of $889.78 in Saint Anthony to a maximum of $1285.07 in Vadnais Heights. The tax differed by almost $400 for no other reason than the different tax rates. Even within Vadnais Heights, if a family built their $30,000 home on one side of the street, in the 624 school district, their taxes would be $183 higher than if they built on the other side of the street, in the 625 school district.

These disparities in tax resources, it must be pointed out, do not derive from the fact of the multi-centered metropolis itself, as much as from the fact that the multi-centered metropolis relies so heavily for its

TABLE 6-4

MILL RATES FOR 1973 PROPERTY TAXES IN RAMSEY COUNTY

Municipality and School District No.[a]	Local	County	Schools[b]	Misc.	Total Rate
Arden Hills — 621 (R)	9.471	22.241	65.391	4.046	101.149
Arden Hills — 623 (R)	9.471	22.241	64.362	4.046	100.120
Blaine — 621 (R)	14.443	22.241	65.391	4.218	106.293
Falcon Heights — 623	8.734	22.241	64.362	3.644	98.981
Falcon Heights — 623 (R)	8.734	22.241	64.362	4.046	99.383
Gem Lake — 624	3.713	22.241	83.699	3.644	113.297
Lauderdale — 623	5.738	22.241	64.362	3.644	95.985
Lauderdale — 623 (R)	5.738	22.241	64.362	4.046	96.387
Little Canada — 623	6.820	22.241	64.362	3.644	97.067
Little Canada — 624	6.820	22.241	83.699	3.644	116.404
Maplewood — 622	12.090	22.241	69.183	3.644	107.158
Maplewood — 622 (V)	12.090	22.241	69.183	4.462	107.976
Maplewood — 623	12.090	22.241	64.362	3.644	102.337
Mounds View — 621 (R)	12.768	22.241	65.391	4.218	104.618
New Brighton — 282 (R)	11.728	22.241	55.407	4.046	93.422
New Brighton — 621 (R)	11.728	22.241	65.391	4.046	103.406
North Oaks — 621	2.839	22.241	65.391	3.644	94.115
North Oaks — 624	2.839	22.241	83.699	3.644	112.423
North St. Paul — 622	9.942	22.241	69.183	3.644	105.010
North St. Paul — 622 (V)	9.942	22.241	69.183	4.462	105.828
Roseville — 621	11.648	22.241	65.391	3.644	102.924
Roseville — 621 (R)	11.648	22.241	65.391	4.046	103.326
Roseville — 623	11.648	22.241	64.362	3.644	101.895
Roseville — 623 (R)	11.648	22.241	64.362	4.046	102.297
St. Anthony — 282 (R)	7.284	22.241	55.407	4.046	88.978
St. Paul — 625	34.242	22.241	50.779	4.059	111.321
Shoreview — 621	12.711	22.241	65.391	3.644	103.987
Shoreview — 621 (R)	12.711	22.241	65.391	4.046	104.389
Shoreview — 623	12.711	22.241	64.362	3.644	102.958
Shoreview — 623 (R)	12.711	22.241	64.362	4.046	103.360
Spring Lake Park — 621 (R)	11.354	22.241	65.391	4.218	103.204
Vadnais Heights — 621	18.923	22.241	65.391	3.644	110.199
Vadnais Heights — 624	18.923	22.241	83.699	3.644	128.507
White Bear Lake — 624	14.990	22.241	83.699	3.644	124.574
White Bear Lake — 624 (R)	14.990	22.241	83.699	4.046	124.976
White Bear Lake — 624 (V)	14.990	22.241	83.699	4.462	125.392
Town of White Bear — 621	.570	22.241	65.391	3.644	91.846
Town of White Bear — 621 (R)	.570	22.241	65.391	4.046	92.248
Town of White Bear — 624	.570	22.241	83.699	3.644	110.154
Town of White Bear — 624 (R)	.570	22.241	83.699	4.046	110.556
Town of White Bear — 624 (V)	.570	22.241	83.699	4.462	110.972

[a] R = Rice Creek Watershed District; V = Valley Branch Watershed District.
[b] Includes 2.648 mills for Intermediate S.D. 916. Does not apply in S.D. 282 and 625.

Source: Report to Ramsey County Taxpayers: Schedule of Mill Rates for 1973 Taxes, prepared by Department of Property Taxation, Saint Paul, Minnesota.

tax revenue upon locally imposed property taxes. In order to alleviate these disparities, most states have taken steps to provide state aid to local school districts. The state aids normally derive from state sales taxes or income taxes and are normally distributed among the state's school districts according to complex formulas based on the number of pupils and the fiscal needs of the school districts. Federal aid to education has not been of much benefit in alleviating the deficiencies of the property tax.[43]

The most dramatic attempt to alleviate fiscal disparities in recent years was a California Supreme Court decision to strike down property taxes as the means for financing public education.[44] Since financing schools by locally derived property taxes necessarily means that some school children will live in districts that have fewer tax resources than other districts have, it was argued that this method of financing public schools violates the equal protection clause of the federal Constitution. Although this decision was reversed by the federal courts, it sparked considerable interest among the states to find solutions to the problem of fiscal disparities. One of the most imaginative approaches was that of Minnesota. In 1971 the state of Minnesota passed a Fiscal Disparities Act which provided that some property taxes be shared. By this act, 40 percent of all commercial property tax base created in the metropolitan Twin Cities after 1971 is allotted to a metropolitan pool which is then distributed according to an equitable formula among all the municipalities and school districts of the metropolitan region. Even though this law has been in operation for only a short time, and even though it affected the tax base only for commercial property constructed since 1971, it has already begun to redistribute the property tax resources in that metropolitan area.[45]

Despite attempts to iron out the differences in property tax inequities, most suburban municipalities and school districts in the United States still rely heavily on local property taxes for their revenue. As long as this remains the case, the multi-centered metropolis will continue to separate public needs from available public resources. This separation will obviously continue to favor the residents of areas with the public resources (i.e., the suburbs with a substantial tax base) and disfavor the residents of both central cities and suburbs with a poor tax base.

Private Wealth and Public Penury

These fiscal disparities have led to scrimping on public services in the less affluent suburbs. Unless it is extraordinarily rich, a suburb of

10,000 people is hard put to provide all the urban services its residents may demand. Sewer and water lines may have to be provided. Police and fire protection will have to be made available. Libraries, swimming pools, sidewalks will be wanted. And the fast growing suburb will come under pressure to provide them all at once.

The various approaches to providing these services without giving up suburban autonomy will be discussed in the following three chapters. One of the most common strategies of the poorer suburbs is what Robert Wood refers to as the "strategy of the unwashed"; that is, simply to scrimp and do without all but the most necessary of services.[46]

Uncontrolled Sprawl

If there is any one distinguishing physical feature of the North American metropolis, it is the sprawl of the suburbs over the countryside. This sprawl is accentuated by the fact that control over zoning decisions is left in the hands of individual suburban municipalities. A study of zoning disputes in New York concluded that although individual zoning decisions "do not appear to have great significance by themselves, the total metropolitan development pattern is the result of a patchwork of local decisions, overlaid by transportation networks imposed by the state and Federal governments."[47]

The multi-centered metropolis prevents a coherent approach to controlling metropolitan growth, to channeling the growth into areas designed for it, and to preserving other areas for permanent recreational green spaces or drainage, or even for vital groundwater recharge purposes. Despite the suburbs' lower population densities, they often have less park space or recreational space per capita than do the central cities. Typically, suburban growth has occurred before sewer and water lines were constructed, which in many areas has posed a threat to the safety of the water supply. Furthermore, the outer suburbs are characterized by very low density, and the population concentrations are often separated by great distances. When low-density suburbs finally are forced to install public sewers and water supplies, the cost of these is much higher than it would have been if the growth had been planned in conjunction with the need for utilities. In the face of all this, suburban land use policies, particularly zoning laws, have been very unsuccessful in regulating where and under what conditions developers can build. Despite the ineffectiveness of suburban zoning controls, suburbanites tend to oppose vociferously any attempts to transfer zoning powers to a higher level of government, such as the county.[48]

Loss of Accountability for Public Decisions

Although the suburbs were supposed to bring the government closer to the citizen, evidence indicates that on many vital questions the opposite has occurred.[49] Retention of the multi-centered metropolis has necessitated a proliferation of single-purpose governments to provide the services which the suburban municipalities cannot provide individually. Since the municipalities, the metropolitan authorities, and the state and federal agencies all exercise some portion of responsibility in any given suburban municipality, it is virtually impossible for the ordinary citizen to know which government is responsible for what.

Proliferation of Governments

Perhaps the most visible consequence of the multi-centered metropolis has been the proliferation of governments, principally of municipalities and special districts. Beginning early in the twentieth century and extending to the 1960s, state legislatures made it relatively easy for metropolitan fringe communities to incorporate. As will be discussed in the following chapters, part of the motivation for this was to avoid annexation by the central cities.

The Metropolitan Syndrome

In conclusion, a metropolitan syndrome had emerged by the late 1950s. Outlying suburban populations grew faster than the ability of local governments to supply services to them. Small service districts proliferated. Wide disparities developed in the level of public services that were provided in different areas of the metropolis. Similarly, wide disparities developed in the property tax rates. The social consequences of the metropolitan syndrome had deleterious effects on the racial minorities, who were systematically excluded or zoned out of the more prestigious suburbs. The physical well-being of the suburbs themselves was threatened when, because of the inability to provide basic public services such as water and sewers, excessive reliance on septic tanks and private wells led to pollution of water supplies. And the proliferation of muncipal governments and special districts seemed to indicate that the whole pattern of metropolitan growth had gotten beyond control. Clearly some drastic steps were in order.

BIAS IN THE MULTI-CENTERED METROPOLIS

The foregoing discussion has shown that certain people derive benefits because of the governmental and political structure of the multi-centered metropolis. Certain other people are disfavored.

The poor and the racial minorities are most directly disfavored by the multi-centered metropolis. Because the multi-centered metropolis separates public needs from available resources and because of the discrepancy between private wealth and public penury, local governments in the metropolis are not able to apply all of their potential resources to programs that deal with the special problems of the poor and the racial minorities. Because local municipalities can use their zoning powers to minimize the moving in of low-income residents, low-income families (both white and black) are prevented from living near the places where the most dynamic growth is occurring both in jobs and in economic opportunities — around the suburban shopping centers.

Some researchers have presented evidence that the suburbs are not promoting extensive integration either racially or socioeconomically.* This bias of the multi-centered metropolis has had several results, particularly on public education. The poorest school districts are populated with the lowest-income residents and the most affluent school districts with upper-middle-income residents. In metropolises with large minority populations, central city schools have higher percentages of minority pupils. Furthermore, the greater the proliferation of governments in a metropolis, the more likely that metropolis is to have large disparities in average income between its municipalities.[50]

Theoretically, this bias against the racial minorities and the poor *does not necessarily have to result* from the multi-centered metropolis. It is conceivable that within the existing pattern of suburban development, property taxes could be equalized, minorities could be given access to the better school districts, transit systems could be built to give inner city residents easy access to suburban job locations, and low-income public housing could be relocated into the suburbs. But the controversy that has erupted over attempts to put these measures into practice indicates that significantly reducing the bias will be terribly difficult. Considerable progress has been made over the past decade,

---

* A study of suburbs of Buffalo, New York, and Milwaukee, Wisconsin, found very little class integration [Richard F. Hamilton, *Class and Politics in the United States* (New York: Wiley, 1972), pp. 155–180].

and progress will probably continue to be made in coming years. But, on balance, the contemporary state of governmental dispersion in the suburbs remains biased against the poor and the racial minorities.

A second bias of the multi-centered metropolis favors those who profit from uncontrolled sprawl — particularly land speculators, real estate developers, and large retailing enterprises. Local municipalities, which make zoning decisions in most metropolises, seldom turn down proposed real estate developments that will increase the local community's tax base, such as shopping centers or expensive single-family homes. Nor do they consider how the development fits into area-wide growth patterns. And once the overall permission for a shopping center is granted, specific decisions as to the kinds of shops and their owners or managers may be left to the shopping center management, without input from the local municipality or residents.

Although it is clear that the multi-centered metropolis favors large-scale developers by granting them considerable autonomy in their operations, it is not as clear who is directly hurt by this process. Nor is it clear that the direct profits of development would be more widely shared if zoning decisions were made at the metropolitan rather than the municipal level. As Chapters 10 and 11 discuss, considerable pressure has been brought on legislatures and the federal government to enact more rigorous land use regulations.

A third bias may exist in the multi-centered metropolis: a bias against the public good. To the extent that the "public good" consists of the objectives of minimizing pollution, protecting open space, equalizing the availability of public services, and equalizing access to housing, shopping, employment, and educational facilities, then contemporary suburbia is probably biased against the public good. But it is doubtful that universal agreement exists that these objectives constitute the public interest. Furthermore, many steps have been taken toward many of these objectives in the past decade.

Finally, the multi-centered metropolis is biased against effective citizen input. With such a wide variety of government agencies dealing with any given geographical region, concerned citizens may find it extremely difficult to express grievances effectively because they do not know which agency has responsibility for their particular grievance. In theory, suburbanites are very close to their city council and their school board, and they are much more likely to know one of these officials personally than are central city residents. But they also are likely to discover that some of the most important governmental activities that concern them — street light location, sewerage, transit service, welfare problems, and in some suburbs even water supply, fire protection, and police protection — are not handled by these local officials. The description that follows shows by how much the *theory* of small-town Jeffersonian democracy differs from the *fact*.

> So when a group of Port Washington parents decided in September of 1970 that a light was needed on Main Street to help shepherd children between the elementary school and the library, they found a jumble of jurisdictions. The school on the south side of the street was located in an unincorporated area of Port Washington, therefore controlled by the township. The library on the north side was located in the Village of Baxter Estates. The street itself was a county road, but located in and patrolled by the Port Washington Police District, which is independent of the village, town, and county. Traffic lights on county roads are the responsibility of, naturally, the county. However, parking on the street falls under the jurisdiction of the town. As a result, the parents' request for the traffic light, made through the library board of trustees, ended up being passed from one jurisdiction to another. Finally, the county in December turned down the request and recommended that the police district propose to the town the elimination of parking on a section of the street, on the spurious theory that speeding drivers and anxious children would have a better view of each other.[51]

THE MULTI-CENTERED METROPOLIS: VIABLE? DESIRABLE?

Questions naturally arise whether the multi-centered metropolis, with its consequences and biases, is a desirable phenomenon and whether it is even viable. The question of desirability is basically a value question in which one's response will largely depend on how one assesses the consequences and biases mentioned above. Those who think that these consequences and biases are inherent to the system generally seek an overall restructuring of metropolitan government. Those who think that the system is basically sound seek to preserve and perfect it by amendment.[52]

The question of the viability of the multi-centered metropolis is essentially an empirical question. If the heart of the multi-centered metropolis is the independent suburban municipality, what measures must be taken to preserve suburban autonomy and still provide the services which suburban residents demand? If the multi-centered metropolises have caused the consequences and biases indicated above, what measures must be taken to cope with these consequences and biases? The next three chapters analyze the approaches taken to solving these problems.

Some Suggested Readings

Scott Donaldson, *The Suburban Myth* (New York: Columbia University Press, 1969). An interesting and readable critique of the antisuburban literature.

Frederick M. Wirt, Benjamin Walter, Francine F. Rabinovitz, and Deborah R. Hensler, *On the City's Rim: Politics and Policy in Suburbia* (Lexington, Mass.: D. C. Heath, 1972). This is the most comprehensive book to date on suburban politics.

Herbert J. Gans, *The Levittowners: Ways of Life and Politics in a New Suburban Community* (New York: Vintage Books, 1967). Gans, a prominent sociologist, moved into Levittown in order to conduct this important study.

Robert C. Wood, *Suburbia: Its People and Their Politics* (Boston: Houghton Mifflin, 1958). Although somewhat dated, Wood's book is important for its interpretation of suburbia as a reincarnation of the Jeffersonian ideal of small-town democracy.

Bennett M. Berger, *Working Class Suburbs* (Berkeley and Los Angeles: University of California Press, 1960). Somewhat dated, but a useful description of a suburb which does not fit the stereotype of suburbs as upper middle class.

Leo F. Schnore, "The Social and Economic Characteristics of American Suburbs," *The Sociological Quarterly* 4, no. 2 (Spring 1963): 122–134. Makes the distinction between employment, residential, and mixed suburbs.

William H. Whyte, Jr., *The Organization Man* (Garden City, N.Y.: Doubleday, 1957), part VII, "The New Suburbia: Organization Man at Home." A study of the upper-middle-class suburb of Park Forest, Illinois. This book was a major contributor to creating the stereotype of a homogeneous, upper-middle-class suburbia.

John Kramer, ed., *North American Suburbs: Politics, Diversity, and Change* (Berkeley, Calif.: Glendessery Press, 1972). A collection of readings on suburbs.

Karl A. Lamb, *As Orange Goes: Twelve California Familes and the Future of American Politics* (New York: Norton, 1974). An in-depth, three-year study of people and politics in one of America's most famous suburban counties.

Chapter 7

A major task of governments in metropolitan areas has been to cope with the consequences of the multi-centered metropolis, outlined in the previous chapter. *At a minimum*, pressures have increased rather than decreased for urban governments to provide services for the growing populations in the suburbs. But the pressures upon urban governments are rarely put in minimal terms. Urban governments are usually pressured by a variety of groups not only to provide at least minimum levels of service for all residents, but also to equalize tax inequities, to find the resources to satisfy public needs, to control suburban sprawl,

Strategies for Avoiding Metropolitan Government

and to simplify the overlapping and complex structure of governments in metropolitan areas.

DEALING WITH THE CONSEQUENCES OF THE MULTI-CENTERED METROPOLIS

How urban governments should cope with the problems associated with the multi-centered metropolis has been the subject of considerable dispute involving a wide spectrum of opinions and value judgments. At one end of the spectrum are those persons who believe that the problems cannot be dealt with unless the whole system of governments is scrapped and a new, general-purpose government is established at the metropolitan level. At the other end of the spectrum are those who believe that adequate methods of governing the metropolis can be achieved without resort to a metropolitan government as such. The disagreement between these two fundamentally different approaches to coping with metropolitanization underlies the conflicts over metropolitan political reforms which are discussed in the next four chapters. Before looking at specific strategies for metropolitan governmental reform, it will be useful to contrast these two theoretical approaches. Some acquaintance with the spokesmen for and the basic tenets of each approach is necessary in order to understand the fundamental changes which are occurring in the governance of the metropolis.

The Scrap-the-System-and-Start-Over School of Thought

According to those who would scrap the whole contemporary system of metropolitan governments and start over, the flaws of the multi-centered metropolis are so deeply rooted in its chaotic governmental structure that the structure itself must be rebuilt. The efficacy of the present governmental apparatus is brought into question. And the apparatus itself is seen as antidemocratic, not accountable to the electorate, inefficient, and unconducive to meaningful citizen participation. This is a devastating indictment of the present system, and it is presented by some distinguished scholars and prestigious organizations.

The argument that the present system is antidemocratic is made most forcefully, perhaps, by political scientist Robert Wood.[1] Participation in suburban political affairs is very limited. Election turnouts in suburban municipal elections are much lower than are turnouts for corresponding elections in the central cities or even for county offices. And the attempt of the suburbs to recapture the Jeffersonian ideal of small-town democracy very close to the people is misleading, for such small-town governments are seldom truly democratic. Even the famed town meetings of colonial New England inevitably fell under the dominance of a few local elites. For Wood, the big, "gargantuan" city provides a much better forum for the exercise of democratic values than does the proliferation of hundreds of small municipalities in suburbia.

The notion that small suburban governments are somehow closer to the people than large city governments is also challenged. Sociologist Scott Greer claimed that because the large city governments deal with more important issues than do small suburban governments, they dominate the media and capture people's attention. Suburban governments, in contrast, deal with such small issues that they "trivialize" local politics. Consequently, in the sense of getting people's attention and dealing with issues that are important to them, "the government of the greater urban polity is 'closer to the people' — they see its symbols with their morning coffee."[2]

Perhaps the most common complaint against the multi-centered metropolis is its seeming inability to equalize the costs and benefits of government.[3] The Advisory Commission on Intergovernmental Relations (ACIR) has focused considerable attention on this issue, has attributed many of the inequities to the fragmentation of governmental authority, and has made several recommendations to improve the structure of local government.[4] The commission especially recommended a reduction in the number of special districts and local governments and encouraged steps that would lead to metropolitan and regional-level governments.

Finally, and perhaps most forcefully, a general-purpose government at the metropolitan level is felt to be needed for reasons of efficiency, administrative competence, and matching the level of government with the level of problems.[5] Political scientist Luther Gulick argues that many metropolitan problems — such as water supply, sewage disposal, and air pollution — are area-wide problems that can only be handled on an area-wide basis. To handle them on any other basis is to take indivisible problems and try to divide them up among many governments.[6] Two other scholars, Amos H. Hawley and Basil G. Zimmer, have argued that the contemporary multi-centered metropolis is characterized by the traits of "governmental chaos, of producing and service inefficiency and of administrative impotence."[7] In their minds, the only reasonable solution to this chaos is to "consolidate the many political units under a single, overarching municipal government."[8]

Institutionally, the most prestigious advocate of metropolitan government in recent years has probably been the Committee for Economic Development (CED), an organization of civic-minded businesspeople. CED was concerned about the two interrelated problems of efficacy at the metropolitan level and responsiveness to citizens at the local level. To meet these two needs, CED recommended that governments in metropolitan areas be entirely reshaped into a two-tier, federative-type system. As an excellent example of how this should be done, the CED cited the reorganization of government in metropolitan Toronto.[9]

The Metropolitan-Governance-without-a-Metropolitan-Government School of Thought

Despite these arguments for performing major surgery on the structure of governments in the metropolis, very few major surgeries have taken place.[10] Seldom has it been concluded that the Jeffersonian ideal of small-town democracy ought to be scrapped in suburbia and replaced with a general-purpose metropolitan government. Suburban residents are generally unconcerned about the proliferation of governments in the metropolis.[11] And rather than make sweeping changes in governmental structures, local officials generally prefer to make incremental changes when they become necessary to deal with specific problems that arise. These incremental changes tend to protect and preserve the status quo and avoid any fundamental alterations in the governmental apparatus.

It would be a mistake, however, to think that metropolitan reform is opposed only by self-seeking, petty, small-time politicans. Some prominent scholars have raised several disturbing questions about the logic of those who would make basic alterations in the government of the metropolis.

Political scientist Charles Adrian has charged as unrealistic many of the assumptions that underlay the proposals to establish general-purpose metropolitan governments.[12] One of these assumptions was the belief that the central city must continue to prosper and expand with the central business district as the main focal point for the metropolis. This assumption may be incompatible with the ways in which metropolises grow. As pointed out in Chapter 2, the uni-centered city, built around a central business district, may be simply one stage in the history of urban growth. And Chapter 12 will show that the tendency of metropolitan growth to spill beyond the boundaries of central cities is a process that occurs in other countries as well as in the United States. Thus metropolitan growth is more than simply the proliferation of suburban municipalities.

Adrian also charges that reformers are unrealistic when they argue that metropolitan governments should be created so that needed services can be provided much more efficiently and economically. The suburban "merchant or homeowner may value other things higher — in particular, access to decision-making centers and representativeness of local government."[13] A study of suburbanites' attitudes in six different metropolitan areas also found that suburbanites were not greatly perturbed over the inadequacy of their public services. Even where they were concerned about the inadequacy of services, they seldom believed that a metropolitan government would improve the service.[14] Furthermore, the reformers' belief that metropolitan government would save money through its professional administration and its practice of economies of scale is not very convincing to many opponents of metropolitan government. Political scientists Vincent and Elinor Ostrom have argued that recent public administration studies of selected public services tend to refute the notion that highly bureaucratized and centralized administration is more efficient than a proliferation of autonomous, smaller administrations that can compete with one another.[15] Political scientists Edward C. Banfield and Morton Grodzins discuss a point of diminishing returns beyond which economies of scale do not save money. Costs per unit of services decrease up to about 50,000 people, but they do not seem to decrease after that.[16] Also, since the level of public services in suburbia is likely to vary greatly, any attempts to even out these services could only mean bringing the service levels of the poorer suburbs up to the levels of the richer suburbs. And this undoubtedly would mean more expenditures. Although nobody has conducted an extensive empirical analysis of this question, an appraisal of metropolitan government reforms in Toronto, Nashville, and Dade County concluded that expenditures in fact had increased since the adoption of metropolitan government.[17] Even though expenditures increased, the services could still have been operating at greater efficiency than previously. But average voters are more likely to be concerned with the net impact of the services on their property tax bill than with internal administrative efficiencies or with the costs per capita of the services. And empirical evidence does indicate that average suburbanites think that the creation of a metropolitan government would indeed raise their taxes.[18]

Finally, according to Adrian, the reformers' belief that professional administration is preferable to part-time, amateur administration may be at odds with the preferences of the majority of suburbanites. To the homeowner, "amateur fire fighters provide enough services to meet his demands."[19] Many of the volunteer services such as fire fighting perform an important symbolic function in suburbia. Countless suburbs in the United States view the volunteer fire department as a source of local civic pride. The local newspaper proudly notes how swiftly the volunteer firemen can respond to the fire siren, arrive from their scattered locations, and meet the fire truck just as it arrives at the scene of the fire. Local suburban Lions Clubs and Rotary Clubs generate enormous symbolic support for local governmental structures when they engage in money-raising activities to purchase rescue squad equipment, thus saving the local taxpayers thousands of dollars.

In addition to Adrian's questions of whether the demand to create general-purpose metropolitan governments is based on realistic assumptions, a second question is whether one can even talk realistically of such an entity as a metropolitan community. Political scientist Norton Long, who is a veteran of one major metropolitan government battle,* has argued persuasively that such a thing as a metropolitan community exists only in the minds of planners and metropolitan reformers.[20] For most people, the sense of community on public policy rarely encompasses the entire metropolis.

A third question that has been raised is whether creation of a metropolitan government is necessary in order to correct the flaws of the multi-centered metropolis. Opponents of metropolitan reform contend that many of the flaws can be corrected simply by continuing to tinker with the existing system. Banfield and Grodzins assert that many of the problems currently referred to as metropolitan problems involve only a portion of the metropolitan area. They therefore question why all the public water supply districts, for example, should be brought under one government. The same question may apply to other services such as solid waste disposal, sewerage, public health, recreation, police, and fire protection.[21]

Closely associated with the argument over what constitutes an area-wide problem is the argument over what ought to constitute the political boundaries of a metropolitan area. Banfield and Grodzins attack the notion that political boundaries ought to correspond to features of the natural environment; in many parts of the country, they point out, no clear-cut delineation exists between one area and another. According to the logic of the reformers — that the natural geographic metropolitan area should be under a single government — the numerous contiguous SMSAs along the megalopolis of the Atlantic seacoast should all be under one form of government.

Finally, several important value questions are involved in restructuring metropolitan government. Two of the most important relate to the political voice of the racial minorities and the problems of equalizing services and taxes throughout the metropolis. Concerning the first, Frances Fox Piven and Richard A. Cloward have argued that the creation of metropolitan government would dilute black influence in many central cities. They argue very persuasively that "many urban problems remain unsolved, not for lack of areawide planning, but for lack of political will."[22]

The arguments that the benefits and costs of the government in any given metropolitan area ought to be equalized also run into opposition. Should all services be equal throughout the metropolitan area? Or should all areas simply be required to provide minimal standards of

* Long was involved in the battle for the home rule charter in Cuyahoga County. This is analyzed in Chapter 9.

services? Once the minimal standards are achieved, should wealthier areas be allowed to maintain levels of services that are above the minimum? Banfield and Grodzins answer the last two questions affirmatively.[23] But among the vital services involved are education, public health facilities, and libraries. And it is difficult for this writer to admit that some residents of the metropolis should have inferior schools, hospitals, and libraries simply because they live in a portion of the metropolis that has no shopping center or commercial real estate, while other residents should have superior schools, hospitals, and libraries simply because their area of the metropolis is benefited by such tax-generating establishments.

A more sophisticated version of the same argument is presented by Vincent Ostrom, Charles M. Tiebout, and Robert Warren, who compare metropolitan governance to a free market economy. Just as business firms compete with each other by producing or marketing goods, so do metropolitan municipalities compete with each other by producing or marketing public services. And this creates a "quasi-market choice for local residents in permitting them to select the particular community in the metropolitan area that most closely approximates the public service levels they desire." The net result is a "very rich and intricate 'framework' for negotiating, adjudicating, and deciding questions that affect their diverse public interests."[24]

Three problems arise with this free market economy as the model for producing and distributing public services in the metropolis. First, the availability of certain public services becomes dependent upon whether the citizen can afford to live in a given muncipality. The school district with the highest per-pupil expenditures is likely to be found in the suburban areas with the most expensive homes. Citizens who cannot afford such homes have no free market choice for their decision not to take advantage of these superior expenditures on public education. While some private goods may legitimately be distributed on the basis of higher-quality goods to different classes of recipients, public services are normally distributed indivisibly on an equal basis to all classes of recipients.[25] In the realm of public education, at least one attempt has been made in state courts[26] to establish the concept that such free market models of providing public services may violate the Fourteenth Amendment to the United States Constitution, which states: "No state may deny any of its citizens the equal protection of the laws."*

---

* It should be noted, however, that the federal courts eventually rejected the contention that locally financed school districts violate the equal protection clause of the Constitution. See *Rodriguez v. San Antonio School District*, 93 S. Ct. 1278 (1973).

Second, the free market model of metropolitan governance apparently assumes that the provision of public services needs no more governance than the provision of private goods and services. Even in the theoretical free market model of the economy, however, some overall regulation of the economy is necessary, either by the government or by a supposedly invisible hand which guides the market place. If the provision of public municipal services in the metropolis performs according to free market rules, then the regulation of public services of necessity becomes, as Matthew Holden has so aptly phrased it, a problem in diplomacy.[27] To state that there is a limited analogy between metropolitan governance and either a free market economy or international diplomacy is one thing; to posit it as a model for the way in which urban services ought to be provided in the metropolis is quite another thing. That transforms an empirical judgment into a normative judgment. Furthermore, it provides a theoretical justification for what is in most metropolises a very inequitable distribution of public services.

Finally, the free market model of the metropolis is valid only to the extent that the free market model of the economy is valid. And if free market economies ever existed in the world, they certainly do not today. To posit the free market model as a norm to be adopted in the political sphere in urban America is to promote an economic model that does not exist even in the economic sphere.

Still undiscussed is the proposal that the people obviously want a multi-centered metropolis. Simply by moving to suburbia, post–World War II Americans have chosen small-town governance. They have also voted for it with their ballots; as Chapters 8 and 9 will show, voters have rejected an overwhelming majority of metropolitan government referendums put before them. For services that the small suburban municipalities could not handle, voters preferred that these services be removed from the arena of partisan politics by establishing a big-business type of special district organization to handle them on a supposedly nonpolitical basis. But establishing a metropolitan-level, general-purpose government would return politics to the administration of these services. And that was undesired. In the words of Robert Wood, the choices of the residents of the metropolis were limited to two: "Grassroots democracy or big business — no other vehicle is trustworthy in the United States."[28] Confronted with such an apparent array of citizen preferences for the multi-centered metropolis, any arguments against it were often dismissed as elitist, antidemocratic, or politically unrealistic.

There is a grain of truth in this assertion that a metropolitan-level government might be antidemocratic. But there is also an anti-democratic strain in the prevailing structures of governments in the multi-centered metropolis. To the extent that the governing institutions in the multi-centered metropolis are not accountable to the electorate and to the extent that they are more responsive to functional interest groups than they are to the citizenry at large, then to that extent the multi-centered metropolis itself is also elitist and antidemocratic. Furthermore, to the extent that the very structure of the multi-centered metropolis systematically excludes certain classes (such as racial minorities) or certain geographic areas (such as those suburbs that lack a high property tax base) from equal access to the major tax revenues of the metropolis, then to that extent it violates the spirit if not the letter of the constitutional provision that no state may deny any of its citizens the equal protection of the law. This argument, however, has not been accepted by the United States Supreme Court.*

These considerations show the sharp differences in value orientations between the approach that would scrap the whole system and the approach that seeks governance without a metropolitan government. It is not quite so apparent, however, that one approach is more democratic than the other. The notion that the multi-centered metropolis is nothing more than the democratic, free market choice for millions of post–World War II Americans certainly has to be rejected, for the very choices that were available to the millions of migrants to suburbia were structured by decisions and nondecisions that had been taken by both the federal government and the state governments.

FEDERAL AND STATE ROLES IN CREATING THE MULTI-CENTERED METROPOLIS

The federal and state governments played significant roles in the evolution of governmental structures in the metropolis, and these roles will be described in detail in Chapter 11. This chapter only indicates how they supported the creation and maintenance of the multi-centered metropolis. The federal government did this in three ways. First, Federal Housing Administration (FHA) and Veterans' Administration (VA) mortgages provided an enormous subsidy for the construction of new residences on a large-scale basis beyond the central city boundaries.

* The United States Supreme Court has, on questions of financing public schools, explicitly rejected this argument [Rodriguez v. San Antonio School District, 93 S. Ct. 1278 (1973)].

Federal highway programs, especially the establishment of the interstate highway system and the highway trust fund by the Federal Aid Highway Act of 1956, facilitated the development of the transportation network that would be needed for a widely dispersed population to be integrated into the metropolitan community. Together, these programs contributed greatly to suburbanization.

A second aspect of the federal role, which will be discussed later in this chapter, is the encouragement it gave to the formation and maintenance of special districts to administer federal programs dealing with public housing and with natural resources. Third, and perhaps most significantly, until 1965 the federal government took little action to coordinate its various programs, to tie them to general urban policies, or to relate them to community development. One result was to stimulate not only uncontrolled suburbanization but, at least in the Northeast, to subsidize the transformation of the central city into, as Norton Long expressed it, a "reservation for the poor, the deviant, the unwanted, and for those who make a business or career of managing them for the rest of society."[29]

The federal role in stimulating the multi-centered metropolis was the result of positive actions which the federal government took to establish programs to meet specific needs. The state roles, to the contrary, were largely roles played through inaction rather than action. The state role can be seen principally in the areas of legislative apportionment, state tendencies toward annexation and consolidation of governments, and limitations which have been established on the powers and debt limits of general-purpose local governments. The last two roles are discussed later in this chapter in reference to special districts and annexation. Legislative apportionment relates to the multi-centered metropolis primarily because the rural-dominated state legislatures tended to be unsympathetic to urban problems and for so many years tended to ignore them. But ignoring the urban problems did not cause them to disappear, and local governments in the metropolis were obliged to resort to a variety of devices to cope with the problems within the limitations of powers that state governments granted them. Consequently, the major thrust of recommendations for state action in metropolitan governance focuses on legislation to strengthen general-purpose local governments and legislation to strengthen state-level capabilities to cope with metropolitanization.[30] As reapportioned state legislatures during the 1960s began to reflect more accurately the population concentrations of the metropolises, the legislatures have in fact become more active on urban problems.[31]

STRATEGIES TO PRESERVE THE STATUS QUO

Given the ideological biases against general-purpose metropolitan government and the peculiar roles played by both the federal and state governments in the emergence of metropolitan United States, it is not surprising that the earliest strategies for coping with metropolitan problems tended to protect the status quo. One of the most serious suburban problems was that of finding the physical and financial resources needed to supply urban services such as streets, sidewalks, sewers, water, lighting, schools, and police and fire protection. The traditional ways of financing these improvements through locally imposed property taxes obviously became more and more impossible as the services themselves, especially schools, became exceedingly expensive. The attempts to reimplant small-town democracy on the fringes of the metropolis caused most suburban cities to end up, financially speaking, with the worst of both worlds. On the one hand, they were too small to possess the broad tax resources of the central city or to practice its economies of scale. And on the other hand, they were too numerous, and too competitive, for any one of them to become the commercial center for a broad geographic region, as was characteristic of rural small towns. In the rural small town, a natural ecology limited the population growth to the number of families and business enterprises needed to serve the surrounding rural area. The suburban small town had no such natural limit on population growth. And the suburban cities' services quickly became overburdened. The most obvious way to compensate for these disadvantages was for each city to (1) attract commerce or industry in order to broaden its tax base, and (2) restrict its housing supply to relatively expensive homes that would add to the property tax base.

Although this course of action was a reasonable one for individual suburbs to follow, for metropolitan areas as entities it was a formula for disastrous competition for commercial and high-value residential real estate which would increase the local property tax base. Since there was seldom enough industry to go around, there were more losers than winners in the competition.[32] This compounded the problem of attracting high-value residential property; and again there were as many losers as winners. In 1972 the city planner of one suburban municipality of Minneapolis–Saint Paul estimated that the break-even point for new housing was approximately $28,000. Houses above that value brought more property tax into the school district than municipal and school district expenses. Houses below that value brought more expenses than they did tax revenue.[33] Consequently, the suburbs were encouraged to restrict new homes to those valued above the break-even point.

At approximately the same time, a study showed that only ten of eighty-one selected municipalities in the same metropolitan area had an average home market value exceeding that amount.[34] In other words, seven of every eight communities were destined to be losers in the competition for high-value homes, no matter what they did. In the community in question, the average home market value was more than $8,000 below the desired amount. And for the metropolis as a whole, the cost of individual homes was driven up to the point where, it was estimated, over 80 percent of the families in the region could not afford to purchase an average-priced new house.[35] The Advisory Commission on Intergovernmental Relations reported similar disparities in the tax structures of most metropolises.[36]

In the quest to provide a reasonable level of services without forsaking the political autonomy of the small town, some alternative had to be found which would at the same time enable the suburbs to use economies of scale in providing services, keep the costs of local government reasonable, and enable them to retain their small-townish image.[37] Special districts and the device of purchasing services from other units of government provided two imaginative and immediate answers to these problems.

Contracting for Services: The Lakewood Plan

When a suburban community was too small to practice economies of scale in supplying services, the most ingenious device created was to separate the production of services from the provisions of services.[38] The production could be left to the municipalities, counties, or special districts large enough to take advantage of economies of scale. The smaller communities could then handle the provision of services by purchasing them from the larger unit. This practice is sometimes referred to as the Lakewood Plan, because the Los Angeles suburb of Lakewood was the first in the nation to exist completely on the basis of purchasing almost all its basic services from another unit of government. In just the four years from 1950 to 1954, Lakewood grew from a sparsely settled farmland to a suburban municipality of 50,000 people. Because Lakewood is the most renowned example of providing its public services by buying them from other governments, its plan is well worth examining for its advantages and its disadvantages.

Prior to 1954, Los Angeles County was allowed to provide its services only in unincorporated areas. The services provided in these unincorporated areas were paid for not only by taxes derived from those areas but also by taxes derived from municipalities that did not receive any of the county's services. Residents of these incorporated municipalities complained that they were being charged for services that went only to the unincorporated areas. And in the unincorporated areas, the residents were beginning to desire more control over their own territory. However, if they incorporated in order to get that control, they would not only lose the services that the county was providing, but they would be subject to the extra tax burden that was levied on the residents of municipalities.[39] The impasse was resolved in 1954 by the compromise known as the Lakewood Plan. The plan allowed suburban municipalities incorporated after 1954 to purchase a package of services from the county. The plan also authorized local sales taxes as an incentive for incorporation. Under the provisions of the Lakewood Plan, Los Angeles County signed over 1600 agreements with all seventy-seven municipalities for over fifty-eight types of services which the county supplies. Some of the major services and the number of cities which purchased each one are shown in Table 7-1.

TABLE 7-1

SERVICES PROVIDED TO CITIES BY THE LOS ANGELES COUNTY GOVERNMENT: 1972

Standard Form Agreement	Cities Contracting for Service	
	Number	Percentage of all cities in the county
Maintenance of city prisoners in county jail	76	99
City health ordinance enforcement	74	96
Subdivision final map checking	70	91
Emergency ambulance program	67	87
General services agreement	65	84
Animal control services	38	49
Hospitalization of city prisoners	37	49
Industrial waste	31	40
Building inspection	30	39
Law enforcement services	29	38
Street constuction and maintenance	28	36
Parcel map checking	14	18
Tree planting and maintenance	5	7

Source: Advisory Commission on Intergovernmental Relations, *Report A–44. Substate Regionalism and the Federal System: The Challenge of Local Governmental Reorganization* (Washington, D.C.: U.S. Government Printing Office, 1974), vol. III, p. 71.

From one perspective, the Lakewood Plan and the device of contracting for services was an overwhelming success. It guaranteed local suburban municipalities both their autonomy and the ability to utilize economies of scale in providing municipal services to their residents. Not only did the Lakewood Plan guarantee the existence of suburbs, it even gave them several alternative producers from whom they could purchase the services. They could, in many instances, produce a needed service themselves; they could purchase it from another municipality; they could enter a joint powers agreement with another municipality to provide the service jointly; and, in some instances, they could purchase the service from a private firm. In summary, the Lakewood Plan created a mechanism for translating into reality the free market model of the metropolis. The suburban government was like a shopper entering a supermarket and purchasing the most appropriate products at the lowest price. If the county wanted too high a price for a given service, the purchaser could look elsewhere for a cheaper price.

If the Lakewood Plan solved the immediate dilemma of providing large-scale urban services without sacrificing local autonomy, it was not without its critics. Because of its position as the major producer of services, the county dominates in any bargaining with local municipalities over the quality of services and the costs at which they will be provided. Because of this, local control over services is more an illusion than a reality. The Lakewood Plan also led to a proliferation of municipal government incorporations in the county, because the passage of the plan in 1954 gave tax incentives to suburban residents to incorporate rather than become annexed to the City of Los Angeles or even remain unincorporated. Whereas only two cities incorporated in the county between 1930 and 1950, thirty-two cities have incorporated since the inception of the Lakewood Plan. Some of these new cities were special-interest cities created to secure particular tax advantages. The City of Industry is a tax shelter for factories and warehouses. Another suburb, Dairy Valley, is a farming enclave. In Rolling Hills, all the streets are owned by a private company. And Hidden Hills is literally walled-in. When its gates are closed, outsiders cannot enter.[40]

The Lakewood Plan did not cause the incorporation of these municipalities, but by enabling them to purchase services that they were incapable of producing for themselves, it gave them a tax incentive to incorporate. Since it guaranteed the county government's position as the preeminent producer of public services in the region, county officials or bureaucrats had no incentive to seek a broader, metropolitan-wide government.[41]

Whatever might be the merits of these criticisms, the practice of municipalities purchasing some of their governmental services from other units of government has become very popular. A survey of eighty-six metropolitan counties found that 65 percent of them reported some form of intergovernmental cooperation in the provision of public services among the municipalities within their counties and with neighboring counties.[42] These forms ranged from interlocal agreements, to transfer of functions to a higher level of government, to consolidation of functions.

Special Districts

A second mechanism created to enable vital services to be performed without basically altering the structure of the multi-centered metropolis is the *special district*. The special district is simply an independent government created to perform a specific function such as water supply, sewage disposal, or fire protection. As such, the special district is an autonomous government with its own jurisdiction, its own procedures for selecting its governing board, and usually its own taxing powers. It is not simply an agency of a government, such as a legislature or a given department. It is a government in its own right, just as a city is a government or a school district is a government.

The use of special districts has increased steadily over the past few decades. Until the 1940s there were only about 9000 special districts in the entire country. By 1972 there were 23,000. Of these, over 8000 were found in metropolitan areas in every state except Alaska. Table 7-2, which tabulates changes only in SMSAs, shows that changes in the number of special districts account for over three-fourths of the increases in local governments between 1967 and 1972. The number of school districts declined 12 percent through consolidation, from 5421 to 4758. During the same period, the number of noneducational special districts increased 6.4 percent, from 7569 to 8054, making special districts the most popular device among the metropolitan areas' 22,000 governments. Also evident from the table is the rapid increase in special districts which perform more than one function, although the overwhelming preference is still for single-purpose special districts. The proliferation of special districts has bothered many observers of metropolitan government, and at least five states — California, Nevada, New Mexico, Oregon, and Washington — have taken measures to limit their continued proliferation in SMSAs.[43]

The major reason for the popularity of special districts undoubtedly

TABLE 7-2

INCIDENCE OF SPECIAL DISTRICT GOVERNMENTS IN SMSAs: 1962, 1967, 1972

Kind of Local Government	Number in SMSAs			Change from 1967 to 1972[a]	
	1962[a]	1967	1972	No.	%
School districts	7,072	5,421	4,758	−663	−12.2
Towns and townships	3,282	3,485	3,462	−23	−0.7
Counties	447	447	444	−3	−0.7
Municipalities	4,903	5,319	5,467	+148	+2.8
Special districts	6,153	7,569	8,054	+485	+6.4
Single-purpose	NA	7,288	7,492		
Multi-purpose[b]	NA	281	562		
	19,589	22,241	22,185	−56	−0.3

[a] The 1962 data refer only to the SMSAs existing at that time. The increase or decrease computations refer only to changes from 1967 to 1972 in the 264 SMSAs existing in 1972.
[b] The 1967 number of multi-purpose districts refers only to number of multi-purpose districts in 1967 SMSAs, not 1972 SMSAs.

Source: United States Bureau of the Census, Census of Governments: 1972, Volume I: Governmental Organization (Washington, D.C., U.S. Government Printing Office, 1973), p. 10.

lies in the fact that they can raise money for needed services at the same time that they maintain a low political and fiscal visibility. Municipalities and counties are quite often restricted by state laws from assuming responsibility for the needed services or from raising their debt to the level that would be needed to provide the services. In these instances the problem can be solved by creating special districts with their own taxing powers and their own debt level. Because the taxes generated by these districts are normally collected by the county, many voters are confused about the origin and distribution of the property taxes they pay. This confusion gives special districts low fiscal visibility and helps shield them from criticism when citizens groups protest against rising taxes. A final reason for the proliferation of special districts can be traced to the federal government's grant-in-aid programs. Federal grants for public housing, urban renewal, soil conservation, and other natural resource purposes increasingly were given to newly created special districts rather than to general-purpose local governments.[44] Table 7-3 shows that special districts which perform these four functions account for over 2100, or about 25 percent, of the 8000 special districts in metropolitan areas.

TABLE 7-3

SPECIAL DISTRICT GOVERNMENTS IN 264 SMSAs BY FUNCTIONAL CLASS: 1972

Functional Class	Total of Special Districts in SMSAs Performing the Function Indicated	
	No.	%
Single-function districts	7492	93.1
Fire protection	1547	19.2
Natural resources[a]	1371	17.0
Urban water supply	888	11.2
Sewerage	866	10.7
School buildings	619	7.7
Housing and urban renewal	731	9.7
Parks and recreation	378	4.7
Other single-function districts[b]	1092	13.6
Multi-function districts	562	6.9
	8054	100.0

[a] Includes drainage, flood control, irrigation, water conservation, soil conservation, and miscellaneous natural resources.
[b] Includes districts for cemeteries, highways, health, hospitals, libraries, electric power, gas supply, transit, and other purposes.

Source: United States Bureau of the Census, Census of Governments: 1972, Volume I: Governmental Organization (Washington, D.C., U.S. Government Printing Office, 1973), p. 10.

Despite the evident popularity of special districts, their proliferation has caused some serious problems both for the governance of the metropolis and for making the government responsive to the electorate and to the citizens' needs. A study of over 500 special districts in the San Francisco Bay area[45] found that few citizens knew that the special districts existed, let alone what they did. Once created, districts are hard to dissolve because of vested interests that grow up around them and incumbent office holders who often are understandably reluctant to lose their positions.

In addition to these problems of low political visibility, in some instances land developers have created and used special districts for their own purposes. In the San Francisco Bay area, the Estero Municipal Improvement District was created to allow a real estate developer to issue tax-exempt government bonds worth $55 million to cover his development expenses of land fill, street paving, and utilities installation for a projected community of 35,000 people. The developer then sold the lots to builders, who in turn erected and sold the homes. The

$55 million bonded debt of the district became a first lien on the property of the homeowners. The net result of this transaction was to create a new government primarily for the purpose of allowing one real estate developer to make much higher profits than he would have made had he developed the land exclusively on private terms.[46] Since houses usually sell for the highest price that the market will bear, it seems doubtful that these extra profits were passed on to the home buyers in the form of lower prices.

Metropolitan Districts

The *metropolitan district* is a special district that produces a specific service on either a county-wide or a multi-county level. The number of metropolitan districts, like the number of special districts, has increased in the larger SMSAs until there are currently over a thousand such districts in existence.[47] The services performed by the metropolitan district are those which transcend most municipal boundaries and can be performed most efficiently on a regional or county level. Typically, such services include transit, sewerage, water supply, parks, and sometimes airports.

The most famous and most successful metropolitan district is undoubtedly the Port Authority of New York and New Jersey.* It was established in 1921 by an interstate compact between New York and New Jersey to develop commercial and transportation facilities in the region. It is directed by a twelve-member governing board of commissioners appointed by the governors of New York and New Jersey. Once appointed, the commissioners become virtually immune from removal. The commissioners are selected from upper-level executives of the major corporations in the two states.

The Port Authority was given no taxing powers; but, once created, it quickly developed lucrative profit-making enterprises. By 1931 it was operating four toll bridges and the Holland Tunnel. The next year it opened a freight terminal. In 1944 it opened a grain terminal, and in 1948 it took over its first airport. During the 1950s it acquired the rest of New York's major airports. During the 1960s it entered the real estate

---

* Until 1972 it was called the Port of New York Authority. The Census Bureau refers to the Port Authority as an independent government rather than as a special district. However, it is a metropolitan district if one uses the criteria established by John C. Bollens that the district "performs an urban function and includes the central city (or at least one central city if there are more than one) and a major part of the remainder of the territory or population of a metropolitan area" [John C. Bollens, *Special District Governments in the United States* (Los Angeles: University of California Press, 1957), p. 53].

business and constructed the 110-story twin towers of the World Trade Center. By the end of the 1960s, the Port Authority's assets had grown to nearly $3 billion. Its operating revenues exceeded $200 million by 1974. And its facilities included six interstate bridges and tunnels, two bus terminals, six airports, ten truck terminals, the World Trade Center, facilities for international shipping and other commercial activities, and one railroad system. It was the last of these facilities which caused the Port Authority one of its most severe headaches.

Despite the Port Authority's enormous success, critics have long complained that it was neglecting commuter rail service, one of its original responsibilities. Rather than relieving New York's traffic problems, it was charged, the Port Authority's bridges and tunnels were making New York's traffic congestion worse by bringing in more automobiles. The Authority was increasingly pressured to invest some of its ever increasing revenues into commuter rail transit. After a long, drawn-out battle in which the Port Authority eventually was attacked on the issue by the governors of both states, the Metropolitan Rapid Transit Commission, the New Jersey legislature, the mayor of New York City, many local leaders in New Jersey, a committee of the United States Congress, and a variety of groups and citizens concerned about the transit problem in New York, a compromise was finally arranged in 1962. The Port Authority agreed to purchase one small commuter railroad. In exchange, it was given permission to enter the lucrative New York real estate business in competition with private business by constructing the World Trade Center. In the intervening years, public transit in New York has continued to deteriorate and the Port Authority is still under fire for not assuming greater responsibility for the transit problem. It met some of these objections in 1973 when it agreed to construct a rapid rail transit line that would link midtown Manhattan with the Newark and Kennedy airports.[48]

Although the profitability of the Port Authority and the extensiveness of its operations make it unique among metropolitan districts, its very uniqueness illustrates the major advantages and disadvantages of metropolitan districts. The major advantage is that a given service can normally be performed on a metropolitan scale very effectively, efficiently, and economically. Operating expenses will often be covered by fees collected from the service, and capital expenses for constructing new facilities will normally be covered by an issue of public bonds which are paid off from the operating revenue plus a small property tax. Federal grants are often available to the district under many federal grant-in-aid programs. Because of the federal grants, the

"For once, let's start the day without you telling me there's a taller one going up in Chicago."

This *New Yorker* cartoon about the Port of New York Authority's World Trade Center captures some of the absurdity of runaway technological progress. The twin towers of the Trade Center use more electrical energy than a city of 100,000 people. Through the people, traffic, and utility services which the towers demand, they have added immeasurably to the congestion of lower Manhattan.

Drawing by Richter; © 1971 The New Yorker Magazine, Inc.

bonding authority, and the fees collected from operating the public services, the metropolitan districts enjoy considerable financial independence from city councils. And this financial independence can make metropolitan districts very popular with economy-minded public officials.

Metropolitan districts such as the Port Authority of New York and New Jersey, the Southern California Metropolitan Water District, and Chicago's Metropolitan Sanitary District sell vitally needed services — and, as shown by the example of the Port Authority of New York and New Jersey, can often sell them at a profit. For these kinds of services, the metropolitan district approach works very well. But many vital metropolitan services such as mass transit or air pollution control must operate at a deficit rather than a profit. And as the case of the Port Authority of New York and New Jersey demonstrates, getting profitable metropolitan districts to take on needed but unprofitable services is often difficult.

This aspect of metropolitan districts means that despite their obvious financial advantages, they present political disadvantages to the metropolitan area as a whole. The example of the Port Authority of New York and New Jersey indicates that the relative financial independence of the metropolitan district makes it very difficult to adapt its operations to changing needs. Political authorities have responsibilities for defining the priorities of the state or the metropolis, but often no mechanism exists by which policies of metropolitan districts can be brought in line with new priorities. This was certainly true of trying to get the Port Authority to assume greater responsibility for public rail transit.

A related problem posed by metropolitan districts is that of coordinating the different functions each of them perform separately. The transit problem of a metropolis can only get worse if the plans of the automobile and highway planners are not coordinated with those of the public transit planners. Similarly, if metropolitan sprawl is to be contained, there must exist a high level of coordination between plans for sewer construction, water line construction, highway construction, construction of public transit lines, shopping center construction, solid waste disposal, and open space preservation, to name a few major metropolitan concerns that are often handled by isolated metropolitan districts. It does little good if water lines run in one direction, sewage lines in another, highways in a third, and transit lines in another, and no provisions are made for the preservation of open space.

In order to subordinate metropolitan districts to elected political officials and to coordinate the activities of different metropolitan districts, three tactics have been attempted: the constituent unit method of representation, the multi-purpose district, and the use of a review and planning authority.

The *constituent unit* method of representation seeks to subordinate the metropolitan districts to the major elected government bodies by having the most important government bodies represented directly on the boards of the metropolitan districts. A metropolitan transit commission, for example, might be composed of council members or mayors from the central city and the principal suburbs. The rationale for such representation is that these government representatives will oblige the metropolitan district to be responsive to their constituents. All too often this does not work in practice. In many instances, the commission is torn by political conflicts between commissioners who represent the interests of their own cities.* Even where the constituent unit method of representation does succeed in subordinating a metropolitan district to the local elected officials, *different* officials will be on *different* metropolitan districts and consequently cannot coordinate the activities of various districts. Nevertheless, because it enables some control by elected officials, the constituent unit method of representation has been quite popular.[49]

A second approach to coordinating the activities of metropolitan districts has been to consolidate several isolated single-purpose metropolitan districts into one *multi-purpose district* that would exercise overall policy control over each function and ensure that the various services were coordinated. The most recent examples of this have been in Seattle, Washington, where sewage disposal and transit are combined under a metropolitan district called the Municipality of Metropolitan Seattle, and Portland, Oregon, where the Metro Service District coordinates the policies of all the metropolitan districts in that metropolis. But these multi-purpose districts have not been very far-reaching.[50]

A third approach to coordinating the activities of metropolitan districts was adopted in Minneapolis–Saint Paul. The Metropolitan Council, created in 1967, was given very broad review powers to reject plans and programs of metropolitan districts within the Twin Cities metropolitan area. These powers have largely been negative rather than posi-

---

* For example, in Minneapolis–Saint Paul, the Metropolitan Airports Commission came under criticism from many suburban leaders because it had representatives from only the two central city governments. The suburban leaders maintained that they, too, should have input on decisions on a future airport location, because the location would vitally affect the course of land development in some of the suburbs. Partially as a result of these criticisms, the Minnesota Legislature in 1974 replaced the constituent unit method of representation with one based on districts.

tive, since the Metropolitan Council can veto actions of the metropolitan districts but cannot impose its own plans upon them. When major policy conflicts arose between the Metropolitan Council and the Metropolitan Airports Commission and the Metropolitan Transit Commission, a long, drawn-out, divisive impasse occurred in both transit and airport planning. Finally, a major restructuring of the metropolitan agencies in 1974 shifted the arena for decision-making on the issue of a mass transit system from the metropolitan level to the state legislature. This inability of an agency with purely negative review powers to settle the stalemate between two recalcitrant agencies does not bode well for metropolitan coordinating devices that lack positive enforcement powers.

Metropolitan districts are partly a device to maintain the status quo in metropolitan governance and partly a device to create new forms of governance. In the respect that they provide a mechanism to deal with specific functional problems on an area-wide basis, they represent a break with the parochialism characteristic of suburban municipal politics. But they are protective of the status quo in several respects. Because of their uni-functional orientation, controlling and coordinating the policies of several districts is difficult. Like contracting for services and like special districts, metropolitan districts do not restrain the proliferation of governments in the metropolis. Finally, because of the way in which their boards are constituted, metropolitan districts are not normally held accountable to the electorate. There is no known instance of the voters rising up and throwing out of office the members of any metropolitan board.

STRATEGIES FOR CENTRAL CITY EXPANSION

Unlike the strategies to preserve the status quo, the strategies for central city expansion do represent possibilities for metropolitan government. There are two such strategies: annexation and the granting of extraterritorial powers to cities.

Annexation

Prior to World War I, metropolitan growth occurred largely through the expansion of the central city boundaries by annexing outlying territories. In this way the city's physical growth could keep up with the growth of its population. During these years few people resided beyond the boundaries of the central cities, and fewer municipalities sprang up as autonomous suburbs on the fringes of the cities. The consolidation of incorporated municipalities during this period was a frequent occurrence. Because of the frequent annexation to and consolidation with the central city, the growth of suburban fringe populations posed few problems until late in the nineteenth century. By 1900, however, successful annexation attempts became less popular and less frequent. Consequently, the growth of the central city through annexation peaked about the time of World War I.

This peaking resulted from two mechanisms. First, most state legislatures made incorporation easier for municipalities; and second, they made annexation more difficult. Particularly important were requirements that annexation be approved by dual referendums of the voters both within the city doing the annexation and within the area to be annexed. Because strong opposition to annexation existed among the new suburbanites, such annexation referendums were very difficult to pass in the suburban areas.* By the time the first phase of suburbanization ended during the Great Depression, the central cities of the Northeast and the Midwest were mostly encircled by a first tier of suburbs. Attempts by central cities to annex noncontiguous land beyond the first tier of suburbs were generally frowned upon by the courts. Following World War II, most states relaxed their annexation restrictions, and a new phase of annexation occurred. Except for the South and the Southwest, however, this second phase of annexation primarily consisted of unicorporated territories being annexed by suburbs and smaller cities, not by big central cities.†

Extraterritorial Powers

The most imaginative approach to using annexation for central city expansion occurred in Texas. The Texas approach involved *extraterritorial powers*, which consist of a city's jurisdictional right to control

---

* Historian Kenneth T. Jackson asserts that suburbanites' opposition to annexation was in great part a moral issue. They looked upon the central city immigrants as the cause of much of the vice and corruption that characterized the politics of many central cities. See his "Metropolitan Government Versus Suburban Autonomy: Politics on the Crabgrass Frontier," in *Cities in American History,* ed. Kenneth T. Jackson and Stanley K. Schultz (New York: Knopf, 1972), pp. 442–446.
† The Advisory Commission on Intergovernmental Relations reports that post–World War II annexations have been most likely to occur in smaller cities with reform-style governments, cities whose residents are similar socioeconomically to the residents about to be annexed, and cities outside of the Northeast and Mid-Atlantic regions. See the commission's *Report A–44 Substate Regionalism and the Federal System: The Challenge of Local Governmental Reorganization* (Washington, D.C.: U.S. Government Printing Office, 1974), vol. III, pp. 82–84.

subdivision practices in unincorporated territories contiguous to its borders. These powers were conferred by the Texas Municipal Annexation Law of 1963, which, in effect, allowed a city to combine its annexation powers with the exercise of extraterritorial powers. The larger a city was, the further it could extend its control over suburban subdivisions. Also, without referendum, the city could annually annex up to 10 percent of its territory and any public land it wanted.[51]

The most dramatic use of these powers was made by Houston, which annexed right-of-ways along highways and railroads and thus increased tremendously the amount of outlying area within the five-mile limit in which it could exercise subdivision control. As a consequence of these policies, Houston was able to grow as fast as its suburbs. By 1970, Houston was the only one of the twenty largest metropolitan areas to have more people living in the central city than in the suburbs. The fact that it is also the only large United States city with no zoning laws may have reduced suburbanites' fear of annexation.

For annexation to be a viable strategy of metropolitan control, then, there are two prerequisites. First, the central city must border substantial amounts of unincorporated territory. Second, state legislation must make annexation easier than new incorporation. Most cities of the Northeast and the Midwest fail on the first count for most of them are completely surrounded by incorporated suburbs. On the second count, most areas of the country fail. The only fast-growing areas of the country where these two conditions have been met have in fact seen substantial use of central city annexation during the 1950s and the 1960s — the South and the Southwest. Some notable examples are Houston, Dallas, Fort Worth, San Diego, Phoenix, and Oklahoma City.

SUMMARY: BIAS IN THE STRATEGIES TO AVOID METROPOLITAN GOVERNMENT

This chapter has reviewed several approaches to coping with the consequences of the multi-centered metropolis. All of the approaches have one common aspect: in practice they all serve as devices for avoiding the creation of a metropolitan government. As seen above, the very purposes behind such approaches as contracting for services, special districts, and metropolitan districts are to preserve the continued existence of independent, autonomous suburban municipalities. By making economies of scale available to these governments, they make possible the provision of many services that the governments themselves may be too small to provide.

In theory, the devices of annexation and extraterritorial powers have potential for making the central city government a metropolitan government. In practice, however, they have not been very useful for this. Their potential is greatest in the newer metropolitan areas where the proliferation of suburban governments has not yet occurred and where state laws are more favorable to annexation. Even in these areas, however, the utility of annexation for metropolitan governance is dependent upon how effectively the central city government is organized and whether it has control over the functionally organized bureaucracies and special districts.

Because the strategies discussed here support the status quo, they also support the existing biases of the multi-centered metropolis. As seen earlier, sharp differences in value orientations emerge between the approach that seeks one general-purpose metropolitan government and the approach that seeks governance without a metropolitan government. The strategies reviewed in this chapter generally support the values and biases of the second type of approach. Consequently, they are biased against an equal sharing of property tax revenues in the metropolis. The reliance upon special districts and metropolitan districts also strengthens the biases of the functional fiefdoms that were discussed in Chapter 5. The reason for this is that most special districts and metropolitan districts become very independent of direction by elected officials and very isolated from the electorate.

Finally, there is a bias to the pattern by which governmental functions have been assigned to metropolitan districts or contracted to large-scale county governments. Political scientist Oliver Williams distinguishes between *systems-maintenance functions*, such as water supply or sewage disposal, which are essential for the sheer physical maintenance of the metropolis, and *social-access functions*, such as zoning, subdivision control, and land use controls, which determine who will have access to the better schools, the most dynamic economic growth areas, and the most desirable residential areas.[52] While there has been little hesitation to create metropolitan districts or make other large-scale arrangements to perform the systems-maintenance functions, there has been considerable reluctance to allow land use controls or residential zoning practices to be turned over to metropolitan-level agencies. In fact, the reliance upon single-purpose metropolitan agencies to perform some of the systems-maintenance functions has enabled some suburban municipalities to persist in their discriminatory exercise of social-access functions.

It is conceivable that a metropolitan government as such would remove such social-access functions from the control of small suburbs. This possibility will be examined in Chapter 8.

Some Suggested Readings

The Scrap-the-Whole-System Approach

These readings articulate very clearly the concept that metropolitan problems can best be solved through the creation of a metropolitan-level government in each metropolis.

Luther Gulick, *The Metropolitan Problem and American Ideas* (New York: Knopf, 1962).

Amos H. Hawley and Basil G. Zimmer, *The Metropolitan Community: Its People and Government* (Beverly Hills, Calif.: SAGE Publications, 1970).

Reshaping Government in Metropolitan Areas (New York: Committee for Economic Development, 1970).

The Governance-without-a-Government Approach

The four articles listed below have become classic critiques of the concept that metropolitan governance can be achieved only by creating a metropolitan-level government. Adrian points out several flaws in the logic of the reformers. Long portrays metropolitan political economy as the intricate interplay of various games which are played in various sectors of metropolitan politics and economics. The need for a general-purpose government to control these interactions is portrayed as dubious. Ostrom, Tiebout, and Warren present the free-market model of metropolitan governance. Holden presents the diplomatic model.

Charles R. Adrian, "Metropology: Folklore and Field Research," *Public Administration Review* 321, no. 3 (Summer 1961): 148–157.

Norton E. Long, "The Local Community as an Ecology of Games," *American Journal of Sociology* 64 (November 1958): 251–261.

Vincent Ostrom, Charles M. Tiebout, and Robert Warren, "Organizing Government in Metropolitan Areas: A Theoretical Inquiry," *The American Political Science Review* 55 (December 1961): 831–842.

Matthew Holden, Jr., "The Governance of the Metropolis as a Problem in Diplomacy." *Journal of Politics* 26 (August 1964): 627–647.

A Social-Access Approach to Interpreting Metropolitan Governance

Oliver P. Williams, *Metropolitan Political Analysis* (New York: The Free Press, 1971). Williams interprets metropolitan politics in terms of controlling locational decisions which give access to the social amenities of the metropolis. He argues that whereas control over systems-maintenance functions often is transferred to a metropolitan level, control over social-access functions seldom is.

Studies on Some Specific Strategies

Richard M. Cion, "Accommodation Par Excellence: The Lakewood Plan," in *Metropolitan Politics: A Reader,* 2nd ed., ed. Michael N. Danielson (Boston: Little, Brown, 1971).

Advisory Commission on Intergovernmental Relations, *Report A–22: The Problem of Special Districts in America* (Washington, D.C.: U.S. Government Printing Office, May 1964).

Kenneth T. Jackson, "Metropolitan Government versus Suburban Autonomy: Politics on the Crabgrass Frontier," in *Cities in American History,* ed. Kenneth T. Jackson and Stanley K. Schultz (New York: Knopf, 1972). An excellent portrayal of the rebellion against annexation at the turn of the century.

Chapter 8

In some metropolitan areas, bold attempts have been made to reorganize local governments into new, general-purpose governments at the metropolitan level, governments that could cope with the consequences of the multi-centered metropolis. Such metropolitan governments have been adopted in very few metropolises, however, and even where adopted the results have been less far-reaching than their original promoters hoped. Nevertheless, battles to establish these metropolitan governments dominated metropolitan politics during the 1950s and much of the 1960s.

Strategies to Attain Metropolitan Government

Three types of metropolitan reorganizations have occurred. Most useful in metropolitan areas contained within one county have been reorganizations entailing either (1) consolidation of the central city government with the government of the county, or (2) internal reorganization of the urban county to make it an effective instrument of government. The third type of reorganization involves the creation of a *two-tier* form of government, the first tier responsible for area-wide functions, the second tier for local functions. Each of these three strategies of metropolitan reorganization involves basic restructuring of existing levels of government.

CITY-COUNTY CONSOLIDATION

One of the most theoretically appealing approaches to metropolitan government has been to consolidate the city and county into one governmental unit and strengthen the governing capabilities of that unit. Such a plan necessarily works best in the smaller SMSAs where the entire metropolis is contained in a single county. Of the 265 SMSAs, 100 are one-county SMSAs. These are mostly small- and medium-sized SMSAs, and it is among them that city-county consolidation has its greatest theoretical potential. But some potential for consolidation as a means of metropolitan government also exists in the large SMSAs, even though they may not be contained in a single county. Over a fifth of the population of the entire country lives in twenty-three counties of more than one million population. Only one of these twenty-three counties has attempted a consolidation.* Considerable theoretical potential thus exists for using the county as a basis for metropolitan government, both among large counties and among small counties.[1] This was recognized by the Committee for Economic Development (CED), which in 1966 suggested that the county should be the basic governmental unit for dealing with area-wide problems.[2]

In the nineteenth century, in fact, consolidation of cities and counties occurred in New Orleans in 1805, in Boston in 1822, in Philadelphia in 1854, and in New York in 1898. Since the consolidation in Honolulu in 1907, however, only four major consolidations were successful out of at least twenty-three attempts.[3]† These were Baton Rouge (1947), Nashville (1962), Jacksonville (1967), and Indianapolis (1969). Despite this pronounced lack of success, new city-county consolidations are currently being considered in at least forty other locales, including some major metropolitan areas.

Because so many areas are considering city-county consolidation, the most important features of the four major consolidations merit investigation. Five basic questions arise: Why was consolidation proposed? How did it change the structure of government and representation in elected bodies? How did it change the handling of public services? What has been accomplished as a result? And what was the effect of consolidation on the racial minorities? The first four questions will be examined here, and the last question will be examined at the end of this chapter.

Why Consolidation Was Proposed

In the places where successful consolidation has occurred, three background factors have usually been associated with the movement to-

---

* Miami–Dade County, Florida. It could be argued that a form of consolidation exists in New York City in which five counties have been subordinated to the city government.
† A major consolidation is considered here to be a consolidation that involves the governance of more than 250,000 people.

ward consolidation. First, the provision of public services has usually broken down or at least encountered serious complications. Second, special political conditions have facilitated the movement toward con- solidation. Third, most of the suburban areas and populations were not already contained in other, incorporated municipalities.*

A city-county consolidation that was motivated by a deterioration in the provision of public services is best exemplified by the situation in Nashville–Davidson County, Tennessee. By the 1950s, most of Nash- ville's population growth was occurring in the suburban areas. An estimated 100,000 suburbanites were using septic tanks for the dis- posal of human waste, and at least 25 percent of these septic tank systems were operating faultily. This posed a severe threat to the safety of the water supply, which was primarily obtained from private wells. Police and fire protection were very deficient.[4] Because of this, people turned more and more to private subscription for private police and fire services. Several firms competed to provide fire protection in the sub- urbs, and the inconsistent quality of this fire protection made the cost of fire insurance higher in the suburbs than in the city. Things came to such a pass that in one instance, firefighters employed by a private fire company responded to the alarm of a burning house not to put out the fire — the burning house was not insured by their company — but to prevent the fire from spreading to a neighboring house, which was company-insured. They stood by and watched the one house burn to the ground.

In summary, Nashville's metropolitan area was characterized by sharp city/suburban political divisions, few area-wide special districts, and deficiencies in the provision of public services in the suburbs. Tax- able resources were distributed very unevenly throughout the metro- politan area. County expenditures, which benefited primarily the ur- banized area, were often duplicated by the city's expenditures.

In each of the other three counties where consolidation occurred, a similar situation existed. Baton Rouge had been plagued with a prolif- eration of special districts and a sprawling of the population beyond the city's boundaries.[5] Jacksonville was threatened by a loss of accredit- ation of its school system and a breakdown of its sewerage system, which was polluting the Saint Johns River.[6] Only in Indianapolis had the metropolitan problems not reached a crisis stage. Through the cre- ation of county-wide service districts, Indianapolis had handled the problems of suburbanization with considerable success. The major

---

* These factors do not necessarily cause the movement toward consolidation, however, because the same factors were sometimes present in metropolises that did not experience a consolidation movement. But in the absence of some combination of these factors, consolidation is very unlikely to occur.

complaint there seemed to be that the proliferation of these districts had gotten beyond the control of the elected county and city officials.[7]

A second feature common to these consolidations was the existence of special, favorable political conditions. The legal hurdles to achieving city-county consolidation are usually formidable. First, either state constitutions must be amended to provide for the consolidation, or a legislative enabling act must be passed that will permit the county to assume the powers of an urban government. In either case, major action is required by the state legislature. If a substantial number of local officials oppose such legislation, the legislators are often reluctant to pass it. Even after such legislation is secured, a second hurdle arises because consolidations usually require referendum approval by the majority of voters both within and outside of the city.

In each of the four cities in question, special factors eased the difficulty of overcoming these hurdles. In the case of Baton Rouge, Louisiana's Constitution was easy to amend.[8] Once the constitutional amendment was passed authorizing a new charter, the referendum on the charter itself needed only a parish-wide majority to be put into effect.* Even so, it passed by a slim margin of only 307 votes out of a total of 14,000 votes cast. In Jacksonville and Indianapolis, no constitutional amendment was needed, and the local legislative delegations from these cities were powerful forces on local matters in their respective legislatures.

In Indianapolis, Jacksonville, and Nashville, the consolidation movements were also facilitated by special, temporary political situations. In Jacksonville–Duval County, the consolidation movement was accompanied by a long, drawn-out exposé of corruption in city government which led to indictments of eight city government officials on counts ranging from grand larceny to bribery and perjury. One observer commented that "things seemed to have sunk so low that almost any change would have been welcome."[9] The consolidation referendum passed by a substantial margin.

In Nashville the passage of the consolidation charter in 1962 was linked not to public corruption but to extreme voter dissatisfaction with the city officials. A very similar consolidation proposal had been resoundingly defeated by the voters just four years earlier. What led to the final victory of the consolidation plan in 1962 was widespread discontent with two unpopular political moves during the intervening period: the annexation of considerable land and population without

---

* In Louisiana a county is called a parish.

holding a referendum,* and the passage of a so-called "green sticker tax" which obliged suburbanites to purchase green stickers and display them on the windshields of their cars when they drove on the streets of Nashville.

When a new consolidation referendum was put before the voters in 1962, it was approved by substantial margins both within the city and in the suburbs.[10] Voters were urged to vote for the plan because the mayor of Nashville opposed it. He had been associated with and blamed for the unpopular green sticker tax and the annexation. Thus, a vote for the charter was considered to be a vote against the mayor. The procharter campaign in 1962 was waged on the basis of what sociologist Scott Greer called the purification ritual of metropolitan reform. One could vote for the consolidation in effect by casting a vote to throw out the unpopular rascals who previously had inhabited city hall.[11]

In Indianapolis, consolidation was greatly aided by the fact that it needed no voter approval. The entire matter was handled in the state legislature. As Chapter 9 will show, the legislature provides a more flexible forum for dealing with metropolitan reform than does a voter referendum.

If the consolidations in these four places were facilitated by peculiar political circumstances, they were also facilitated by the fact that not very many incorporated areas existed in the suburbs. Nashville–Davidson County had only six incorporated municipalities, and they were allowed to retain their separate existence. Baton Rouge had none. Jacksonville–Duval County had four small cities that were allowed to retain their separate existence. Indianapolis–Marion County had sixteen small suburbs which were consolidated along with the city of Indianapolis; four larger suburbs were allowed to retain their separate existence. Thus, in none of these four areas did consolidation pose a threat to any large suburban governments.

Consolidation, the Structure of Government, and Representation

The most visible governmental change in consolidated governments is normally the creation of a new, county-wide council to replace the previous city council and county legislative bodies. These new councils have usually been large (forty members in Nashville, twenty-nine in Indianapolis, and nineteen in Jacksonville) and have used a combination of at-large elections and single-member district elections. A result

* The Tennessee Constitution permitted such annexations.

is that control over the new councils has gone, immediately or eventually, to the suburbanites. In the case of Indianapolis, the Republicans got an immediate and apparently permanent dominance. The representation of blacks was critically affected by the reorganizations (this will be discussed at the end of this chapter).

In terms of the government structure, consolidation brought drastic reorganizations in some of the cities. In Nashville, many public services, which had previously been performed separately by the city and the county were merged into one: instead of two school systems, there was now just one; instead of two public health departments, there was just one. In Jacksonville, the integration of public services under the control of the new council was less extensive than it was in Nashville. In fact, about two-thirds of the public spending in Jacksonville is conducted by independent agencies that are subject to very little control from the consolidated government.[12]

The least complete integration of the governmental structure came in the Indianapolis–Marion County consolidation. All of the existing governmental units were left intact. There are still eleven separate school districts, sixteen townships, some small cities, and some public authorities. The new government, entitled Unigov, consisted of the same elected county officers as prior to the consolidation, and there was no change in the county Welfare Board, county assessors, or county Tax Adjustment Board. Police and fire protection services remained virtually untouched.[13] Nevertheless, Unigov accomplished a major reorganization of the administrative agencies of the old county and the old city and subordinated them to the mayor. In the opinion of one observer, this has led to "a much stronger degree of coordination than previously existed."[14]

Consolidation, Public Services, and Taxes

As pointed out in Chapter 6, one of the most persistent features of the metropolitan political economy is the wide disparity that exists in the quality of public services and the tax rates paid for these services. The four consolidated city-counties have dealt imaginatively with this problem by dividing the county into different service zones. Usually there is a rural zone which receives a minimum of public services and an urban zone which receives the maximum of public services. Since the rural zone residents receive fewer services, they pay a lower property tax rate. The residents of the urban zone, who receive more services, pay a higher property tax rate. Provision is made for the urban zone's boundaries to expand as population grows in the rural areas.

In Nashville, for example, all county residents pay a tax on the general-services district. This tax finances schools, public health facilities, police protection, courts, welfare, public housing, urban renewal, streets and roads, traffic, transit, library, refuse service, and building codes. In addition, the more densely populated urban areas, which need more extensive provision of government services, constitute an urban-services district. Residents of these areas pay a higher tax rate, and for this they receive fire protection, intensified police protection, sewage disposal, water supply, street lighting, and street cleaning. The charter provided for a gradual expansion of the boundaries of the urban-services district as the population continued to grow in the suburbs. As late as 1972, however, the urban-services district still had not expanded beyond the area of the former city of Nashville.[15]

A very similar two-zone system of services is also utilized in Jacksonville–Duval County,[16] while Baton Rouge has a three-zone system. The third zone is an industrial district which enjoys a special taxing situation. The most complicated method of providing services and paying for them is found in Indianapolis–Marion County. Nine separate services each have their own taxing district which overlap with each other. And, depending on where a person lives in the county, he will pay a tax rate ranging from one to all nine of these services. In fact, this structure of services and taxation changed very little with the consolidation.[17]

An Assessment of Consolidation's Accomplishments

The general assessment seems to be that consolidation has led to greatly improved public services — but that the very nature of improving public services has meant increased expenditures and increased property taxes.[18] It must be recognized that the course of inflation would have made property taxes rise anyway. In fact, they have risen precipitously even in areas which did not undergo any metropolitan reorganization. In Nashville and Jacksonville, the consolidated governments have made significant headway in installing sewer lines and central water supplies. In Indianapolis, the greatest impact of the consolidation was described as

> political-psychological. . . . In a very considerable measure, the Unigov reorganization, in spite of all its compromises and exclusions and limitations, has created a new political constituency, a political community different from the ones which existed before. This community of about 800,000 people now chooses a single political leader and a single political deliberative body. They are perceived by all to be their central spokesmen.[19]

In Nashville the new government brought about a general upgrading of public schools. For the first time, government was able to purchase open land for future recreational facilities. It initiated a massive sewer construction program. A voter opinion survey conducted two years after the new charter was accepted found that 71 percent of the voters were satisfied with Metro's operation. The survey also discovered that citizens felt that the new government made it easier for them to know whom to call or see when they had a problem.[20]

The biggest failings of the consolidated governments have been in coping with suburban sprawl and in dealing with social issues. In both Indianapolis and Nashville, the SMSA now extends beyond the boundaries of the consolidated city-counties. Jacksonville–Duval County is a one-county SMSA and, for the foreseeable future, most of the growth of that metropolis should occur within the county.

On the vital social issues, the consolidated governments (and other metropolitan government schemes as well) have fared poorly. One author writes that "the current record of metros in redistributing resources which are raised locally is almost uniformly bad."[21] Nor have any of the governments moved very dynamically toward decentralizing decision-making and service delivery to the neighborhood level, although Indianapolis has taken some timorous steps in this direction.

STRENGTHENING THE URBAN COUNTY

Whatever the popularity of city-county consolidation, the device can only be as effective as the county government that is established. The problem is that most county governments traditionally have not been organized very effectively for the purpose of coping with urban ills. In particular, county government has lacked the capacity for decisive executive leadership. Almost 60 percent of all counties are governed by the traditional county governing body known as the board of commissioners.[22]* This board has responsibility for overseeing the operations of all the agencies and departments of the county. In practice, however, the boards of commissioners are usually ineffective in doing this. County agencies have tended to become very autonomous, and very little coordination has existed between them. Big county agencies, such as welfare departments, public hospitals, public health bureaus, or highway departments, have tended to create large bureaucracies and have gained the autonomy characteristic of the functional fiefdoms described in Chapter 5. The smaller agencies, such as tax assessors,

* Traditional county boards of supervisors are also included in this 60 percent.

license bureaus, registers of deeds, or bureaus of vital statistics, have in many instances become the patronage preserves of isolated political factions that strongly oppose centralized administrative control. Especially where the head of such a department is elected to his position (as is often the case with registers of deeds and sheriffs), the boards of commissioners have little leverage to oblige these fiefdoms to implement general public policies.[23]

Most proposals for modernizing county government center on creating an executive office that would have the authority to subordinate these disparate agencies to some form of centralized control. Three particular proposals have received the most attention: the elected county executive, the county manager, and the county administrator. The elected county executive is analogous to the strong-mayor form of city government. Because the executive would be elected, he would have a large political base of support; and because he would be given substantial appointive powers, he would exert considerable leverage over all county agencies. Finally, because in most urbanized areas he would have the largest constituency of any local government officials, he would undoubtedly eclipse the public visibility of all other urban political officials. Perhaps this is why very little support has been shown for the proposal of an elected county executive. Only about 6 percent of all counties have adopted this innovation.

The county manager is analogous to the city manager. He is directly accountable to the board of commissioners. Although he lacks an electoral base of political support, he is given broad supervisory and budgetary control within the county government. County managers have been used with considerable success in Dade County, Florida, since 1957. But the county manager as a form of government has not been very popular; it has been adopted by only 6 percent of all counties.

Similar in concept to the county manager is the county administrator. The major difference between the two is that the county administrator is given much more limited supervisory control. He is less effective in coordinating various county agencies and thus is less threatening to them. This may be why the county administrator form of government has become fairly popular; it has been adopted in 29 percent of all counties.

Other proposals have been advanced for strengthening county government. These include: expanding the number of services performed by counties, improving the tax-raising abilities of counties, adopting merit systems of hiring and promoting employees, upgrading bureaucratic personnel, granting land use powers to counties, and consolidating all counties within an SMSA into a gigantic supercounty.

TWO-TIER GOVERNMENT: MIAMI AND TORONTO

The third form of metropolitan government to be considered here is the two-tier approach, which has been promoted by the prestigious Committee for Economic Development (CED). The CED was primarily concerned about two overriding needs of government in contemporary urban America, two needs which appear to be mutually exclusive. On the one hand is "the need for jurisdictions large enough to cope with problems that pervade entire areas," while on the other hand is the need "for jurisdictions small enough to allow citizens to take part — and take pride — in the process of government."[24]

Divisions of Powers in Two-Tier Governments

Recommendations for two levels of government often are based on what political scientists refer to as an incorrect "layer-cake" concept. The layer-cake concept perceives each different level as performing distinct and separate functions. Such a concept is misleading, because any given function in a metropolis usually has municipal, county, state, and federal officials involved in its performance. And a given local official will, in the course of carrying out his local duties, also perform federal and state services.[25]

Any rigid division of functions between levels of government, then, is based on a layer-cake perception of federalism which fails to account for the intertwining complexity of intergovernmental relations. Nevertheless, local governments are obliged to operate in this environment, and the result has been myriad unsystematic patterns to the structures of intergovernmental relations.[26] Especially where two-tier systems of government are proposed, the problem of dividing functions between the tiers is inescapable. The CED proposals on two-tier government attempt to avoid the simplicities of layer-cake federalism by suggesting a "sharing of power" rather than a "division of functions." Although some governmental functions will be assigned to the local level and some to the metropolitan level, "most will be assigned in part to each level."[27] A rough division of powers is suggested in Table 8-1. In reality, the division of functions between tiers is very difficult to apportion on the purely logical grounds of assigning specific functions to their most appropriate levels.[28] Attempts to designate the appropriate levels for each function usually lead to considerable bickering. One government official commented in frustration, "the rationale for taking over something is how bad is the service — everything is potentially metropolitan in scope."[29]

TABLE 8-1

DIVISION OF POWERS IN TWO-TIER GOVERNMENT

Primarily Metropolitan	Shared	Primarily Local
Transit (with community participation)	Planning	Solid waste collection (with no recommendation on disposal)
Water supply	Housing	Welfare (with financing at the national level)
Sewage disposal	Police	

Adapted from Reshaping Government in Metropolitan Areas (New York: Committee for Economic Development, 1970), pp. 45, 51, 56.

There are no clear-cut examples in practice of the kind of two-tier government the CED suggested for metropolitan areas. In North America, the two closest approximations are Miami, Florida, and Toronto, Canada. Although both areas established a two-tier form of government, Miami's utilized the existing county as the basis for metropolitan government and Toronto's established a true federative form. Because they are so distinct, each will be considered separately.

Miami: A Two-Tier Urban County

In 1957 Dade County, Florida, established a two-tier form of metropolitan government that seemed to promise a solution to the problem of metropolitan governance. The movement to establish this government was promoted by an increasingly widespread belief among business and good government leaders that intergovernmental antagonisms and excessive parochialism on the part of the county's twenty-six municipalities were seriously impairing the efficient provision of public services in the region. Traffic conditions in particular had become intolerable. There were no expressways or overpasses. Because each town could set its own speed limits and other traffic regulations, some towns became renowned locally for the fines they collected through speed traps.[30] Civic leaders in Miami expressed open resentment at the parochialism practiced by some of the suburban communities, particularly Miami Beach. And the resentment was openly returned. When the mayor of Miami Beach denounced the plans for the new metropolitan government, a member of the Miami–Dade Chamber of Commerce retorted that Miami Beach was almost completely dependent upon the city of Miami. "We Miamians furnish them with water, we burn their garbage, we house their servants, we furnish them with roads leading to Miami Beach . . . we even carry it to the ultimate extreme, we bury their dead."[31] The City of Miami's government was plagued with charges of corruption. Police were accused of not enforcing the city's ordinances on gambling and vice. In contrast, the county government was relatively well regarded. Over the years several public services had been transferred from municipal control to control by the county government.

Since the end of World War II, business and civic leaders in Miami had put forward various plans for consolidating city and county services. These civic leaders forged a working alliance with the Dade County delegation in the state legislature which guided through the legislature a constitutional amendment which granted a home rule charter to Dade County in 1955. The amendment was approved by the voters, a new charter was drafted, and in 1957 the new charter was narrowly approved by a county-wide majority of 44,404 to 42,620.

The new charter established a two-tier government. A restructured and modernized county government was given responsibility for what were deemed the area-wide functions. These included mass transit, public health, planning, and some central police and fire services. In the twenty-six municipalities, which currently house about 57 percent of the county's population, other functions have effectively been left to local municipalities, special districts, or school districts. These include police patrolling, public education, and control over local zoning and land use. For some of these functions, the county was authorized to establish minimum service standards. If a local government failed to meet these standards, the county was empowered to take over the service. The charter also allowed the local governments to maintain higher zoning and service standards if they so chose.[32]

This division of functions coincides very neatly with Oliver Williams's distinction between systems-maintenance functions and life-style functions.[33] All the functions turned over to the county involve maintaining the physical operation of the metropolis — keeping the traffic flowing, the water unpolluted, and the public services in operation. The functions that had the most sensitive relationship to controlling people's access to the most highly prized social amenities of the region — public education and residential location — remained in the control of the local governments.

This two-tier system of governance applies only in the municipalities. The unincorporated areas of the county, which house about 43 percent of the population, have no two-tier system. In these areas, the county government handles both local and area-wide functions.

The new county charter also replaced the traditional commission style of government with a county manager form of government. The county manager was given substantial executive responsibilities, and the county commissioners were removed from any direct control over the departments of government. The county board of commissioners became, in effect, a legislative body. Eight commissioners represent geographical districts, but they are elected at large. A ninth commissioner representing the whole county is also elected at large, and he is given the title of mayor. The mayoral position is very weak, however, since the executive authority resides in the county manager. The mayor is simply the first among equals on the board of commissioners.

The early years of the two-tier government were characterized by bitter conflicts between the county and the municipalities. These conflicts were sparked by the county's attempts to take over functions that had traditionally been performed by the municipalities.[34] The board itself was deeply divided over many of these issues, and as a consequence, the first county manager was unable to exercise effective leadership. He was dismissed in 1961 and was replaced by a manager who was able to allay some of the municipal officials' resentment against the county. The second manager lost his position four years later, however, when widespread resentment erupted against a doubling of the property tax assessments in the county. The charter was revised in 1963 to strengthen the county board of commissioners and a new manager was appointed in 1965. The new manager enjoyed greater confidence among the board members than did his predecessors, and the Metro government entered a period of political stability. A proposal to strengthen the executive branch by replacing the county manager with a strong mayor was resoundingly defeated in a 1972 referendum.[35]

A county-wide, council manager form of government having been settled on, the government faced a second problem: securing an adequate revenue base for its operations. While Metro was given greatly expanded urban functions in 1957, it was not given the tax base needed to perform these functions adequately. Because of a peculiarity of Florida law, Metro was denied such traditional urban fund-raising sources as excise taxes, franchise fees, a share of the state cigarette taxes, and the authority to impose taxes on utility bills.[36] Consequently, it was forced to rely almost exclusively on property taxes to finance the new services. This problem has been eased considerably in recent years by broadening the county's revenue sources. By 1970–71, the county's reliance on property taxes had diminished to the point that they provided only about a third of the total county revenue.[37] Even with this broadening of the fiscal base, considerable revenue problems remain. The county still does not have the revenues needed to finance all of the services it is responsible for providing. Residents of the municipalities complain that their taxes are supporting services which are delivered primarily in the unincorporated areas.[38]

Despite its difficulties, Miami's Metro has many significant accomplishments to its credit. First among these, undoubtedly, is the fact that it is the only successful two-tier experiment in the United States. As late as 1970, two of the country's leading scholars on metropolitan governance wrote that the "permanency of the two-level arrangement in Metropolitan Miami is still in doubt."[39] Since 1970, that doubt has fairly well disappeared. Metro has endured in Miami. And that in itself is a significant accomplishment. Since inception it has successfully integrated a haphazard county government. It has drawn up the area's first general land use plan. It has established uniform, county-wide traffic laws and uniform subdivision ordinances. It has taken steps toward the establishment of an area-wide bus system. Master plans for water and sewers have been prepared but a county-wide sewer system still does not exist. Other public services have been improved considerably. Expensive duplication of many services by county and the municipal governments has been greatly reduced. And the provision of services to the minority populations has been significantly upgraded.[40]

Toronto: A Federative Government

In contrast to Miami, Toronto represents a true federative government.[41] Dade County has unincorporated areas in which the two-tier system does not operate. In Toronto, by contrast, two levels of government operate throughout the entire metropolitan area. A second difference lies in the nature of representation. In Miami, the city governments are not represented in the county government. In Toronto, in contrast, the city governments themselves have been represented from the very beginning on the Metropolitan Council.

By the 1950s Toronto was plagued with the same metropolitan growth problems that plagued United States metropolises. Because of governmental fragmentation, there was an inability to plan regionally. The metropolis was without adequate water and sewage facilities and a modern, coordinated public transit system, and individual jurisdictions were unable to finance major projects and programs.

In 1947 a Toronto and Suburban Planning Board was established to propose an equitable means of providing water, sewage, transit, parks, and public education services. Two years later it issued a report recommending the progressive amalgamation of the thirteen municipalities in the metropolitan area. This proposal was rejected by suburban officials, who suggested instead a form of metropolitan government that would guarantee the existence of the thirteen municipalities. The Ontario Province Municipal Board studied the two plans and in 1953 issued a report, know as the Cumming Report, which recommended a federal system that was very similar to the plan proposed by the suburban officials.

Based on most of the recommendations of the Cumming Report, the Ontario province legislature passed the Municipality of Metropolitan Toronto Act, which created a 24-member Metropolitan Council. Twelve of the members were municipal officials from the city of Toronto. And the other twelve were municipal officials from each of the twelve suburbs. The Metropolitan Council selected its own chairman, who was not obliged to be one of the twenty-four councilmembers.

The Metropolitan Council was made responsible for providing services which transcended local boundaries. These primarily included property assessment, construction and maintenance of freeways, and development of regional parks. Other functions such as street lights, provision of public health services, fire protection, and marriage licenses were left to the individual municipalities.

The early years of metropolitan government in Toronto were a time of unmitigated success in providing services which had been neglected. The water and sewer systems were greatly expanded. More schools were built. An extensive program of expressway construction was undertaken. Subway and bus lines were extended. A regional park system was created. Because of the very high financial rating given the Metropolitan Council, it is estimated that having Metro handle all the capital financing costs saved over $50 million in interest charges during the first ten years of its existence.[42]

Despite these successes, a split occurred in the Metropolitan Council in the early 1960s which nearly destroyed it. In 1963 the Toronto representatives on the council proposed a subsidy for the Toronto Transit Commission, which had suffered a severe drop in passengers since Metro's inception in 1954. The subsidy was bitterly opposed by the suburbanites who were not served by any of the subway lines. When the council finally approved a $2.5 million subsidy, two suburbs retaliated by filing a suit challenging the legality of this subsidy. The *Toronto Telegram* wrote a blistering editorial which clearly indicated the basic problem with the Metropolitan Council. "Metro is a balkanized state where each municipality subordinates the interests of the whole to its own interests."[43]

The net result of the conflict over transit was a reorganization of the Metropolitan Council in 1966 which eliminated Toronto and the thirteen old suburbs and replaced them with six new boroughs of a new municipality. Rather than allocate each suburb a seat on the Metropolitan Council, as had been done previously, seats were now allotted among the boroughs on the basis of one-person, one-vote.

A general assessment of Metropolitan Toronto after almost two decades of operation indicates that two-level federation in the metropolitan area is a viable form of government. Toronto does possess one advantage which does not exist in any state in the United States, however. Both at the creation of Metro in Toronto and at the time of the divisive split over transit in 1963, a provincial government existed which was capable of taking decisive action. The closest approximation to this in the United States occurred in Indianapolis and the Twin Cities, where the state legislatures created the new metropolitan units without recourse to referendums.

METROPOLITAN GOVERNMENT AND THE RACIAL MINORITIES

Creation of metropolitan governments has had an immediate and apparently negative impact on the voting *potential* of central city blacks. Especially in Jacksonville and Nashville, blacks had constituted a large and growing portion of the central city populations prior to the consolidations and could reasonably have looked forward to wielding an increasing influence over the city government. After consolidation, however, their percentage of the populations was considerably reduced. Similar situations have led black leaders to oppose metropolitan reforms proposed in several metropolises. In Jacksonville, most black leaders supported consolidation, but opposition came from two black leaders who feared dilution of black voting strength and from one black who had been previously aligned with the old city government.[44] Black voters approved the plan by a margin of 59 to 41 percent.[45] In Nashville, the black leadership was also divided, while the black electorate voted against the plan by a margin of about 56 to 44 percent.[46]

Whether the *potential* decline in black voting strength actually occurred is dubious. Nashville blacks had been guaranteed a district system of representation in the new council, and this was a marked improvement over the complete lack of representation which they had suffered under the old at-large system of electing councilmen in Nashville.[47] Furthermore, an analysis of all postconsolidation elections in Nashville found no evidence that any black candidates were defeated because of the dilution of black voting strength.[48] In Indianapolis, Unigov's district system of electing councilmembers not only ensured blacks of representation on the new council, but it gave the black militants and activists a stronger voice in both city and political party affairs.[49] In Jacksonville, the district system of election also guaranteed some black representation on the new council,[50] although some observers commented that the number of 'black seats ended up being fewer than the number tacitly agreed upon prior to the consolidation.[51] In summary, then, the numerical representation of blacks seems to have met or exceeded expectations in Nashville, Indianapolis, and Jacksonville. The establishment of metropolitan governments has not necessarily reduced black representation in terms of numbers.

Numerical representation is not the same thing as effective representation, however. And how the creation of metropolitan government affected the political efficacy of blacks seems to vary from city to city. In Indianapolis, Unigov has been much more successful than previous Democratic administrations in the city at getting federal grants for programs which operated primarily in black neighborhoods.[52] This no doubt is due to the fact that the Republican-dominated Unigov has been able to maintain good relations with the Republican administrations in Washington. In Jacksonville, observers report that both black and white leaders view the postconsolidation system "as a vast improvement over pre-consolidation days."[53] Black employment increased under the new consolidated government, and black representatives have been appointed to every advisory board. Systematic efforts have been made to hire more black policemen and firemen. In contrast to an underrepresentation in the preconsolidation council, black representation on the consolidated government council reflects the black percentage of the area's population. Apparently as a move designed to show good faith to the black population, the first sewers installed under the consolidated government's sewer construction program were in black neighborhoods.[54]

The example of metropolitan reorganization in these three cities does not provide a definitive answer to the questions of what minority populations can expect from metropolitan government. But they do indicate that the question is a good deal more complicated than simply asking whether metropolitan government will dilute the voting potential of blacks.* Some important trade-offs are involved. In Jacksonville,

* This seems to have been the primary concern of much literature on the impact of metropolitan reorganization on the black population. [See Frances Fox Piven and Rich-

for example, blacks who already comprised 40 percent of the old city's population before consolidation looked forward to the day when they could have a majority and win the mayor's office. But it would have been the mayoralty of a city that was definitely on the decline. This trade-off was expressed succinctly by one local black leader who was subsequently elected to one of the consolidated government's at-large council seats. "I might have been the black mayor, but I would have been only a referee in bankruptcy."[55] Immediate influence in a viable government was preferable to dominance over an unviable one. Some scholars think that metropolitan reorganizations can be structured in ways that will protect the black population.[56] Finally, one scholar has pointed out that the special district forms of government which have proliferated in metropolitan areas have been "so rarely open to black influence . . . [that black leaders] . . . may become strong advocates for metropolitan forms that are answerable to the voters and that are not obstructed in decision making by ad hoc boards, and single function oriented agencies and districts."[57]

On balance, then, metropolitan government has not diminished black representation in Nashville, Jacksonville, or Indianapolis. It may even have made that representation slightly more effective. But the emphasis would have to be on the word *slightly*. The available evidence seems to suggest that metropolitan government has had very little impact, positive or negative, on black power. Black influence remained relatively unchanged.[58]

RESTRUCTURING METROPOLITAN GOVERNMENT: CONSEQUENCES AND BIASES

Consolidation, strengthening the urban county, and two-tier government: what conclusions can be drawn about these devices for restructuring metropolitan government? Are they really effective mechanisms for coping with the consequences of the multi-centered metropolis? Do they provide effective means for responding to the needs of unorganized citizens as well as the demands of organized groups? And, whatever the merits of these reorganizations, are they really indicative of change when only four major consolidations have occurred in the last thirty years, only 6 percent of metropolitan counties are using the

---

ard A. Cloward, "What Chance for Black Power?" *The New Republic* 185, no. 13 (March 30, 1968): 23; and Lee Sloan and Robert French, "Race and Governmental Consolidation in Jacksonville," *Negro Educational Review* 2, no. 1 (April–July 1970): 72–78.]

most advanced form of county government, and no United States metropolis has adopted a federative scheme of government? Have the reorganization movements brought substantial change? Or have they simply been sound and fury, signifying nothing?

A response to these questions must first address the problem of division of powers between the local and area-wide governments. None of the systems has provided a definitive resolution to this problem. In Miami, disagreement over these issues was so disruptive that it almost destroyed the Metro. In Jacksonville, problems have been recurring over the inclusion of existing municipalities under the urban zone services provided by the consolidated government. And the reorganization of metropolitan counties so that they can assume more governmental functions, as was recommended by the Advisory Commission on Intergovernmental Relations, inevitably causes conflict with existing municipalities that already provide services which the strengthened county government may attempt to assume.

Metropolitan governments are uniformly much more successful in dealing with the physical questions such as sewers, water supply, or parks and recreation than they are in dealing with social issues such as fiscal disparities, race relations, open housing, and the location of public, low-income housing in the suburbs. In terms of controlling metropolitan development and suburban sprawl, the metros do not seem to be much more effective than are the governments in metropolitan areas where metros have not been created. The proliferation of suburban incorporations has been greatly slowed down, but only recently has suburban development been tied to any metropolitan development plans.

Nevertheless, metropolitan government, as it exists in Nashville, Jacksonville, Indianapolis, and Miami, has some inherent biases. First, it has a greater bias toward professional values in determining metropolitan priorities and in settling metropolitan problems than did the prereform governments.[59] The professionalism of the city planner and the public administration specialist becomes much more institutionalized in metropolitan government than it does in suburban or old central city government. The party politician and the ward alderman do not necessarily disappear under metropolitan government, but they necessarily have to conduct themselves in the language of the professionals and on the terms of the professionals when they deal with certain items. A comprehensive development plan, for example, may be necessary to get some kinds of federal grants. And it must be drafted in language that is at least understandable if not acceptable to the federal planning officials involved in making the grants. Not only do the planning professionals determine the language to be used, they also play a significant role in setting the agenda for issues that the metropolitan governments will confront.[60]

Some observers have suggested that this bias toward professionalism in metropolitan government also involves a bias toward public regardingness.[61] The professional planners will supposedly have in mind the overall interests of the public in the entire metropolitan area. Such an assertion is based, however, on the assumption that planners are public regarding. As will be seen in Chapter 10, such an assumption is difficult to verify.

Second, metropolitan governments have not eliminated the biases of the multi-centered metropolis on the social-access issues of zoning, education, and housing. These governments have been much more successful at tackling physical construction problems about which a consensus exists than at tackling social-access problems about which there often is no consensus. As Oliver Williams has noted, the tendency has been to rebel against efforts to transfer such social-access functions to metropolitan-level governments.[62]

Third, metropolitan governments are biased against citizen participation in their affairs. Voting turnouts for the election of metropolitan councils have usually been low. And none of the metropolitan governments created to date has moved very effectively to involve citizens in their activities.

Fourth, because the leaders of many urban groups take metropolitan government seriously enough to oppose its formation, these leaders probably *think* that metropolitan governments will be biased against their interests. The opposition by suburban municipal officials, special district officials, and the administrative officers of city and county governments leads one to suspect that metropolitan government has the capacity to counter some of the existing biases toward the functional fiefdoms that now exist in the metropolis. Considerations of the impact of metropolitan government upon the black communities indicate that the inevitable dilution of black voting strength can be mitigated by certain structural arrangements to guarantee blacks a voice in the resulting metropolitan government. Consequently, the evidence suggests that metropolitan government, if it is designed appropriately, does have the potential to make some noticeable alterations in the structure of bias toward the existing functional fiefdoms.

Finally, the possibility exists that metropolitan governments themselves might be biased against citizen input. In Chapter 5 the movement toward community control was explained as a reaction against the unresponsiveness of big central city governments to citizen demands. The same unresponsiveness would seem likely to occur in metropolitan governments unless some forms of control sharing accompanied the metropolitan reform. Two developments give encouragement along these lines. First is the attempt made in Indianapolis to establish neighborhood councils. If these prove successful in lessening citizen alienation in the relatively limited sphere in which they will operate, then the stage may be set for expanding their sphere of operations in Indianapolis and adopting the device in other areas. The second encouraging development involves the increased authority that the metropolitan governments are given over special districts. As noted, this could lessen the autonomy of certain functional fiefdoms and at least make them more accountable to the political leaders elected by the citizenry. There would then be at least a tenuous link between the vote of the citizen and the kinds of policies that are carried out in his neighborhood.

This chapter has painted a relatively optimistic picture of the consequences of metropolitan government, showing it as partially effective and probably more effective than continuing the status quo. But the nagging fact remains that only a minute fraction of American metropolises have adopted metropolitan governments. What good is metropolitan government if it cannot be achieved? This is a reasonable question. An even more reasonable question might be: Under what conditions can it be achieved? This topic is discussed in the next chapter.

Some Suggested Readings

Melvin B. Mogulof, *Five Metropolitan Governments* (Washington, D.C.: The Urban Institute, 1973). Uses a comparative format to analyze the consolidated government of Jacksonville, the urban county of Miami, the federated government of Toronto, the multi-function special district in Portland, Oregon, and the planning and policy coordinating Metropolitan Council of Minneapolis–Saint Paul.

Reshaping Government in Metropolitan Areas (New York: Committee for Economic Development, 1970). A forceful argument for the creation of two-tiered governments in United States metropolises.

Advisory Commission on Intergovernmental Relations, *Report A–41. Substate Regionalism and the Federal System. Volume II, Regional Governance: Promise and Performance — Case Studies* (Washington, D.C.: U.S. Government Printing Office, 1973). Of the six-volume series on substate regionalism, this volume is probably the most useful to political scientists. It contains special articles by prominent scholars on several of the major attempts to reorganize governments in metropolitan areas.

Joseph F. Zimmerman, "Metropolitan Reform in the U.S.: An Overview," *Public Administration Review* 30, no. 5 (September/October 1970): 531–543. A summary of attempts to create metropolitan governments up to 1970.

Major works for some of the metropolitan governments discussed in this chapter are indicated below.

Brett W. Hawkins, *Nashville Metro: The Politics of City-County Consolidation* (Nashville, Tenn.: Vanderbilt University Press, 1966).

Edward Sofen, *The Miami Metropolitan Experiment* (Bloomington: Indiana University Press, 1963).

Frank Smallwood, *Metro Toronto: A Decade Later* (Toronto: Bureau of Municipal Research, 1963).

Harold Kaplan, *Urban Political Systems: A Functional Analysis of Metro Toronto* (New York: Columbia University Press, 1967).

William C. Havard, Jr., and Floyd C. Corty, *Rural-Urban Consolidation: The Merger of Governments in the Baton Rouge Area* (Baton Rouge: Louisiana State University Press, 1964).

Chapter 9

The metropolitan reorganization schemes discussed in the previous chapter are much more important for what they aspired to accomplish than for their practical applications. Whatever the accomplishments of existing metropolitan governments in Miami or Nashville, the fact remains that very few consolidations or two-tier governments have been established. It would be a mistake, however, to conclude that campaigns for metropolitan reform are a thing of the past. In the early 1970s over forty areas were considering some form of governmental consolidation, and in many of these areas metropolitan reform campaigns are

The Politics of Metropolitan Reform

likely to occur for several years. Because of this continuing impulse toward reform, it would be useful to examine the politics of metropolitan reform in order to identify the reasons why it has been so difficult to accomplish.

In Chapter 9 two major unsuccessful attempts at county government reform (Saint Louis and Cleveland) will be contrasted with two successful attempts (Nashville and Miami). Since the structure of the reformed governments in Nashville and Miami have already been described, this chapter will focus only on the question of why the reforms were successful there. It will then examine a major metropolitan reform in the Twin Cities which, like Indianapolis, avoided a referendum by having the reforms enacted directly by the state legislature. Finally, some of the arguments and assumptions of the reformers are evaluated in light of the reform campaigns in these metropolises, which leads to the question of biases in the reform movement struggle.

These five examples are chosen for analysis because they illustrate well the factors which have dominated metropolitan reform campaigns in general. When scholars analyze the recent defeats of metropolitan government proposals in places such as Durham, North Carolina, and Portland, Oregon, they will probably find the same forces at work there that are described here. And proponents for metropolitan governmental reform in the many places now considering them would be well advised to study these campaigns very carefully.

TWO FAILURES AT FRONTAL ASSAULT

Saint Louis: Defeat of the City-County Multi-purpose District Plan

In 1959 a multi-purpose district proposal called the Greater Saint Louis City-County District was rejected by the voters. A relatively mild metropolitan reform measure, the City-County District would not have replaced any existing local government. It would have taken over the functions of only one existing metropolitan district, the Sewer Board. But in addition to sewer services, it would have been given responsibility for a variety of other county-wide services, including a metropolitan road system, mass transit facilities, all property tax assessments, and the preparation of a comprehensive development plan. The new district would have been governed by an elected council. The reasons for the rejection of this proposal are very important, for they present a classic explanation of the defeat of metropolitan government reform proposals that has broad application.

The Setting

For almost a century Saint Louis–area politics have been characterized by a sharp division between the city and the county politicians. Since 1876 the county government has operated only beyond the city boundaries. Within the city, traditional county functions, such as welfare or public health services, have been performed by the city government. This has provoked a sharp division in the city between two political forces. On the one hand, a set of public offices grouped around the mayor constitute the focal point of those interests concerned with broad questions of public policy. They tend to be supported by the newspapers, the downtown business interests, and voters in the middle-class wards. Contrasted to this mayor's office group is a set of county offices which perform the traditional county government services in the city. Together these offices make very little policy, but they provide nearly a thousand non–civil service jobs.[1] While the mayor's office group adheres to the symbols of good government and has little patronage to dispense, the opposite is true of the county office group. Officials of the latter serve a constituency of organized labor activists and political leaders from low-income wards.[2]

Saint Louis uses the strong mayor–council form of city government. While the aldermen are elected from wards and are usually dominated by a Democratic prolabor faction, the mayor represents an electoral coalition between the ward-based politics of the lower-income areas and the middle-class politics of the so-called newspaper wards.[3] Because of this broader constituency, the mayor's office has served as a focal point for those persons interested in general policy questions for the city.

One scholar, noting the existence of the ward politics, the strong labor unions, and the preponderance of lower-income people, commented that the city is governed "better than she should be."[4] Although the existence of strong unions, ward-based politics, and a high percentage of low-income people have often constituted a background that facilitated corruption in local politics, Saint Louis politics have been relatively honest and clean for almost two generations. The city has normally been governed by the Democrats since 1949, while Republicans ruled from 1941 to 1949. The central city of Saint Louis has been losing population steadily over the last two decades (from 856,796 in 1950, to 622,000 in 1970). By 1970 the central city contained barely a quarter of the total metropolitan population. Also, by 1970 the city was about 41 percent black, as compared to about 28 percent in 1960 and 18 percent in 1950.

In contrast to a fairly unified city government and a declining city population, the county has been characterized by a growing population and a highly fragmented government. At the time of the battle over charter reform, the county contained ninety-eight municipalities which ranged in population from 50 people to over 50,000. There were twenty fire protection districts, twenty-seven school systems, and a county-wide school district for the handicapped. Since 1950, the county government has operated under a home rule charter with an at-large elected supervisor serving as the chief executive. However, since several other county department officials are elected separately, the chief executive has limited control over the administrative apparatus. In contrast to the partisan ballot for county offices, local municipal elections are nonpartisan and are dominated by the local Republicans.

Because of this fragmentation in county government, the animosities between city and county, the partisan differences between the suburban municipal officials and the Saint Louis city officials, and the vivid separation of the city and county, very little formal cooperation existed between the city of Saint Louis and suburban governments in the county.[5] Very few mechanisms were available to coordinate public

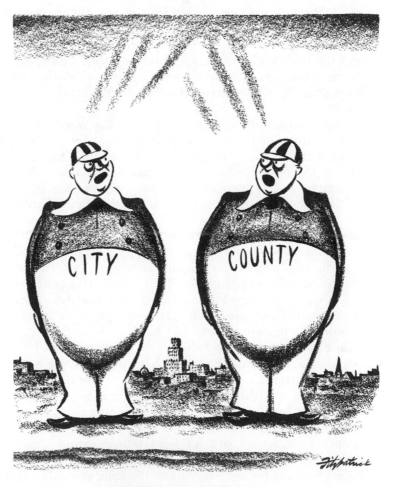

"MEET ME AT ST. LOOIE, LOOIE, —

The difficulty of bringing county and city together is portrayed in this cartoon by Fitzpatrick.

Fitzpatrick in the *St. Louis Post-Dispatch*, December 12, 1956.

services or to handle the suburban sprawl. The history of attempts to end the fragmentation and to bring about a general governmental unification did not bode well for reformers. Out of five previous charter revision attempts to improve governmental relations between the city and county, only one had passed.

How the District Plan Was Created

Particularly disturbing to the reformers was the defeat of a referendum in 1955 which would have established an area-wide transit authority. In response to this defeat and in response to the need to attain area-wide control over transit, the mayor of Saint Louis and the county supervisor formed a committee to study the transit problem. While that study was being conducted, an ambitious alderman named A. J. Cervantes formed a Citizens' Committee for City-County Coordination to seek a new metropolitan charter. Cervantes was candidate for president of the Board of Aldermen at the time and was seeking an issue on which he could base his candidacy. He decided to promote the plan for city-county consolidation.[6]

Cervantes' first move was to gather the petition signatures needed to create a board to draft the consolidation charter. This brought him into conflict with Saint Louis Mayor Raymond Tucker, who apparently looked upon Cervantes as a potential candidate for his position and did not wish to see this rival given any advantage.[7] The mayor countered Cervantes' initiative with a plan to have Saint Louis University and Washington University conduct a survey of the area's governmental problems.

After a year's study, the survey team produced a recommendation for a multi-purpose special district very similar to the one which was finally put before the voters in 1959. A charter committee, called a Freeholders' Board, was created to draft a new charter that would create such a district.

No sooner was the Freeholders' Board created than it encountered two difficulties which plagued its efforts to get a new charter accepted. First, none of its members enjoyed major political stature in the community. And second, it was divided almost evenly into two irreconcilable blocs. One bloc was based mainly among the city representatives who favored a city-county consolidation, and the other was based mainly among the county and suburban representatives who favored the university survey's recommendation of a multi-function metropolitan district. Four members were neutral and their votes could swing either way. After almost a year of hearings and arguments over five different plans, in April 1959 the board, by a vote of 10 to 9, proposed the multi-purpose district solution. So divisive had the arguments of the two factions become that some of the members of the losing faction even refused to sign the final report. Nor did the board members campaign for the new charter once they had approved it.[8]

Who Was For the Plan and Who Was Against It

Lining up in favor of the new plan were, first of all, the major business leaders. They did not find the fragmented government conducive to good business practices. They felt not only that a metropolitan government would produce a better investment climate, but that it had a public relations value for them. The reorganization was also backed by several religious spokesmen, including the Church Federation of Greater Saint Louis, the Catholic newspaper, and a prominent rabbi. Their support of the district plan had a public relations value for the churchmen as it had for the businessmen in that it was consistent with their general support for good government. The League of Women Voters and the American Association of University Women campaigned in favor of the plan. The local chapters of the Institute of Architects and the American Institute of Planners endorsed the plan. Finally, both metropolitan daily newspapers endorsed the plan.

Notably absent from this list of supporters were some of the most politically powerful groups in Saint Louis. The leaders of the Saint Louis AFL-CIO Labor Council actively opposed the plan because they did not think it went far enough. Since they already had considerable influence on city government, they preferred a city-county merger that would enable them to extend their influence to the metropolitan level. As for the political party leaders, the city leaders were cool to the plan for reasons similar to those of the labor leaders. In the county, the leaders of both parties actively opposed the plan: the Democrats because it would force them into closer ties with the city Democrats, and the Republicans because they feared any move that would spread the city Democratic machine's influence into the suburbs.

In addition to the party and labor officials, many municipal officials in the suburbs spoke against the plan. Many of them were part-time office holders who may have felt their positions threatened if the plan went through. In the suburban areas, twenty-two of the twenty-nine weekly newspapers opposed the reorganization.

Black leaders were notable for their absence either as supporters or opponents of the plan. Although blacks constituted almost a third of the city's population, the district plan did not affect the issues that concerned them most vitally.

A key political figure was Mayor Raymond Tucker of Saint Louis. Although he had been responsible for establishing the original university study group, Tucker maintained a judicious silence on the district plan itself until one month before the election. At that time he announced his opposition to it. His motives seem to have been mixed between a political desire to avoid creating a rival status position and a sincere belief that the plan did not go far enough in solving the area's problems. When it became obvious that the mayor was not going to back the plan, many other civic leaders began to lose their public enthusiasm for it as well.

Perhaps the only major political figure actively engaged in fighting for the plan was Alderman A. J. Cervantes, whose City-County Coordination Committee decided to head up the campaign. But his office as an alderman did not give him the position or the stature to overcome the opposition and the apathy which surrounded the campaign.

On balance, the forces were obviously weighted more heavily against the plan than for it. One very knowledgeable team of observers commented that "the forces at work against it were too powerful, and the groups for it too uncommitted to bring about the proposed changes."[9]

Conducting the Campaign

Not only was the campaign in Saint Louis biased heavily against the reformers from the start, the campaign itself was conducted without zeal or enthusiasm. Having received generous campaign contributions, the proponents hired a public relations firm to undertake a mass media campaign for them. Informational discussion groups were organized in neighborhoods, but precinct work as a tactic failed. Some of the influential persons who had endorsed the concept in the beginning failed to campaign actively on its behalf, and the campaign organizers were not even able to secure a prominent civic official to serve as campaign chairman.

The opponents of the plan were not very active, either. Several citizens' groups arose in different areas of the county to oppose the plan, but their effectiveness is difficult to measure. After the mayor of Saint Louis finally came out in opposition to the plan, even he did not campaign actively; he gave only two speeches on the subject. The most grass-roots opposition came from a Citizens' Committee for Self-Government, which scheduled over two dozen meetings to discuss the subject. But the meetings failed to arouse any interest among the citizenry, and attendance was generally very small.

Analyzing the Vote

When the plan finally came to a vote in November 1959, it was resoundingly defeated. The count was 43,478 to 21,343 in the city and 82,738 to 27,633 in the county. Through an analysis of the voting returns on the referendum, political scientist Henry J. Schmandt and his associates made several conclusions.

First, although the overall voter turnout was only about 40 percent, the turnout was positively related both to social rank and to partisan activity. Particularly in the city, the highest turnout occurred in the wards with the highest socioeconomic rank and in those few wards where a grass-roots campaign had been conducted.

Second, a positive relationship was found between social rank and support for the district plan. The strongest support came from the middle-class newspaper wards; the strongest opposition came from the Negro wards and the low-income wards.

Third, the most effective arguments of the metro opponents were that it would cause a tax increase, that it would promote super-government, and that it would cause a loss of local autonomy. These arguments were much more effective upon homeowners than they were upon renters.

Last, and most important, was the conclusion of Schmandt and his associates: "No metropolitan plan *can* pass over active opposition of the political parties. No such plan *is likely* to pass without partisan support."[10]

Cleveland: Defeat of the Cuyahoga County Home Rule Charter

On the same day that Saint Louis voters rejected the City-County District Plan, voters in metropolitan Cleveland also rejected a home rule charter proposal for Cuyahoga County, although by a much smaller margin. A short comparison will help to establish the generality of the patterns observed in Saint Louis.

The Setting

Two background factors in Cleveland were very similar to background factors which provided an unfavorable setting for the campaign in Saint Louis. Demographically, both Cleveland and Saint Louis suffered sharp population declines after reaching a peak about 1950. In Cleveland, the population declined from 914,878 in 1950 to 751,000 in 1970. The Negro population had increased from 16 percent of the city's population in 1950 to 34 percent in 1960 and to about 38 percent in 1970. Furthermore, while the central city population was declining, the suburban population was increasing.

Additionally, Cleveland and Saint Louis were similar in their previous history of unsuccessful attempts to achieve metropolitan reform. Cuyahoga County's home rule charter of 1959 was the tenth in a long series of charter reform proposals which had been put before the voters since the Great Depression. Despite all these reform proposals, Cleveland's municipal boundaries and the county's powers were basically the same in 1959 as they had been when the first charter reform proposal was voted on in 1932.

How the Plan Was Created

Like Saint Louis's plan in its creation, Cleveland's 1959 home rule charter proposal was the product of a metropolitan survey conducted from 1956 to 1958 by the Cleveland Metropolitan Services Commission. The commission was carefully selected to draw support from as many sectors of Cuyahoga County as possible and to draw opposition from as few as possible. With Ford Foundation financing, in 1958 it produced a report that urged an extensive expansion of the powers of Cuyahoga County government.[11]

Who Was For the Plan and Who Was Against It

The proponents for the plan in Cleveland were much more successful in finding persons of political stature to support them than were the proponents in Saint Louis. They received endorsements from prominent businessmen, leaders of both political parties, and several major politicians. However, they failed to get support from either the mayor of Cleveland or the leaders of the city's increasingly important black community. In fact, the Metropolitan Services Commission had deliberately refused to make any special concessions to leaders of the black community, by neither offering them special positions on the commission nor guaranteeing them employment on it. The mayor of Cleveland and several black community leaders actively campaigned against the plan. The heads of two city agencies whose jobs would be transferred to the county government under the new charter also joined the opposition.

Conducting the Campaign

In both Saint Louis and Cleveland the campaigns were conducted on the basis of making an intellectual appeal for greater efficiency and modernity in government. This appeal is referred to as a capitalist-realist approach by sociologist Scott Greer. Its heroes are "the technicians who are experts in government, businessmen who want to see government run at least as well as the business corporation."[12] But in neither Saint Louis nor Cleveland did the reformers combine their efficiency appeals with an attack on any deficiencies in the status quo government or its incumbent office holders. Greer commented:

> This belief in the integrity of existing government combined, in St. Louis and Cleveland, with a desire to neutralize the political parties, since it was thought that they might defeat any charter that threatened their organization and patronage systems. The campaigns deliberately avoided antagonizing the party chieftains. At most the supporters of the plans said, "We will give you administration by experts, under elected officials responsible to the voters."[13]

Because of their attempts to avoid antagonizing the existing power holders, the charter proponents were put on the defensive when the charter came under attack by the city department heads whose jobs were to be taken over by the county. The departments made colorful statements which got them newspaper headlines, while the educational approach of the charter proponents made much drabber copy for the reporters.[14] One of the department heads was quoted, "I'd say to them, 'Say — what's wrong with the present situation? You got a good government. What's wrong? Show me.' I'd get right down to specifics. — 'What's been done wrong?' "[15]

Not wishing to provoke animosity from other political leaders attached to the status quo, the reformers were unable to pinpoint abuses. They were reduced to arguing that the new charter would produce a more efficient, more representative government that would provide better services. The problem with this argument was that surveys in both Saint Louis and Cleveland indicated that most voters were content with the existing level of services. In Saint Louis, a public opinion survey discovered that of 150 units of government, only one was thought to be operating poorly. And that one, ironically, was the sewer district, which was a metropolitan agency.[16] In Cleveland, a voter opinion survey obtained similar results. Of nine major services which would come under the authority of the new charter government, a majority of the respondents said they were completely satisfied with all but bus and transit.[17] And the governmental areas that evoked strong dissatisfaction, such as housing and juvenile delinquency, were not to be handled by the new charter government. Consequently, the reformers in both Saint Louis and Cleveland were fighting uphill battles. They were asking people to reform the agencies which provided the services with which the people were the most satisfied. And for the services about which people expressed dissatisfaction, the reformers offered no relief.

In conducting their campaigns, the reformers in Cleveland and Saint Louis faced another problem as well. They did not have a natural constituency of voters to whom they could appeal. Political scientist Henry J. Schmandt and his associates commented that this problem is faced by good-government reformers generally.

> This coalition of good government forces and business is further handicapped in issues requiring popular referendum by lack of a constituency that can be readily mobilized. The group's effectiveness in winning electoral support is therefore severely limited unless it can entice into the cause such mass-based groups as the political parties and labor. The press is similarly handicapped. Although it has a mass audience, its ability to mobilize the public in a civic cause is restricted by the interests and predispositions of its readers, their readiness to listen, and their capacity to understand issues.[18]

Analyzing the Vote

When the issue finally came to a vote in Cleveland, it was narrowly defeated by a margin of 29,000 out of 193,000 votes in the city and 8,000 out of 226,000 votes in the county. Two political scientists conducted an intensive analysis of the vote and drew a number of conclusions about Cleveland's elections for metropolitan reform.[19] First, they discovered that voters were much more likely to approve the drafting of reform charters than they were to approve the charters themselves. In fact, Cleveland voters had approved the drafting of charters three times (in 1934, 1949, and 1958), but they had not approved any charter change.

A second aspect of the Cleveland vote was very similar to the vote in Saint Louis. In both cities the higher socioeconomic areas voted more strongly for metropolitan reform while lower socioeconomic wards and black wards voted heavily against reform. In Cleveland this was particularly noteworthy, because blacks had consistently supported metropolitan reform proposals in eight previous referenda from 1933 to 1957. In 1958 and 1959, however, the black vote went heavily against the charter. This reversal has usually been attributed to an unwillingness among blacks to dilute their voting potential by transferring power out of the city government to a county government that would be beyond their influence.[20]

A third pattern in Cleveland was found in the suburban vote. The suburban communities with a substantial tax base supported metropolitan reform more than did the suburbs with a poor tax base. The strongest suburban opposition came from the small industrial enclaves in the suburbs.

In summary, the reasons for defeat of the reform proposal in Cleveland were very similar to the reasons for the defeat of reform in Saint Louis. In neither place were the reformers able to generate any widespread excitement for their proposals. The balance of political forces for and against the charters were heavily weighted in favor of the opponents. The minority communities were not brought into the campaign for reform. The interests of certain status quo supporters were at stake, and they opposed the plans. There was no evidence that many voters were dissatisfied with the service areas that were to be turned over to the new metropolitan governments. And the plans themselves offered no prospect for improving the services with which voters were considerably dissatisfied. Finally, the plans did not evoke support among numerous working-class and lower-middle-income neighborhoods, because the plans were solidly defeated in those areas.

TWO FRONTAL ASSAULTS THAT SUCCEEDED: ELEMENTS OF SUCCESSFUL CAMPAIGNING

Since the reform charters of Miami and Nashville were discussed in considerable detail previously, there is no need to describe them again here. What has not yet been analyzed are the ways in which the campaigning for metropolitan government in Miami and Nashville differed from the patterns observed in Cleveland and Saint Louis.

Levels of Public Discontent

In Saint Louis, Cleveland, and some other cities where voter surveys have been conducted,[21] voters were not markedly dissatisfied with the provisions of government services.* In Nashville, voters were dissatisfied.[22] And for several years prior to the charter reform, voters in

---

* In Flint, Michigan, a survey discovered that not a single service was felt to be unsatisfactory by a majority of the population.

Miami were not only concerned over tax inequities, but they were upset about charges of corruption in police services in the city of Miami. It would seem, then, that substantial public discontent with public services creates a climate favorable to metropolitan reform if the proposed new governmental structure can offer some hope for satisfying that discontent.

The Purification Ritual

A second major difference between the successful and the unsuccessful reform attempts is closely associated with this first difference. The reform proposal has a much better chance for success if there is widespread public dissatisfaction with government officials, government agencies, government practices, or particular politicians. The new government can then be sold as a device for purging the government of its unpopular elements; and the campaign can be run as what Scott Greer terms a purification ritual. In Nashville, the extremely unpopular green sticker tax and the city's annexation moves were successfully blamed on Nashville Mayor Ben West. Thus a vote for the charter in 1962 could be sold as a vote against the mayor and his unpopular practices. In Miami, the charter proponents pointed out that the new charter government would be able to confront tax inequities and other aspects of government which drew strong feelings in much of the county.[23] In Cleveland and Saint Louis, the charter proponents were unable to do either of these things. Thus, charter campaigns appear to have a better chance to succeed if their organizers can make a credible attack on some aspect or feature of the incumbents that is unpopular with a substantial part of the electorate.

Neutralizing Potential Opposition

A third factor was the ability of the charter proponents to neutralize their potential opposition. In Nashville, the effectiveness of Mayor Ben West's political opposition in 1962 was neutralized by his own unpopularity. In Miami, the political party leaders and labor organizers were never very important in city politics. The metropolitan dailies, which had limited influence in Saint Louis, were among the major molders of opinion in Miami. Thus, one of the keys to victory was to turn the balance of politically important forces in favor of the charter, as in Miami and Nashville, rather than against it, as in Saint Louis. Even this tactic is not a guarantee of success, however. In Cleveland substantial political party support existed for the plan, but it was still defeated.

Background Factors

Another difference between the successful and unsuccessful plans lies in the demographic and developmental background factors. The major city-county consolidations established through referenda have all occurred in the South. Part of this must be attributed to the traditional reliance in the South upon counties as the basic political and administrative units. Southern metropolises have typically been surrounded by fewer incorporated suburbs than have Northern metropolises, so fewer local municipal officials have a vested interest that would be harmed by a metropolitan government. In both Saint Louis and Cleveland, the officials of many suburbs could and did oppose the new charter. In addition, in Miami the suburbanites are generally emigres from other areas of the country rather than ex–Miami City residents. They therefore have fewer attachments to traditional political structures in Miami and fewer emotional ties to the Miami area.[24]

Considering these differences, Nashville and Miami are more atypical than typical of most American metropolises. Unlike in the cases of Miami, Nashville, and Jacksonville, widespread dissatisfaction with governmental services apparently does not exist in most metropolises. This limits the utility of the purification ritual as a campaign device. Furthermore, the balance of political forces is normally more supportive of the status quo than it is of drastic change. Some years ago, political scientist Edward Banfield persuasively argued that the balance of political forces in most metropolises is more likely to be against metropolitan reform than in favor of metropolitan reform.[25] Events since then have mostly confirmed Banfield's judgment.

Similarities between Successful and Unsuccessful Campaigns

Successful and unsuccessful attempts at metropolitan reform have had important similarities as well as differences. All four instances had a very low voter turnout. Despite the months of public relations campaigns for and against the charter reforms, most voters failed to understand them and many voters did not even know about them. A poll taken in Miami several months after the charter was passed found that almost two-thirds of the people did not know that a big change in county government had occurred.[26] It is not clear whether voter apathy is detrimental to metropolitan reform. A survey of eighteen refer-

endum votes on metropolitan charter reforms from 1952 to 1961 indicated that charters were defeated more often in heavy turnouts than in
light turnouts.[27]*

Besides low voter turnout, all four metropolitan elections showed a
similarity in the kinds of people who support metropolitan reforms and
the kinds who vote against them. As Table 9-1 shows, the strongest
supporters of metropolitan reform are also the groups which, as
pointed out earlier, are the weakest in their ability to mobilize an electorate. If central city radio and television stations, downtown commercial interests, real estate interests, banks, Leagues of Women Voters, or
academic spokesmen are never heard opposing a city-county consolidation and, on the contrary, are always highly visible in their support of
it, their political influence may well be discounted by many voters
before the campaign even begins. In contrast, some of the groups in
opposition to metropolitan reform quite often have a local constituency which they are able to mobilize when their interests are vitally
affected. Particularly important are the suburban government officials,
county employees, suburban government employees, suburban neighborhood groups, and racial minority leaders.

Perhaps the most important groups are those whose response to
metropolitan organization is not automatic, such as organized labor or
county officials. Although the study shown in Table 9-1 was conducted
during the 1950s, most of the patterns remained the same through the
1970s. The major changes since then have been a decline in the willingness of city officials and employees to support metropolitan reform
proposals. This occurred in the Jacksonville referendum in 1967 when
the city's daily newspaper opposed the new consolidation and local
officials attempted to put several obstacles in the path of an orderly
transition.[28]

IN THROUGH THE BACK DOOR:
THE TWIN CITIES

Miami, Nashville, Cleveland, Saint Louis, and Jacksonville all represent frontal assaults on the status quo in the sense that each of these
reform movements went directly to the voters to approve far-reaching
governmental changes. The metropolitan reforms achieved in Minneapolis–Saint Paul and Indianapolis differed from these others in that the

---

* Heavy turnout was defined as exceeding 50 percent of the turnout in the last preceding
presidential election.

TABLE 9-1

COMMUNITY ELEMENTS INVOLVED IN METROPOLITAN REFORM CAMPAIGNS 1950–1961

Community Element	Number of Metropolitan Areas in Which the Indicated Community Elements Played the Indicated Roles[a]							Total Score
	+3	+2	+1	0	−1	−2	−3	
Community Elements Strongly in Favor of Metropolitan Reform								
Metropolitan newspapers[b]	16	—	1	—	—	1	—	47
Leagues of Women Voters	11	4	1	1	—	—	—	42
Central city Chambers of Commerce	8	7	1	—	—	—	—	39
Central city commercial interests	6	6	5	—	—	—	—	35
Central city real estate interests	4	9	3	—	—	—	—	33
Radio and television stations	5	5	3	1	—	—	—	28
Banks	5	3	2	2	—	—	—	23
Central city officials[b]	5	3	4	2	2	—	—	20
Academic groups or spokesmen	2	6	2	1	—	—	—	20
Manufacturing industry	4	1	5	3	1	—	—	18
Utilities	4	3	1	—	1	—	—	18
Municipal Leagues or similar research groups	5	2	—	—	—	—	1	17
Central city homeowners	2	3	5	—	3	—	—	14
Community Elements Ambivalent toward Metropolitan Reform								
Central city employees	4	1	4	—	1	2	2	7
Suburban Chambers of Commerce	2	1	1	2	2	—	—	6
Taxpayers groups	—	4	1	1	—	—	1	6
Church groups	—	1	4	—	—	—	—	6
Central city political organizations	—	3	1	2	2	—	—	5
Central city neighborhood improvement groups	1	1	2	—	1	—	1	3
Labor unions	—	4	2	—	3	2	1	0
Parent Teacher Associations	—	1	1	—	—	—	1	0

reform was achieved entirely by the state legislature with no appeal directly to the voters. The consolidation plan in Indianapolis was discussed in the previous chapter. The Minneapolis–Saint Paul reform differed markedly from those previously discussed and merits a brief description.

In essence the Twin Cities Metropolitan Council is a metropolitan planning and policy coordination agency. It has four major powers. First, as the metropolitan planning agency, it is responsible for preparing the metropolitan development guide. The development guide is a statement of policies on topics that range from airports to a develop-

TABLE 9-1, continued

Community Element	Number of Metropolitan Areas in Which the Indicated Community Elements Played the Indicated Roles[a]							Total Score
	+3	+2	+1	0	−1	−2	−3	
State political leaders	—	—	2	—	—	1	—	0
Government suppliers	1	—	1	—	—	2	—	0
County political organizations	—	3	1	2	2	—	2	−1
County officials[b]	1	2	3	5	2	2	2	−2
Suburban homeowners	2	1	2	3	2	4	1	−3
Suburban neighborhood improvement groups	—	—	1	3	—	2	2	−7
Minority racial elements[c]	—	1	1	—	1	2	2	−8
Rural real estate interests	1	1	1	—	6	4	2	−8
Community Elements Strongly Opposed to Metropolitan Reform								
Suburban commercial interests	—	3	2	3	3	3	3	−10
Suburban real estate interests	—	2	3	—	3	3	2	−10
Farm organizations	1	—	1	—	2	2	3	−11
Officials of other local governments	1	—	1	2	2	2	3	−11
Employees of other local governments	—	—	1	1	2	1	3	−12
Other newspapers	2	1	2	1	3	2	6	−13
County employees	—	—	3	2	1	4	5	−21
Rural homeowners	—	1	—	2	5	4	4	−24
Farmers	—	—	—	—	1	10	4	−33

[a] +3 = A leading, active, unified element *for* the plan
+2 = A unitedly favoring element, but not in a strong or leading role
+1 = Predominantly for, but with some splitting or reservations
0 = Strong but divergent positions taken by some important components of group
−1 = Predominantly against, but with some splitting or reservations
−2 = A unitedly opposing element, but not in a strong or leading role
−3 = A leading, active, united element *against* the plan
[b] Opposed metropolitan reforms in some recent campaigns.
[c] Favored metropolitan reforms in some recent campaigns.

Source: Advisory Commission on Intergovernmental Relations, *Factors Affecting Voter Reactions to Governmental Reorganization in Metropolitan Areas* (Washington, D.C.: U.S. Government Printing Office, 1962), pp. 69–70.

mental framework. Second, the council is the federal A–95* review agency. Most federal grant applications must be cleared through a metropolitan review agency before they will be awarded. Since the Metropolitan Council also is the region's planning agency, it theoretically can use its review powers to coordinate federal grants around certain policies. For example, in 1973 the council successfully used the threat of a negative review to oblige one suburban municipality to provide

* A–95 refers to the memorandum from the Office of Management and Budget which establishes the guidelines to be used by the metropolitan review agencies.

low-income public housing. With more than 600 grant applications in the past two years, the council has given a negative review about 9 percent of the time.[29] Third, the state legislature has granted the council a veto power over the plans of metropolitan districts in the region. This is strictly a negative power. Although the council can veto the plans of metropolitan districts, it cannot force its own plans upon those agencies. Thus, when the council vetoed the Metropolitan Transit Commission's (MTC) plans for a rapid rail mass transit system, it was unable to impose its own plans for an expanded bus system on the MTC. The issue became deadlocked between the two agencies, and eventually the state legislature was called upon to resolve it. Finally, the council can suspend the plans of municipalities for up to ninety days if it feels those plans are inconsistent with the metropolitan development guide. It then can use the ninety-day period to negotiate a solution with the municipalities involved.

The Metropolitan Council was established by legislative act in 1967.[30] Prior to 1967 the Twin Cities region was plagued for many years by governmental fragmentation, tax inequities and disparities, and inconsistent provision of services throughout the region. The two central cities were ringed by over 130 incorporated suburban municipalities. This made central city annexation and city-county consolidation strategies useless for coping with metropolitan problems. And the need to provide services in the suburbs led to a proliferation of municipalities, metropolitan agencies, special districts, and joint-powers agreements. By the middle 1960s, the region had over 300 governments with very little coordination between them. The lack of coordination was beginning to produce a crisis in sewerage and water supply. A state Health Department investigation in 1959 discovered that 250,000 people in thirty-nine suburbs were getting their drinking water from contaminated wells. Over 400,000 people used septic tanks rather than sewers.[31] When the Federal Housing Administration announced that it would no longer insure mortgages that did not provide for central sewer and water hookups, it became clear that some kind of metropolitan-wide coordinating action was necessary.

Concerning the kind of action that was needed, at least eleven major groups put forward ideas to establish some form of metropolitan coordinating agency. Much interest was expressed in the Toronto federative experience, and several reformers traveled to Toronto to gain first-hand impressions of its operations, but federation was rejected as unsuitable and politically unfeasible. More conservative reformers were much interested in establishing a council of governments for the Twin Cities.

Perhaps the crucial event was the court-ordered reapportionment of the state legislature in 1965, which gave the metropolitan area its fair share of legislators for the first time. With the newly apportioned legislature, the breakdown in providing sewer services, the threat to the safety of the water supply, the noncoordination of metropolitan agencies, and the variety of civic groups pressing for action, by the time the legislative session opened in 1967 it was no longer a question of *whether* the legislature would establish some new metropolitan agency. The question had become: What powers would be given to the new agency and how would it be constituted?

Because of this evolution of consensus, metropolitan reform in the Twin Cities never went through a voting campaign. And the kinds of groups which surfaced in Saint Louis, Cleveland, and other cities to defeat metropolitan reform schemes never argued against the creation of the Metropolitan Council. Suburban officials, who may have viewed the new Metropolitan Council suspiciously, never organized themselves against its creation. In fact, their spokesman agency, the League of Minnesota Municipalities, put forward a proposal for the Metropolitan Council which was more far-reaching than the bill which eventually passed the legislature. County officials in the metropolitan area formed an Inter-County Council in 1966 to offer an alternative to the Metropolitan Council. And a chain of suburban newspapers opposed the idea of a Metropolitan Council with teeth and proposed in its stead that the legislature create a Council of Governments for the Twin Cities. But the very fact that these interests spoke of an alternative rather than in opposition indicates how much consensus existed that the status quo had to be changed.

This lack of any significant opposition to the Metropolitan Council was explained by one observer as the result of a consensus of opinion that "something needed to be done, and [that] there was no push for a comprehensive home rule metropolitan government consolidation."[32] This lack of substantial opposition among the suburban officials might also have been a reflection of the particular nature of the political culture in Minnesota. This political culture has been described by Daniel J. Elazar as more moralistic than the political cultures of Cleveland or Saint Louis. According to Elazar, a moralistic political culture is more receptive to governance for the common good than is either the individualistic or the traditional political culture.*

* In Elazar's terminology, the individualistic culture has a utilitarian concept of government which prefers a minimal amount of governmental intervention in what are considered private, individual matters. The traditional political culture is ambivalent toward governmental intervention in the private sphere and looks upon public office holding as the perquisite of the social and economic elite. The moralistic political culture has no

Another very important factor was the fact that the debate occurred in the forum of the legislature rather than in the forum of a voter referendum. When an issue comes to a referendum, one has only two choices; one can vote for the issue or against it. Given this choice, suburban newspapers, county officials, and municipal officials in the Twin Cities might have opposed such a referendum just as similar officials had done elsewhere. But in the forum of the legislature, the normal process is one of negotiation, bargaining, and compromise rather than adamant opposition, especially when strong interest groups are pushing for action on an issue which clearly needs legislation.

A final important feature about metropolitan reform in the Twin Cities has been the incremental nature of the way in which the reforms have occurred. As indicated above, the creation of the Metropolitan Council was the culminating event in a long history of developing a consensus that some area-wide approach to metropolitan problems was needed. Nor did the metropolitan reform cease with the creation of the Metropolitan Council in 1967. In every legislative session since then, the council's powers have been expanded, refined, and clarified. If the only forum for debating the council's powers had been a referendum, it is highly unlikely that the council's powers would have continued evolving after its creation.

Reflection on the Twin Cities' approach to metropolitan governance shows some advantages and some disadvantages. The major disadvantage is that a metropolitan reform enacted by a state legislature is not likely to be as far-reaching as one drafted by a charter commission and submitted to the electorate in a referendum. The interest groups which oppose metropolitan government are able to bargain with the legislators to dilute the scope of the reform. The Metropolitan Council created by the Minnesota legislature, for example, is not nearly as far-reaching a metropolitan government as are the governments created by referendum in Miami, Jacksonville, and Nashville.

The major advantages are two. First, as indicated above, the legislative approach to creating metropolitan reforms increases the likelihood of some kind of reform governance being established, since most city-county consolidation proposals and other metropolitan government proposals are defeated at the ballot box. A weak legislatively

---

ambivalence about governmental intervention in the private sphere and believes that governments have a responsibility to act for the public rather than the private good. [See Elazar's *American Federalism: A View from the States* (New York: Thomas Y. Crowell, 1966), pp. 89–97.] The importance of Minnesota's political culture to the establishment of the Metropolitan Council and the appropriateness of Elazar's concept of a moralistic political culture was suggested in private communication by Frederick M. Wirt.

created government may be better than no reform at all. Second, the legislative approach is more conducive to an incremental evolution of the powers of the metropolitan government once it is created. In contrast to the gradual refinement of powers of the Twin Cities Metropolitan Council, the Miami–Dade County Metro can change its charter only through a referendum. The most recent of the proposed changes, an elected county executive, was rejected by the voters in 1972.

MINORITIES AND METROPOLITAN REFORM

In the creation of metropolitan governments, the role played by the minority communities has often been very important. It was least important in the creation of Miami–Dade County Metro and in the two legislatively created metropolitan reforms — Indianapolis and Minneapolis–Saint Paul. In Jacksonville, Nashville, Saint Louis, and Cleveland, however, the role of the blacks in particular was very important. In Saint Louis, blacks were important primarily by their absence. No effort was made to enlist their support for the district plan and no support was forthcoming. In Cleveland, where the home rule charter for the county was defeated by a very small margin, the black interests had been needlessly ignored. Black leaders campaigned against the charter, and black wards voted resoundingly against it. The most success in getting black support came in Jacksonville and Nashville. In both places, blacks were given important positions on the commissions which drafted the consolidation charters, and a large council elected from districts was created in order to maximize black representation. The result of these concessions was that prominent blacks supported the consolidation in both places. Black wards strongly supported consolidation in Jacksonville but rejected it narrowly in Nashville.

From the foregoing, several propositions can be advanced. In some metropolises, such as the Twin Cities or Miami, the racial minority electorate may be so small that it will have a negligible role in the attempt to establish the new reform. Second, the approach of creating metropolitan governments by state legislative action minimizes minority influence. In most state legislatures, minority communities are severely underrepresented. Even the one-person, one-vote principle does not preclude a gerrymandering of legislative districts to divide minority populations among several districts. And this has occurred with the black populations in several cities. In contrast, a referendum at least gives the minority voters a chance to exert as much influence as their numbers warrant.

Third, the metropolitan governments can be structured in ways that will minimize the dilution of the minority voting potential. In particular, large councils in which the members are elected from districts rather than at large will ensure some minority representation on the council. This assurance can be enhanced by promises to draw the council district lines so that the minority communities will have the maximum number of representatives warranted by their numbers. In addition, the charter can include guarantees for civil rights and equal opportunities in public employment. Such guarantees will be very important to those minority leaders who fear that the whole purpose of the metropolitan government is to keep them from appointive positions and jobs in the city government.

Finally, the metropolitan government promoters can include minority leaders in the planning, drafting, and promotion of the new charter. Certainly, the act of having minorities on the charter commission can be billed as an act of good faith that the new government will deal fairly with the black community.

POLITICAL REFORM AND POLITICAL BIAS: SOME CONCLUSIONS

The attempts to achieve metropolitan reform demonstrate certain political biases. The first of these involves the question of stasis or change in metropolitan governance. The attitudes of the general metropolitan population and the leadership of many powerful interest groups seem biased toward stasis rather than change; many more reform campaigns have been lost than have been won.

Second, the perceptible changes that have taken place suggest that the attitudinal biases are more inclined toward incremental and limited changes than they are toward drastic and far-reaching changes. Although the reforms in Indianapolis and the Twin Cities were far less extensive than complete consolidation of governments, they did, nevertheless, increase the capacity to deal with the metropolitan problems in their respective areas. And even though very few metropolitan counties have adopted the most advanced forms of urban county government (the county manager and the elected county executive), increasing numbers of metropolitan counties are adopting some reorganization proposals and assuming more responsibility for urban functions of government. Accomplishing limited reforms in metropolitan governance in an incremental fashion is apparently much easier than accomplishing sweeping reforms in one dramatic action.[33]* This is the major lesson of the Twin Cities and Indianapolis — especially the Twin Cities, where the creation of the Metropolitan Council not only culminated years of incremental changes, but the council itself has been subject to incremental growth since its creation.

These attitudinal biases themselves are subject to change. In the late 1950s and early 1960s, some very prominent and respected political scientists argued that the voters were so adamantly opposed to metropolitan government that such governments were virtually impossible to create.[34] Since then, general attitudes and expectations about metropolitan reorganizations may have changed. Melvin Mogulof wrote recently: "There is a sense of malaise about local government in metropolitan areas and a sense that too much has been surrendered to the 'invisible' governance of special purpose agencies in the desire to avoid metropolitan government."[35] When this sense of malaise can be tied in with a new electoral majority, as happened with the 1968 victory of Republicans in Indianapolis, then some of the preexisting political biases can be overcome.

To the extent that the public mistrusts metropolitan government, however, the examples of Indianapolis and the Twin Cities indicate that substantial changes can best be obtained by limiting the metropolitan reform proposals to those that can be accomplished by legislatures without requiring voter approval in referendums. Although this may seem to be an undemocratic attempt to skirt the will of the electorate, the legislature is actually a much more appropriate forum for conducting metropolitan changes, as was shown above. In a referendum, the electorate is given a simple yes or no choice over a charter that, more likely than not, has been drafted by a blue ribbon committee of civic-minded reformers who lack electoral experience. Legislative committees, in contrast, are not limited to a take-it-or-leave-it option. They can debate any conceivable aspect of the proposal that any interest group or politician cares to raise. Whether this method of dealing with metropolitan reform is less democratic than the referendum approach depends primarily upon how democratic the legislative committees are in their procedures. If one accepts the Madisonian preference for repre-

---

* Thomas M. Scott demonstrates how changes in suburban governance occur in an incremental fashion as governments learn from one another. He concludes that innovations in government are viewed with less hostility in communities that can see the effects of such innovations in the neighboring communities. [See his "The Diffusion of Urban Governmental Forms as a Case of Social Learning," *Journal of Politics* 30, no. 4 (November 1968): 1091–1108.]

sentative government over direct democracy,[36] then seeking metropolitan reform through the legislative approach is not so much an attempt to skirt the will of the people as it is an attempt to provide a forum where the people's representatives can work effectively.

All this considered, it must be admitted that very few metropolitan governments have been created. What has been the aftermath of the defeats of consolidation? If metropolitan government is rejected, what can be done? In fact, several options exist. And a considerable amount of incremental change has occurred. These will be examined in Chapter 10.

Some Suggested Readings

Scott Greer, *Metropolitics: A Study of Political Culture* (New York: Wiley, 1963). A brilliant analysis of the relationship between cultural values and the politics of metropolitan reform. Includes coverage of the major battles for metropolitan reorganization during the late 1950s and early 1960s.

Advisory Commission on Intergovernmental Relations, *Factors Affecting Voter Reactions to Government Reorganization in Metropolitan Areas* (Washington, D.C.: U.S. Government Printing Office, 1962). Although this booklet is dated and does not cover the more recent campaigns, most of the interpretations are still valid.

Analyses of Saint Louis

Robert H. Salisbury, "Interests, Parties, and Governmental Structures in St. Louis," *The Western Political Quarterly* 13, no. 2 (June 1960): 498–507.

Henry J. Schmandt, P. G. Steinbicker, and G. D. Wendel, *Metropolitan Reform in St. Louis* (New York: Holt, Rinehart and Winston, 1961).

Analyses of Cleveland

James A. Norton, *The Metro Experience* (Cleveland: The Press of Western Reserve University, 1963).

Estal E. Sparlin, "Cleveland Seeks New Metro Solution," *National Civic Review* 69, no. 3 (March 1960): 142–144.

Richard A. Watson and John H. Romani, "Metropolitan Government for Metropolitan Cleveland: An Analysis of the Voting Record," *Midwest Journal of Political Science* 5, no. 4 (November 1961): 365–390.

Analysis of Minneapolis–Saint Paul

Stanley Baldinger, *Planning and Governing the Metropolis: The Twin Cities Experience* (New York: Praeger, 1971).

Analysis of Miami

Edward Sofen, *The Miami Metropolitan Experiment* (Bloomington: Indiana University Press, 1963).

Analyses of Nashville

Brett W. Hawkins, *Nashville Metro: The Politics of City-County Consolidation* (Nashville, Tenn.: Vanderbilt University Press, 1966).

Daniel R. Grant, "Metropolitics and Professional Political Leadership: The Case of Nashville," *Annals of the American Academy of Political and Social Science* 353 (May 1964): 72–83.

Analyses of Jacksonville

John M. De Grove, "The City of Jacksonville: Consolidation in Action," in Advisory Commission on Intergovernmental Relations, *Report A–41. Substate Regionalism and the Federal System. Volume II, Regional Governance: Promise and Performance — Case Studies* (Washington, D.C.: U.S. Government Printing Office, 1973).

Joan Carver, "Responsiveness and Consolidation: A Case Study," *Urban Affairs Quarterly* 9, no. 2 (December 1973): 211–250.

Analysis of Indianapolis

York Willbern, "Unigov; Local Government Reorganization in Indianapolis," in Advisory Commission on Intergovernmental Relations, *Report A–41. Substate Regionalism and the Federal System. Volume II, Regional Governance: Promise and Performance — Case Studies* (Washington, D.C.: U.S. Government Printing Office, 1973).

Analysis of the Role of Minorities

The impact of blacks on metropolitan reform movements has not been dealt with very systematically. Some of the following do address this question.

Willis Hawley, *Blacks and Metropolitan Governance: The Stakes of Reform.* (Berkeley, Calif.: Institute of Govermental Studies, University of California, 1972).

Dale Rogers Marshall, B. Frieden, D. W. Fessler, *The Governance of Metropolitan Regions: Minority Perspectives* (Baltimore: Resources for the Future, 1972).

Tobe Johnson, *Metropolitan Government: A Black Analytical Perspective* (Washington, D.C.: Joint Center for Political Studies, 1972).

Lee Sloan and R. M. French, "Black Rule in the Urban South," *TRANS-action*, (November/December 1971), 29–34.

Chapter 10

The persistent defeat of so many metropolitan government reforms during the 1950s and 1960s suggests that the 1970s can be termed a postreform period. The demand for change in the 1970s has shifted away from charter battles for metropolitan governments and toward other, more limited, incremental approaches to dealing with the problems of the multi-centered metropolis. These problems did not disappear. Nor have the demands let up to increase the capabilities of urban governments to deal with these problems. From the middle 1960s to the present, metropolitan areas have responded to the problem

The Politics of Incremental Change in the Postreform Metropolis

of metropolitan governance with a vitality and creative imagination which only a decade earlier seemed out of the question. While all-encompassing proposals to create metropolitan governments had failed during the 1950s and early 1960s, the late 1960s and the 1970s saw an increasing number of limited reforms and limited attempts at cooperation.

Three developments stand out. First, a distinction has been made between systems-maintenance issues of metropolitan politics and life-style issues. Second, under federal incentives a proliferation of metropolitan planning has combined with a metropolitan agency review over federal grant applications. Third, a new metropolitan institution, the council of governments (COG), has emerged to handle these planning and review functions.

A MATTER OF LIFE STYLES

One feature of change that this chapter will discuss is the increased willingness to turn control of certain kinds of governmental functions over to centralized metropolitan agencies. But not all governmental functions are being turned over. Oliver Williams has posited what is called the "life-style model" of metropolitan politics, which seems to fit contemporary trends in metropolitan governance. Where there is no outside intervention by the federal government, Williams states that "policy areas which are perceived as neutral with respect to controlling social access may be centralized; policies which are perceived as controlling social access will remain decentralized."[1] The objectives of social access are the life styles of upper-middle-class suburban areas, particularly the life styles of the expensive suburban school districts and the exclusive residential areas. The devices which control access to these life styles thus become the issues about which suburbanites fight the most vehemently to retain local control. And the most obvious public issues which strike most directly at maintaining the exclusivity of these life styles are: bussing of pupils for the purpose of achieving racial balance, low- and moderate-income public housing, zoning, and possibly the equalizing of fiscal disparities in the metropolis. Suburban officials show great reluctance to allow these issues to be controlled by a centralized metropolitan government.

In contrast to these life-style issues, many of the problems of the metropolitan syndrome — such as sewerage, water supply, health facilities, or solid waste dispoal — represent what Williams labels systems-maintenance functions of government. Equal access to sewers does not threaten anybody's life style in the suburbs, but it is essential to maintain the health and safety of the majority of the population. As the seriousness of these systems-maintenance problems began to be recognized and as they began to be perceived as nonthreatening to the suburban life style, municipal officials became less and less opposed to centralizing and coordinating their operations in agencies that were large enough to practice economies of scale. Even in metropolises such as Toronto, Miami, and the Twin Cities, where major metropolitan reorganizations have been achieved, the new governments have been much more effective in the physical-development issues than they have in the social issues where questions of life style are at stake.[2]

This suggests that the major battles of metropolitan politics during the later 1970s will be less over the forms of metropolitan governance than over the substance of issues that are threatening to suburban life styles. The outlines for this may have been set in court battles over bussing, the fiscal disparities inherent in relying on property taxes to finance public schools, and the extension of low- and moderate-income public housing into the suburbs.[3] It is not clear yet whether the Supreme Court will sustain these state- and lower-court decisions, nor, as political scientist Paul Friesema has pointed out, "is it certain that the Court decision can be enforced, even if sustained. We may learn what 'massive resistance' is really like before the decade is through."[4]

In stressing the much more difficult problem of coming to terms with the life-style issues of the contemporary metropolis, however, it would be a serious mistake to underestimate the importance of the increased willingness of local officials to seek regional cooperation on the systems-maintenance issues. These issues are far from settled. What has changed has been the willingness of local officials to cooperate on centralizing control over the resolution of these issues. Much of this centralization, as Williams suggested, has resulted from the desire to provide the services as cheaply as possible. But much of it also has come from federal incentives to form metropolitan planning agencies and councils of government.

THE ORIGIN AND IMPACT OF METROPOLITAN PLANNING

City Planning: Background, Attitudes, and Structures

Metropolitan planning is a historical outgrowth of urban planning. Urban planning is the attempt to make future urban development conform to prestated priorities and guidelines. Such attempts in the United States have a long history that dates back to colonial plans for cities such as Boston, Philadelphia, Savannah, and New Orleans. L'Enfant's plan for Washington is only the most famous of several such city plans. These plans, however, did little more than map out the central core of the city, and they were never able to keep pace with rapid city growth during the nineteenth century. In New York City, for example, the early nineteenth-century planners expressed pride that they had planned for a city large beyond their wildest expectations. Within a generation the city had outgrown their plans. West of the Appalachians, cities were designed in grid patterns in the attempt to impose order on future growth.

Contemporary urban planning dates not so much from these early endeavors as it does from the City Beautiful movement at the turn of the century.[5] In 1893, the city of Chicago commissioned the design of an elaborate lakeshore development of lagoons, parks, boulevards, and classicial architecture to house the Columbian Exposition. From then until about 1915, many progressive urban reformers sought to alleviate the social problems of the cities by beautifying them, by planning large, physical construction projects that were aesthetically pleasing. The most elaborate of these plans was undoubtedly the plan of development for Chicago, which provided for reversing the flow of the Chicago River to preserve the purity of Lake Michigan, land fills and park construction along the lakefront, forest preserves on the western edge of the city, and broad avenues that reached far into the hinterland. This City Beautiful stage was succeeded by the City Functional or the City Efficient stage. This stage began with the drafting of a plan in 1909 for the development of Boston. Just as the Chicago plan had focused on physically beautifying the city, the Boston plan added the dimension of anticipating economic as well as physicial needs. It focused on making the city more efficient. Public finances were to be made more open and honest. Public health facilities were to be provided and the regional economy was to be strengthened.[6]

The City Efficient stage of planning dominated until after World War II, when the concept of the comprehensive development plan came into general acceptance. Such plans attempt to present precise blueprints for the development of cities as they will look twenty or thirty years in the future.

Underlying all three of these stages was the assumption that city planning should be conducted for the general public interest of the city as a whole rather than for the private interest of particular clients. This assumption came under attack in the 1960s when the concepts of "pluralism in planning"[7] and "advocacy planning"[8] were put forward to justify the use of professional planners by groups of citizens (especially the poor and the racial minorities) whose private interests were not being served well by the supposed public interests being advocated by the city planners.

All of these stages of planning have left their imprint upon contemporary planning attitudes and institutions. One of the most important influences on planning was the progressive reform movement discussed in Chapter 4. In the words of political scientist Francine Rabinovitz, city planning was "conceived as a set of rules and structures designed to keep politics out of urban development."[9] By setting down in advance the rules of land use control and by dividing the city into a series of zones for different kinds of activities, it was hoped that the meddling of politicians in locational decisions could be minimized. Professional planners generally developed a scorn for politics and politicians that even today has not been entirely eradicated.[10] Partly as a result of this attitude, the earliest municipal planning commissions were isolated as much as possible from the political process. The planning commission was usually composed of prominent businessmen and civic leaders who were independent of the local political machines, and the commissions themselves were independent of the mayor's office. But as time passed, the independence of the planning commission from the city's political leaders was found to be a liability in getting the plans accepted by the political officers. And recent decades have seen a move to incorporate planning into the administrative offices of the city government.[11] Presently, about two-thirds of all city planning agencies are directly subordinated to the chief executive of the city.[12]

In addition to the planning commissions, other key actors in city planning are the city councils, the city planners, the chief executive officers of the city, federal officials, and the business enterprises that wish to construct residential or commercial developments in the city. The city planner, who is the central person among these actors, is responsible for working with the planning commission to develop a comprehensive development plan for the city and for carrying out the plan once it is approved. City planners have historically tended to come out of the engineering and architecture professions and have concentrated on physical concerns such as building size, lot size, and zoning regulations. Since World War II, however, the educational background of planners has included more social science instruction, and many of these planners focus on social services such as health facilities, community development, poverty, and social problems.[13] The physical planners tend to predominate in the city planning departments,[14] while the social planners are found in other public and private agencies such as neighborhood councils, community action agencies, and health and welfare planning councils.[15]

One of the most noteworthy developments in city planning during the 1960s was the number of suburban municipalities which engaged in city planning. At the end of the 1950s, less than half of the cities of 10,000 or more people had spent money to develop city plans. By the middle 1960s, 92 percent of such cities had developed city plans. The major reason for this increase was the demand of the federal government that city plans be drawn up before the city could be eligible for federal urban renewal funds.[16]

The physical layouts of many suburbs were originally designed by real estate developers who plan curving streets, shopping centers, and other amenities which will give the suburban development an aesthetic appearance that is appealing to the residents and will put them within an acceptable commuting distance of shopping and other service facilities. When the development incorporates, its residents may wish to retain their residential character of single-family homes, but the local officials responsible for planning very often find that their aesthetic concerns conflict with the need to approve developments such as industry, fast-food franchises, or apartment buildings that make a positive contribution to the suburb's property tax base. Even though they may have approved a comprehensive plan for the suburb's development, they often look favorably upon deviations from the master plan if these deviations will contribute to the tax base of the suburb.

If the suburban city is large enough to afford the expense, it will hire its own professional planning staff. Many municipalities are too small to hire such a staff, however. They contract with a professional architect or planning consultant to provide a package deal consisting of a land use survey, population projections, a general plan, and recommendations on zonings. These packaged contracts were most popular during the 1950s and 1960s when suburban growth was very rapid. They had little effect on controlling or regulating suburban growth. The planning consultants often had little long-range involvement with the communities, and the local planning officials lacked the training and expertise to transform the planning document into an ongoing process of guiding municipal growth.[17]

The devices used by the city planner to implement the objectives of the comprehensive master plan are basically two — zoning and subdivision control. Through zoning, the planning commissioners can set aside certain blocks of the city for single-family homes, other blocks for multiple-unit dwellings, other blocks for light industry, other blocks for heavy industry, other blocks for commercial retail facilities, and so forth. Under subdivision control, the planner can oblige subdivision developers to install streets, sidewalks, sewers, water facilities, lighting, and perhaps recreational facilities. The costs for these improvements are then passed on to the home buyers and need not be paid for from general taxes.

When a real estate developer presents a proposal that is contrary to the city zoning code or to the general master plan, he has to apply for a variance, which is an official exemption from the code. If the developer is large enough to make a significant impact on the community, he can normally get his projects approved by offering some minor concessions to the planning commissioners. In this way a convenient relationship is worked out between the developer and the suburban officials. The developer gets essentially what he wants, and the suburban officials are able to extract enough compromises from the developer to prove to the suburban residents that they, the officials, are doing their jobs.

An excellent, if perhaps extreme, example of this is described by Herbert Gans in his account of planning in Levittown.[18] The local township planning officials "knew little about city planning," so they contracted with a consultant to serve as their city planner.

> The planner's sympathies were more with Levitt than with the residents. . . . His planner's philosophy and his judgment of where the power lay dictated that he work closely with the builder in planning for the township, and that he adapt his recommendations to the builder's proposals. As a result, the preliminary plan, completed in 1959, coincided closely with Levitt's own scheme.
>
> Yet even when [the public officials] had effective veto power over Levitt's operations, they did not often think to exercise it, because they felt Levitt was trying to do a good job and would make the township the best in the country.
>
> When the Township officials did question the Levitt proposals, it was almost always on matters of detail. On the larger issues they agreed. . . .[19]

The general trend in suburbia has been to use zoning powers to provide for very clearly and carefully segregated uses of land. Single-family homeowners tend to resent the construction of apartments or townhouses close to them. Consequently, in recent years buildings such as townhouses and apartments have commonly been constructed along the freeways, where the land is less desirable for single-family residences and where these larger buildings can serve as noise buffers for the single-family homes. Commercial activity is also quite clearly segregated, usually with the most extensive commercial retail activity being located in large shopping centers designed to be reached by automobile rather than by foot. A number of architectural critics have lamented the tendency toward segregated land use patterns in central cities as well as in suburbs.[20] The major exceptions to segregated land use are found in *planned unit developments* and in suburban new towns, such as Reston, Virginia, or Columbia, Maryland. Planned unit developments (PUDs) are relatively large neighborhoods of a city or suburb that have been zoned for development with a mixture of housing styles, commercial activity, and land uses.

In addition to zoning and subdivision controls as tools to implement the master plan, the city fathers also rely on a *capital improvements budget* to finance a long-range, planned schedule of public projects. The capital improvements budget will normally be drawn up and implemented by a separate capital improvements commission, but three-fourths of the city planners indicated that they are involved with the capital improvement programs.[21] Since the capital improvements budget has a source of funds to locate public projects throughout the city, it is very important for implementing the master plan.

In the central cities and the larger suburbs, the planning process is much more professional than the process described above for the small suburbs. These larger municipalities hire their own planning staffs, which are usually subordinated to the mayor or the city manager. The focus of planning attention is also likely to differ from the focus in the suburb. In the fast-growing suburbs, planning attention focuses on controlling future population growth and geographic expansion of the developed areas. By the time a suburb reaches a population large enough to afford the expense of a full-time planning staff and by the time it has transformed its government structure from that of a rural village or township to a municipal corporation, its physical growth pattern has normally been set and quite often its geographic area is practically filled with residential and commercial development. To impose strict development controls at this stage in suburban growth is really to gain control over very little. Nevertheless, if it wishes to get urban renewal funds or housing funds or some other funds from the federal government, the suburb may have to produce a comprehensive master plan for the function involved. Consequently, much of the planning activity in urban areas is defined in terms of urban renewal, urban redevelopment, highway construction, and other large-scale activities that depend on federal funding.

Metropolitan Planning

Because city planning is normally confined to the geographic areas within its municipal boundaries, it has difficulty in coping with problems that transcend municipal boundaries and in coordinating its plans with those of neighboring communities. The realization of this in the post–World War II era sparked an interest in planning at the regional or metropolitan level.

The first metropolitan plan was probably the regional plan for New York and its environs sponsored by a private foundation in 1929. Key provisions of the plan were not implemented, however.[22] And left on their own, few other metropolises attempted to formulate their own metropolitan plans. Even as late as 1962 there were only sixty-three metropolitan planning commissions. These agencies were generally understaffed, underfinanced, and without authority to influence regional development. Less than half of the thirty-eight largest planning agencies, in fact, had even developed comprehensive plans. Consequently, they concentrated on population studies, economic analyses, and traditional land use planning.[23] By the end of the decade the number of metropolitan planning agencies had tripled to almost 200, and they were becoming increasingly active. In 1965 the Housing and Urban Development Act authorized funds for research and planning activities to be undertaken by regional planning agencies. This was a marked departure from the planning incentives written into earlier housing legislation in 1949 and 1954. Whereas those acts had provided planning incentives at the municipal level for general housing plans, the 1965 incentives were made available to metropolitan agencies which could use the funds for a broader range of planning activities. This availability of funds was a significant spur to the officials in many metropolises to create metropolitan planning agencies in order to acquire the federal funds.

The 1965 Housing and Urban Development Act was followed in 1966 by the Demonstration Cities and Metropolitan Development Act (Model Cities Act), which demanded that a wide variety of federal loans and grants be approved by metropolitan review agencies before the grants could be awarded. Metropolitan planning commissions could qualify as the review agencies. The procedures for exercising this review power were spelled out by the Office of Management and Budget in its A–95 circular in 1969. Hence the metropolitan review power is commonly referred to as the A–95 power.

A third significant congressional initiative that provided a stimulus for metropolitan planning was the Intergovernmental Cooperation Act of 1968. This act stated, "To the maximum extent possible, . . . all federal aid for development purposes shall be consistent with and further the objectives of state, regional and local comprehensive planning."[24] This provision further strengthened the metropolitan planning agencies, for it enabled the metropolitan review agency to subordinate federal grants to the priorities and plans developed by that agency.

Because of these provisions — the availability of federal funds, the emphasis upon research, and the review power — metropolitan planning could be taken seriously for the first time in America. The metropolitan planning agencies now had the funds to hire professional staffs and to contract out particular jobs to consultants who could specialize in given areas. This gave the metropolitan plans a quality that could not be duplicated in most of the smaller municipalities. The metropolitan planning agencies also have a larger focus which enables them to tackle certain planning issues that the local municipalities are incapable of dealing with effectively. Some of these are land use, transportation, water supply, community facilities, air pollution, open space preservation, and recreation.

On these issues metropolitan planning has performed a very valuable service to the local suburban planners who have neither the staff nor the viewpoint to undertake the studies conducted by the metropolitan planning agency. This was particularly evident in Detroit, where carefully exercised leadership by the director of the Detroit Metropolitan Area Regional Planning Agency led to the formation of an extraordinarily cooperative Inter-County Committee of County Supervisors,[25] the forerunner of the councils of governments (COGs). Some of the planning commission studies found most valuable by the suburban officials were population research, industrial trends, land use, zoning regulations, and local public improvement plans.[26]

The Impact and Politics of Metropolitan Planning

Despite the tremendous proliferation of metropolitan agencies over the past decade, it is highly doubtful whether the results of the planning have been very far-reaching. David Ranney writes that these agencies "have not been able to bring about a metropolitan planning policy which is followed by the governments comprising the metropolitan areas."[27] Geographer John Friedmann asserts that "the manifest purpose of this style of planning [i.e., comprehensive development planning] — to shape the development of cities and nations in accord with a preconceived design, and to do so on the basis of functionally rational criteria — was not being accomplished. Where it was tried, and judged by its own claims, comprehensive planning turned out to be a colossal failure."[28]

One reason for the limited effectiveness of metropolitan planning can be traced to the estrangement between politicians and the professional planners. As the self-styled guardians of the public good and as the promoters of long-range policies, the planners inevitably confront the politician who is supposedly concerned with short-range private benefits for his constituents. This confrontation was described succinctly by political scientist Edward C. Banfield, who wrote: "No competent politician will sacrifice votes that may be needed in the next election for gains, however large, that may accrue to the public 10, 20, or 30 years hence."[29] Another reason for the limited effectiveness of metropolitan planning has been the absence of agreed-upon metropolitan goals which can be implemented through a metropolitan development plan. Planners may promote such goals. But they can implement them only if they are accepted by other political actors and if they also control budgets, investment decisions, locational decisions, and zoning practices.

Some evidence indicates that the spate of metropolitan planning since 1965 has apparently been little more than an exercise in drawing

The difficulties of coordinating federal, state, and local planning are aptly portrayed in this 1965 cartoon by Herblock. Note the monkey wrench which somebody has thrown into the works. Also note the 1754 cartoon. The 1754 unification proposal was the Albany Plan authored by Benjamin Franklin. After the eventual fruition of his unification efforts at the Philadelphia Constitutional Convention, Franklin is supposed to have glanced over his shoulder at a painting of the sun and declared that he believed the sun was rising over the dawn of a new union. It is not clear from Herblock's cartoon whether the sun is rising or setting.

From *The Herblock Gallery* (Simon & Schuster, 1968)

up plans merely to get federal money.[30] How useful such plans then become is questionable. One study by the Urban Land Institute found that of 102 cities surveyed that have a planning commission, only ten made specific use of the plans produced by these commissions.[31]

Other inhibiting factors stem from the high value placed on local autonomy. Local officials fear that strong metropolitan plans will force upon them development that they do not want and will deny them development that they may want. Particularly, they are reluctant to allow control over zoning, public schools, and other life-style issues to be taken from local hands. Finally, the overwhelming majority of metropolitan planning agencies are not tied to a strong political base.[32] In contrast with a central city planning agency, which can be tied directly to the mayor and benefit from his base of support, the metropolitan planning agency has no electoral constituency of its own nor any major elected political figure who can lend support to it. For all of these reasons, the planner tends to view politics as an inhibiting factor that places an upper limit on what can be accomplished through planning.[33]

Advocacy Planning

Because of these obstacles to effective planning, successful planners adopt tactics and objectives that are commensurate with the prevailing organization and dispersion of power in their respective metropolises.[34] Quite often this causes the planners, like other political actors, to be much more responsive to the demands of the functional fiefdoms than to the needs of isolated citizens. Indeed, the uninformed, nontechnical, and often emotional input of the isolated citizen may well be disparaged by the persons planning the development projects in the metropolis. Very few private real estate developers seem inclined to invite citizen participation in the planning of their projects. From the developer's viewpoint, citizen input is negative since citizens usually object to some feature of any project. And since most citizens do not even hear about projects until considerable money has been spent on them and they are presented to a planning commission or zoning board for approval, there is no mechanism for citizen input to be anything but negative. Nor is this inhibition of citizen participation limited to private developers. Big-city planning staffs, highway planners, urban renewal planners, or metropolitan planning agencies tend to be just as unreceptive to citizen groups as are the private developers. Many federal programs require citizen participation in the planning process. But such participation has usually occurred after the plan was drafted, so participation meant it was presented at a public meeting for the purpose of enlightening the public. Rarely have citizens played a significant role in drafting city plans or urban renewal plans.[35]* The result, quite often, has been a widespread feeling of alienation and helplessness in the face of drastic neighborhood changes caused by construction of locally unwanted freeways,[36] motels, commercial establishments, urban renewal projects,[37] university expansions, or any number of big projects. There is a basic tension between the traditional wish of the early-twentieth-century reformers to depoliticize politics and the Jeffersonian ideal of citizen participation. Political scientist Thomas Scott has traced much of contemporary urban alienation to this tension. "In many ways, the present level of alienation toward political institutions is the result of the fact that we have moved very swiftly, especially in suburbs, to government by technocrat without raising and resolving the fundamental issues of the relationships between the governmental professionals and the part-time, semi-interested citizen."[38]

One proposal to remedy this citizen malaise has been advocacy planning. The major spokesman for advocacy planning has been city planner Paul Davidoff, who argues that the planning bureaucracies have aligned themselves with the prevailing local establishments and have neglected the legitimate needs of the poor and the racial minorities. To remedy this, Davidoff proposes that citizens' groups hire professional planners to prepare their own plans and propose them to the appropriate public agencies. In this way citizens can initiate positive proposals to the city government; and since they are represented by a professional planner, they are not overwhelmed by technical jargon.[39]

The concept of advocacy planning has provoked a serious split within the planning profession. The dominant, more conservative faction demands that planning promote the public good rather than advocate the private good of specific clients. These planners also tend to believe that city planners should restrict their official acts to land use planning and abstain from political or social issues. The smaller, proadvocacy planning faction rejects both of these beliefs.[40]

The Conservative Bias of Urban Planning

If the advocacy planners are correct in their charges, then urban planning as such has an inherent conservative bias. This statement is supported by empirical evidence at least in the areas of highway planning,[41] urban renewal planning,[42] and comprehensive development planning[43] in which the planners have been responsive primarily to

* In the model cities and community action programs, to be sure, there has been extensive citizen participation in the planning process.

their respective bureaucracies and functional fiefdoms. Such planning is conservative, because the plans reflect the biases of past decisions and seek to protect the agency and the program from future encroachment.[44] Sociologist Herbert Gans argues that the dominant faction of the American Institute of Planners is conservative.[45] Finally, some observers argue that all planning, even advocacy planning, is inherently conservative because it seeks merely to reform existing institutional practices rather than to overthrow them.[46]

Most of the arguments for the conservatism of urban planning focus on city-level planning for highways or urban renewal. Metropolitan planning may be a more liberalizing force than these other kinds of planning, for it does represent a challenge to the status quo of municipal autonomy. And *if* the comprehensive metropolitan land use plans were implemented, they would have a sharp effect on the future of suburban sprawl. They would also, *if implemented*, broaden the social access to residences, schools, and jobs in the metropolis. The fact that they have not achieved these things is more a testimony to the strength of the status quo than it is to the conservatism of the metropolitan planners. In this sense the planners are exerting a liberalizing and not a conservative influence on metropolitan politics. The plans would provoke a change in the power relations. A slow, incremental change to be sure, but change nevertheless.[47]

COUNCILS OF GOVERNMENTS

For performing the metropolitan planning function and the A–95 clearinghouse function of reviewing federal grant applications, the most popular form of metropolitan agency has been the *council of governments* (COG). A council of governments is a voluntary association of local municipalities and counties that join forces for the purpose of coordinating their activities on regional problems. COGs as a governmental device date back to 1954 and the establishment of the Supervisors Inter-County Committee in the Detroit, Michigan, area. Other COGs were created in Washington, D.C. (1957), San Francisco (1961), Salem, Oregon (1958), Seattle, Los Angeles, Atlanta, Philadelphia, and New York.

The Washington Metropolitan Council of Governments

A good example of the reasons for founding a COG and the possibilities and limitations it offers is presented by the Washington, D.C., Metropolitan Council of Governments.[48] This COG (WMCOG) grew out of a cooperative effort in Washington governance, which by the late 1950s was beginning to reach the limits of attacking area-wide problems on a function-by-function basis.

There had been a long history of cooperation on functional activities in the Washington region. Eleven special authorities had been set up to regulate particular services in and around Washington. Considerable interstate and interjurisdictional agreement had been worked out on such matters as water supply, sewage, roads, and recreational space. Nevertheless, most of these jurisdictional agreements had been adopted piecemeal for specific needs, and there was little coordination between them. Each organization was designed in functional terms, and within each functional sector there were often subregional jurisdictions. Maryland, Virginia, and the District of Columbia, for example, all had special agencies dealing with the function of recreational open space. Most of these agencies were underfinanced, and no general body had planning or coordinating responsibility for the whole area.

In 1957 the Washington Metropolitan Regional Conference was organized, and five years later in 1962 it changed its name to the Washington Metropolitan Council of Governments. Designed to stimulate cooperation between the federal government, the two states, and the various counties and municipalities involved, the WMCOG concentrated on noncontroversial issues such as demonstrating the need for mass transit, water supply, and pollution abatement.

The WMCOG developed an elaborate organization that has become typical of most COGs. Its ultimate governing body is the Conference, which meets semiannually and has representation from each of the constituent unit governments. In between the semiannual meetings, policy is established by an executive board, and day-to-day operations are carried out by an executive secretary and his staff. The WMCOG, was originally financed by voluntary assessments from each of the constituent units of government, but with the enactment of the 1965 Housing Act, these voluntary assessments have been supplemented with federal planning grants. Five policy committees were formed to cover transit, water supply and pollution control, land use, public safety, and health and welfare. In addition to these policy committees, the staff organized technical advisory committees.

During its early years, the WMCOG carried out a relatively successful program in the functions that have been referred to here as systems maintenance. Through its studies on transit, it recommended and saw created a National Capital Transportation Agency and subsequently a Washington Metropolitan Area Transit Commission which has successfully undertaken the construction of Washington's subway. WMCOG also drew up a year-2000 Regional Development Plan in an attempt to focus public attention on several land use problems created by extremely rapid population growth. On the life-style issues, WMCOG has been less successful, but it did create the United Planning Organization, which became the local community action agency once the federal antipoverty program was started in 1965.

The Proliferation of COGs

COGs experienced their most rapid period of growth during the 1960s. As late as 1960 only seven COGs existed in the country. By 1972 there were over 300.[49] This rapid increase is due primarily to the availability of federal government planning grants and to federal demands for a metropolitan review process. Many metropolitan planning agencies became councils of governments when the 1965 Housing and Urban Development Act made COGs eligible to receive grants for planning and research in a broad range of activities. These included professional staffing, administrative expenses, organizational, fiscal, and planning studies, data collection, land use planning, transportation, housing, economic development, resource development, community facilities, and general improvement of the living environment.[50] Federal grants accounted for an estimated two-thirds of all COG expenditures.[51] In addition to federal funding as a stimulus to creating COGs, a further federal stimulus was the designation of COGs as the A–95 review agencies. In areas such as Nashville and Jacksonville, where very strong metropolitan government structures existed, these governments were not given the review power. The power was given instead to local COGs.

A second stimulus for the proliferation of COGs was simply that they are so easy to create. All that is required is a joint statement of principles by the affected local governments and the incorporation of an organization to implement those principles. Because the COGs are created voluntarily, the local governments can ensure that the COGs have less teeth than some other forms of metropolitan governance.[52]

Another important stimulus to the creation of COGs was the establishment in 1967 of a staff and program by the National Service to Regional Councils. The National Service now serves as a clearinghouse for information important to COGs. It consults with local councils and assists them with specific problems, providing information on federal programs.

An Assessment of COGs

COGs possess some very important advantages for intergovernmental cooperation. Not only are they relatively easy to create, but once created they become a mechanism for studying metropolitan problems and for formulating solutions to the problems. Most metropolitan areas never had such a mechanism prior to the formation of the COG. The COG also may have more influence on local governments than some other agencies by virtue of the fact that it is composed of elected officials. Although its proposals may not be as far-reaching as those of institutions further removed from locally elected officials, the very fact that locally elected representatives on the COG have backed the proposals may increase the possibilities of their acceptance.

Nevertheless, COGs also possess extreme limitations as a tool for metropolitan governance. Three limitations in particular stand out: the constituent-unit form of representation, the limitations on COGs' authority, and their lack of success in dealing with the social-access or life-style issues. The fact that COG members are also officials of local governments means that COGs have a constituent-unit form of representation. This has caused disruptive bickering between the units of government in many COGs, but especially in San Francisco[53] and Cleveland.[54] In both places the problem was eventually resolved by moving toward granting each city representation that was roughly proportionate to its population. In Cleveland this was attained only after a bitter conflict in which the Department of Housing and Urban Development threatened to remove from the COG its status as the A–95 review agency.

If the representational problems of COGs can be solved by applying the one-person, one-vote principle to its constituents, the second major problem, that of sufficient authority, is not so easily resolved. The coercive authority of most COGs lies exclusively in their status as the review agency for federal grants. Other than this, they lack taxing powers and powers to enforce their decisions. Nor is there any guarantee that the federal granting agency will uphold a COG's review decision. Except for a few states, such as Texas (which has made financial aid available), most COGs rely for their finances upon local government assessments and federal planning grants. Beyond the problem of money lies the fact that COGs can do little to make local governments follow their decisions. In fact, in the Washington, D.C., COG, one of the constituent counties from the state of Maryland temporarily withdrew from WMCOG in disagreement with the general direction of the organization. Cleveland temporarily withdrew from its COG. Because of this possibility of withdrawal, COGs cannot take decisive and effective action unless an overwhelming majority of members support any given proposal. And, of course, overwhelming majority support does not normally occur on the controversial life-style issues. Even in exercising the A–95 federal grant review power, COGs have been reluctant to exercise their authority to the fullest. A study of eleven COGs in Texas found that the review process was perfunctory. Only two COGs in Texas had ever made a negative review.[55] Melvin Mogulof, who is probably the most knowledgeable student of COGs, has commented that "the COG finds it extremely difficult to do things such as make critical comments about applications of member governments for federal funds, establish priorities which affect member governments, or influence local governmental actions in an attempt to make them consistent with regional planning."[56]

Finally, COGs have been very ineffective in dealing with the social-access and life-style issues discussed at the beginning of this chapter. There are two reasons for this. First, the 1966 Model Cities Act which created the review power specifically limited it to "federal loans or grants to assist in carrying out open-space projects or for the planning or construction of hospitals, airports, libraries, water supply and distribution facilities, sewerage facilities and waste treatment works, highways, transportation facilities, and water development and land conservation projects within any metropolitan area."[57] This language clearly ignores the social-access issues of tax disparities, low-income public housing in the suburbs, and bussing of pupils to achieve racial balance in the schools. The second reason for the weakness of COGs in dealing with the life-style issues stems from the constituent-unit structure of COGs. This structure effectively grants a veto to the very suburban governments that do not want to lose control over the life-style issues. Consequently, the number of COG successes on social-access or life-style issues such as housing are very few.* A study of ninety-eight COGs, in fact, found that they rejected the idea that central city problems should be one of their focal points.[58]

This ability of COGs to define metropolitan problems in a way that excludes central city problems has provoked some sharp conflicts be-

---

* In Washington, the WMCOG prepared a model fair-housing ordinance which its constituent governments were urged to adopt. In Dayton, a procedure was established for allocating responsibility among the governments for low- and moderate-income housing. [See Domestic Council Committee on National Growth, *Report on National Growth, 1972* (Washington, D.C.: U.S. Government Printing Office, 1972), p. 29.] In the Twin Cities, the Metropolitan Council used its A–95 review powers to oblige one suburb to develop its plans for low- and moderate-income housing.

tween the COGs and the central city. The sharpest conflict of this sort probably was that between Cleveland and the Northeast Ohio Area-wide Coordinating Agency (NOACA). Formed primarily to meet federal A–95 review demands and to obtain federal grants, NOACA was heavily dominated by the suburban governments. NOACA rejected a Cleveland proposal that the COG take action to ensure middle- and low-income housing in the suburbs.[59] NOACA then refused to deal with the question of rapid transit and instead favored a state-highway-department-proposed freeway that was opposed by both Cleveland and several eastern suburbs. Cleveland then withdrew its financial support from NOACA and sued for representation on the one-person, one-vote principle. NOACA retaliated by barring Cleveland from voting at board meetings. The immediate issue of representation was resolved when HUD threatened to strip NOACA of its A–95 review power if NOACA did not adopt the one-person, one-vote principle. But even with the proportional representation on the council, Cleveland is still entitled to only one-fourth of the NOACA board members, and the deep-rooted suspicions of the central city have not disappeared among the other 75 percent of the board.

CONCLUSIONS: CHANGE AND BIAS IN THE PLANNING AND REVIEW FUNCTIONS

Metropolitan planning and the A–95 review process since the mid-1960s represent a small but significant change in the politics of metropolitan governance. They illustrate well the incremental nature of urban political change. They represent change because they are a marked departure from the devices to preserve the status quo that were discussed in Chapter 7. However, they represent *incremental* change because they are not as drastic or as far-reaching as the city-county consolidations, the urban county governments, and the two-tiered metropolitan governments discussed in Chapter 8. Since, as discussed in Chapter 9, very few such metropolitan governments were actually created, and since those that were created were the result of extraordinary conditions, the drastic, far-reaching changes are not very attainable. One commentator wrote:

> Probably, most reform proposals failed in the transformation from theory to reality because the problems of urban America were being solved, even if the solutions were inefficient, unplanned, and lacking in design and purpose. People got to work, even with poorly planned streets and much traffic congestion; the garbage was picked up eventually; children were educated

as well as or better than their parents; and urban life for the majority was not too disruptive.[60]

With drastic change out of the question and with the consequences of the multi-centered metropolis still unsolved, the most successful innovations for governing the metropolis have been the combination of metropolitan planning with the A–95 review process. In some metropolises, such as Minneapolis–Saint Paul, this federal review process has been augmented by state-granted review powers. In most metropolises, these functions have been given to the COGs. This change is incremental because it does not go very far, but it leaves open the possibility for further evolution of the COG to becoming a stronger institution. The change is primarily stimulated from without.

The incremental nature of the review process can best be seen in the distinction between the systems-maintenance and life-style issues. As indicated above, the A–95 review power works best on the systems-maintenance issues and in most metropolises has not yet been applied to the life-style or social-access issues. This is incremental change because it touches only one small increment of the sum total of issues of metropolitan politics. As Oliver Williams suggested, the major cleavage in metropolitan politics in the late 1970s seems to be occurring over the question of equal access to upper-middle-class life styles as exemplified in the very few exclusive suburbs. The cleavages are basically race and class related. The issues which provoke these cleavages are zoning, the expansion of low- and moderate-income public housing into certain suburbs, bussing to achieve racial balance in the public schools, and the elimination of fiscal disparities in the metropolis.

Because of this, the A–95 review processs and metropolitan planning are not very effective in removing the class and racial biases of the multi-centered metropolis that were discussed at the end of Chapter 6. Theoretically they could be effective for this. Given the stipulation of the Intergovernmental Cooperation Act of 1968 that federal grants be consistent with the objectives of metropolitan planning, there is no theoretical reason why the A–95 review agencies could not use their planning and review power to remove the biases of the multi-centered metropolis. They could write into their metropolitan plans provisions for low- and moderate-income housing in the suburbs, for example, or provisions for coordinated land use zoning, and then use their review power to deny unrelated federal grants to those municipalities that refuse to follow the plan's provisions. The agencies could also lobby before the state legislatures to make significant modifications in tax disparities in the metropolis and to equalize the financing of public education.

Metropolitan planning agencies *could* do these things. But it is obvious that most metropolitan planning agencies, especially the COGs, are not doing them. Because of the limitations on COGs discussed earlier, COGs are very unlikely to reverse the biases of the multi-centered metropolis, although they have demonstrated that they can deal effectively with some of the systems-maintenance problems.

Finally, the most striking aspect of contemporary metropolitan politics has been the emergence of the federal government as a force behind change. Legislation in 1965, 1966, and 1968 has transformed the federal government from a stimulator of the multi-centered metropolis and the expansion of functional fiefdoms to a promoter of metropolitan planning and coordination. It is primarily from actions by the federal courts and some agencies of the executive branch that substantial inroads have been made on the capacity to deal with the systems-maintenance issues.

This trend toward increasing involvement of the federal government in metropolitan affairs does not seem likely to be reversed. The federal government is likely to continue to be under pressure to deal with the life-style issues. These prospects raise serious questions about whether or not the federal involvement, which has been fragmented, program oriented, and inconsistent, can be unified under a national urban policy. These questions will be discussed in Part IV.

Some Suggested Readings

Oliver P. Williams, *Metropolitan Political Analysis* (New York: The Free Press, 1971). Williams makes the basic distinction between life-style issues and systems-maintenance issues and argues that the metropolitan politics of the 1970s will be dominated by the conflict over life-style issues rather than the conflict of forms of metropolitan government that dominated the 1950s and early 1960s.

H. Paul Friesema, "Cities, Suburbs, and Short-Lived Models of Metropolitan Politics," in Louis H. Masotti and Jeffrey K. Hadden, eds., *The Urbanization of the Suburbs,* vol. VII of *Urban Affairs Annual Reviews* (Beverly Hills, Calif.: SAGE Publications, 1973), pp. 239–252. Places Williams's life-style model of metropolitan politics in the context of earlier models.

David C. Ranney, *Planning and Politics in the Metropolis* (Columbus, Ohio: Merrill, 1969). An excellent short overview of and introduction to various types of planning and their relation to the political process.

Mel Scott, *American City Planning Since 1890* (Berkeley: University of California Press, 1971). This is probably the most comprehensive history of American city planning available. An excellent reference text.

Alan A. Altshuler, *The City Planning Process: A Political Analysis* (Ithaca, N.Y.: Cornell University Press, 1965). Focuses on the strategy of planners, the structure of planning, and the substance of policy in separate case studies.

Francine F. Rabinovitz, *City Politics and Planning* (New York: Atherton Press, 1969). A comparative study of planning in separate New Jersey cities.

H. Wentworth Eldredge, ed., *Taming Megalopolis: vol. II, How to Manage an Urbanized World* (Garden City, N.Y.: Anchor Books, 1967). Contains several articles on planning and the implementation of the planning process.

Melvin B. Mogulof, *Governing Metropolitan Areas* (Washington, D.C.: The Urban Institute, 1971). A study and evaluation of the effectiveness of councils of governments in various metropolitan areas.

Philip W. Barnes, *Metropolitan Coalitions: A Study of Councils of Government in Texas* (Austin: Institute of Public Affairs, University of Texas, 1969). Studies and evaluates eleven COGs in Texas.

Frances Friskin, "The Metropolis and the Central City: Can One Government Unite Them?" *Urban Affairs Quarterly* 8, no. 3 (June 1973): 395–422. Analyzes the political problems of the COG in Cleveland.

John Friedmann, "The Future of Comprehensive Urban Planning: A Critique," *Public Administration Review* 31, no. 3 (May/June 1971): 315–326. Analyzes the reasons for the failure of comprehensive planning and urges that such planning be rejected in favor of a style of planning devoted to urban policy analysis.

Anthony James Catanese, *Planners and Local Politics: Impossible Dreams*, vol. VII of SAGE Library of Social Research (Beverly Hills, Calif.: SAGE Publications, 1974). Catanese compares the planners' apolitical perspective to Don Quixote's tilting at windmills. He argues that the planners must become more like politicians and the politicians more like planners if urban problems are ever going to be dealt with rationally.

Robert Goodman, *After the Planners* (New York: Simon & Schuster, 1971). This is a polemical book that blames much of the urban crisis on oppressive planning. An urban planner himself, Goodman advocates planning for liberation.

PART IV

The increasing involvement of the federal government in the political affairs of the metropolis has had a marked effect on both the tone of metropolitan politics and the structures of metropolitan governance. Primarily because of pressures from the federal government, the life-style issues are kept alive. And primarily because of pressures from the federal government, metropolitan planning, metropolitan planning agencies, and councils of governments have markedly increased. Whereas federal involvement prior to 1965 on balance supported the multi-centered metropolis and the functional fiefdoms, federal involvement since 1965 has been characterized by an ambivalence toward these. On the one hand it supports them. On the other hand, it seeks greater centralization of authority at the metropolitan level.

TOWARD A NATIONAL APPROACH TO METROPOLITANIZATION

Because of this ambivalence, it is often argued that a national urban policy is needed to tie together the hundreds of separate urban programs into coherent operations that strive to attain compatible objectives. Some attempts have been made to subordinate the hundreds of urban programs to the urban priorities of the president. These developments and their relationship to the changing federal role in urban affairs are examined in Chapter 11.

In trying to determine what should be involved in a national urban policy, it is instructive to examine the attempts of other countries to establish policies to cope with their metropolitan growth. These attempts and their relevance to the United States are discussed in Chapter 12. Chapter 13 speculates on the likely political changes in the American metropolis by the period 1980–1985. Chapter 14 presents a general summary of the major urban changes and the political biases which are related to them.

Chapter 11

All the developments discussed in Chapter 10 (metropolitan planning, the review process, and councils of governments) share one feature: their current, widespread usage is due primarily to the intervention of the federal government in urban affairs. Federal involvement in urban affairs extends to many other areas as well. Urban renewal and urban freeway systems have resulted directly from federal activity. Urban welfare programs, criminal justice programs, and health care programs are heavily financed by the federal government. So extensive has the federal involvement become and so far-reaching have been the changes

The Changing Federal Role in Metropolitan Affairs

in the nature of its involvement that the changing federal role in urban affairs requires some detailed explanation.

Four broad changes can be discerned in the federal role. First was the invention of the grant-in-aid as a device for urban problem solving. This device received its greatest impetus in the 1930s and the 1960s. Second were the grand designs of the Lyndon Johnson presidency. Third has been the proposal of revenue sharing as an alternative to grants-in-aid and to the Great Society programs. This was the major contribution of the Richard Nixon presidency to the evolution of the federal role. Finally, beginning in the late 1960s there has been a demand for the articulation of a national urban policy. These changes cannot be grouped into four distinct historical periods, each with its own beginning and end. On the contrary, each change is accompanied by the development of permanent constituencies that benefit from the institutional programs and of agencies whose creation constituted the change. These institutions, programs, and constituencies thus become a permanent feature of the urban political landscape.

THE GRANT-IN-AID APPROACH TO URBAN PROBLEM SOLVING

By the time that President Richard M. Nixon in 1973 announced his intention to terminate nearly a hundred federal urban programs in anticipation that Congress would pass his special revenue sharing measures, the federal government already had 530 grant-in-aid programs in operation. By 1975 the total federal spending on these programs amounted to over $50 billion, and the sum was growing at an annual rate of about 17 percent. A decade earlier there had been barely 100 grant-in-aid programs, and they had amounted to about $10 billion. By 1975 these programs were contributing about 22 percent of all state and local government revenue. A decade earlier they had contributed barely 11 percent of state and local government revenue.[1]

Despite this tremendous growth in federal programs during the 1960s and despite the magnitude of the expenditures involved, there was no consensus that these programs were improving the quality of life. And for the federal programs that operated in metropolitan areas, hardly a major program existed that was not under attack from one group or another. The federal grant programs themselves were accused of distorting the ability of states and localities to establish their own priorities.[2] The welfare programs were accused of breaking up families, destroying people's initiative, and condemning people to live their entire lives on permanent public welfare.[3] The urban renewal programs were accused of engaging in "Negro removal" and destroying more housing than they replaced.[4] The Office of Economic Opportunity was accused by the president's former urban advisor, Daniel Patrick Moynihan, of decimating the antipoverty program efforts through unthinking acceptance of the dogma of maximum feasible citizen participation.[5] The model cities programs were supposed to bring about a concerted interagency effort in target neighborhoods, but the funds were too few and were scattered over too many sites to have such an impact.[6] Even within the federal government, attempts to utilize federally owned land in key cities for the purpose of creating demonstration "new towns in-town" were dismal failures.[7]

Not all of the federal programs were failures, of course, and many of the accusations were unfounded. There were also some startling success stories. Legal aid programs initiated procedures for using the courts to force changes upon living conditions in urban slums. Community action programs trained a generation of black youths in organizing techniques and pressure tactics. Head start programs provided stimulating learning experiences for small children. Day care centers were established for mothers who wished to work or needed to work.

But all these efforts did not eradicate poverty, rejuvenate the cities, or even provide a single city as a stunning success story which other cities could emulate. The best thoughts of the best minds had been brought to bear on urban problems during the 1960s. The budgets for the three domestic agencies which administered most of the urban programs — Health, Education and Welfare (HEW), Housing and Urban Development (HUD), and the Department of Transportation (DOT) — sky-rocketed to a total of over $90 billion annually by the end of Nixon's first term in office. And after all these years of effort by all these experts, when a conservative president asked for an accounting, the liberal intellectuals and the recipients of the federal aid had in great measure become the greatest critics of the programs. The president's chief advisor on urban affairs, Daniel Patrick Moynihan, could only assert that "Too many programs have produced too few results."[8]

What happened?

Grants-in-Aid

To appreciate what happened, it is necessary to examine the basic mechanism through which the federal government becomes involved in urban programs. Few programs are actually operated by the federal government itself. Rather, the federal government provides the major share of funding for programs through the grants-in-aid device, and the actual operations of programs are undertaken by special agencies created or designated by state or local governments. A grant-in-aid is simply a federal payment to a state or local government to perform some specified activity. Before the state or local government can receive the federal payment, it often has to match a certain percent of the funds being advanced by the federal government. The actual operating agency which administers the program is then required to draft plans on how it will perform the service. It is also required to adhere to federal performance guidelines and to submit its performance to supervision by the federal agency that administers the program. A prominent example of this would be the community action agencies (CAAs) created by city governments to receive antipoverty grants from the Office of Economic Opportunity (OEO), created in 1964. The CAAs drafted plans which outlined the programs they would establish to combat poverty, and they submitted their plans to the OEO for funding. The actual programs were then administered by the CAAs, not the OEO.

Historically, grants-in-aid extend back at least to the Morrill Act of 1862, which gave land to states for the purpose of establishing the land-grant colleges. Subsequent acts provided for grants of funds and for matching grants by the states. About ten such programs existed by 1930.[9] Beginning with the Great Depression of the 1930s, the number of grants-in-aid programs steadily grew, but even as late as 1960 there were only 100 such programs. They were used to finance highway construction, public works, public assistance, public housing, airport construction, hospital construction, vocational education, and many other purposes. During the 1960s, with the promotion of President Lyndon B. Johnson's Great Society, two important changes occurred in the use of grants-in-aid. First was the proliferation of grant-in-aid programs from about 100 to over 500. Second, the grant-in-aid programs were designed more and more to accomplish nationally defined objectives rather than to help state governments accomplish state objectives.[10]

There are four different types of grants-in-aid, and they are differentiated by two criteria. First, grants-in-aid can be distinguished by the narrowness or broadness of the programs for which they grant funds. Categorical grants are specified for very narrowly defined purposes, and they give recipient governments very little discretion in spending the funds that they receive. When several categorical grants are consolidated under a single, broad grant in which greater discretion is given to the recipient agency, the result is a block grant. Most grants-in-aid are of the categorical type rather than the block-grant type. A prime example of a block grant is the Partnership in Health Act of 1966, which consolidated under one program separate grants for tuberculosis control, heart disease research, radiological facilities, venereal disease control, and research into several other diseases. Under this block grant, recipient governments can allocate the grant funds according to their needs. If a recipient community has a greater need for venereal disease control than it does for tuberculosis control, then it can allot its funds accordingly. Under a categorical grant program, this would not be possible.

A second criterion for classifying grants-in-aid is the degree of discretion permitted the federal granting agency to deny grants to applicants that fail to meet the agency's specifications. If the federal agency has no discretion but must allot its funds to states or communities by the terms of a rigid formula established by Congress, that grant is a formula grant. In contrast to formula grants are project grants. These are awarded for proposed projects that meet criteria established by the granting agency. The chief example of a project grant until 1974 has been the urban renewal program. A proposed workable program had to be submitted to and approved by the Urban Renewal Administration before the urban renewal funds were granted. It is apparent that the project grant entails greater federal control than does the formula grant. An example of a formula grant would be the Aid for Dependent Children (AFDC) program, which is operated through county welfare departments. Under this program the county is obliged to give AFDC assistance to any mother who qualifies. And the federal government is obliged to make AFDC funds available to any welfare department that meets the specifications of the law.

Federal Highway Programs

The federal government has provided assistance for highway construction and purposes since 1916.[11] But it was the highway legislation of 1944 and 1956 that had the greatest impact on urban development. The Federal Aid Highway Act of 1944 approved a 41,000-mile interstate highway system to connect the major urban centers. The Federal Aid Highway Act of 1956 provided the means of financing this interstate highway construction. It established a federal highway trust fund which was derived from a four-cents-per-gallon federal tax on gasoline. The Bureau of Public Roads was given authority to determine the routes for the new interstate highways. Ninety percent of the construction was to be financed from the highway trust fund. And the other 10 percent was financed by the individual states whose individual departments of highways assumed responsibility for the actual construction and maintenance of the new highways.

The interstate highway program has had four major consequences on the metropolitan centers. First, as pointed out in Chapter 2, the urban freeways constructed under this program contributed to the migration of population and shopping facilities to the suburbs. Second, by tearing up enormous tracts of residential housing in the cities, they displaced countless numbers of people and destroyed many viable urban neighborhood communities. Third, because the local residents whose neighborhoods were torn up found themselves powerless to stop the freeways, their construction and the manner in which they were constructed was one of several contributing factors to the increased public alienation with city government during the 1960s and early 1970s. Finally, by effectively subsidizing the construction of roads for automobiles, the federal government neglected the needs of public transit, and public transit facilities throughout the nation deteriorated progressively in the years since World War II.

By the 1970s several explosive reactions to these consequences began to occur. Strong opposition grew to the construction of freeways in cities and to the earmarking of the highway trust funds exclusively for highway construction. In Boston, a coalition of citizens' groups protested so successfully against the construction of a freeway through their neighborhoods that the governor of Massachusetts ordered an end to all freeway construction in the city.[12] Congress, in 1966, reacted to lobbying from conservationist groups and forbade the construction of freeways through public park systems unless there were no alternative routes. And in 1971 the Supreme Court upheld a suit filed by conservationists against a proposed freeway through a park in Memphis, Tennessee.[13] The heart of the battle over federal freeway programs has centered on attempts to broaden the purpose of the highway trust fund so that the moneys could be used for mass transit as well as for construction of highways. Congress and the presidents, however, have traditionally preferred maintaining the highway trust fund intact and instead making separate appropriations. Until 1974, however, such appropriations have never been commensurate with the needs of mass transit. In 1973 Congress finally opened the highway trust fund for mass transit uses and in 1974 authorized an extra $12 billion for mass transit.

Federal Housing and Urban Renewal Programs

Housing

Federal housing programs date back to the 1930s when federal action was required to limit the foreclosing of mortgages and to keep the mortgage-lending institutions from going bankrupt.[14] These actions were followed by the long-term, low-interest, low-down-payment, guaranteed mortgages of the Federal Housing Administration (FHA) and the Veterans' Administration (VA). As previously noted, these FHA and VA programs served the suburban white working-class and lower-middle-class housing markets rather than the central city poor and the racial minorities. FHA loans were barred to noncaucasians as late as 1962.

To provide housing assistance for the poor, the Housing Act of 1937 was passed. This act provided federal funds for local housing authorities to purchase land in blighted urban areas, tear down the old buildings, construct apartments, and rent them out at subsidized rates to low-income persons.[15] Although the local housing authorities were established by the city governments, the funds for the housing projects and the direction of the projects' construction were furnished by a federal agency, the Public Housing Administration. For a variety of reasons, most of these housing projects failed to solve the housing problems of the poor. The buildings were often high-rise apartments with little or no open space or recreational facilities surrounding them. As of the middle 1960s the programs had actually torn down more housing than they had constructed.[16] They led to increasing concentrations of blacks in the big-city ghettoes, and in some cities, they were even used deliberately to relocate the blacks from scattered locations throughout the cities to a few large ghettoes.[17]

Urban Renewal

One major problem with public housing was its subordination to urban renewal through the Housing Act of 1949 and its subsequent amendments, particularly the amendments of 1954. Urban renewal operated very similarly to the earlier public housing in that it provided federal funds to local public agencies (LPAs) to condemn land, clear it, and make provisions for its redevelopment. Urban renewal differed from public housing in two key respects. First, whereas the 1937 Housing Act had prescribed that *all* of the redeveloped area must be used for residential development, the 1954 act and subsequent amendments allowed up to 30 percent of the cleared land to be used for commercial purposes rather than for residential redevelopment. This enabled LPAs to tear down substantial areas of slum housing and use the land for a variety of purposes ranging from central business district redevelopment (Saint Paul) to university campus construction (Chicago) to shopping center construction (Bridgeport). For reasons of the local property tax base, urban renewal was more attractive to city governments than was public housing. Whereas the replacement of privately owned slum housing with publicly owned low-income apartments took property off the property tax roles, the redevelopment of central business districts increased the property tax base. Twenty-seven renewal projects in Chicago more than doubled the property tax values of the land that was redeveloped.[18]

A second difference between urban renewal and public housing was the involvement of the private sector under urban renewal. Public housing was both constructed and operated by public agencies, the local housing authorities. Under urban renewal, however, after the land was cleared by the LPA, it was then sold to a private redeveloper who developed it at a profit in accord with agreements he had reached with the LPA. In some respects, this put the urban renewal plan at the mercy of the real estate market. Private redevelopers naturally were reluctant to purchase sites in undesirable neighborhoods. In Newark, for example, the LPA (the Newark Housing Authority) found that its first urban renewal project was stalled for several years because it could not find a private developer willing to build on the site that the Housing Authority had cleared. In subsequent projects it first negotiated with private developers what sites they were interested in purchasing and then condemned the buildings and cleared those sites. In the words of two political scientists, "The responsibility for site selection, planning, and decisions about land reuse is thus defined in terms of profit for the redeveloper, as well as of professional criteria."[19] Studies of urban renewal in New York indicate that the same kinds of criteria were applied there as well.* In contrast to public housing, then, urban renewal is much more attractive both to private real estate developers looking for profits and to city officials looking for ways to increase rather than decrease the city's property tax base.

Both public housing and urban renewal have been heavily criticized for their destructive effects on cities. As indicated above, more housing units have been destroyed through these programs than have been constructed.[20] They have increased rather than decreased racial segregation[21] and have destroyed viable, functioning, urban neighborhood communities.[22] The housing projects themselves have been turned into dangerous, high-rise slums.[23] So dangerous and unpleasant was the Pruitt-Igoe public housing project in Saint Louis, for example, that people refused to live in it. Its 2700 apartments never maintained high occupancy rates. And in 1972 the failure of this project was publicly admitted when some of the buildings were torn down.[24] The relocation of families from slum areas being demolished has been conducted with the utmost financial and psychological hardships for these families.[25] The public housing programs have never related housing to the social and cultural environment.[26] In summary, in the words of two commentators, public housing was virtually meant to fail.[27]

Many of these problems have been dealt with (but certainly not eliminated) by subsequent legislation. By the 1970s a plethora of federally sponsored housing programs existed in a variety of agencies. Some

---

* Urban renewal director Robert Moses would turn the title over to the redeveloper before the site had been cleared, thus allowing the developer to make a profit by renting slum housing even though he had paid the price for the cleared land, not for the buildings [Jeanne Lowe, *Cities in a Race With Time: Progress and Poverty in America's Renewing Cities* (New York: Random House, 1968), pp. 68–72].

stimulated federally financed purchases of land, as in urban renewal. Others stimulated private investors to construct new housing. Others provided tax incentives to improve the existing supply of housing. Others provided rent supplements. Finally, the urban renewal program itself underwent drastic changes in 1973 and 1974. In 1973, President Nixon impounded funds which had been appropriated for urban renewal purposes and for public housing. This brought a virtual halt to new urban renewal and public housing construction. In 1974, the Housing Act of that year eliminated urban renewal as a separate grant-in-aid program. Urban renewal grants were consolidated with nine other urban grant programs, thus giving individual cities much more discretion on how the consolidated funds would be spent.

THE GREAT SOCIETY AND THE GRAND DESIGN FOR URBAN PROBLEM SOLVING

Of all the presidential administrations, that of Lyndon Johnson produced the greatest number of urban programs.[28] With typical overstatement, Johnson named his domestic programs the Great Society. But the overstatement notwithstanding, Johnson's urban programs were outstanding by comparison with those of any previous president. The most significant urban successes of the Great Society were:

1. The creation of two cabinet-level departments to deal with urban problems. A range of transportation programs were brought together under the Department of Transportation (DOT). With the passage of the Urban Mass Transportation Acts of 1964 and 1966, DOT was authorized to make grants to cities to improve their mass transit systems. The Department of Housing and Urban Development (HUD) was created in 1965. It was given responsibility not only for most of the housing and urban renewal programs, but it was also made the central agency for coordinating some federal urban programs and for stimulating urban and metropolitan planning.
2. The Elementary and Secondary Education Act of 1965. Not only did this act provide extensive funding for elementary and secondary education, but its Title I provisions established the principle of compensatory education by earmarking funds for schools with large numbers of economically disadvantaged children.[29]
3. The Economic Opportunity Act of 1964. This act established the war on poverty and the Office of Economic Opportunity (OEO). The OEO saw its purpose as creating experimental innovations that the estab-

lished bureaucracies were too timid or too conservative to initiate. Its most controversial creation was the community action program (CAP), which sought to involve local citizens in the planning and implementation of programs designed to end their poverty. The community action programs were designed and administered by community action agencies.

4. Fair Housing Act of 1968. This act outlawed discrimination in the sale or rental of housing.

5. Public Housing Legislation of 1968. This act authorized 400,000 units of public housing. Unlike the 1949 housing act, the 1968 act was supported by appropriations.

6. Model Cities Act of 1966 (see below).

Through these massive programs, the Great Society made three changes in the relationship between the federal government and the urban centers. First, it broadened the federal involvement extensively. As Suzanne Farkas has noted, until the middle 1960s the entire debate over the federal role in urban affairs was structured in terms of the housing and urban renewal programs instituted in 1949. For the next fifteen years, the entire content of debate about urban issues focused almost exclusively on questions such as relocation for the persons displaced by urban renewal, the percentage of the urban renewal project that should be devoted to housing, and the percentage of financing that should be local.[30] The Great Society programs raised a whole series of issues such as the participation of the poor in the planning and operation of the programs, compensatory education, advocacy action in legal services and planning, equal opportunity in housing and employment, the role to be played by militant movements,[31] and a host of social or human-related issues. Second, this very broadening of issues and programs for the first time forced the federal government to look seriously at coordinating all the programs which it had unleashed. Third, under the Great Society, the grant-in-aid programs were designed for the first time to attain nationally defined objectives rather than state or locally defined objectives.[32] The program which presents the best illustration of these three changes is probably the model cities program.

The Model Cities Program

Shortly after assuming the presidency, Lyndon Johnson was advised by Council of Economic Advisors chairman, Walter Heller, of a Kennedy administration proposal to completely rebuild blighted neighborhoods of a few cities on an experimental, demonstration basis.[33] All existing federal programs would be concentrated on these areas. They could be used as models of what concerted and coordinated federal action might accomplish by working in partnership with the local government. Other cities would then institute similar programs to emulate the model. Johnson liked the idea but informed Heller that such a program would have to include more than just a few cities if it were ever to pass through Congress and appease blacks. Just a few demonstrations would be interpreted by black leaders as mere tokenism. Johnson preferred instead something "big and bold."[34] In August 1964, a presidential Metropolitan and Urban Affairs Task Force was formed and given responsibility for designing practical suggestions for implementing the model cities proposal. The task force included some of the country's most thoughtful scholars of metropolitan and urban affairs. They had a strong and deep commitment to coordinated action by the various agencies of the federal government. The task force criticized existing federal programs, including the OEO, for operating in ways that fragmented logically related services. Included in the task force's final proposal was a suggestion that the federal government "adopt two or three large cities and in addition build a brand-new one in order to show what could be accomplished by well-conceived, large-scale, concerted effort."[35]

Although this recommendation was not incorporated in the president's legislative requests for 1964 or 1965, because he thought that the recommendations were too theoretical, it did lead to the formation of a second task force in 1965 which was charged by the president with making a practical proposal that could be implemented and show results while Johnson was still in office. Whereas the first task force had been dominated by "thinkers," the second task force was dominated by "doers," or, as in the case of Budget Director Charles L. Schultz, thinkers who were also doers. Schultz preferred to concentrate federal spending at a saturation level in five cities and to make a careful analysis of the results. The task force briefly considered the idea of concentrating all federal spending on just one demonstration city, but this was rejected because the administration would have been forced to choose between two of the most powerful Democratic supporters in the country: Mayor Richard Daley, who would propose Chicago, and labor leader Walter Reuther, who would propose Detroit. The task force also rejected Schultz's suggestion of five cities, because five cities would not attract enough Congressmen to vote for the bill. The task force report finally recommended that sixty-six demonstration cities be approved.

Cities would be invited to make an application that would identify a neighborhood to be redeveloped by the demonstration cities treatment. The applicants would be judged on the quality of their plans for redeveloping the model city area. Once selected, two kinds of federal assistance would be available. First the demonstration city neighborhoods would be eligible to receive all existing federal grants on a priority basis. Second, to make up any difference between what was available under existing programs and the costs of their demonstration cities experiment, they would receive supplemental grants on an eighty-twenty matching basis. For every $80 of federal supplemental grants, the city government would have to provide $20. These supplemental grants would ensure cooperation of all the federal agencies. Since the locally approved model cities program could get whatever supplemental grants it needed (at a cost of 20 percent), it would thus be in a good bargaining position to get other federal agencies to join in what promised to be a very glamorous program.

In order to get the bill through Congress, administration supporters tacitly promised over 100 congressmen and senators that their cities would be chosen for model cities sites. In order to get Senator Muskie to be floor manager of the bill in the Senate, he was informally promised that three cities from his home state of Maine would qualify for the program. When the Demonstration Cities and Metropolitan Development Act was finally signed into law, one of the president's public relations–conscious advisers noted that with all of the riots and demonstrations occurring in the cities during those days, it would be much more diplomatic to refer to the program as the model cities program rather than the demonstration cities program.* The Model Cities Administration invited cities to make application for model cities programs; and in 1966, sixty-three cities were chosen to participate in the first round of model cities grants. Laredo, in the president's home state of Texas, did not even submit an application, but it received a grant anyway. Smithfield, Tennessee, was an appropriate winning city, since it was the home town of the chairman of the House Appropriations Subcommittee that dealt with HUDs budget. Another appropriate winner was Pikesville, Kentucky, which was the home town of another key subcommittee chairman. Montana, the home state of Senate Majority Leader Mike Mansfield, had two cities among the winners. And Maine, floor leader Muskie's home state, got the three winners which Muskie had been promised. To ensure that the program

* The term *demonstration* has connotations of riots and protest movements that were not popular.

would not be blamed for political favoritism, Banfield writes that "at least one large city represented in Congress by a Republican had to be on the list. Happily, one — Columbus, Ohio — was found."[36] The next year, another round of winners was chosen, more than doubling the total number of model cities to 150.

Because of its emphasis on the coordination and concentration of all available federal programs in urban neighborhoods, the model cities program is different from any other federal program. The parent federal funding agency is HUD. And the local operating agency is a city demonstration agency (CDA). Unlike the CAAs of the antipoverty program, the model city CDAs were closely linked to city halls. The CDAs also put much more emphasis than did the CAAs on long-range, comprehensive planning for their neighborhoods. CDAs were also obliged to involve local residents in the program planning and operations. Thus there were high hopes that the model cities approach would be able to stimulate the kind of community development in poor neighborhoods that the CAAs had failed to accomplish. Rather than alienate community residents from city hall officialdom, it was hoped that model cities would bind them together in a joint effort. And model cities offered the possibility that for the first time the hundreds of separate, functionally organized federal programs would be subordinated to the needs of both community residents and elected city hall officials.

Early evaluations of the model cities programs suggested that they had enormous potential for accomplishing their goals.[37] However, Congress never appropriated the full amount of money authorized for model cities, and the amount of money actually spent never added up to the amount appropriated. Furthermore, the White House never lent its full prestige to the implementation of model cities. And the federal agencies in charge of the categorical grant programs were never as cooperative with the model cities planners as had been anticipated.[38]

In 1973, the Nixon administration impounded money that was appropriated for model cities, thus bringing the program to a standstill while a long court battle ensued to determine the legality of impoundment. The Housing Act of 1974 consolidated model cities with nine other urban grant programs into a large block grant for community development. The practical effect of this consolidation will be to minimize the model cities role as a coordinator and concentrator of federal programs and to change it into one more urban action agency. In many cities, the greater discretion over allocation that is given city governments by the block grant will mean the demise of model cities, because they will choose to use the funds elsewhere.

THE COORDINATING APPROACH TO
URBAN PROBLEM SOLVING

The demise of the model cities program in 1973–74 illustrates one of the key problems confronting the contemporary federal role in metropolitan areas. Since federal involvement in metropolitan and urban affairs operates through more than 500 different grant-in-aid programs, how can all those programs be coordinated so that they operate for common purposes rather than work at counter purposes? In addition to the unsuccessful model cities approach, two other coordinating devices have been attempted.

First, the Model Cities Act of 1966 and the Intergovernmental Cooperation Act of 1968 created the metropolitan review process. This is more commonly known as the A–95 review, as has been mentioned before. Under A–95 guidelines, applications for over 130 federal categorical grants must be submitted to review by a metropolitan review agency designated by HUD. The review agency can comment negatively on the application if it violates metropolitan priorities established for the given area. The granting agency may then refuse to honor the grant application. Although this is a potentially strong device for coordinating federal programs in metropolitan areas, in practice it has turned out to be a weak coordinating instrument. As noted in Chapter 10, negative reviews are rarely given. And the review agencies are reluctant to challenge the suburbs on the life-style issues such as zoning or low- and moderate-income housing.[39]

A second approach to coordinating federal programs has been to decentralize federal management functions to ten administrative regions and to create within each region a federal regional council.[40] These councils are composed of the heads of all the federal regional offices in the region. They are responsible for meeting regularly and coordinating their operations. However, the federal regional councils have not been very effective. The regional offices of federal agencies remain more attentive to the demands of their parent agencies in Washington than they do to the demands of other agencies' regional offices.[41]

THE GRANT-IN-AID APPROACH: AN ASSESSMENT

All of the above approaches to urban problem solving have relied in one way or another on the grant-in-aid as the basic mechanism for involving the federal government in metropolitan and urban affairs.

The 1960s saw the proliferation of grant-in-aid programs and the creation of attempts to coordinate the federal programs. But the basic mechanism remained the same — the grant-in-aid. As the basic instrument for federal involvement, the grant-in-aid programs have had several strengths and weaknesses. These are analyzed below.

The Positive Impact of Federal Programs

The federal grant-in-aid programs have had at least five positive features. First, these programs stimulated the states and municipalities to act on and spend considerable money on urban problems. Since most federal programs had matching grant features in which the state or municipality could buy into a federal program by providing 10 percent of the cost (interstate highways) or 20 percent of the cost (model cities), state and local governments bought into a great many programs. Local conservatives complained that buying-in was a trap. They argued that the federal funds would eventually be terminated and the local governments would be obliged to absorb the total cost of running the programs because they would be reluctant to curtail the services once they were in operation.

Second, the federal programs provided some very badly needed services. Although welfare programs may be as deficient as their critics maintain, the fact remains that for the first time, through the federal programs established during the 1930s, American governments began providing aid for the blind, the disabled, the unemployed, and the deserted, widowed, or single mothers with dependent children. The community action programs also may be as inefficient and unsuccessful as their critics maintain; but again for the first time, through the antipoverty and Great Society programs of the 1960s the federal government established a very important symbolic concern for the poor. Even if the programs did not eradicate poverty, they trained many people in the tactics of community organization and they did provide some badly needed jobs for CAA employees who otherwise might have been without jobs. And many of the programs were successful. In great measure, these programs served as conduits by which federal funds could be channeled into local service and self-help agencies. As Michael Reagan has pointed out, "To say that grant-in-aid funds account for over 20 per cent of state-local revenues is to say that those governments would do one-fifth less for their citizens without federal aid."[42]

Third, the multitude of federal programs created a multitude of ways in which local governments could tie into federal programs, which is very consistent with the fragmented nature of metropolitan governance. Requests, applications, or contacts with the federal government occur in parochial context but seldom in a metropolitan context. Political scientist Michael Danielson has characterized this as a "system in which the many pathways to the national capital attract numerous metropolitan actors, each motivated by a different perspective of the urban landscape and none representing the metropolis as a whole."[43] It could be argued that the fragmented nature of the grants-in-aid program made federal aid more accessible than it would have been if it had all been centralized and coordinated.

Fourth, the federal urban programs have served as a stimulus to the local economy.[44] Urban renewal, highway construction, and housing programs have provided a great many jobs and have invested billions of dollars in the local economies. Although it is probably true that very few of these jobs went to the poor or to the racial minorities, the jobs did go to people who needed them. Urban renewal programs in particular have stimulated almost every major central city in the country to rebuild its central business district.

Finally, and most importantly, grant-in-aid programs have enabled the federal government to deal with national problems. Problems of urban poverty, public welfare, urban transportation, and public housing are widely recognized as national problems, not local problems. Without the grant-in-aid programs, these problems could not be dealt with nationally. Each state or locality would have to cope with its portion of the problem on its own and in isolation from other states and localities that were also trying to deal with their portions of the problem.

The Negative Impact of Federal Programs

Despite these positive contributions, the grants-in-aid approach to urban problem solving has been subjected to severe criticism. First, they have seriously aggravated already existing imbalances in the urban political ecology. The federally sponsored freeway systems and interstate highways were designed to save the central cities. Instead, they led to the physical dispersion of shopping centers which have siphoned retail shoppers away from the central cities. Federal housing programs were supposed to eliminate slums, yet after a decade of New York's housing program just as many people lived in slum housing as had lived there at the start. The FHA/VA-insured home mortgages did provide a significant prop for the home mortgage system, but they also completely ignored community development. They stimulated growth in suburban areas which were already receiving more growth than they could regulate. No attempt was made to set up a preferential condition for guaranteeing loans which would rank applicants according to community criteria rather than individual criteria. Such an action would have forced local communities to establish criteria for land development and would have given local communities a strong incentive to support metropolitan planning.[45] Urban renewal programs were similarly treated without any relation to metropolitan development planning.

Second, federal programs led to extreme functional specialization. The local housing and redevelopment authorities which operate the urban renewal programs often became highly autonomous and isolated from mayors and city councils. Federal welfare programs operated through state and county departments of public welfare which often were totally unrelated to the activities of the housing authorities whose redevelopment activities were so important to the welfare recipients.

Third, and as a consequence of these first two negative impacts, federal programs compounded the problems of accountability and control. By creating agencies which were semiautonomous and quasi-independent of mayors and elected local officials, the most important agencies for the physical development of a city were put beyond the reach of the local electorate.

Finally, the grants-in-aid skew state and local budgets into the areas determined by federal programs. And this makes it more difficult for state and local governments to meet problems in areas not supported by grants-in-aid.[46]

REVENUE SHARING

The criticisms of the grant-in-aid approach to urban problem solving were severe enough that many persons began to suggest alternative approaches either as replacements for grants-in-aid or as supplements to them. One proposal was to replace the multitude of categorical grants with a limited number of block grants. Another idea suggested that if locally operated programs could not be coordinated from Washington, then federal funds should be turned over to the local governments and let them operate their own urban programs as they saw fit with very few federal strings attached. This approach was consistent with the generally conservative thinking of President Nixon, who for years had maintained that too much domestic power was being concentrated in Washington. Once in office, Nixon spoke of a "new federalism" in which the states would emerge from their dominance by the federal government. In practice, this meant initially a withdrawal of White House support from attempts to achieve racial desegregation through bussing children from one school to another for the purpose of achieving a racial balance. Concerning the welfare system, Nixon adopted a variation of the guaranteed income combined with a mandatory work requirement for certain recipients and proposed that this income maintenance plan be phased in to replace many of the existing welfare programs.[47] This plan was consistent with the new federalism, because the administration of the plan would in great measure be left to the states.

But the key proposal for Nixon's new federalism emerged in 1971 when the president revealed his federal revenue sharing proposals. Federal revenue sharing had first been proposed by President Kennedy's chairman of the Council of Economic Advisors, Walter Heller. Heller argued that the federal government had preempted the most lucrative source of tax revenue when it adopted the graduated progressive income tax. Because the federal income tax and the social security taxes absorbed a major share of a worker's paycheck, the states were very limited in their ability to tax income. Despite these difficulties, thirty-nine states currently use income taxes and by 1970 such taxes (both individual and corporate) provided states with about 28 percent of their revenue. The greatest portion of their revenue, 30 percent, came from general and selected sales taxes, and only about 2 percent came from property taxes.[48] Local governments received the major share of their revenue from property taxes.[49] Neither property taxes nor sales taxes are believed to grow with the economy as fast as the national income tax. In fact, however, state and local revenue collections have been increasing *faster than those* of the federal government, rising from $31 billion in 1956 to $122 billion in 1971, almost quadrupling during the fifteen years. Over the same period, federal revenues increased about 2.5 times from $78 billion to $200 billion. Even if state and local revenues were increasing faster than federal revenues, the state and local sources of revenue (sales taxes, property taxes, and basically nonprogressive income taxes) are fairly regressive forms of taxation, causing lower-income people to pay out in taxes a higher percentage of their income than is paid by people with higher incomes. Even in states with progressive income taxes, the taxes are not as progressive as the federal income tax.

For all of these reasons, the states and localities were thought to lack the tax resources to provide needed urban services. This could be remedied, according to Heller's thinking, by having the federal government annually turn back to the states and localities a fixed portion of the federal income tax revenues. This sum would be divided among the states according to a formula based principally upon population.

For different reasons, revenue sharing initially appealed to both liberals and conservatives. From a conservative point of view, revenue sharing would strengthen state and local governments and make it easier for them to perform the needed urban services without having to rely upon the initiative of the federal government. From the liberal point of view, the revenue sharing concept appeared to enlarge the total governmental capacity to provide needed services. And since the funds would come from the federal income tax, they would be raised in a much more progressive manner than would be possible in any of the states.

Nixon's Proposals

There were other arguments in favor of revenue sharing as well. There were also strong objections.* Because of the debate over these arguments, over a decade passed before revenue sharing went from Heller's proposal to enactment into law in 1972. A crucial point of Nixon's revenue sharing proposal was its division into two programs. The first, which was enacted in 1972, was called *general revenue sharing*. General revenue sharing allotted $5 billion per year for five years to the states and communities for them to use virtually as they saw fit. The only strings attached were that the funds had to be used on priority projects and could not be used to promote racial segregation. About 40 percent of the general revenue sharing funds went to the state govern-

---

* Some arguments in favor of revenue sharing are: the unreliability of some categorical grants, the tendency of categorical grants to become hard and narrow, and the hope that revenue sharing would make the states more viable fiscally. The major arguments against revenue sharing include the following. The unit which spends the tax money should also raise the tax money. The availability of many categorical grant programs gives the local government many options from which it can choose. State governments are too inadequate and in many instances too corrupt to be trusted with the funds and discretion they would receive through revenue sharing. The notion that the states are laboratories for governmental innovation has been overdone. The states in actuality are not any closer to the people than is the federal government. Particularly for the racial minorities, the federal government has been more responsive than have the state governments. Revenue sharing might mean less funds going to urban and metropolitan problems. Finally, in Michael Reagan's words, revenue sharing "moves us back to the level of separate state political cultures (and to the extent that the pass through is required, even to the level of separate local political cultures) as the context-setting environment in which public expenditure decisions will be made." Reagan, in *The New Federalism* (New York: Oxford University Press, 1972), summarizes the case for revenue sharing (pp. 92–101) and the case against revenue sharing (pp. 102–132). The quote is taken from pp. 126–127 of his book.

ments, and the rest were passed directly to the local communities. The program was to run for five years through fiscal year 1977 and was to allocate a total of $30 billion to the states and local governments. The funds were to be appropriated directly from the United States Treasury into a newly created State and Local Government Fiscal Assistance Trust Fund. The trust fund then apportioned the money out to the states and localities every six months according to a formula adopted by Congress. Although Nixon sent the general revenue sharing bill to Congress early in 1971, it was not enacted into law until late in 1972.

Nixon's second proposal was *special revenue sharing.* Special revenue sharing was intended to replace about 70 of the 530 federal categorical grant programs. These programs would be phased out and their funds picked up under four special revenue sharing programs,* which are shown in Table 11-1. As long as the state or locality spent its funds in the appropriate area, few restrictions were placed on how it was spent. Unless the discontinued federal programs were picked up and funded by the states or communities under the funds which they received from the special revenue sharing, the programs would fold. From a conservative point of view, this had the added advantage of allowing each state and locality to decide for itself what its priorities would be. If city A decided to use the funds for a model cities program, it could use special revenue sharing funds to run it. And if city B decided that it did not need a model cities program, then it could use its special revenue sharing funds for a different purpose.

In addition to replacing the categorical grant programs, Nixon's special revenue sharing proposals were characterized by three other features. First, the funds would be dispensed by complicated automatic formulas. Second, 20 percent of the better community funds and 15 percent of the manpower training funds were reserved for the secretaries of HUD and the Labor Department, respectively, to use at their discretion. Third, a hold-harmless provision guaranteed that no city would get less money under special revenue sharing than the average of what it had received from existing categorical grants over the preceding four years.

On the face of it, Nixon's special revenue sharing looked like an enormous bargain for state and local governments whose officials had for years complained that the categorical grant programs preempted their freedom of action. In fact, however, the proposal was greeted with little enthusiasm. And, as Table 11-1 shows, only one of the pro-

* These were the terms of the 1973 proposals for special revenue sharing. Nixon had originally proposed in 1971 that six special revenue sharing programs replace 129 categorical grant programs.

TABLE 11-1

1973 SPECIAL REVENUE SHARING PROPOSALS

Proposal	Level of Funding for FY 1975	Ultimate Disposition
Better schools program	$2.8 billion	Died in August 1974 with the passage of an omnibus Elementary and Secondary Education Act. Out of an original request of 32 grant consolidations, only a small number were in fact consolidated.
Better communities program	$2.3 billion	Died in August 1974 with the passage of the 1974 Housing Act. This act consolidated ten grants-in-aid including model cities and urban renewal. But the revenue sharing approach was rejected through the imposition of federal regulations on the grant expenditures.
Law enforcement program	$0.8 billion	Died August 1974 with the extension of the Law Enforcement Assistance Act through 1976.
Manpower program	$1.3 billion	Partially enacted through the Comprehensive Employment and Training Act of 1973. Consolidated manpower grant-in-aid programs and decentralized their operations.

Source: Congressional Quarterly Almanac, 1973, pp. 349, 749. Congressional Quarterly Weekly, February 3, 1973, pp. 222–223; and August 24, 1974, pp. 2319–2322.

posals, manpower, was translated into law.* For reasons which the White House never fully explained, in 1973 Nixon began unilaterally dismantling the programs which were subject to being phased out if Congress should pass the special revenue sharing bills. But he did not wait until the bills were passed before phasing out the programs. In some instances, such as the model cities program supplemental grants, the federal programs were to phase out a full year in advance of the time that the states and localities were to get their first payment under special revenue sharing. Because of these premature acts, Nixon ran

* The better communities consolidation of ten categorical grants is sometimes referred to as revenue sharing. In the strict sense of the term, however, it is not revenue sharing, because the federal government imposes restrictions on the grant expenditures.

into enormous opposition in 1973 in Congress from liberal and urban congressmen.

An Assessment of Special Revenue Sharing

Even granting President Nixon the best of intentions, his revenue sharing proposals represented a step backward in terms of formulating national urban policy or coordinating programs in metropolitan areas. Political scientist Michael Reagan refers to revenue sharing as a federal government "cop-out." By eliminating the categorical grant programs and turning the money for those programs over to the states and localities, the federal government in effect was backing away from the attempt to establish national priorities in dealing with national domestic problems.[50] Furthermore, because the federal programs to be phased out dealt with problems around which a new set of interest groups had emerged and because these interest groups found the national government more receptive to their problems than state or central city governments, the special revenue sharing proposals might have diminished the effectiveness of those interest groups.

> Having succeeded at the federal level, usually after years of protracted bargaining and political coalition building (i.e.: logrolling), the leaders of major interest groups representing the needs and demands of the schools, the children, the poor, the ethnic minorities, and the cities are not going to accept without a real fight the message that they should now begin over again in all the state capitals. After all, they have focused on Washington in the first place largely because of the proven unresponsiveness of those capitals. Again, it is a question of which priorities shall prevail, those of the national community or those of the lesser, narrower communities; those of the most inclusive majority, or those of the most exclusive status quo dominated pressure system?[51]

One feature of general and special revenue sharing which reduces the federal capacity to establish urban priorities is the automatic formula for distribution of funds to state and local governments. Under the categorical project grants, some cities had participated at a very low level in federal urban programs. In some cases the state legislatures and constitutions restricted local government spending, and the smaller cities were sometimes hindered from buying into the federal programs. In other instances, the local leaders were not very effective in seeking federal grants. Particularly left out were the small rural towns which lacked the know-how and the channels to take maximum advantage of the federal grant programs. This meant that large, highly organized city governments like that of Chicago, for example, got more than their share of the categorical grants. Under the special revenue sharing better communities proposal, the $1.6 billion reserved for urban community development would be spread around the more than 250 cities with populations of 50,000 or more. Consequently, the federal agencies would have no capacity to allocate the funds to cities that were meeting federal priorities and not to allocate them to cities that were failing to meet federal priorities.

Finally, in a metropolitan sense, it is difficult to see how the special revenue sharing can help promote metropolitan planning and the establishment of metropolitan priorities.[52] The most effective tools yet created by the federal government for the imposition of a metropolitan set of priorities were the 1965, 1966, and 1968 provisions which funded metropolitan planning efforts and instituted the A–95 review process. Through the initial special revenue sharing provisions, about a fifth of all federal grant programs and about a third of all their expenditures would pass directly to the local governments and would not be subject to the A–95 review process. Because of this, the 1971 special revenue sharing proposals reduce by a fifth the ability of the designated federal review agencies to coordinate policies in metropolitan areas. Furthermore, the money not only bypasses the metropolitan review process, it goes directly to the most vociferous opponents of the review process, the municipalities themselves.

TOWARD A NATIONAL URBAN POLICY

The Need for a National Urban Policy

The major criticism of Nixon's revenue sharing proposals, then, was that they moved away from articulating a national urban policy.[53] But the multitude of programs presented several problems of coordination. And, by the early 1970s, many felt that the federal government vitally needed to articulate a set of national urban policy goals and objectives to coordinate the formulation and implementation of all federal urban programs.* Nixon's former urban affairs adviser, Daniel Patrick Moynihan, argued that the multitude of federal urban programs do not add up to a policy,[54] and former HUD Undersecretary Robert Wood made the same point.[55] Programs deal with only specific aspects of the metropolis; and until the creation of a metropolitan review power in 1966,

---

* A *goal* is a broad statement of something to be accomplished. An *objective* is a more specific statement of something to be accomplished. An objective operationalizes the goal. Whereas a goal need not always be measurable, an objective's attainment is always measurable.

the federal government made little attempt to ensure that the more than 500 federal programs complemented each other rather than worked at cross purposes. Given the crisis atmosphere of the 1960s and the rapid and sudden growth of the federal interest in urban affairs, it was perhaps inevitable that programs proliferated in isolation from one another and with little thought as to how they fit into overall goals and objectives. But once the crisis atmosphere passed, it is difficult to understand why more effort was not given to coordinating all of these activities. Without national goals, objectives, and priorities to tie the programs together, nothing provides an overall guidance for all the federal urban programs. Consequently, the sheer magnitude of existing federal urban programs demands the articulation of national policy goals and objectives.

A second argument for establishing a national urban policy derives from the magnitude of the population growth and migration. Even if the declining birth rates stabilize the American population, that stabilization cannot come until the end of the century. In the intervening years, the American population will increase by between 75 million and 100 million people.* Not only do demographers know that an increase in this range will occur, they know where it will occur. Barring a complete reversal of present trends, the increase will occur almost entirely in the four emerging megalopolitan complexes. Central cities and inner suburbs will stabilize or continue to decline, while outer suburbs and the small rural towns within commuting distances will continue to grow. In practical terms, during the next thirty years about half as many houses, schools, streets, sewers, and power plants will have to be constructed as have already been built in metropolitan areas in the entire history of the United States. No national policy currently speaks to this future construction, to the migration trends, or even to the population growth itself.

---

* The most conservative population projection for the year 2000 is for an increase of 40 million people over the 1970 population. It is based on the assumption that the average number of children per child-bearing woman will decline from the 3.1 average that prevailed since World War II to an average of 1.7. If the average declines only to 2.7, then the projected population increase is put at 83 million by the year 2000. And a national population of 300 million will be reached by about the year 2005. If the birth rate drops to the replacement level of 2.1 children per woman, then the projected population increase by the year 2000 is 58 million, and the population mark of 300 million is not reached until the year 2025. The main difference between having a birth rate of 2.7 and the replacement level of 2.1 seems to be that it will take an extra twenty-five years for the population to reach the 300 million mark. The projections are made by the Bureau of the Census. See United States Bureau of the Census, *Current Population Reports*, ser. P-25, no. 541, "Population Estimates and Projections" (Washington, D.C.: U.S. Government Printing Office, 1975).

The discussions in the four preceding chapters make it clear that currently existing alternatives to megalopolitan sprawl cannot handle this projected growth. One suggested alternative has been new towns. But new towns are not a viable solution.* If an average new town contains 50,000 people, then 2,000 such new towns would be needed to house this population increase, or approximately 80 new towns per year in the last twenty-five years of the century. The total contemplated public and private new town projects does not approach even a small fraction of this number. In the meantime, suburban subdivisions continue to sprawl. Consequently, under current nonpolicies this hundred million population increase inevitably will occur in and just beyond the suburban fringes of the four emerging megalopolises. Without a national urban policy, this growth cannot be accommodated without aggravating the already serious metropolitan problems discussed in Chapters 6 and 7.

A third reason for establishing a national urban policy is that urban problems are national problems. The fundamental causes of the urban problems are found in such unexciting statistics as the national ratio of births to deaths and national migration figures. No given metropolis or state can hope to cope with these factors on its own. The number of people receiving aid for dependent children (AFDC) at any given time is likely to be very closely related to changes in the gross national product, and state or local governments acting individually can do very little to affect it. Nevertheless, they are left to cope with the brunt of the problems which face most AFDC recipients — the need for adequate housing, the need for competent and often compensatory education, the need for a variety of social services, and, in many instances, the need for jobs. Very few of the causal factors of the urban problems can be dealt with by individual states and municipalities acting in isolation. Only the national government can coordinate the efforts of states and municipalities so that they act in concert rather than in opposition to one another.

The Elements of a National Urban Policy

Demonstrating the need for a national urban policy is much easier than creating one. Even formulating such a policy at the highest levels of government would give no guarantee that it would be more than a few words on a piece of paper. Just as Chapter 10 demonstrated that there is

* Urban planner Marshall Kaplan has assailed the designation of government funds for new towns as diverting funds from more urgent urban needs [Kaplan, *Urban Planning in the 1960's: A Design for Irrelevancy* (New York: Praeger, 1973), pp. 40–41].

a distinction between planning as a document and planning as a process, so there is a distinction between policy as a document and policy as a process. The material covered so far in this chapter presents ample evidence for this distinction. President Johnson articulated a policy statement that ordered the creation of new towns in-town, but his policy statement was never translated into action. Congress in the Elementary and Secondary Education Act of 1965 established policies of compensatory education, but such policies were frustrated by state departments of education and local school districts. Congress and the president together in 1966 articulated a model cities program. Yet after almost a decade of model cities activities and several billlon dollars expended, not a single urban neighborhood has been rejuvenated to the point where it serves as a model for the rest of the country. Furthermore, the present system of grants-in-aid has created urban interest groups that stand to lose influence if the grant programs are subordinated to national policies.

With these limitations on national urban policy, what can be done is to indicate the changing role of the federal and state *actors* in urban policy making, to isolate the issues which should form the *content* of a national urban policy, and to note the importance of urban policy as *a process.*

Federalism and a National Urban Policy

The changing federal role in urban affairs is directly related to changes in the concept of federalism. The Constitution makes no mention of federal-urban relations. Indeed, it does not mention urban affairs or cities at all. The direct relations between cities and the federal government is a recent innovation which indicates that some profound changes have occurred in the meaning of the concept of federalism. The Constitution specifies only two levels of government, the state and the federal. For the first century and a half, relations between these two levels of government were understood under the concept of *dual federalism.* Within their respective spheres, each level of government was considered sovereign and independent of the other. The proliferation of grants-in-aid since the 1930s has shown, however, that the two levels of government were not at all independent of each other. Rather than dual federalism, political scientist Daniel J. Elazar asserted that *cooperative federalism* was a more appropriate term.[56] That is, government action in most functions occurred through the cooperation of the two levels of government rather than through sovereign and independent action over particular functions. Morton Grodzins used the metaphors of *layer cake* and *marble cake federalism* to illustrate the distinction between dual federalism and cooperative federalism.[57] By the end of the 1960s the federal involvement directly with local governments in urban areas had become so dominant that even the cooperative model of federalism no longer seemed appropriate. Michael Reagan used the term *permissive federalism*[58] to describe this new relationship. Programs are established nationally and carried out by the state or by state-created agencies. In effect, the federal system of government has become what James Sundquist called a *single system of government*.[59] In such a single system, the states necessarily play an important role in implementing national urban policies. Consequently, the state role in urban affairs is inextricably intertwined with the federal role in urban affairs.

State Actors in a National Urban Policy

An often-made and considerably true quip about federalism and urban affairs is that the cities have the problems, the federal government has the money, and the state governments have the legal authority. Thus the success of any attempts to apply national resources to urban problems will greatly depend upon the efficacy of the states in using their legal authority. For many years the states, dominated by rural-oriented legislatures, virtually ignored urban problems and took few initiatives. Their major role was creating or allowing the creation of the multitude of special districts and new government agencies that were the recipients of the federal grant-in-aid programs. As the population became increasingly metropolitan, however, the state legislatures were forced to reapportion, which gave fair representation to the suburbs for the first time.* The states then came under increasing pressure to act on urban problems. Much of this pressure was articulated by several prestigious organizations which were seeking either to decentralize the American federal system or to improve the capabilities of state governments. Three of these in particular played an important role in developing the agenda for state action on urban problems.

---

* The United States Supreme Court forced reapportionment in accord with the one-person, one-vote principle upon the lower houses of state legislatures in *Baker v. Carr*, 369 U.S. 186 (1962), and upon the upper houses of state legislatures in *Reynolds v. Sims*, 377 U.S. 533 (1964). Most studies have concluded that reapportionment has had a minimal impact on public policy in states. [See Herbert Jacob, "The Consequences of Malapportionment: A Note of Caution," Social Forces, 43 (December 1964): 256–261; and Thomas R. Dye, "Malapportionment and Public Policy in the States," *Journal of Politics* 27 (August 1965); 586–601.]

Michael C. Le May made a contrary assessment of the impact of reapportionment. [See his "The States and Urban Areas: A Comparative Assessment," *National Civic Review* 61, no. 11 (December 1972): 542–548.]

First, the Advisory Commission on Intergovernmental Relations (ACIR) was established in 1959 to promote legislation that would make the federal system more effective. The commission is composed of existing political officers, governors, legislators, mayors, and county officials. Although it has been concerned with the entire gamut of federal relations, it has made three major recommendations concerning state action in metropolitan areas. First, state governments were urged to pass legislation to facilitate many of the metropolitan reform proposals described in Chapters 7 and 8, particularly annexation, federative schemes, urban counties, multi-purpose districts, the transfer of metropolitan functions to large units of government, and intergovernmental cooperation. Second, the ACIR has recommended the creation of state offices for local affairs. And third, it has recommended making it more difficult to create new municipalities.[60]

A second agency urging urban reform has been the Council of State Governments (CSG), established in 1925. Its recommendations are published regularly in its journal, *State Government*, which not only announces the council's policy statements but keeps its readers apprised of developments in state government. With particular references to urban affairs, the CSG has urged the states to:[61]

1. Pass legislation that would facilitate the establishment of metropolitan reforms such as multi-purpose districts, federations, urban county home rule governments, city-county consolidations, annexations, or transfer of functions to larger authorities.
2. Provide technical assistance to local governments to help them meet their development responsibilities.
3. Broaden the financial resources of local governments.
4. Regulate local government activities which require intergovernmental cooperation, and increase the requirements that need to be met before new municipalities can be incorporated in SMSAs.
5. Take over the exercise of certain local functions, such as highway planning or transportation planning.

Because the thrust of the CSG suggestions would place the initiative in state hands rather than in the hands of city governments and because it has sought for federal aids to be administered through the states rather than given directly to the cities, the Council of State Governments has sometimes been viewed as antiurban.[62] Such initiatives would diminish the influence of urban interest groups such as black organizations, representatives of the poor, and the big-city mayors.

A third agency involved in metropolitan affairs is the Committee for Economic Development (CED), composed primarily of progressive-minded businessmen. The CED has produced three influential publications over the past decade: *Modernizing State Government,* 1967;[63] *Modernizing Local Government,* 1966;[64] and *Reshaping Government in Metropolitan Areas,* 1970.[65] The general thrust of CED recommendations have been toward greater efficiency and improved accountability of the government to the electorate through a clearer delineation of governmental functions and lines of responsibility. While many of its recommendations concerning state and local government have been adopted, its 1970 recommendation that two-tier schemes of metropolitan government be established (see Chapter 8) has not once been adopted.

Except for the proposals to establish metropolitan governments, these recommendations have been fairly well implemented. By 1973 all of the states had adopted at least one of the recommendations and most of the states had adopted several.[66] States have tended to establish state offices of local affairs to coordinate state activities, advise and assist local governments, encourage local cooperation, and serve as clearing houses for information. They may even become directly involved in the operation of traditionally local activities. In New Jersey, for example, the state Department of Consumer Affairs has operated its own program to increase the supply of moderate-income housing and has also contributed to the operations of the model cities programs in that state.[67]

The most significant state activity in urban affairs has occurred on a functional basis. The states have become increasingly active in problems of open space, mass transit, freeways, water supplies, air and water pollution, and reorganization of metropolitan governmental arrangements.[68] An assessment of these actions, however, leaves a mixed picture. At best, effective action has been taken on specific functional problems; state air pollution regulations, for example, have improved the quality of air in many urban centers. At worst, state action has supported the functional fiefdoms discussed in Chapter 5 and has led to increasing the problems of fragmented government in metropolises. A study of state action in New York concluded that despite its effective action on a functional basis, it in fact had increased governmental fragmentation.[69]

The most dramatic state action has been the establishment of publicly owned urban development corporations. In New York an Urban Development Corporation (UDC) was created in 1968 to identify and redevelop target urban areas. It was given $1 billion in bonding authority, complete authority to develop a project from beginning planning stages to completion, eminent domain powers to enhance its ability to acquire land, and authority to override local zoning and building controls when necessary. The UDC is a state enterprise that is beyond the control of either local voters or local officials. It appeared to have considerable potential for dealing with urban housing problems until it defaulted on a bond issue in 1975.[70] Whether the troubles of New York's UDC will discourage the further use of such agencies in general is not yet clear.

The Content of National Urban Policy

If a national urban policy is to be developed out of the melange of urban programs, of what would it consist? Daniel P. Moynihan has identified some of the elements which a national urban policy should contain,[71] but most scholarly writing addresses narrower functional questions and questions on specific programs. Nevertheless, a national urban policy ought at least to provide guidance on the major issues of contemporary urban life. Four particular issues are of the utmost importance.

First, and perhaps most important, a policy should be established on the distribution of future population growth. Although nobody really knows how many people can fit into the Northeast megalopolis, for example, the recurring brownouts and power shortages over the past decades plus the severe crisis in fuel oil and gasoline in the winter of 1973–1974 suggest that we may be approaching the limit under present technology. The federal government should begin discussing *where* the yet coming hundred million people should be housed and *what kinds of incentives* can realistically induce them to live there.

Second, a national urban policy must confront the deterioration of the older center cities. Although hundreds of programs exist for these cities, many of them work at cross purposes, and many disrupt the governing capabilities of city governments. Many nonurban government policies, such as the agricultural subsidy policies, have had an adverse effect on the central cities by driving sharecroppers off farms and into the cities. The federal government needs to decide what it wants for these urban centers, and the city governments need to define what they want for themselves. Unless broad goals and objectives can be formulated, federal involvement cannot be anything other than piecemeal and ad hoc. Unless federal and local governments can each formulate its broad objectives in a meaningful way, they will not be able to establish control over the existing functional fiefdoms. The federal urban objectives need to be stated every bit as clearly as the federal objectives were stated when it was determined to place a man on the moon. Once the objective is stated, the programs can be tied to the objective. Without an overriding objective, nothing ties the programs together.

Third, a national urban policy would demand that the federal government consistently confront the life-style issues of social access that were discussed in Chapter 10. Unless the gross inequities in the distribution of public goods and services in housing, jobs, and schools that characterize most metropolitan areas can be reduced, the nation probably cannot avoid the two-societies fate predicted by the Kerner Commission, "Our Nation is moving toward two societies, one black, one white—separate and unequal."[72] Why should any white parents who can really afford the choice live in a neighborhood where their children must attend inferior schools and confront what they *think* is a relatively high probability of physical assault? And the answer, of course, is that very few people will live there if they can afford not to. For entirely rational reasons, they migrate into better neighborhoods where their children can have what they think are better and safer schools. And they strongly resist any efforts of local governments to make them share their advantages with the residents of less-advantaged neighborhoods. Continued federal pressure thus is an absolute must if the life-style issues are to be faced.

Fourth, a national urban policy must address the problems of suburban sprawl. Federally stimulated metropolitan planning has not done this. New town proposals have not done it. Incalculably valuable natural resources of farm land, recreational space, open space, water supply, and natural beauty have been plowed under and paved over in the past thirty years. And over the next thirty years they will continue to be wasted unless federal incentives and priorities are established. The failure of Congress in 1974 to pass a bill to provide incentives to states to regulate land use more carefully was a major setback for the articulation of a national urban policy.

The four aspects of urban policy indicated here refer to *national* problems, not local problems. And the existence of national problems involving federal expenditures of over $50 billion demands that national policies be articulated to guide the purposes for which and the ways in which that money is spent.

The Process of National Urban Policy

Just as important as articulating national policy goals and objectives is the process of implementing such policies. The president was charged by the 1970 Housing and Urban Development Act with formulating a national urban growth policy and with sending Congress every two years a report on urban growth. The task of preparing this report was given to the Domestic Council Committee on National Growth, and it sent its first report to Congress in 1972. Rather than articulate a national urban growth policy, however, the committee rejected even the possibility of doing so. "This document makes no claim . . . to present a single, comprehensive national growth policy. The hard unavoidable fact of the matter . . . is that no single policy, nor even a single coordinated set of policies, can remedy or even significantly ameliorate all of our ills. As our problems are many and varied and changing, our national solutions must be multiple and diverse and flexible."[73]

This statement reflects an understanding of the difficulties involved in translating policy statements into policy actions. The urban history of the 1960s provides abundant examples of federal policies that were unimplemented or poorly implemented because the federal government did not possess the means or the unity to enforce them. On the other hand, the 1960s also present abundant examples of federal initiatives that worked very well and accomplished their policy objectives. In order to assess whether the White House can fulfill its congressionally mandated obligation to formulate a national urban growth policy, it would seem useful to try and distinguish between the kinds of policies that the federal government is currently capable of implementing and those that it is not. Some things it does very well; other things it does very poorly.

First, the federal government poorly implements those policies which are adversely affected by traditional congressional logrolling. For example, the model cities programs' prospects for success were seriously hampered from the beginning because the programs were spread among cities in so many congressional districts that no single model city ever got enough funds to carry out its objectives. If the goal behind model cities was in fact the creation of a demonstration project which all cities could emulate, then congressional logrolling was dysfunctional for the attainment of such an objective.

Second, during the 1960s coordination of federal policies was a dismal failure. The Office of Economic Opportunity was so unable to fulfill its legislative mandate to coordinate urban programs that it simply ignored the mandate and devoted itself to stimulating innovation and experimentation.[74] Model cities were specifically created to coordinate federal programs at the neighborhood level, but their success at this was extremely limited.[75] The A–95 review process was devised to enable all federal grants to be coordinated at the metropolitan level, but the results have been largely unencouraging.[76] Federal regional councils were created as a coordinating device, but these too have been largely ineffective.[77] And just the simple task of constructing housing projects on surplus federal land in cities, a situation in which the federal government possessed complete control over the land and money, required just enough cooperation between the Departments of Defense, Housing and Urban Development, Justice, Health, Education and Welfare, and local city governments that the project failed.[78]

Third, the federal government has a spotty record of ensuring that federal funds are spent in compliance with federal guidelines. For example, the Elementary and Secondary Education Act has been unable to fulfill its Title I mandate for compensatory education.[79] And HUD has not overseen effectively the use of credit provisions for new towns programs.[80]

There are federal activities in which the implementation process has worked very effectively; for example, transfer payments. Transfer payments are simply payments of cash from the federal treasury to individuals. They are called transfer payments because they in effect collect income taxes from some people and distribute (or transfer) those revenues to other people. The prime examples of transfer payments are social security and veterans benefits. There may be disagreement about the adequacy of benefits or whether Congress has put too many obligations onto the social security tax or on the general regressive nature of the social security tax, but once people qualify and register for social security benefits, the Social Security Administration accomplishes its objective of mailing checks to them with a minimum of disruption. A contrast of the Social Security Administration with the Office of Economic Opportunities suggests that it is much easier to do an effective job of mailing checks to people who are badly in need of money than it is to create programs that will help those same people have an effective voice in how their neighborhoods are run.

Second, the federal government operates some kinds of programs much better than others. Its most successful programs are characterized by (1) well-defined agency responsibilities, (2) tangible, measurable objectives, (3) adequate resources, and (4) the absence of strong opposition among interest groups or government agencies that could divert the program from its original intentions. The Apollo mission to land a man on the moon was clearly characterized by these characteristics, but the federal housing programs lacked them. In the Apollo program, NASA's responsibilities were clearly defined, the objective of placing a man on the moon was tangible and measurable, adequate resources were provided, and some of the most powerful interest groups in the country strongly supported the economic boost which the program would give to the economy. In the federal housing programs, a multitude of agencies have had overlapping missions. The objectives were tangible, but appropriations to meet them were inadequate; and, at least since 1949, a number of powerful urban actors have subordinated public housing objectives to more lucrative renewal objectives. In comparing the space program with the public housing programs, NASA was clearly given much better control to accomplish its program objectives than was the Public Housing Administration.[81]

Third, the federal executive branch has been fairly successful at carrying out orders of the federal courts. Although desegregation of public schools and compliance with affirmative action orders have been slow, considerable progress has been made. Pursuant to court orders, children are now attending racially desegregated schools in places and numbers which only a few years ago would have seemed impossible.

These statements comparing the things the federal government does well with those it does poorly are highly tentative. More systematic research is needed on the dynamics of implementing federal policies. If the above analysis is valid, however, important implications follow for the success and requirements of establishing national urban policies.

First, the coordination problem is horrendous. Nothing that has yet been tried has worked well. Under the Johnson administration, first the Office of Economic Opportunity and then the Department of Housing and Urban Development was named as the agency to coordinate all federal urban programs. The Nixon administration probably devoted more effort toward coordinating and controlling urban policies than any previous administration. Under Nixon, a Domestic Council was created to enable the White House to coordinate the formulation of domestic policies. The Domestic Council was to be chaired by the president, and membership consisted of the vice-president and the heads of the major departments and agencies concerned with domestic affairs. To ensure that the policies formulated by the Domestic Council were actually carried out, the Office of Management and Budget was given responsibility for evaluating the various domestic agencies in relation to the policies established by the Domestic Council. President Nixon, however, never exhibited the concern for urban problems that was needed to make this apparatus function effectively. His major policy considerations apparently centered on eliminating as many urban programs as possible and turning the funds for their operation over to the state governments. The powerful interest groups at the state capitals were much more likely to have been Nixon supporters than the urban interest groups built around the Great Society programs of the late 1960s. Consequently, Nixon's urban policies appeared to be predicated on the political principle of neutralizing as much as possible the influence of his political adversaries.

Second, the problem presented by traditional congressional logrolling is equally horrendous. How can model-cities-type programs, community action programs, or mass transit programs have a measurable effect anywhere if the appropriations are never adequate and if the funds are parceled out to the districts of every rural or small-town congressman who happens to head a subcommittee?

THE BIAS OF THE FEDERAL INVOLVEMENT

Because the federal involvement in urban affairs is so massive and so heterogeneous, it is difficult to categorize its overall biases. If some federal programs (such as public housing) seemed biased toward the status quo, others (such as the community action programs) seem equally biased toward rapid social change. Furthermore, the multitude of federal programs makes it difficult to categorize an overall bias of the federal involvement in terms of individual group benefits. Each program generates its own constituency. And if the residents of low-income residential neighborhoods are often disproportionately injured by some federal programs (such as those supporting urban renewal and freeway construction), other federal involvements (such as transfer payments, Aid for Dependent Children, and day care centers) disproportionately benefit these low-income peoples.

In order to assess the overall bias of the federal involvement, a concept is needed to calculate *net bias* or *net impact* of federal programs upon identifiable constituencies and upon major urban and metropolitan problems. If the total of federal programs biased against some identifiable urban constituency (for example, poor blacks) is outweighed by the total of federal programs biased in favor of that constituency, then the *net bias* or *net impact* of federal programs would be biased in favor of that constituency. If the total of federal programs promoting social change is outweighed by the total of federal programs protecting the status quo, then the net bias or net impact of federal involvement would be biased against social change.

To translate the concept of net bias into operational terms is very difficult, however. The constituencies of urban programs are not easy to identify precisely, and the criteria for deciding whether a program works for social change or for the status quo are not clear. Consequently, the task of operationalizing the concept of net bias lies beyond the scope of this book. What follows, instead, is an attempt to delineate six general patterns of the federal involvement which strongly suggest a definite net bias. These patterns involve: (1) the creation of interest groups for the urban poor and minorities, (2) the attempts to equalize social access to middle-class life styles, (3) the attempts to control suburban sprawl, (4) attempts to improve governmental accountability to the electorate, (5) attempts to subordinate urban programs to comprehensive national urban policies, and (6) attempts to use urban policies and programs as a device for redistributing income and resources.

Bias and the Creation of Interest Groups for the Urban Poor

Certain programs of Lyndon Johnson's Great Society were biased toward the creation of interest groups to represent the interests of the urban poor and the racial minorities. Particularly the community action programs and the model cities experiment greatly broadened the scope of community leadership in inner city communities, particularly in the black communities. This leadership has been far from unified, but it did not disappear with the demise of the war on poverty. Consequently, the black community in the 1970s was much stronger than a decade earlier in confronting urban governments about their operation in black neighborhoods. Particularly in relation to black communities, the federal programs created in the 1960s have solidified a number of urban interest groups that cannot be ignored: the Urban League, the Urban Coalition, the Conference of Mayors, and most of the racial improvement groups, including the NAACP and Congress on Racial Equality. The defeat of President Nixon's special revenue sharing proposals must in part be attributed to the realization among these interest group leaders and their congressional allies that they would be treated much more harshly if federal funds were channeled through state capitals than they are with funds coming directly from the nation's capital.

The obverse of this bias of the Great Society, however, is that neither the national nor the state capitals are very responsive to the unorganized urban needy. The highest rates of urban poverty exist among the Indians and the elderly (both black and white). The most disorganized urban communities are probably the Indians and the Appalachian white working-class poor. Neither group has benefited significantly from federal urban programs, which are biased toward the organized groups. These programs are biased more in favor of organized, middle-class economic groups (for example, urban renewal and the construction industry) than they are toward the organized poor (for example, Aid for Dependent Children and the Welfare Rights Organization). The unorganized poor benefit least of all from federal programs (for example, those elderly who live exclusively on their social security income).

The revolutionary aspect of the New Deal in the 1930s was its institutionalization of organized labor as a mechanism for representing the interests of the working-class poor who were organized in unions. The failure of the Great Society during the 1960s was its inability to create a similar mechanism which could represent the interests of those poor who were unorganized or not part of the unionizable labor force.

Bias and Social Access to Middle-class Life Styles

A second net bias of the federal involvement has been against measures that would equalize social access to middle-class life styles. Federal housing programs illustrate this most clearly. Some federal housing programs, such as rent subsidies and HUD 235 and 236 programs, have indeed improved the access of moderate-income people to middle-class life styles, because they made it easier for these people to live in middle-class neighborhoods, and under urban homesteading they provide incentives for the middle class to move into poor neighborhoods. However, none of these programs has had a very far-reaching impact on integrating communities along either class or racial lines. Furthermore, as indicated by the estimates given in Table 11-2, the housing programs that facilitate social access are heavily outweighed by the housing programs which diminish social access and promote both racial and economic segregation. Federal Housing Administration (FHA) mortgage guarantees have been used overwhelmingly in the suburbs and have promoted almost no housing for the poor or for the racial minorities. Public housing has been largely confined to the poor neighborhoods of central cities, and has had the net impact of increasing racial segregation.*

Bias and the Containment of Suburban Sprawl

Third, federal programs have a net bias against attempts to contain suburban sprawl. The major federal programs to contain it, as indicated in this and the previous chapter, have been the stimulation of metropolitan planning and councils of governments. However, these

---

* Even though public housing does not improve social access for the poor, it must be noted that it *does* lower the cost of housing for those who live in the public projects and in that respect *does* constitute a redistribution of income. Because public housing is used by poorer people than those who use the HUD 235 and 236 programs, it can be considered more redistributive than those programs even though it does not do as much as they do to improve social access to middle-class life styles. For an analysis of the redistributive aspects of federal housing programs, see Henry J. Aaron, *Shelter and Subsidies: Who Benefits From Federal Housing Policies?* (Washington, D.C.: The Brookings Institution, 1972), pp. 121–126, 136–140.

TABLE 11-2

SELECTED FEDERAL PROGRAMS AND THE EQUALIZATION OF
SOCIAL ACCESS TO MIDDLE-CLASS LIFE STYLES

Some Federal Programs That <u>Diminish</u> Lower-class Access to Middle-class Life Styles[a]		Some Federal Programs That <u>Increase</u> Lower-class Access to Middle-class Life Styles[b]	
Program	Dollars (millions)	Program	Dollars (millions)
Urban renewal: 1953–1974[1]	9,468	Rent supplements: 1966–1973[3]	403
Low-rent public housing:		HUD–235: 1968–1973[4]	766
1953–1974[1]	6,644	*Home ownership assistance*	
VA mortgage guarantees:		HUD–236: 1968–1973[4]	407
1945–1970[2]	4,005	*Rental housing assistance*	

[a] Urban renewal and public housing diminish social access because they have destroyed more slum housing than they have replaced. They have contributed to the residential concentration of low-income families and racial minorities, and they have seldom provided low-income housing in the suburbs. VA mortgage guarantees diminish social access because they seldom are made to low-income people. In 1970, the average VA-loan home purchaser owned liquid assets of $2454, paid $21,264 for his home, and had an after-tax monthly income of $720. This was an estimated before-tax annual income of $9600. This was slightly higher than the 1969 median family income ($9433) and more than twice as high as the poverty-level income for a family of five. (For source of data, see text note 4.)
[b] These programs increase social access because they provide assistance to low- and moderate-income households and they allow for these households to be dispersed among middle-income residential neighborhoods.

Sources:
[1] These data are extracted from United States Department of Commerce, Bureau of the Census, *Statistical Abstract of the United States* for the years 1974 (p. 249), 1968 (p. 383), 1965 (p. 398), 1962 (p. 385), and 1958 (p. 406).
[2] United States Department of Commerce, Bureau of the Census, *Statistical Abstract of the United States:* 1971, p. 262.
[3] Harold Wolman, *Politics of Federal Housing* (New York: Dodd, Mead, 1971), p. 146, for years 1966–1969. For 1970–1973, the sources are the same as the ones listed for note 4, below.
[4] Budget of the United States Government (Washington, D.C.: U.S. Government Printing Office). Fiscal year 1970, Appendix, pp. 520–521; fiscal year 1971, Appendix, pp. 500–501; fiscal year 1972, Appendix, pp. 496–497; fiscal year 1973, Appendix, pp. 509–510; fiscal year 1974, Appendix, pp. 497–498; fiscal year 1975, Appendix, pp. 492–493.

have been extremely weak control mechanisms. Furthermore, as Table 11-3 shows, the federal funds invested in them are small compared to the amount of federal funds invested in programs which stimulate suburban sprawl — especially guaranteed mortgages in the suburbs and the urban portion of the interstate highway system. It is difficult to conclude that the net bias of the federal involvement in urban affairs has been anything other than against containing suburban sprawl.

Having noted the net bias against containing suburban sprawl and the net bias against equalizing access to middle-class life styles, however, it must also be recognized that the federal government's investment toward containing sprawl and improving social access is growing

TABLE 11-3

CONTROLLING SUBURBAN SPRAWL AND THE BIAS OF SELECTED FEDERAL PROGRAMS

Some Federal Programs That Contribute to Spreading Suburban Sprawl[a]		Some Federal Programs That Contribute to Controlling Suburban Sprawl[b]	
Program	Dollars (millions)	Program	Dollars (millions)
Federal highway trust fund outlays: 1955–1972[1]	53,328	Metropolitan, regional, and interstate planning: 1954–1972[3]	182
VA mortgage guarantees: 1945–1970[2]	4,005	Urban mass transit aid: 1965–1974[4]	1,403
		Projected urban mass transit aid: 1975–1980[5]	11,900

[a] The highway trust fund contributed to sprawl because of the influence of freeways on metropolitan growth. It must be noted, however, that much of the highway trust fund outlays was spent in nonmetropolitan areas and thus did not contribute to sprawl. VA mortgage guarantees contributed to sprawl because most of the VA loans were made in the suburbs and contained no provision for community planning.
[b] Planning helps to control land use. Mass transit contributes to controlling sprawl because it diminishes reliance on the automobile and concentrates growth around the transit lines.

Sources:
[1] Bureau of the Census, *Statistical Abstract of the United States* for the years 1974 (p. 224), 1969 (p. 382), 1965 (p. 392), and 1962 (p. 381).
[2] Bureau of the Census, *Statistical Abstract of the United States: 1971*, p. 262.
[3] Bureau of the Census, *Statistical Abstract of the United States: 1974*, p. 708.
[4] Bureau of the Census, *Statistical Abstract of the United States* for the years 1974 (p. 249) and 1970 (p. 409).
[5] *Congressional Quarterly*, November 23, 1974, p. 3184.

much faster than its investment against them. The $12 billion Mass Transit Aid Act passed in 1974 was a massive commitment to a measure which would help contain sprawl. And the consistent commitments to affirmative action programs and to a more flexible approach to housing programs, as indicated by the 1974 Housing Act, should also help equalize social access. Finally, both of these negative biases are related to the urban interest groups that were enhanced by the proliferation of urban programs under the Johnson administration. Groups such as the Conference of Mayors, the Urban League, and the Welfare Rights Organization have a vested interest in increasing social access and limiting continued suburban sprawl. They lobby accordingly.

Bias and Governmental Accountability

Until at least the end of the 1960s the net impact of government programs was clearly to diminish the accountability of urban governments to the electorate. Many grant-in-aid programs stimulated the proliferation of special districts. Many other programs stimulated the creation of semiautonomous housing and redevelopment authorities. Welfare programs have been administered under a Byzantine system of administrative rulings that practically defied the accountability of the program to local elected officials. Several of the coordinating devices created since the middle 1960s have at least aimed at making the operation of federal programs more accountable to identifiable officials. These devices include the A–95 review process, the stimulation of councils of governments, the federal regional councils, and the creation of the Domestic Council in the Executive Office of the President. None of these devices, however, except perhaps for the councils of governments, bolsters the authority of local elected officials. It could be argued that they may, in fact, diminish that authority. The A–95 process, if it ever worked effectively, would subordinate the local officials to a metropolitan-level review agency which would be beyond the control of local voters.

Two conclusions are warranted. First, because federal programs have stimulated the creation of independent special districts and semiautonomous public agencies that are not accountable to the voters, they have diminished the democratic principle. Second, because federal programs are so important for the major developmental aspects of city and suburban politics, they have stimulated a usurpation of power away from the elected governing officials and toward the local, state, and federal bureaucratic functional fiefdoms. Even if recent innovations succeed in subordinating these functional fiefdoms to the White House, the residents of individual metropolises can expect to exert very little influence over the White House.

Bias and Policy Making

The net bias of the federal urban involvement is against subordinating urban programs to comprehensive, systemic national urban policies. The reaction of urban interest groups against special revenue sharing shows this clearly. Although special revenue sharing can hardly qualify as a national urban policy, the initial Nixon proposals would have shifted influence away from those groups that are powerful at the national capital and toward those that are powerful at the state capitals. This would have been extremely detrimental to local big-city groups which had emerged around the model cities programs, the community action programs, and several others of the more than 100 grant-in-aid programs which Nixon was going to consolidate into special revenue sharing. The results were predictable. These groups and their allies in Congress and the federal bureaucracies fought bitterly against the proposals. The net result was a substantial amount of consolidation but within the framework of a compromise that effectively diluted the concept of special revenue sharing and ensured the big-city mayors and the major urban bureaucracies in HUD, DOT, and HEW that they would not suffer any setbacks.

With the present political configuration of Washington, which seems likely to prevail at least until late in the 1970s, a national urban policy would be difficult to implement. Such a policy would require strong leadership from the White House. Such leadership was impossible under the Nixon administration once his Watergate troubles surfaced early in 1973. And the early days of the transition into the Ford administration gave no indication that President Ford was even concerned with the problem. Furthermore, little incentive exists for any president to try to subordinate urban programs to national policy. To meddle with the $50 billion worth of grant-in-aid programs is to meddle with a hornets' nest. Even if the programs are brought under policy control, little dramatic payoff can occur within the four-year time span of the presidential term of office, as one can see historically. Given the energy problems and gasoline scarcities of the middle 1970s, clearly the contemporary metropolises would be much better off if the 1974 Mass Transit Aid Act of $11 billion had been passed twenty years or even ten years earlier. But what president would have gained politically by promoting such a concept in those days?

Bias and the Redistribution of Income

The preambles of federal urban legislation usually suggest that their objectives are to improve the lot of the disadvantaged. This was true of the Economic Opportunity Act, the Model Cities Act, the Elementary and Secondary Education Act, and many other acts which establish the urban-oriented grant-in-aid programs. One might therefore conclude that the objective of urban programs has been to redistribute income. By establishing programs to provide services for people who lack the resources to provide the services for themselves, the urban programs raise revenue from some people and turn it over to other people in the form of new services. This theoretically constitutes a redistribution of income.

Such a conclusion would be difficult to sustain, however. The effect of urban programs is not so much to redistribute income as it is to create wealth and to give a portion of that wealth to the constituencies of the programs, to the recipients of the new services. The major portion of such new wealth, however, goes not to the poor but to middle-class people connected to the organized groups that belong to the constituency of the program. By infusing new federal money into the economy, federal programs create jobs, purchasing power, and business activities. And the fact that the federal budget has operated at a deficit rather than being balanced since the inception of urban programs in the 1930s suggests that the money being poured into these programs was newly created money, money borrowed against the future rather than money taken out of the pockets of the middle and upper classes through the income tax.

This may all seem rather obvious and unimportant, but it has two significant ramifications. First, the pattern for federal involvement has been to justify urban programs in rhetoric that implies a redistribution of the wealth. This is of symbolic importance, for it suggests that something is really being done to alter the living conditions of the urban poor. Second, the programs themselves infuse newly created wealth into the economy rather than redistribute old wealth. This new wealth is thus distributed through the prevailing economic institutions. Thus the major share of the new wealth will go to the middle and upper classes, and only a minor share will go to the poor. The bias implication of this is that under present conditions any urban program, no matter how radical its rhetoric, is preservative of the prevailing class structure. It does not stimulate radical social change nor does it redistribute the wealth.

The one possible exception to this may be transfer payments. In transfer payments, the money is paid out directly to the needy. Bureaucracies are kept to a minimum. And functional tie-ins between the federal bureaucracies and the local bureaucracies do not constitute functional fiefdoms which destroy the governing capabilities of local governments.

CONCLUSIONS

The federal involvement in urban affairs has evolved to the point where increasing pressures demand the coordination of urban programs under some form of executive-directed national urban policy. In summary more and more policy *documents* will probably be forthcoming from the White House, federal urban-related departments, and urban-oriented interest groups. However, the preconditions do not yet exist for transforming policy documents into the *policy-making process.*

The dynamics of the federal involvement thus suggest that several things will continue to happen throughout the middle and late 1970s. First, the total of federal aids destined for state and local governments will continue rising. The total figure for FY 1975 was $52 billion, and it rose during the first half of the decade at an annual rate of 17 percent. Second, if the grant consolidations of 1973 and 1974 in community development, education, manpower, and law enforcement prove satisfactory to the urban interest groups, more grant consolidations will probably be made in the future. Third, attempts to make the melange of federal programs accountable to the White House and to councils of local elected officials will probably continue through such institutions as councils of government. Fourth, these federal actions probably will not significantly improve the access of the poor to middle-class life styles or significantly alter suburban sprawl. Finally, the biases of the federal involvement that were outlined above will change very little.

If this analysis is correct, then pressure will increase throughout the balance of the 1970s to create a national urban policy. Because of the difficulties involved in creating such a national urban policy in the United States, one of the most fruitful things that the contemporary student of urban affairs could do would be to examine the urban policies of other countries to see how they have dealt with problems analogous to urban problems of the United States. Some of the approaches to urban growth used elsewhere might have applicability in the United States. These approaches and their relevance to the United States will be examined in Chapter 12.

Some Suggested Readings

Douglas M. Fox, ed., *The New Urban Politics: Cities and the Federal Government* (Pacific Palisades, Calif.: Goodyear Publishing Company, 1972). An excellent collection of readings on cities in the federal system, the federal policy-making process, and the politics of policy implementation.

Michael Reagan, *The New Federalism* (New York: Oxford University Press, 1973). Criticizes federal revenue sharing as less desirable than an improved system of grants-in-aid as the basic instrument for channeling federal funds into state and local governments.

James L. Sundquist, *Making Federalism Work: A Study of Program Coordination at the Community Level* (Washington, D.C.: The Brookings Institution, 1969). Argues that the federal system has become a single system. Analyzes coordination of federal programs in both rural and urban communities. In the urban communities, Sundquist is highly favorable toward the model cities approach.

Daniel J. Elazar, *The American Partnership* (Chicago: University of Chicago Press, 1962). Argues that dual federalism has been replaced by cooperative federalism.

Morton Grodzins, "The Federal System," in the President's Commission on National Goals, *Goals for Americans* (New York: Prentice-Hall, 1960), pp. 265–282. Articulates the marble-cake theory of federalism as distinguished from the layer-cake theory.

Roscoe C. Martin, *The Cities and the Federal System* (New York: Atherton Press, 1965). Includes an excellent discussion of the increasing importance of grants-in-aid and how they operate.

Alan K. Campbell, ed., *The States and the Urban Crisis* (Englewood Cliffs, N.J.: Prentice-Hall, 1970). A collection of descriptive articles on various aspects of state involvement in urban affairs.

Harold Kaplan, *Urban Renewal Politics* (New York: Columbia University Press, 1963). An inquiry into the politics of urban renewal in Newark.

Jewell Bellush and Murray Hausknecht, eds., *Urban Renewal: People, Politics and Planning* (Garden City, N.Y.: Doubleday, 1967). A reader containing articles on the goals of urban renewal, the politics of urban renewal planning and decision making, the execution of urban renewal, and evaluation of urban renewal.

Martin Anderson, *The Federal Bulldozer* (Cambridge, Mass.: M.I.T. Press, 1964). A conservative critique of urban renewal on the grounds that it is wrong to expropriate some people's private property and turn it over to other people for them to make a profit.

Oakland Task Force, *Federal Decision Making and Impact in Urban Areas: A Study of Oakland* (New York: Praeger, 1970). Examines the difficulty of coordinating federal programs.

Daniel P. Moynihan, *Maximum Feasible Misunderstanding: Community Action in the War on Poverty* (New York: The Free Press, 1969). Criticizes the attempt to involve the poor in the planning of the antipoverty programs.

Edward C. Banfield, "Making a New Federal Program: Model Cities, 1964–1968," in Allan P. Sindler, ed., *Policy and Politics in America: Six Case Studies* (Boston: Little, Brown, 1973), pp. 124–158. Details the process through which the governmental procedures needed to create the model cities program virtually ensured that the program would not be able to accomplish its objectives.

Jerome T. Murphy, "The Education Bureaucracies Implement Novel Policy: The Politics of Title I of ESEA, 1965–1972," in Allan P. Sindler, ed., *Policy and Politics in America: Six Case Studies* (Boston: Little, Brown, 1973), pp. 160–198. Paints a pessimistic picture of the ability of federal agencies to make sure that their state and local counterparts implement the intentions of new federal policies — in this case of the policy of compensatory education.

Martha Derthick, *New Towns in Town: Why a Federal Program Failed* (Washington, D.C.: The Urban Institute, 1972). Largely because of the inability of federal bureaucracies to cooperate and because of local opposition, an ingeniously simple housing proposal by the president never got off the ground.

Suzanne Farkas, *Urban Lobbying* (New York: New York University Press,

1971). Shows the impact of various actors on the politics of formulating federal urban policies.

Alan Lupo, Frank Colcord, and Edmund P. Fowler, *Rites of Way: The Politics of Transportation in Boston and the U.S. City* (Boston: Little, Brown, 1971). Describes the successful fight to achieve a moratorium on more freeway construction in Boston. Places the Boston conflict in the broader perspective of regional and national planning for transportation.

Daniel P. Moynihan, *Toward A National Urban Policy* (New York: Basic Books, 1970). Contains Moynihan's essay calling for the establishment of a national urban policy. Also contains twenty-four other articles on various topics which a national urban policy would have to confront.

Chapter 12

Because our own urban crisis is so intense, we in the United States tend to ignore the fact that the process of urbanization here is related to the process of urbanization in other nations. The causes of urbanization are basically no different in the United States than elsewhere. Throughout the world, population has been growing beyond the capacity of the agricultural sector to provide employment. In enabling fewer farmers to produce more food, improvements in agricultural technology only accentuate the migration of people out of rural areas. The drive toward modernization and economic development has demanded an ever in-

National Approaches That Have Been Tried Elsewhere

creasing number of people to work in the bureaucracies of corporations and government agencies. All of these are the causes of urbanization, whether it be in highly developed United States or in less developed Brazil.

If the causes of urbanization are not unique to the United States, what about the problems which result from urbanization? These too tend to be found in great abundance throughout the urban world, regardless of country or ideology. Inadequate housing, insufficient job supply, ineffective transit, suburban sprawl, and ineffective mechanisms of governance are problems that confront all metropolises, whether they exist in highly totalitarian Russia or highly democratic United States. Even our highly publicized racial problems find parallels elsewhere in the world. And in some respects blacks and whites actually mix better in the United States than do Arabs and Jews in Jerusalem, Moslems and Hindus in India, or Catholics and Protestants in Northern Ireland.

340

What *is* different about the United States is the peculiar way in which we approach both the causes and effects of urbanization. Many other nations attempt to cope with urbanization through comprehensive urban growth policies that seek to identify the causes and the problems of urbanization and to relate specific programs to these causes and effects. In the United States a national policy of this sort has never become a subject of national debate.[1] Congress tends to deal with bits and pieces of urbanization through specific bills that are seldom conceived of as part of an interacting system of programs. As will be seen below, England, France, and Brazil have each enacted broad policies attempting to deal with the causes of urbanization. They are not neccessarily better because they can take strong national action. Nor are we necessarily better because we protect local autonomy. However, something can be learned about metropolitan politics by comparing the experiences of various countries at various stages of metropolitanization in their attempts to formulate national policies of urban growth.

The method of comparison will be to examine in England, France, and Brazil three facets of their urban policy development: (1) the overriding urbanization problems that confront each country, (2) the evolution of their approaches to national urban policy, and (3) some assessment of the effectiveness of their policies. One experiment from Scandinavia will be examined. Finally, the applicability or inapplicability of these approaches to the United States will be discussed.

ENGLAND AND A NATIONAL URBAN POLICY

The Overriding Problems

As the urban development problems of England have evolved, four major themes seem to have predominated. First is the problem of fitting the relatively large British population of fifty-three million people into a relatively small land area of 94,000 square miles. England proper, which excludes Scotland, Wales, and Northern Ireland, is about the same size as the United States Northeast megalopolis and contains a population slightly larger than that of the megalopolis.

Closely related to this concentration of such a large population is the second problem of managing the internal population migrations within Great Britain. For many decades people have migrated into southeast England, especially into London, where most of the economic growth has occurred. This has left many areas of northern England and Scotland in an economically depressed condition for years.

Because of the population migration into London and the other urban regions, these metropolises have been plagued with deterioration at the core and sprawl in the suburban fringes. Controlling this deterioration and sprawl has been the third major urbanization problem, particularly in and around London. The fourth major problem has been the governance of London itself.

The Evolution of Urban Policy

The concern for urban problems began very early in England, dating back to two late-nineteenth-century movements. The first was an outgrowth of the Fabian socialist movement. The Fabians rejected the Marxist dogma of violent revolution and believed that a just socialist society could be achieved through the use of parliamentary democracy. On their agenda to improve the living conditions of the working class they included reforms of housing and community conditions as well as reforms of the capitalist economy. A second movement grew out of the writings of the earliest town planner, Ebenezer Howard. In his book, *Garden Cities*,[2] Howard argued that large industrial cities were inhuman and were by nature prone to breeding slums. He proposed supplanting them with what he called garden cities which, like the new towns of today, would be designed to accommodate small populations.

The urban conditions that were criticized by the Fabians and the garden city advocates grew worse as the years passed. During the Great Depression of the 1930s, when unemployment in the depressed areas reached levels of up to 50 percent of the work force, the government accelerated the migration to London by adopting a policy of bringing the workers to the jobs. If continued permanently, such a policy could only deepen the economic deprivation of the north and increase urban overcrowding in the south.

In 1939 a Royal Commission on the Distribution of the Industrial Population (Barlow Commission) was created to study these two problems, and it suggested that a national planning agency be created to rebuild the urban centers and disperse industries to the stagnating areas of the country. By dispersing industry, the depressed areas could be made economically viable and their populations would not have to migrate to London in order to find employment.[3] None of these suggestions could be adopted immediately, however, because of the urgencies of World War II. The war itself only accentuated the need for urban policy making. By delaying immediate action on urban problems, the problems grew worse. And the damage inflicted on industrial cities by German bombing raids was so severe that considerable post-war urban reconstruction was inevitable.*

This postwar reconstruction was shaped by two monumental pieces of legislation. In 1946 the New Towns Act was passed. This act planned relatively small, self-contained communities of about 60,000 people scattered around the country's major metropolitan areas. Twenty-eight such new towns were built in the next decade and a half under this program, and by 1960 over a million people lived in various new towns. A second act was even more far-reaching. It was the Town and Country Planning Act of 1947 which imposed stringent land use controls throughout England. It obliged all counties to prepare development plans and to update them every five years. It subjected all commercial or residential development to the control of the county governments. And it required industrial firms to get permission from the national Board of Trade for all new buildings or extensions of over 5000 square feet.

With these tools, the national government was given extensive leverage to control urban sprawl and to disallow construction in areas that did not fit in with national priorities. Thus, by midcentury, the British had established two broad planning strategies. The first promoted economic development in the stagnating areas of the north. The second tried to limit and guide the growth of the large urban centers, especially London.[4]

Over the next three decades these two objectives remained as the focal point of national urban policy under both Labor governments and Conservative governments. During the 1950s a developing areas program identified depressed areas where industries could be relocated in order to reduce unemployment. In 1960 the Conservative government established a National Economic Development Office. It decided to build a second generation of new towns which would be located mainly in the north and would be large enough to serve as foci for growth centers. It also improved the tax incentives to encourage more industries to move, and it began relocating government offices from London to the north. This policy was continued by the succeeding Labor government, and by the end of the decade some 60,000 government-related jobs had been diverted to the target areas.[5] While this did not greatly affect the London economy, it gave a significant influx of economic activity into the depressed areas.

* In Coventry, for example, the German blitz destroyed 5500 homes and inflicted serious damage on many others. [R. W. G. Bryant, "The Reconstruction of Coventry," in *Taming Megalopolis: Vol. II, How to Manage an Urbanized World,* ed. H. Wentworth Eldredge (Garden City, N.Y.: Doubleday, 1967), p. 765].

These developments of the 1950s and the 1960s were basically refinements of the original strategy plotted out in the late 1940s. Although these efforts have not halted the growth of London nor brought economic prosperity to the depressed areas of the north, the planners have developed an impressive array of tools for managing urbanization.

The Growth and Governance of London

With a metropolitan population of over 12 million people, London is the major center of what one analyst sees as a "linear megalopolitan complex" extending from London through Birmingham to Liverpool and Manchester.[6] Despite its great population, London, with an inner city density of 27,000 people per square mile, is much less dense than the inner city of Paris (73,152), Manhattan (44,139), or Copacabana in Rio de Janeiro (43,770). Nevertheless, like many big cities, London is characterized by extreme congestion at the core, a declining central city population, and a sprawling suburbanization beyond the city proper. Four major government actions over the last generation have shaped the growth of London since World War II. These four actions were the Green Belt Act of 1938, the Abercrombie Plan of 1944, the New Towns Act of 1946, and the creation of the Greater London Council in 1963.

In 1938 Parliament passed the Green Belt Act which established a permanent girdle of open space about five miles wide around the outer reaches of the London population at that time. This belt begins about twelve to fifteen miles from the center of London and coincides with an area defined by planners as the Greater London conurbation. Conurbation is a British word created by combining the two words "continuous urbanization."[7] The green belt also roughly coincides with the boundaries of the city established for the Greater London Council in 1963. Through these measures, the statistical and administrative definitions of London thus were made to coincide with the physical boundaries of the city, a feat that is extraordinary in any metropolis.[8] This area comprises 620 square miles and in 1971 contained 7.5 million people, a decline of half a million from the 1961 census.

The Green Belt Act of 1938 was important for several reasons, not the least of which is that the integrity of the green belt concept has been adhered to by succeeding generations of government officials. This has made a realistic political definition of London's government boundaries possible. Unlike New York, Chicago, or most large American cities in which the city drifts indistinguishably into suburbia without any physically demarcated boundary, London now has a political boundary that is marked off by a sharp physical change in the countryside. The green belt also marks the limits of the interwar suburbs which were built from 1919 to 1939 along the subway lines which extend out from the center of London. Because of the green belt, future growth of London was highly constrained. In the beginning it was feared that continued growth of the city within the green belt would lead to much higher densities. But time showed that population growth within the city would be highly constricted and that future population growth would spill over beyond the green belt.

Such a spillover, in fact, was precisely what the Abercrombie Plan of 1944 recommended. While supporting the green belt concept, it rejected the idea of higher population densities in the city. By limiting population densities very severely, it made inevitable a population overspill of more than a million persons who would have to be resettled beyond the green belt. To absorb this spillover population and at the same time prevent suburban sprawl, the New Towns Act of 1946 was enacted. It would channel about half of this projected population growth into eight new towns to be constructed just outside the green belt.

If the population growth of the London region had remained within the projections of the Abercrombie Plan, the new towns would have sharply limited the suburban sprawl. In fact, however, London's outer ring absorbed 40 percent of the total population growth of the entire country between 1945 and 1960. This growth far outstripped the projections of either the Abercrombie Plan or the New Towns Act. Despite their evident success in themselves, the London new towns had obviously not contained the urban sprawl.

Another problem also became apparent in the post–World War II years. London, like many American cities, was plagued with excessive fragmentation of governmental authority. Over a hundred local units of government existed within the green belt. This included six counties, three county boroughs, and sixteen special-purpose metropolitan authorities. In some services, such as transit, very little coordination existed between the various agencies which had planning or operating responsibilities for highways, trains, subways, and buses.

The parliamentary response to the inadequacies of London government was an act creating in 1965 the Greater London Council which established a two-tier form of government within the green belt. The Greater London Council was given responsibility for town and country planning, ambulance service, fire service, housing review, and other problems of a metropolitan concern. For services which could most adequately be delivered on a smaller level, the government of London was decentralized into thirty-two boroughs. The boroughs ranged in population from 165,000 to 329,250 people, with an average of about 250,000. These boroughs were given administrative responsibility for personal health and welfare services, children's services, housing, education, and environmental health services.[9] Each borough elected its own governing council.

Assessment

The decline of London's population and the continued growth beyond the green belt since the formation of the Greater London Council suggest either that the four postwar growth measures were eminently successful or that they were superfluous. For while the congested population inside the green belt declined by half a million to 7.5 million, the total London region population continued to grow. This indicated that the national development districts program still had not curbed the population migration out of the depressed areas into the London region. Furthermore, the strong development controls exercised by the Greater London Council within the green belt were not matched by equally strong controls beyond the green belt, and fringe area sprawl continued beyond London proper. One journalist writing for the London *Economist* complained that the suburban sprawl beyond the green belt was "creating a ghastly form of rural suburbia."[10] Within the green belt, not only was the population declining, but it was declining in a pattern strikingly reminiscent of demographic patterns in the older American metropolises. While the middle class migrated out beyond the green belt, the city itself was increasingly becoming more populated by low-income persons and racial minorities who were immigrating from the West Indies, Africa, and India.

The limited success of these policies is probably due as much to the magnitude of the problem as to the limitations of the policies themselves. Whatever their limitations, they are certainly imaginative approaches to very real problems. Especially noteworthy are the new towns, the green belt, the attempts to control population migrations and industrial locations through the use of incentives, and the control over physical development under the provisions of the Town and Country Planning Act. Whether these approaches are appropriate to the United States will be discussed at the end of this chapter.

FRANCE: NATIONAL EQUILIBRIUM METROPOLISES VERSUS A POLYCENTRIC PARIS

The Overriding Problems

The overriding problem of urbanization in France is centered in the relation of Paris to the rest of the country. Paris dominates France in ways that London never dominated England. This dominance was dramatized in 1947 by a provocative report entitled *Paris et le Désert Français*, which was written by a Ministry of Reconstruction geographer named Jean François Gravier.[11] So complete had been the historical dominance of Paris over the rest of France, according to Gravier, that life in the provinces constituted a barren desert culturally, economically, and administratively. During the century preceding Gravier's report, Paris had absorbed the entire net increase in France's population.

Two debilitating features of French life resulted from this excessive centralization. First, by siphoning the country's population and economic activity into the national capital, Paris was, in effect, sucking the life blood out of the provinces. Second, the increasing concentration of people and industry in Paris led to an overbearing congestion in that city.

Concerning the first of these features, *le désert français*, the population and industrial growth of France was severely unbalanced. Paris dominated the economic scene as the financial, industrial, and administrative center of the country. Other relatively prosperous areas were concentrated in the north around Le Havre, along the Mediterranean coast around Marseilles, and along the valley of the Saone and Rhone rivers. Each of these areas possessed either favorable agricultural conditions or mineral deposits, cheaply available hydroelectric power, tourist attractions, or a major shipping port to stimulate economic activity. But outside of these few regions, the entire western and southwestern portions of the country suffered under the burden of a stagnating economy. By the late 1950s the average income in these areas was 50 percent of that in Paris. French growth was so dominated by Paris that few other areas became metropolitan. Aside from Paris, only Marseilles and Lyons contain central cities possessing over half a million people.

In addition to the debilitating effects of Paris's dominance on the rest of the country, grave concern was expressed that it was debilitating to the quality of life in Paris itself. The Paris of the urban planner is a different world from the Paris of the tourist who stays in the historic parts of the city which are so lavishly furnished with museums, galleries, restaurants, and spacious, tree-lined boulevards.

Like London, there are various definitions of what constitutes Paris. The tourist's Paris consists of the twenty *arrondissements* into which Paris was divided in 1860 when the city received its final extension. These boundaries of the city are marked by the outer terminals of the subway system. The total area of the twenty *arrondissements* is 105 square miles and they contain a population of about 2.6 million people, a decline of almost 300,000 since 1954. Even with its declining population, the central city of Paris is one of the most densely populated cities in the Western world.

Beyond the boundaries of the historic city of Paris are the areas developed after World War I to the east and west of the city. These are the Paris suburbs, known as the *banlieue*. The outer boundaries of this area comprise the Parisian agglomeration, an area of 463 square miles. While central Paris's population has been declining, the population of the *banlieue* has been growing at the rate of about 135,000 people per year. By 1968 the total agglomeration had a population of 8,196,000. Finally, beyond the *banlieue* the influence of Paris extends out about sixty to ninety kilometers from the center of the city and covers an area of 5,000 square miles known as the *région parisienne*, where at least another 1.5 million people live.

Throughout its metropolitan region, Paris is plagued by the same two problems which confront older American metropolises; deterioration in the city's center and sprawl in the suburban fringes. The deterioration and congestion of the twenty *arrondissements* of historic Paris had, by the 1960s, gone far beyond the deterioration of American cities. The subway lines did not extend into the suburbs where most of the population lived. Nor did they connect with the terminals of all the commuter railway stations located on the outer edges of the inner city. Consequently, some of the commuter trains caused a daily traffic jam as their passengers debarked at the railroad terminals and sought taxis or buses, for they were still too far from their destinations to walk to work. Despite the spacious boulevards in the center, few of the city's streets are amenable to heavy automobile traffic. Nevertheless, French automobile production continues to increase each year. And as more and more people drive, the same vicious circle occurs that plagues American cities — increasing automobile congestion and proliferating road space.

Probably no major American city can equal Paris for its housing deterioration. The bulk of the housing was constructed before World War I. Half of all dwelling units in 1962 contained two rooms or less, and fewer than a third of all dwelling units had their own toilet and washing place.

Similar deficiencies occurred in the social and economic infrastructure needed for a large city. At least half of the sanitary sewage generated in Paris is deposited directly into the Seine River without any treatment. Beyond the highly traveled tourist routes in Paris, there is a notable lack of parks and open space. Outside the city, the suburbs are very deficient in secondary schools, higher education facilities, hospitals, and even government facilities. Three suburbs with a total population of 293,000 people in 1962 lacked even a single police station.

The Evolution of Urban Policy

A few years after the publication of *Paris et le Désert Français,* the Ministry of Reconstruction and Urbanism in 1950 called for a population distribution plan.[12] The ministry advocated several measures to decentralize new industries, modernize agriculture, promote tourism, and decentralize cultural facilities such as universities and museums. Throughout the 1950s the central government gradually developed the planning controls to carry out these objectives. In particular, three kinds of measures were adopted.

First, the government encouraged the formation of mixed public-private corporations, composed of local government and private companies, to promote economic development in target regions outside Paris. The national government also provided financial backing for these mixed enterprises.

Second, the government divided the country into twenty-one regions and encouraged each region to formulate regional economic development plans. Special aid was channeled to high unemployment areas in the hopes of curbing migration from those areas to Paris.

Third, the French government tried to limit the growth of Paris itself.[13] As a consequence of these measures, the growth of Paris was greatly slowed, but not stopped. Whereas Paris had accounted for almost all the population growth in France in the century preceding Gravier's report, in the dozen years following the report, Paris accounted for only about a third of the nation's population growth.

As these measures were applied during the 1950s and 1960s, two broad policies gradually emerged. Regarding Paris, the inability to curb the growth of the Paris region led to the idea of channeling that growth through the policy of a polycentric Paris. Regarding the hinterland, the government adopted a policy of building up eight equilibrium metropolises to balance Paris.

Polycentric Paris

The policy of developing a polycentric Paris was framed in 1960 with the formulation of the *Plan d'Aménagement et d'Organisation Générale de la Région Parisienne* (PADOG). This plan involved three elements: limiting the growth of the Paris region, guiding the development of the *banlieue*, and rejuvenating the twenty *arrondissements*. Curbing the population growth was a crucial aspect of the plan. If the immigration could be cut from its rate of over 100,000 per year during the 1950s to about 50,000, this decrease combined with the natural population increase would give the region a manageable population increase of about 100,000 per year. These measures would hopefully hold the population to twelve million at the end of the century.

The second aspect of the PADOG plan was to channel the expected growth into a few gigantic nodes where employment, social facilities, and housing would be concentrated.[14] The entire Paris region was divided into zones in order to locate industrial growth where it was wanted. A land use plan for the area was developed, and extensive relocation incentives were instituted. One regional node was to be located in a zone known as *La Défense*, about 2.5 miles west of the Arch of Triumph. The second node was to be located immediately east of Versailles and south of *La Défense* at a location called Villacoublay. A third node was to be northeast of the city adjacent to the second Paris airport, Le Bourget, the site of the annual Paris Air Show.

Unlike the British plan of creating new towns on the suburban fringe of London beyond the green belt, the French rejected both the green belt concept and the concept of new towns. Instead of a green belt, they decided to guide population growth into wedges which would be centered on the development nodes. They rejected new towns because they might attract more people into the region in an uncontrollable fashion. Rather, the nodes were to be developed on the sites of existing communities. The node at *La Défense* will ultimately house about 800,000 people. Located along the major freeway and extended subway lines running west of the city, it has become a major center for the construction of office space. Consequently, it is hoped that *La Défense* and the other nodes will avoid some of the sprawl which has been characteristic of suburban development in the post–World War II era.

The third aspect of the PADOG plan was to rejuvenate the inner city of Paris. This was to be accomplished partially by dividing the city into three zones which would each handle a specific activity. One zone is reserved for *les affaires* (commerce and the professions), a second is reserved for government administrative offices, and a third for the university. New expansion of commerce, government, or the university will be allowed only within its appropriate zone. When the expansion exceeds the space left in the zone, the expansion will be obliged to occur in one of the major nodes outside of Paris. Thus *les affaires* will be channeled to *La Défense* and administration to the node at Villacoublay. In conjunction with this zoning scheme is a parallel zoning plan aimed at preserving the historic buildings and monuments of central Paris while reconstructing the abysmal housing in the working-class *arrondissements* that come under a new zone of reconstruction.

The PADOG plan to limit the growth of Paris, however, failed. Whereas the target population for 1970 had been set at 9.4 million people, in fact that number was reached in the middle 1960s. Since the success of the PADOG plan depended on its ability to limit the population growth, some adjustments to the scheme had to be made.

Those adjustments were made in 1965 by a new plan called the *Schème Directeur d'Aménagement et d'Urbanisme de la Région de Paris.* This plan increased the year 2000 population projection from twelve to fourteen million, and it also projected an increase of two million jobs, 75 percent of them in the tertiary service sector of the economy, a doubling or tripling of the number of automobiles in the region, and a twofold increase in housing units. The built-up area within the region was designed to increase from 460 to 850 square miles. This development will be guided in an axial development pattern along the banks of the Seine. More urban nodes will be built and interspersed with new towns. They will be linked together by 500 miles of proposed expressways that run along the banks of the Seine through the heart of Paris. And 150 miles of express subways will be constructed to link the urban nodes with the center of Paris. The channeling of development into the urban nodes will give Paris a polycentric pattern and, it is hoped, avoid the suburban sprawl that spilled beyond London's green belt.

Equilibrium Metropolises

A corollary and integral element of the proposal to limit the growth of Paris was to develop provincial metropolitan centers that could siphon off the population from Paris. This policy was established in the Fifth National Plan (1966–1969) which identified eight cities to serve as growth poles to balance Paris.*The eight centers were chosen by the criteria of viability. They needed to be fairly large, to perform vital

* The eight centers are: Lille-Roubaix-Tourcoing, Nancy, Strasbourg, Lyon, Marseille, Toulouse, Bordeaux, Nantes.

economic services for the region, and to have a zone of influence that extended for several miles into the hinterland. From these basic criteria, more than twenty indicators were used to compare the various cities of France. On the basis of these indicators, eight metropolises were chosen.

The policy of equilibrium metropolises had a very appealing simplicity and boldness that quickly caught the imagination of the French.

> The basic territorial problem, the Fifth Plan emphasized, was the appropriate distribution of activities between Paris and the other urban agglomerations. Industrialization of the West was now to be encouraged principally in three major equilibrium metropolises: Nantes–Saint Nazaire, Bordeaux, and Toulouse. It was in these metropolises that general physical development proposals (Schemes Directeurs) were to be prepared: universities, government research establishments, and technical training institutes established or extended, and highway and air activity encouraged. It was in the hinterlands of these urban areas that major agricultural modernization and irrigation schemes were to be undertaken and major regional parks and recreational zones established. An equally impressive list of infra-structure improvements — roads, canals, port facilities, educational establishments, and urban renewal plans — were outlined for the East, in particular for the urban regions of Lille-Roubaix-Tourcoing, Strasbourg, Nancy-Metz, Lyon, and Marseille.[15]

Assessment

The most striking features about French urban policy are the swiftness and boldness with which the government was able to establish national policy and the dominance of the executive branch over the legislative branch in the formulation of the policies. Nevertheless, the 1965 amendments of the polycentric plan were in effect an admission that the policies had not curbed the growth of Paris and that they could not curb it. Even if Paris's growth can be held to the target limit of fourteen million by the year 2000, Paris will continue to grow after that date until it reaches whatever technological and ecological limits exist between primate cities and their surrounding regions. Even if the equilibrium metropolises are successful, nobody knows at this point what the natural limit of metropolises such as Paris might be. Maybe it is fourteen million. Maybe it is twenty-eight million. Or, if energy substitutes for petroleum and natural gas are not found, maybe it is only three million. Nobody really knows the natural limits of the population that can be maintained in a metropolis.

There is some indication that the French are not completely pleased with the results of the polycentric metropolis. A 1973 Ministry of Planning study ruefully concluded that the emphasis on controlling Parisian growth, developing regional equilibrium metropolises, and provoking economic development in the *banlieue* is inducing many multi-national corporations to establish their European headquarters in European capitals other than Paris.[16] Concern has also been expressed about rising competition to Paris as the artistic, literary, and style center of the Western world.

Part of this concern for the life style of Paris and its attractiveness as an international center may reflect an ambivalence about the deliberate attempts of the government toward decentralization. With their policies of equilibrium metropolises and moving government offices out of Paris, the French are moving toward decentralization. One author suggested that the French could demonstrate a convincing concern for decentralization if they would simply move the capital out of Paris into one of the other cities. "The central government is the one 'industry' that could draw a large portion of the elite from Paris; and it is the one major growth industry which could be located in the Center, the South, or the West and not be disadvantaged vis-a-vis the Common Market."[17]

Whether in fact moving the national capital to another location is effective in channeling growth can be seen by looking at Brazil. For in 1960 the national capital of Brazil was moved out of the historic city of Rio de Janeiro beyond the mountains into a great plains area almost in the geographic center of the country.

BRAZIL: ECONOMIC GROWTH VERSUS CONTROLLING MEGALOPOLIS

The Overriding Problems

Britain and France exemplify two different ways in which national planning can cope with urban growth problems and regional economic disparities. Brazil, in contrast, presents an example which is much more analogous to the United States in several respects — size, wealth of natural resources, potential for economic growth, racial differences, and the relationship between the public and private sectors. Britain and France were never presented with a choice between economic growth planning or urban development planning. In Brazil, this appears to be the nature of the choice.

Brazil is one of the few underdeveloped countries which has the potential to become a major industrialized nation. It is the fifth largest country in the world in territory. And with a hundred million people, it is the seventh largest country in population. It possesses one of the world's richest and most varied reserves of mineral deposits, although it lacks substantial deposits of coal and petroleum. Because of an enormous hydroelectric potential, the provision of electrical energy has been relatively free from dependence on expensive fossil fuels.

Not only does the country possess enormous potential for growth, but since 1964 Brazil has been governed by a harsh military dictatorship that has subordinated all policy to the overriding objective of industrial growth. Partially as a consequence of this single-minded pursuit of economic growth, Brazil's industrial output has grown greater than that of the rest of South America combined. In products such as steel, cement, and cotton, which are crucial products for a newly industrializing nation, Brazil is among the top dozen producing countries in the world. The leader in industrial growth is the automobile industry, which by 1974 reached a production level of 900,000 vehicles.

If the country's wealth must be described in superlatives, however, so must its urban problems. Despite its great natural wealth, the per capita income is below $400 per year, and the income is very unevenly distributed. Per capita income in the industrializing south is more than double that of the impoverished rural areas in the heavily populated northeast. These disparities, combined with a high population growth rate (2.7 percent per year annually during the 1960s), have for several decades stimulated population migrations out of the northeast into the emerging megalopolis of the center-south that is centered around and between the metropolises of Rio de Janeiro and São Paulo.

Despite this urbanization process, the rural population has not declined. On the contrary, the 1970 census found that the rural population was even larger than it had been in 1960. Therefore a greater potential for urban in-migration exists now than at any time in the past. To appreciate this potential, it is necessary to note how rapidly the megalopolis cities have grown. Between the 1960 and 1970 censuses, the city of São Paulo added a population of over two million people, which is greater than the population of Philadelphia. The city of Rio de Janeiro added a population of over a million, as large as the population of Houston. By 1970 metropolitan São Paulo had a population of eight million, and metropolitan Rio de Janeiro had a population of seven million. If the growth rates of the past ten years continue through the 1970s, metropolitan São Paulo will possess over twelve million people and metropolitan Rio almost ten million.

Between Rio de Janeiro and São Paulo and along the growth paths spreading out from these two giant cities are located one other central city of a million population (Nova Iguaçu) and thirty central cities of more than 100,000 population.[18] These are growing together into South America's first megalopolis. In an area slightly smaller than the Northeast seacoast megalopolis of the United States, this emerging Brazilian megalopolis has a total population of more than twenty-five million people. This region not only resembles the North American megalopolis in terms of population concentration, it also resembles it by being the area of greatest concentration of industrial output, economic control, and intellectual and artistic achievement. If the South Americans succeed in spanning the Andes and the Amazon jungle with effective road systems, as they seem likely to do, this Brazilian megalopolis could end this century by dominating not only Brazil's economy but the economy of the entire southern two-thirds of the continent.

For several reasons, the emergence of this megalopolis in an underdeveloped country such as Brazil causes much more serious problems than it does in a developed country such as Great Britain or the United States. For one thing, because of the lower stage of economic development and because of the government's desire to channel all available investments into economically productive enterprises, a very limited amount of funds are available for investment into urban services such as sewers, streets, houses, and social services for the low-income inmigrants.

This unavailability of investment capital is compounded by the rapid rate of urbanization in Brazil. In Brazil, all three stages of urbanization — urbanization, metropolitanization, and megalopolitanization — are occurring simultaneously. In the United States these stages occurred more in succession than simultaneously. Urbanization began in the 1840s, and a century passed before the Northeast megalopolis grew to the size of Brazil's present megalopolis. In Brazil the same growth has occurred in half the time, and the stage of the most massive urban growth has not yet taken place. Furthermore, in the United States, Europe, and Japan, urbanization was preceded by a long, steady growth of industrialization. Cities emerged naturally as a consequence of the mechanization of agriculture and the need for large numbers of people to work in the secondary (industrial manufacturing) sectors of the economy which were predominantly located in urban conglomerations. Since these sectors were labor intensive, they could absorb all of the migrating work force. In Latin America, however, and in much of the underdeveloped world, the reverse process has been the pattern.

Urbanization has preceded industrialization. Many of the great cities of Latin America were planned and platted out long before they became industrialized.

This telescoping of the stages of urbanization into a very short time span when the economy is still in a preindustrial stage has had profound consequences in developing countries like Brazil. Industrial plants established in the 1960s and the 1970s tend to be highly capital intensive rather than labor intensive. As a consequence, not enough jobs are available to employ all the people who migrate into the cities. For the plant managers who seek a surplus of cheap labor and for middle-class families which seek an abundance of inexpensive domestic help, this is an ideal situation. For the in-migrants it usually means living at subsistence levels in unsanitary shanty towns called *favelas* in Brazil and *barrios* in most other Latin American countries. For the urban planners, this process means that the underfinanced and usually ineptly administered cities must provide expensive urban services for the in-migrants. But these cities do not receive commensurate, economically productive output in return because there are not enough production jobs to go around. Where open political systems exist, these severe social dislocations have often led to volatile electoral politics.[19]

For the Brazilian megalopolis, the rapid industrialization and urbanization have produced both positive and negative results. On the positive side, an enormous economic boom has resulted. The nation has become a major exporter of manufactured products. A large middle class is being created. Rio de Janeiro and São Paulo are exciting and dynamic cities. On the negative side, however, both cities suffer from excessive air pollution, traffic congestion, periodic epidemics of contagious diseases, and increasing rates of violent crimes. The economic boom has not yet improved conditions for the working class, which enjoys less earning power in 1975 than it did a decade earlier when the military came to power.[20]

Nearly a million people in Rio de Janeiro live in hillside shanty towns called *favelas* which bear such exotic names as the Catacombs, Boogie Woogie, or the Hill of Monkeys. However, little except the names is exotic about the *favelas*. The homes are constructed from scrap lumber and corrugated metal. Water is often gotten from a single spigot at the foot of the mountain and then carried up the hill by hand by women who balance large cans of water precariously on top of their heads as they tread their way back up to their shanties. Electricity is normally furnished by an enterprising *favelado* (shanty-town resident) at the base of the hill who purchases it from the electric utility company and then resells it at a markup to any other *favelado* who cares to string up the wires necessary to tie into the system. Sanitary sewers consist of open drainage ditches that flow down the hills. The result is an abysmal concentration of diseases associated with unsanitary living conditions. These physical facts of the *favela*'s life are compounded by the social fact that the *favelados* are predominantly Negro. They are often illiterate, and they are disproportionately concentrated in the lowest status occupations.[21]

Some of the most notorious *favelas* have been torn down and their residents completely relocated to suburban settlements which have the urban amenities of water, sewers, and electricity; but this often puts the *favelados* an hour or more by bus from their jobs. Since most of the removed *favelas* have been from the upper-middle-class South Zone of the city where the most affluent residents live and where the tourists stay, the government's critics have charged that its programs of *favela* eradication does not really solve the *favela* problem. It merely puts the *favelas* out of the sight of the upper middle class and opens up extremely valuable land for speculative construction in apartments, hotels, or office buildings.[22]

The Evolution of Urban Policy

Three broad urban problems emerge from this picture of urban growth in Brazil. First are the problems of coping with urban growth within the metropolises. Second are the problems of alleviating the regional economic disparities which cause the in-migration to the center-south megalopolis. Third are the problems of channeling migration away from the large metropolises and into the fertile and underpopulated interior.

Although Brazil has no coherent and unified national urban growth plan to deal systematically with these three broad problems, several *ad hoc* developments over the last two decades have led to sporadic national programs to stimulate economic activity in the underdeveloped regions and to channel the rural-urban migration into places other than the industrialized areas of the megalopolis. Until very recently, national planning concerned itself with economic development by stimulating investments into sectors of the economy such as steel production, automobile production, and mineral resource exploitation that the government wished to encourage. With the tremendous disparities in development between the center-south and the rest of the country, however, national planning was forced to deal with regional and urban concerns.

The first step in this direction came in 1955 with the decision to build a new national capital, Brasília, in the interior in order to attract population away from the crowded northeast and the center-south. The second step came in 1959 with the formation of the Superintendency for the Development of the Northeast (SUDENE). Government and private investments were channeled through SUDENE into new industries and other development projects in the northeast, in the hope that these incentives would create enough jobs to absorb the excess rural labor force, and migration to the center-south could be curbed. The third step occurred from 1968 to 1970 with the formulation of the National Integration Program (PIN). The major aim of this program was the completion of a highway network that would link all the country's major cities. The most spectacular project was the opening up of the dense Amazon jungle to highway traffic and to agricultural settlements. In 1973 the Trans-Amazon Highway was completed. It runs along the southern side of and roughly parallel to the Amazon River from the Atlantic seacoast to the Peruvian border. When the road network envisioned by PIN is completed, not only will the Brazilian cities be integrated into a transportation system, but for the first time they will be linked by direct roads over the Andes Mountains to the capital cities of Venezuela and Peru.

Finally, in addition to these steps to channel population migration away from the megalopolis, the Brazilians have created a system of incentives for metropolitan and urban planning. Portions of municipal budgets are withheld if the municipality does not create a local development plan. Since municipal budgets are received from the national government, this is a very imposing device. An elaborate metropolitan plan has been developed for São Paulo, and a major governmental reorganization has been forced on Rio de Janeiro in hopes of improving the ability of these two metropolises to deal with their urban problems.

Assessment

Whether the Brazilians are in fact developing a national urban strategy, however, is open to question. Three questions in particular arise. First, much of the Brazilian reaction to urbanization appears to have developed on an *ad hoc* basis in response to particular, short-term political demands. The creation of Brasília was basically a politically motivated project of a president who had promised to bring the country fifty years of progress in five. SUDENE was created in response to demands for help from the northeast states. And the drive to settle the Amazon and the interior seems to be motivated less by concerns for a national growth strategy than by concern for guaranteeing a profit for those persons and companies that are speculating in real estate and mining rights in those areas.

Consequently, Brazil presents an intriguing paradox. Without anything that approaches the elegance of the French theory of national planning, the Brazilians are taking concrete measures that far exceed the finely planned measures being taken by the French. If one considers the Amazon colonization programs, the *favela* eradication programs, and other resettlement programs, the Brazilians are moving and resettling as many as seven million people.[23] In addition, substantial population settlement has occurred in the interior along the highways constructed over the past two decades.

A second question arises over the possible incompatibility of urban development planning in Brazil and economic growth planning.[24] The greater the investment in housing, social services, health facilities, sewers, lights, and water for the urban in-migrants, the less the amount of funds available for investment in economic development infrastructure. Since 1964, a basic theme of the government's economic policy has been to promote austerity for the lower classes. Rather than redistribute income, their theory has been to concentrate income into the so-called producing classes, which would reinvest the money into new economic enterprises.[25] Therefore, funds invested in certain urban services for lower-class residents represent a deviation from the government's policy of austerity and nonredistribution of income. Furthermore, any successful containment of the growth of cities in the megalopolis will reduce the supply of excess labor, which will drive up the costs of business and make it more expensive for middle-class people to hire domestic servants.

Finally, effective urban planning in the Brazilian megalopolis will demand stringent land use controls. Up to now urban land has existed much more as a speculative commodity than it has as a public resource. To exert stringent land use controls would put the municipal governments in direct confrontation with real estate speculators, large land owners, and large corporations, many of whom have substantial political influence. For all of these reasons, substantial grounds suggest that effective planning for urban development is incompatible with the government's main objective of rapid and continuing industrial growth.

A final question on the Brazilian experiment concerns political stability. The country probably could not have obtained its dramatic economic growth of the past decade without strong leadership in the national government. But with the single exception of the administration of President Juscelino Kubitschek from 1955 to 1960, there has not been a single era of political stability under a democratically elected national administration since the 1940s. Although the military has in effect governed the country for over a decade and shows few signs of loosening its tight control, ten years is a long time for a government to be in power in a country with the political traditions of Brazil. Eventually it will have to leave power and return the country to civilian rule. When that occurs, nobody knows whether the current urban growth experiments will be sufficiently institutionalized to continue on their own momentum. Because of this, Brazil represents one of the world's most intriguing question marks in terms of urban growth policies.

PUBLICLY CONTROLLED GROWTH IN STOCKHOLM

England, France, and Brazil represent only three illustrations of the steps which many governments are taking to preserve the living quality of their metropolises and to restore some semblance of balance between overdeveloped and underdeveloped regions of their countries. It would be useful to take a short look at some less extensive but equally exciting alternative approaches in urban affairs. One approach which has elicited much praise from urbanists has been that of Stockholm, Sweden. Although it is not a particularly large city, having a population of only 1.5 million, Stockholm is perhaps the only city of this size in the world that is afflicted neither by slums nor by suburban sprawl. One can hike from the center of Stockholm to the city limits in any direction and never leave parkland. No suburban resident is ever more than a ten-minute walk from open spaces. Yet at the same time Stockholm retains a highly urban flavor.

Two features of Stockholm's development display an interesting approach to controlling both suburban sprawl and inner city congestion. First, because of its extensive land holdings, the Stockholm government can exercise decisive control over any development in the suburbs. The government began purchasing land as far back as 1902, and today it owns 80 percent of the land in the suburbs. Subdivisions as they exist in North America are unknown in Stockholm. Rather than allowing developers to buy enormous plots of land on a highly leveraged margin and then subdivide them into small lots which can be sold at an inflated profit for single-family residences, Stockholm leases development sites to builders at long-term, low rates. As long as the developer's design remains faithful to an overall plan for use of the region, he is given considerable latitude to utilize whatever structural styles he wishes. At its best, these mixings of government controls with private incentive lead to exciting, highly imaginative towns such as Valingby, perhaps Stockholm's most famous suburban new town. At its worst it leads to drab, uninspiring towns. But nowhere has it produced either the mile after mile of slums that predominate in West Side Chicago or the voracious sprawl that is eating up the rapidly disappearing open space between San Diego and Los Angeles.

The second feature which has enabled the orderly development of Stockholm has been the concentration of development at new town terminals along the rapid transit lines. Not only does the cluster development around the new towns enable green spaces to exist between suburbs, but within the new towns the residences and commercial buildings are so located that abundant recreational space is provided.

RELEVANCE TO THE UNITED STATES

This chapter has strayed very far from questions of governmental structure and political processes. The purpose in doing this has been simply to introduce alternative approaches to metropolitan growth which are not being practiced in the United States but which might have some relevance to national urban policies in this country. In assessing their relevance to the United States, two questions stand out. Is the United States so culturally and politically different from these other countries that their approaches are clearly inapplicable here? If we are that unique, then trying to learn from the examples of other countries seems useless, unless we use the comparisons to point up strengths and weaknesses in our own governing system. Second, are the strategies effective? If they are not, then trying to emulate them in the United States is pointless.

Political Differences between the United States and the Other Nations

Political, cultural, and historical differences between the United States and these other nations might suggest that experiences in those countries have no applicability in the United States. For example, British institutional concern for a national urban policy began almost three decades ago, but the Americans have yet to formulate a national urban policy. While the English are very conscious of the impact of population growth on their very limited land space, America is blessed with many times the land space of Britain and only about four times the population. This makes it more difficult for us to accept the rationale for strong land use controls which the British readily accept. Further-more, the urbanization process in America is highly complicated by definitely antiblack and anti–lower-class suburban housing practices which have given rise to what Oliver Williams calls life-style issues. Similar racial tensions may arise in Britain because of the immigration of Indians, Africans, and Jamaicans, but to date British racial expe-rience has been much less tense than the American experience. These differences between the British and American experiences has allowed the national government in Britain a much freer hand in develop-ing urban policies than has been given to the American federal gov-ernment.

The differences are even more striking when the comparison is made with the French. It has already been noted that the French govern-ment has demonstrated an ability to establish national policy without having its actions decimated by the interference of local power centers. When compared to the dispersion of funds and resources that dis-sipated the potential effectiveness of American programs such as the model cities program, the audacity of the French in dividing the country into eight equilibrium metropolises solely on the basis of ra-tional criteria is very striking. To be sure, the French planners were obliged to make some compromises to pressures from local officials. The inclusion of Strasbourg among the eight equilibrium metropo-lises, for example, was primarily due to pressures from local officials on the national planners, who had originally anticipated only seven equilibrium metropolises. However, compared to the expansion of the model cities program from a very few selected demonstration cities to 150 underfinanced programs spread throughout the entire country just to get the necessary congressional backing to ensure the bill's passage, the few compromises made in the logic of the French plans seem very small indeed.

Such bold planning in the United States at this time is impossible. The national executive in the United States has no authority to appro-priate funds for a national urban policy. Funds can only be appro-priated by Congress. National policy of this sort in the United States must be made with the collaboration of both the executive branch and Congress. Once the policy proposal enters Congress, however, it runs into two problems. While Congress is remarkably well organized through its committee structure to deal thoroughly with specific pro-visions of specific bills relating to specific programs, this very com-mittee structure makes Congress poorly organized to debate broad questions of national policy. Consequently, only in rare moments such as the civil rights debate of 1964 will Congress as a whole debate and act on questions of policy rather than specific programs. Normally the crucial work of Congress occurs in the committee stage where very specific programs are analyzed.

This committee structure accentuates the second problem that policy questions encounter in Congress, the problem of traditional logrolling. Since Congressmen represent specific geographic constituencies, they naturally like to benefit their constituents. Because of this, appropriations measures are always easier to pass if the bill's sponsors have carefully made certain that some of the appropriations will be spent in the districts of the Congressmen whose votes are needed. While this feature of American politics may increase the chances of success of certain kinds of programs such as the space program (in the early 1960s) which are not hampered by regional dispersion, it virtually ensures that any funds for urban or regional development will be scattered into so many congressional districts that they will be virtually useless.

Closely related to the greater efficacy of French national planning is the difference between the two countries in centralization. France is almost at the extreme of a highly centralized government, while the United States has been almost at the opposite extreme. But this greater decentralization in the United States may not necessarily be a disadvantage. As pointed out in previous chapters, the needs and problems of metropolitan regions have much variety from one metropolis to another in the United States. And since the late 1960s, the disenchantment with attempts to centralize program control in Washington has led to increasing demands for decentralization. Even in France, which is much smaller and much less diverse than the United States, the government planners are moving in the direction of decentralization.

In comparison to both the British and the French, the United States possesses both advantages and disadvantages in relation to establishing metropolitan growth policies. The major disadvantages are three. First, we have been much slower in publicly stating that our urban problems are national problems which need national action. Second, our governmental system is not as well organized to deal with overall strategic questions of urban policy as it is to deal with the more tactical questions of specific programs and projects. Third, political culture in the United States is still more receptive to dealing with urban growth as an opportunity for private enrichment than it is as a problem of protecting national resources.

The advantages of the United States lie primarily in the greater availability of both public and privately owned resources which can be brought to bear on urban problems and also on the decentralized nature of the political system. If the federal government can determine national urban policy, the fact of federalism and decentralized government will enable much greater local creativity in the United States than is possible in either Britain or France. This suggests that urban policies initiated in other countries need not be rejected as inapplicable to the United States simply because the political cultures are different. If this argument of the nontransferability of experiments from one culture to another were valid, then the United States could not have adopted its New Deal social welfare legislation, most of which was inspired by the European Social Democrats. Rather than making blanket applications or rejections of urban policy models of other nations, we should examine specific policy approaches for their success and their specific applicability.

Do the Policies Work? Are They Transferable?

Of the various approaches surveyed above, the concepts of limiting growth in the major metropolises while relocating populations and industry away from them were central to the urban policies of Britain, France, and Brazil. The transferability of this approach should be examined. Other approaches which should also be considered are those which lead to stronger land use controls.

Channeling Population Growth

Considering that the American population is expected to grow by another one hundred million people before zero population growth can be achieved, one of the most important policy alternatives to consider is that of limiting the growth of population and industry in certain metropolitan regions and relocating the population and industrial growth into target areas. The experience of France and Britain in limiting the growth of Paris and London respectively does not cause great optimism. The growth of these two metropolises has obviously neither been halted nor even slowed very much. The experience of Brazil may be more encouraging. Since the construction of the new capital in Brasília and the highway from Brasília to Belem, about two million people have migrated to Brasília and along the new highway. Reports about the Amazon highway projects indicate that large population migrations are occurring into the Amazon from all regions of Brazil. It is too early to know whether the in-migration into the megalopolis has been curbed, however. And even if it has, the cost of the resettlement in terms of the loss of personal liberties and the highly regressive distribution of national income would undoubtedly be unacceptable in the United States.

Although it may be impossible for the United States to take the drastic actions taken by the Brazilian government, we have ample precedents for government-sponsored population relocations which could be tied into a national policy. The homestead policies and the subsidizations of the railroads in the nineteenth century contributed to population resettlements. The creation of atomic energy facilities, hydroelectric projects, and the space program led to population resettlements in the last forty years. And the FHA- and VA-insured mortgages and federal highway subsidies successfully aided in the relocation of millions of people into suburbia during the last thirty years.

While the United States has enjoyed considerable success in promoting population migrations through these projects, it had considerably less success with attempts to curb out-migration from depressed rural areas. In the 1960s the Economic Development Administration (EDA) was created to provide direct federal investment in the infrastructure and public services in depressed rural areas, to provide incentives to firms to relocate in those areas, and to provide employment manpower retraining services to workers who had lost their jobs due to technological or other reasons. Four multi-state economic development districts were established, and a separate region was established in the Appalachian area. This gave the federal government five large target areas in which it used loans, grants, and other incentives to spur regional economic development. The 1970 census indicated that the EDA has not been successful in stemming the out-migration of people from the rural areas or in limiting the population growth of the four megalopolises. With the exception of the state of Oregon, which initiated a public relations campaign to discourage people from migrating into the state, most regions are eager to have their populations grow.

In summary, the United States does not now have an urban growth policy to guide the distribution of future population and industrial growth, and the conditions to create such a policy do not now exist. Even in countries where they have existed, such as France and Britain, the results have been minimal. And attempts in the United States to stimulate the economies of depressed rural areas have failed to curb their out-migration.

Strengthening Land Use Controls

Prevention of suburban sprawl can only be accomplished through effective governmental controls over the use of land. There are two important preconditions for effective land use controls. First, the local political culture must be receptive to the concept that urban land is a public resource rather than a speculative commodity. Second, the land use control mechanisms must be reasonably secure from manipulation by bribery, graft, or political influence. Although considerable progress has been made toward both preconditions within the past decade, neither prevails today. Those who have a stake in urban land as a speculative commodity — realtors, developers, and bankers — fought bitterly (and successfully) for the defeat of a national land use control bill in 1974. And newspapers still carry stories on a regular basis about local officials charged with or convicted of taking money for making zoning decisions that are favorable to certain developers. The scandal of former Vice-president Spiro Agnew accepting money from suburban developers was only the most prominent example of a practice that, in one form or another, has become standard operation procedure in many local governments.

Where the preconditions do prevail, exciting concepts can be put into practice. Stockholm was able to purchase suburban land and use it to control development. London was able to preserve a permanent green belt. England was able to resettle nearly a million people in new towns scattered throughout the country. France was able to concentrate future Parisian growth around a few, carefully selected development nodes.

The preconditions have not yet progressed to the point where anything comparable is possible in the United States. Housing legislation in the late 1960s authorized significant financial incentives to developers to undertake the design and construction of new towns, but few such new towns have been built. Congress also authorized the construction of experimental cities that would utilize new technological innovations, but no state was willing to participate in the experiment. Finally, in 1974 Congress failed to pass the national land use bill that would have provided generous federal incentives to states to improve their land use control mechanisms.

The land use control bill will undoubtedly be reintroduced in future sessions of Congress, and some form of federal incentives for land use control will undoubtedly be enacted. Oregon has pursued the novel path of discouraging people from settling there. California has passed what is probably the most stringent land use control law in the nation.

The sprawl of private developments along the Pacific coast was the particular target in California, and the construction of such developments has now been made extremely difficult. Minnesota has passed stringent legislation to hinder future development along the shores of its 10,000 lakes. Perhaps the most noteworthy event has been the requirement by the federal government that certain major developments require environmental impact statements before they can qualify for federal grants or loans. Where this requirement has been supplemented by state requirements for environmental impact statements, the burden of proof has effectively been put on the developers to demonstrate that their developments will not be harmful to the environment. Furthermore, because the process of evaluating the impact of a development must be judged by a planning commission, a municipal or county council, a regulatory agency, and a court of law, the possibilities of graft and bribery are significantly lessened. Because a proposal now has to clear so many different officials, securing passage by bribing the key officials has become very difficult.

CONCLUSION

Many of the experiments with urban strategies which have been tried in other countries are directly applicable in the United States. In many instances very similar experiments have been attempted in the United States. What is lacking in the United States, and what will be the most difficult to achieve, is the articulation of broad objectives which can provide some policy guidance within which specific programs can be organized.

Some Suggested Readings

Lloyd Rodwin, *Nations and Cities: A Comparison of Strategies for Urban Growth* (Boston: Houghton Mifflin, 1970). Rodwin compares attempts to establish national urban growth policies in Great Britain, the United States, France, Venezuela, the Soviet Union, and other countries.

Peter Hall, *The World Cities* (New York: McGraw-Hill, 1971). Hall focuses on several giant metropolises such as New York, Paris, and London and analyzes the attempts to cope with their growth.

Frank Smallwood, *Greater London: The Politics of Metropolitan Reform* (Indianapolis: Bobbs-Merrill, 1965). Smallwood analyzes the creation of the Greater London Council.

Jack Goldsmith and Gil Gunderson, eds., *Comparative Local Politics: A Systems-Function Approach* (Boston: Holbrook Press, 1973). This is a collection of articles on various aspects of urban politics in developed and underdeveloped countries.

Arthur J. Field, *City and Country in the Third World: Issues in the Modernization of Latin America* (Cambridge, Mass.: Schenkman, 1970). This is a collection of articles which places urbanization in the broader context of modernization.

Chapter 13

If present-day urban trends in the United States continue for another decade, what are the likely consequences? In order to answer this question, this chapter will make conservative projections of the developmental and political consequences of certain existing trends. First, reasons will be given why the next decade probably will not witness the adoption of drastic national urban policies along the lines of the foreign experiences discussed in Chapter 12. Second, recent demographic and technological trends will be projected into the near future to show what changes can be expected by the years 1980 to 1985.

Political Change in the Metropolis of the Future

That is, how will the metropolis of 1985 differ from the metropolis of 1975? Third, speculations will be offered about likely political consequences of these changes. How will we be governed in the period 1980 to 1985? And what will be the major changes in political processes?

THE DIFFICULTY OF ESTABLISHING A NATIONAL URBAN POLICY

Barring some unforeseen nuclear or ecological catastrophe, present trends indicate that the next generation of Americans is destined to an urban future that will be increasingly megalopolitanized. And the next generation of human beings throughout most of the earth seems destined to an urban future that will be increasingly metropolitan. As seen in the examples of Britain, France, Sweden, and Brazil, many foreign nations are approaching their urban futures with more boldness and centralized direction than is the United States. The lesser boldness of the United States in these matters does not lie in an unwillingness of Americans to experiment with schemes that other nations have found successful. Indeed, the United States has experimented with many approaches dealing both with urban growth and with social problem solving. Approaches dealing with urban growth have ranged from the deliberate creation of new urban centers at places such as Cape Kennedy to the deliberate protection of vast stretches of open space in Oregon and California. Approaches dealing with social problems have ranged from the establishment of militant community action programs to experiments at rent subsidies in slum neighborhoods. Where the United States has been more timid than some other nations, therefore, has not been in our willingness to experiment but in our ability to tie urban experiments together into a coherent and enduring national policy. Especially throughout the 1960s, American urban programs were almost peripatetic in their quest to initiate new experiments without waiting to see if old experiments were successful. Coherent and enduring policy making in such an environment is difficult to achieve.

Coherent and enduring policy making in the next decade will be just as difficult. We will probably move increasingly in the direction of articulating a national urban policy. But such policy changes are more likely to be incremental than sweeping. The reasons for this are deeply rooted in the structure of the American political system and in the nature of the American political culture.

The structure of the American political system has several features which impede the articulation and implementation of long-range policy goals about the kind of urban society we want to become. Foremost among these features are federalism and the separation of powers. Although the national government has clearly become the dominant policy maker in the American federal partnership, national policies are carried out fifty different ways in fifty different states. The separation of powers makes different branches of the government responsive to enough different constituencies that achieving a consensus on controversial matters becomes almost impossible among all the branches and agencies of government. Furthermore, Congress and the executive agencies in particular are organized around the performance of specific service and regulatory functions which all have their own interest group clientele. This organization of government and private structures around specific service and regulatory functions gives the government a preference for making specific decisions that relate to specific pro;ects. Even within given sectors of public life (veterans' benefits, for example), once a service is established, it is very difficult to get either Congress or the appropriate executive agencies to make policy evaluations of the program in relation to its objectives and its performance.

In some functional sectors of public life, a long-range policy goal can be articulated and all efforts and programs subordinated to the achievement of that goal. The Apollo program and the decision to place an astronaut on the moon are prime examples of this.[1] In the operation of urban programs, however, there is no consensus on long-range policy goals to which separate programs can be subordinated. As a result, several hundred federal programs have proliferated in the metropolises in an uncoordinated, unplanned way. In more than one instance, the objectives of one program have been undone by the objectives of other programs.

Finally, the tradition of logrolling in Congress has been detrimental to urban programs such as model cities in which program success depended on large appropriations being made for a few, carefully selected sites. In order to ensure the votes needed for passage, the number of model cities had to be expanded to so many locations that few cities received a sufficient concentration of resources to carry out a successful program. While these geographical considerations have not necessarily proven detrimental to programs which are not essentially organized on a geographical basis (such as the Apollo program), they do work to the disadvantage of programs designed to operate for the select benefit of certain geographical locations (such as model cities).

For all of the above reasons, the very structure of the American political system makes the formation of a comprehensive, long-range national urban policy very unlikely. Urban policies are therefore likely to continue evolving on an incremental basis, which is probably the most that can be expected.

These structural impediments to the creation of a long-range national urban policy are reinforced by certain prominent values of the American political culture. By *American political culture* is meant the sum total of beliefs, attitudes, opinions, and expectations about the way in which the American political system does function and should function.[2] Foremost among the aspects of the American political culture that impede the establishment of a national urban policy is a deep-rooted ambivalence about the desirability of centralized control over domestic problems. Much of this stems from the colonial heritage and the Jeffersonian ideal of small-town democracy. It also stems from the reaction against the excessive corruption of the urban political machines of the late nineteenth and early twentieth centuries. As a result, governmental authority in urban areas has been deliberately fragmented. One semiautonomous agency is given operating responsibility for one functional service sector, another semiautonomous agency is given operating responsibility in another functional service sector, and so on. The ideal of small-town democracy is resurrected in urban America by the proliferation of relatively small municipalities in the suburbs. General-purpose governments at the metropolitan level are so few and so difficult to establish that they can be considered a virtual impossibility as a way of ending the fragmentation of government authority in the metropolis.

Considerable centralization of authority has been achieved on a function-by-function basis in the area of key services needed to maintain the physical existence of the metropolis. However, on issues in which access to middle-class life styles is in question, such as in zoning, school integration, and the construction of low-income public housing in the suburbs, there has been a strong reluctance to centralize control at the metropolitan level. Federal programs have supported the functional organization of authority and the creation of suburbia itself. During the first half of the 1970s, the major battles of federal aid were over the utilization of such aid to force equalization of access on the lifestyle issues. Thus, all levels of American government have a deep ambivalence toward centralizing authority. When the federal government has had the opportunity to deal with the life-style issues, it has behaved in a very ambivalent fashion. Federal courts did order the desegregation of public schools. However, on other matters, such as whether federal revenue sharing should be tied to demands that substantial governmental reform and reorganization be conducted in metropolitan areas, the federal government has been much less bold. This ambivalence makes formulating and implementing urban policies difficult, especially urban policies that will deal with the life-style issues.

This inability to formulate a national urban policy and to form a national consensus about national objectives for our urban areas is perhaps the most apparent conclusion to be drawn about the governance of metropolitan America. Closely related to this lack of consensus is the lack of political power to confront directly the most obvious urban and metropolitan problems, particularly the life-style problems. We do not lack imaginative proposals; if anything, we are embarrassed by a wealth of creatively imaginative proposals which we have not been able to implement effectively. What has been sorely lacking has been the organization of political power to make the programs work over the long run.

TECHNOLOGICAL AND DEMOGRAPHIC EFFECTS ON THE METROPOLIS OF THE FUTURE

A key question about the future of the metropolis concerns its technological viability beyond the next generation. The contemporary metropolis is contingent upon the availability of a highly developed technology of transit, transport, supply, employment, and provision of public services. The vulnerability of the contemporary metropolis is demonstrated at least once a year when some major central city undergoes a strike by transit workers, garbage collectors, teachers, policemen, or other public employees. The famous blackout of 1965 demonstrated how easily a whole network of metropolises can be paralyzed simply by an electrical failure. And the energy crisis of 1973–1974 demonstrated just how dependent the whole system of metropolises is upon not only the continual supply of gasoline, fuel oil, and natural gas, but upon a *steady increase* in their supply. In trying to speculate on the viability of the contemporary metropolis as far ahead as the period 1980 to 1985, certain assumptions have to be made about the state of the economy and the availability of energy sources.

First, it seems likely that there will be sufficient petroleum, natural gas, and electrical energy to maintain the physical existence and continued expansion of the contemporary metropolis for at least another decade and possibly until the end of the century. Much of this petroleum will come from abroad and will be subject to very high prices and to periodic embargo threats caused by world political situations. Before the end of the 1970s, however, foreign oil will be supplemented by petroleum from the North Slope of Alaska. Also, powerful economic interests are eager to exploit Western shale oil, off-shore oil, and enormous deposits of Western coal reserves. These resources are not inexhaustible, however, and under the present technology of transportation, heating, and electrical energy usage, probably not enough energy sources are available to maintain a continuously expanding metropolis beyond the end of the century.

Second, although continued expansion of the metropolis for another decade is physically possible, it will become increasingly expensive. The economy is not expected to grow as rapidly over the next decade as it did during the 1960s.[3] The sources of petroleum, natural gas, and electrical energy will be much more costly to exploit than previous sources have been. Ecological concerns will continue to require investments to reduce air pollution, to restore polluted waterways, and to reclaim land that will be strip mined for coal. All of these factors will reduce the amount of money available for discretionary income and for improving individual standards of living. This, in turn, will limit the number of people who can afford to buy houses in and commute by auto from a new tier of suburbs created by developers who leapfrog beyond the existing suburbs. Leapfrog development thus will probably slow down within the next decade. Ultimately it will stop — but probably not within the next decade. It is likely to be accompanied by population growth in small rural cities just beyond the metropolis.

Third, because of the pressures indicated above, demands will rise for more effective mass transit systems to decrease peoples' exclusive dependence on the automobile. The 1974 Mass Transit Act was a definite move in this direction.

Fourth, the expansion of the job market will probably continue in the pattern of the past quarter century. That is, the private job market will expand the most rapidly in the suburbs, while the public service job market will expand the most rapidly in the central cities.

Predicting what effects these assumed conditions will have on metropolitan development is, of course, impossible. But one or a combination of three scenarios seems most likely.

One possibility which has been predicted in the media is that of an implosion in which the suburban populations begin migrating back into the central cities. For a variety of reasons, however, only a small percentage of the suburban population can do this. The national population will continue to increase by as many as one hundred million people over the next generation, but the central cities will not have enough facilities to handle such a population in-migration. Despite the increased costs of leapfrog development due to the economic and energy factors cited above, leapfrog development is still likely to be cheaper for big developers than will be the costs of buying previously developed central city land, destroying the buildings contained there, and clearing the sites for new construction. Furthermore, millions of workers now have jobs in the suburbs, and moving back into the central city will not necessarily put them closer to their places of employment. For all of these reasons, the preconditions which would sustain a massive in-migration into the central cities do not exist.

A second possible scenario, also suggested by the media, might be a genuine migration back to the country where families can live much more independently of natural resource shortages than they can in the large metropolises. The *Whole Earth Catalog*[4] implies that such a movement is possible. And the Sunday supplements of the big city newspapers periodically carry feature articles about young families that give up the comforts of the metropolitan rat race for idyllic, primitive homesteads in the wilderness. These publications suggest that it might be possible to create another golden age of thriving, small family farms. On a massive scale, however, such a movement is no longer possible. In the nineteenth century age of thriving, small family farms, most of the arable land was originally unowned by private individuals. It was given by the federal government under the terms of the Homestead Act. In the 1970s, the most arable portions of rural land are not only owned, they are increasingly owned by corporations that either want to cultivate them or to exploit their mineral wealth. Furthermore, as agricultural exportation becomes increasingly important to the national economy, arable farmland will become much too valuable an asset to be used merely for subsistence farming. For all these reasons, not much land will be available for the millions of excess metropolitan population wishing to abandon the metropolis.

The back-to-the-country movement is likely to be limited in the future as it is now to two groups of people. One very small group consists of the dropouts from the metropolitan rat race. The other group, not much larger, consists of a new generation of nonfarmers and part-time farmers. These are professionals — doctors, lawyers, writers, artists, teachers, and others — who can afford the time and the money to absent themselves from the metropolis for days or weeks at a time. They often live in expensively refurbished farmhouses in places such as upper New England or the Blue Ridge Mountains from where they can drive back to the metropolis on a few hours' notice.

The third possible scenario, and the one most likely for most of the population over the next decade, consists of continued metropolitan sprawl. Census Bureau data indicate that since the 1970 census there has been a net out-migration of SMSA residents to small towns and new-tier suburbs just beyond the current SMSA boundaries.[5] So suburban sprawl has been continuing during the early 1970s; and when the SMSA boundaries are redefined, they will have spread geographically to include even more counties.

The sprawl of the 1970s and 1980s is likely to grow much more slowly than it has in the past. Developers will probably be subjected to more rigorous land use controls. Metropolitan planning commissions are likely to have more power to channel growth into predetermined areas and keep it out of undesirable areas. Public transit is likely to have recaptured much commuter ridership from the private automobile. But the metropolis of 1985 is not likely to be very much different from the metropolis of 1975 — except that it will be larger and more spread out.

Beyond 1985, however, and certainly beyond the year 2000, some basic alterations will have to be made in the patterns of metropolitan growth. Economically exploitable energy resources, upon which the current technology of metropolitan growth depends, are not inexhaustible and probably do not extend more than a generation into the future. Major changes in the technology of transit and home heating will have to be made. Whenever such changes have occurred in the past, they have always made a stupendous impact upon the patterns of urbanization. The railroads made the coal and canal towns of early nineteenth century Pennsylvania obsolete. The automobile, the interstate highway, and the airplane made most of the late nineteenth century railroad towns obsolete. And when newly emerging technology is applied to transit and home heating, it is likely to make a major impact on many contemporary suburbs and certain metropolises. Even now, if it were economically feasible, considerable electrical energy could be generated from solar cells and the burning of disposed solid waste. The application of solar heat and energy-conscious building construction methods could reduce home heating dependence on natural gas. Natural gas itself could be supplemented by methane gas generated from human and animal waste. Personalized rapid transit could reach all but the neighborhoods of the lowest densities. High-speed, short-distance train travel between cities could diminish contemporary reliance on energy-intensive plane travel.

As some of these methods are applied, the face and structure of the metropolis is certain to begin changing in ways that are not apparent now. By the year 2000 the patterns of metropolitanization are likely to look very different than they do in 1975. By 1985, however, these physical changes will just be emerging and they will not be very perceptible.

POLITICAL PROJECTIONS

What implications do the above projections have for political change in the metropolis in the period 1980 to 1985? Two areas seem to be of the most importance in answering these questions: (1) expected changes in the governing processes and structures, and (2) expected changes in the attempts of the racial minorities to gain equal access to the middle-class life styles.

Projected Changes in Urban Governance

The first likely change is federal involvement in metropolitan affairs. Environmentalists will demand federal involvement to minimize the ecological impact of future metropolitan growth. Adherents of land use controls will demand more federal involvement when they lose battles at the state levels. Racial minorities will demand federal involvement to help them attain access to the middle-class life styles and to break down segregation patterns in housing, education, and employment. Representatives of the housing and construction industries will demand more federal financial support for the construction of housing units. And the elements of the famed highway lobbies will demand federal funds for more highways and for maintenance of existing highways. Despite attempts by the Nixon administration to minimize the federal role in domestic affairs, the federal government cannot possibly withdraw to a minimal role. The many urban interests that depend on federal funds will lobby strenuously for them. Some urban interests, particularly the racial minorities, rely heavily on the political intervention of the federal government to protect their welfare, and such groups will lobby strenuously for a strong federal role, not a minimal one.

A second likely change is that the federal government will give more policy coordination to its urban activities. The White House is likely to play a more forceful policy role. Urban policy on the French or British model will not be possible, but neither will a return to the days when hundreds of grant-in-aid programs were applied piecemeal with no attempt at overall guidance.

At third likely change is that there will be more demands to be satisfied. The urban interest groups created during the turbulent 1960s have not yet and are not likely in the near future to disappear. If anything, other potential groups are learning from the experience of the blacks that gains can be won if people will band together. Urban governments now deal routinely with groups that did not exist a decade earlier — groups for the retarded, for alcoholics, exprisoners, welfare recipients, tenants, senior citizens, homosexuals, Chicanos, Indians, and many others. One of the most potent groups in many states is the Public Interest Research Group, an organization conceived by Ralph Nader and financed by fees collected by colleges from their students. At the national level, Common Cause has consistently advocated measures to deal with urban problems. None of these groups are likely to change the class structure of society, to redistribute the income, or to terminate the functional organization of power in the metropolis. But they are likely to continue making demands that will challenge the prevailing distribution of wealth and power in the metropolis.

A fourth likely change is that centralized metropolitan agencies — COGs, planning commissions, metropolitan councils, multi-purpose districts, and state agencies for metropolitan affairs — will be strengthened. This will be largely mandated by the federal government's desire to coordinate the activities of its grant programs and to have grant applications channeled through metropolitan-level review agencies. It will also be mandated by state governments which are moving in the direction of creating policy-making bodies at the metropolitan level, as the examples of Indianapolis, the Twin Cities, and Atlanta show. The metropolitan agencies will not have the powers of general-purpose governments, for the creation of general-purpose metropolitan governments has usually failed. Consequently, the most realistic way of creating a metropolitan-level, policy-making apparatus is to build on the COG approach and to turn more and more policy-making authority over to COGs and agencies similar to them.

A fifth likely change is an increasing atrophy of general-purpose municipal governments. As noted repeatedly in earlier chapters, consistently over the past forty years general-purpose municipal governments have been bypassed in the creation of new governmental functions. And these newly created governmental functions have usually been made fairly independent of municipalities. With the newly created review and policy coordination agencies at the metropolitan level, there is even less incentive to subordinate new governmental functions to municipalities. On many issues, such as transit, air pollution control, criminal justice planning, or health planning, control over these functions is localized in agencies other than municipal governments for many good reasons. For one thing, there may be a hundred or more municipalities in the metropolis, and to localize control over these functions in each municipality would compound the problems of coordination. Another reason is that the technical expertise and the bureaucratic structure needed to handle the new functions are much more likely to be found in the COG and/or the metropolitan planning agency than they are in any of the existing municipalities, including the central city government. Consequently, municipalities, including central city governments, will most likely either be bypassed entirely in the performance of governmental functions or be subordinated to policies predetermined at higher levels.

Municipal governments are likely to have their authority diminished in the performance of some of their traditional functions, also. As metropolitan planning agencies and COGs are given authority to implement more rigid land use control regulations, municipalities will undoubtedly find restrictions placed on their exclusive control over zoning and the issuance of building permits. Some states already require state-wide building codes which limit municipal discretion to adopt extravagant building codes that drive up the value of homes. And some states are moving forcefully toward state-wide land use control regulations which will restrict the local zoning powers even further.

The only major innovation in the past ten years that has strengthened local general-purpose government has been revenue sharing. Except for revenue sharing, however, most innovations in governmental structure have led to atrophying the municipalities rather than to strengthening them.

A sixth projection which is implicit in all of the above is that the total urban governmental apparatus in 1985 will be less responsive to individual citizen demands and inputs than the government in 1975. With the increasing importance of the COG-type institutions at the metropolitan level and the decreasing scope of authority of the municipalities, we are rapidly moving toward a de facto, two-tier arrangement of government without any prior agreement on the relative roles of each tier. As these changes occur, the emerging institutions are dominated by existing interest groups and public bureaucracies. The spokesmen for isolated and unorganized citizens have increasingly less input.

This change will be felt most dramatically in the suburbs, where the municipal governments are already very weak, except for their zoning powers. As the suburban municipal governments lose their control over zoning, their major raison d'etre will disappear. Suburban governments will still be close to the people, but they will have so little authority and jurisdiction that the people will not be close to anything of any consequence. The major decisions will be made elsewhere — by the school districts, the special districts, the counties, the metropolitan districts, and the COGs.

The projection for citizen input in central cities may be less bleak than it is in·suburbia. More and more cities are adopting some form of decentralized control sharing designed to give neighborhood residents more input into the political decisions of central city governments. Central city governments perform more functions and operate more services than do suburban governments. Because they are larger and because they are still the symbolic focal point for politics in the metropolis, they have more influence on state leaders, metropolitan leaders, and federal officials than do the officials of any given suburban municipality. And because the central city governments still retain some importance, the neighborhood community councils may end up having considerable influence on the course of local governance. They even may become a more effective vehicle for citizen input than the suburban municipal governments.

Political Projections for Questions of Race

In the functional organization of power in the contemporary metropolis, one of the most urgent needs has been to give the powerless a stronger voice in the political system so that the metropolis can better meet their needs. This need has been most publicized among the racial minorities, but it is acute among other powerless citizens as well. Some observers show an almost nostalgic longing for old-style political machines that could advance the interests of the racial minorities today as they once enabled certain ethnic groups to gain effective political power. But a return to the past is impossible. Probably more and more attempts will be made to establish shared control over the city government through decentralized administration or neighborhood governments. But since a high level of technical sophistication is needed to manage many of the services of the metropolis, reversing the functional organization of power would be difficult. Functionally organized power is necessarily power held by elites who are not accountable to a broad cross section of the population. Attempts throughout the 1960s to organize the masses who did not belong to already existing, functionally organized interest groups generally failed. But these organization-building efforts did start a number of interest groups that still actively attempt to speak for the disadvantaged or for the public interest as they define it. Consequently, one of the key unresolved questions about the future of metropolitan America lies in working out the fundamental tension between demands of the racial minorities for improvement in their access to middle-class life styles and the functionally organized power structures in the sectors of welfare, education, renewal, public housing, and suburban development that have been so instrumental in building the segregated metropolis as it exists in the 1970s.

If one extends current trends in these matters into the next ten years, four projections seem most likely.

First, de facto segregation will continue in housing. Increasing numbers of blacks may move into predominantly white suburbs and neighborhoods, but the basic segregation of residential neighborhoods seems unlikely to be reversed. No programs now in existence or even in the planning stages could make a serious dent in the de facto segregation of housing patterns in the American metropolis. Continued pressure for affirmative action programs in the private employment sector and for low- and moderate-income public housing in the suburbs will make small dents in the patterns of segregation, but they are not capable of reversing the basic pattern. The only system of incentives that could possibly break down segregation patterns would be to give neighborhood residents a subsidy to integrate their neighborhoods. But such a proposal is not being considered.

Second, not only will *de facto* segregation continue, but the lessened growth of the economic pie will decrease the ability of the poor and the racial minorities to have access to middle-class life styles. During the 1960s, the percentage of blacks living below the federally defined poverty level declined.[6] Thus it looked as though increasing the size of the economic pie would do for the blacks what it did for the European ethnic minorities, that is, give them a larger piece. As the economy grew, succeeding generations of the European ethnic minorities lived more confortably than did their parents' generations. However, the economy is not going to grow as fast from 1970 to 1985 as it did during the 1960s.[7] Much of the wealth created will go to the foreign, oil-producing countries and much of it will go to exploitation of domestic oil and energy sources. Consequently, much less will be available for redistribution to the population generally for the improvement of living standards. The poor and the racial minorities are likely to get a smaller share of a more slowly growing pie than they got during the 1960s when the racial minorities achieved their most dramatic increase in living standards.

The European ethnic minorities created ethnic networks by moving into sectors of private or public life that were just being created. The big city police departments and fire departments were disproportionately populated for so long by the Irish because the Irish were the dominant minority at the time that police and fire departments were created. The public school teacher professions and social worker professions in New York City were disproportionately populated by Jews for so long because the Jews were one of the most strategically placed minorities to move into those professions precisely at the time that they were created. It is difficult to foresee what new public sector employment opportunities can arise in the 1970s and 1980s that can serve as a growth sector for black and minority employment. The antipoverty program in the 1960s had aspects of performing this service for blacks, but it is hardly a growth sector any more. Health care and criminal justice planning are two obvious candidates. But the best positions in both of these sectors require highly sophisticated training beyond the bachelor's degree level. In the lower echelons, criminal justice administration and health care delivery have been substantially large employers of the minorities.

Third, the poor and the racial minorities will probably rely increasingly on the intervention of the federal government to help them increase their access to middle-class life styles. Their biggest ally is the federal government. The interest group structure of the black communities is much more effective at the federal level than it is at the state levels. With the black caucus in Congress and a sizeable bloc of votes among urban, nonblack congressmen, the ability of blacks to use leverage within the federal government to place demands upon local governments is not likely to disappear. Certain federal agencies, particularly HUD, HEW, and Justice, have direct mandates to carry out and implement congressionally approved programs to equalize access in certain key areas. Furthermore, even the Nixon-appointed Supreme Court has been receptive to black demands — much more so than anyone would have thought possible at the start of the 1970s. Consequently, the immediate future will see more controversy over bussing of students within school districts to achieve racial balance and continued pressure for affirmative action programs in hiring, promotion, and firing. Many minority and women's groups are willing to file suits charging discrimination against both private and public employers that fail to establish affirmative action programs. And as long as the courts appear sympathetic to the goals of affirmative action, many employers will find that it is cheaper to comply with the demands of the minorities than to fight the suit and risk losing.

Fourth, a high potential for violence will continue between the racial minorities and the lower- and moderate-income whites. It is with these whites rather than with the upper middle classes that much of the competition of blacks will take place. Their children, more than the upper-middle-class children, will be bussed into black-dominated schools. These whites will be more vulnerable than the upper middle class to periodic unemployment and hence more resentful of affirmative action programs for hiring. And more so than the upper middle class, they will feel the squeeze on housing that is likely to persist in a more slowly growing economy and metropolis. Consequently, more individual contact and intercourse will take place between working-class whites and working-class blacks by 1985, and much of this intercourse will be forced upon them by federal action. From this author's perspective, the deeply felt resentments that exist among lower- and moderate-income whites and blacks makes the potential for periodic, disruptive violence very high. The racial politics of the late 1970s and early 1980s contain the seeds of very violent and bitter confrontations between low-income whites and low-income blacks who are competing for dominance over the same neighborhoods, schools, and jobs. It may not necessarily work out this way. Hopefully, desegregation can be achieved peacefully. But no preventive actions have yet been taken to defuse the potential violence of the situation. The violence that accompanied attempts to desegregate schools in South Boston in 1974 illustrate well how potentially disruptive the basic situation is. Every city will always have leaders who will try to postpone the inevitable (in this case, compliance with court orders on desegregation) as long as possible. And other leaders will always seek political gain by appealing to racial prejudice. And wherever large numbers of people congregate over highly emotional issues, the potential for mob violence is always very high.

To achieve desegregation peaceably and to promote the equalization of access of the minorities to middle-class life styles will certainly be a most difficult task over the next decade — as it has over the previous decades.

CONCLUSIONS

Metropolitan politics in the period 1980 to 1985 will begin to reflect political adjustments that must be made to a basic change in the preconditions for a continued growth in the post–World War II metropolis. In the period 1965 to 1975, two basic changes occurred in these preconditions. First, post–World War II metropolitan growth was contingent upon the availability of cheap energy and the ability of the economy to sustain both the mass production of single-family homes in a suburban leapfrog development pattern and a mass consumption economy of continuously improving standards of living for most urban and suburban residents. The oil crisis of 1973–1974 cast doubt on the precondition that the energy resources will be available to sustain metropolitan energy usage over the long run under current technology. The recession of 1974–1975 cast doubt on the ability of the economy to sustain continued post–World War II patterns of metropolitan growth over the long term. At the very least, the increased costs of energy and the prospect of a more slowly growing economy suggest that less money will be available for increases in most peoples' standards of living. For over a decade the ratio of single-family homes to multi-family dwellings produced in the metropolis has decreased. This trend will probably continue.

A second basic change in the preconditions relates to the role of the racial minorities. In post–World War II metropolitan growth, the vast majority of racial minorities were systematically excluded from access to middle-class life styles. The urban upheavals of the 1960s reflected the demand of the leaders of these minorities that this systematic exclusion be ended. In the opinion of this writer, this exclusion cannot be ended by the traditional method of relying on a continued growth in the size of the economic pie. It cannot be ended without some redistribution of income and without major alterations in the distribution of political power in the metropolis. Hence urban political issues in the period 1980 to 1985 will be much more intricately involved with national political issues and with economic issues than they ever have before.

What the political complexion of the metropolis will look like beyond the 1980 to 1985 period is highly conjectural. But certain trends seem likely to persist. One of the constants will be the long-range dwindling of supplies of certain natural resources which have been essential for the development of the modern industrial economy. If these long-range shortages mean, as many persons are predicting, that we will move from an economy of abundance to an economy of scarcity, then the life-style issues of urban politics will undoubtedly assume increasing importance. If the benefits of the metropolis have proven impossible to equalize during the greatest growth boom that the world has ever seen, how can they be equalized when the amount of benefits grows relatively smaller rather than larger each year?

If the long-range shortages of natural resources do in fact lead to a long-range leveling off of the national economy while the metropolitan population continues to increase, then most likely demands will increase for both greater federal intervention and the centralization of political authority in general-purpose, metropolitan governments that can exert some control over the functional fiefdoms. Although it is difficult to imagine urban politics becoming any more explosive in the future than they were during the middle and late 1960s, the seeds for an explosive politics are certainly present in the trends discussed above. Leaders of the new urban minorities will understandably fear the freezing of their racial and ethnic groups into a permanent urban underclass. White lower-middle-class and working-class people will fear an end to their social mobility. Upper-middle-class and professional-class people will fear the loss of their affluent life styles. The leaders of functional fiefdoms will rigidly oppose control-sharing schemes that will diminish their own influence over urban governments, and they will support citizen-representation schemes that give the appearance of shared control as long as the substance of their control is unaffected.

Of course, none of this is inevitable. The entire scenario is predicated on the twin assumptions that natural resource shortages will cause a permanent contraction in the growth of the American economy before the life-style issues of urban politics can be settled. Maybe the technological and economic adjustments to the scarcity of natural resources will be made before they reach the crisis stage. Maybe the life-style issues will be settled. Maybe the population growth will cease. Maybe the traditional American practice of muddling through with piecemeal *ad hoc* remedies for specific problems will continue to suffice for the future as it has for the past. Maybe a national urban policy will be formed to deal with these matters. Maybe the present generation of economic and political leaders will act with more foresight and selflessness over the next decade than they have acted over the previous decade.

Then, again, maybe they will not.

Chapter 14

This chapter will summarize the two main themes of this book — political change and political bias. Both themes will be summarized in the form of a series of propositions about the bias of major urban political changes that have occurred and that are occurring.*

THE NATURE OF URBAN POLITICAL CHANGE

Urban political change has been incremental and evolutionary rather than drastic and revolutionary. Revolutionary change implies an over-

Change and Bias in the Politics of the Metropolis: A Summary

turn of the entire class and economic structure and drastic modifications in the value structure. Drastic change of this magnitude has never occurred in the United States (with the possible exception of the destruction of slavery in the South). This incremental nature of change is related to the nature of political decision making. Political decisions are made in relation to previous decisions, rather than from a starting point of zero. Furthermore, they are not expected to be permanent; decisions made today are expected to be modified and amended tomorrow as needs change. This is referred to as incremental decision making.

1. In this incremental, evolutionary process of political change, three broad historical changes can be identified in the organization of

---

* Because this chapter will only summarize material which has been discussed and documented previously, very few footnotes will be used. Sources can be found by referring to the chapters in which the given subjects were discussed.

political power. The first change began with the age of political machines and extensive European immigration. Prior to the 1840s, political power in most American cities and towns was centered in a small commercial and social elite. From the 1840s until the end of the nineteenth century, this political elite structure was gradually forced open, and the leaders of European ethnic groups acquired political power. During this period, the dominant forms of organizing political power were ethnically and geographically based social and political institutions. The dominant institution was the political party, the famed old-style political machine. The parties still exist and the geographic and ethnic organization of power still exists, but they are no longer the dominant forms of political organization. They were eclipsed by a second evolutionary change in the organization of urban political power.

2. The second change began with the progressive movement at the turn of the century and reached its zenith between the 1940s and the late 1960s. During this period, several factors led to the decline of the political machines. At the same time, the increasing complexity of urban life, the increasing involvement of the federal government after 1932, and the distrust of machine politics led to the organization of urban political power along functional lines. Functional fiefdoms emerged. At the core of the functional fiefdoms are the administrative bureaucracies of the federal, state, and local levels of government. Outside of the governmental structures, numerous special-interest groups such as labor unions, church spokesmen, downtown business interests, racial organizations, highway lobbyists, construction contractors, teachers' organizations, professional organizations, and a host of others established ties with the agencies that operate the services of most concern to them. Examples of functional fiefdoms were found in public education, police protection, urban renewal, and public welfare.

One key characteristic of the functional fiefdom is the decreased influence of the electorate over the decisions of the fiefdom. Another key characteristic is the narrow focus of interest among the members of the fiefdom. Urban renewal fiefdoms are not normally very much involved in questions of police protection, public welfare, or public health, even though the ultimate success of renewal projects is deeply intertwined with these other problem areas. This functional organization of power in the metropolises has coincided with a general atrophy of the governing capabilities of general-purpose local governments. Each time a new special district or specialized agency was created independently of the local big-city council and mayor, the governing capabilities of the big-city governments were relatively diminished. By the 1960s, many of the most important governmental functions in big cities — public health, public welfare, urban renewal, public housing, freeway location, and public education — were essentially handled independently of the elected mayors and city council members. Even within the traditional city government, some employees had effectively unionized and achieved significant independence from centralized policy control by the mayors, their nominal chiefs. The police departments were probably the most striking examples of this. In the 1960s, many big-city mayors owed their election to the votes from black neighborhoods. Many residents of black neighborhoods had serious complaints against police officials. Yet, because of the cohesiveness of the police department bureaucracies and the policemen's associations, the mayors were extremely limited in their ability to change police policies. In Oakland, the city council could not even make and enforce a policy on the use of firearms by policemen.

3. The third evolutionary change began in the middle 1960s when the federal government first consciously considered a national urban policy. The federal government has not yet become the dominant actor in urban politics, but it is certainly an indispensable actor. Prior to the 1960s, federal urban involvement through grants-in-aid existed primarily to give financial support to state and local governments for carrying out their own priorities and policies. By the end of the 1960s, over 500 grant-in-aid programs were contributing almost one-fourth of the budgets of state and local governments, and cumbersome problems of program coordination arose. Since federal grants were generally awarded to special districts and semiautonomous, single-purpose government agencies, local governments proliferated, and the accountability of local governments to local residents diminished. Starting in the middle 1960s, the federal government began seeking to control and coordinate its various programs. The 1970 Housing Act charged the president with developing a national urban growth policy. President Nixon tried to reverse some of these developments by diminishing the visible role of the federal government and strengthening the state governments through general and special revenue sharing. He also sought to dismantle the welfare system through a Family Assistance Plan, and he reorganized the executive branch of government so that urban policies were highly organized under the Domestic Council and the Office of Management and Budget. Despite Nixon's actions, the total amount of grants-in-aid increased by about 60 percent during his term of office from about $30 billion at the end of the 1960s to over $50 billion by FY 1975.

Thus, not only have the federal bureaucracies become major actors in urban politics, but they are increasingly implementing policies determined in Washington rather than supporting policies determined in the state capitols.

THE BIAS OF URBAN POLITICAL CHANGE

Each of the above changes has been accompanied by patterns of political bias. That is, major changes in governmental structures disproportionately benefit some categories of people and institutions while they disproportionately disadvantage others.

These biases do not fit exclusively in either of the two major models for interpreting American politics — the class-based model or the pluralist model.* The class-based model does not fit well because some of the major beneficiaries of the bias of the functional fiefdoms were people who could not be categorized as upper class. The public bureaucracies, the labor unions, and the public employees' associations are composed of people who are clearly not upper class; they are working class and middle class. The patterns of bias in urban politics can be explained in class terms only in the sense that most of the recent changes in government have been biased to exclude the input of poor and unorganized citizens.

However, the pluralistic theories for interpreting urban politics are also inadequate. If urban politics were primarily organized on the basis of interest groups, then the poor and the unorganized could form interest groups and affect government policies accordingly. However, the several studies cited in Chapter 5 show that enormous obstacles impede the organization of the poor into influential interest groups. The prevailing, overall structure of power in the metropolis has a bias that is clearly to the disadvantage of the poor and the unorganized.

If neither class nor pluralist models of politics are adequate for explaining the patterns of bias, then what patterns can be perceived? This question can be answered by analyzing the bias implications of the three major evolutionary political changes. What categories of people and what institutions benefit most from specific political urban change? Do the changes expand the political elite structure to new

---

* A recent analysis of political bias at the national level reaches a different conclusion. Edward S. Greenberg describes various interpretative models of national politics — the welfare state, the pluralist, and the Marxist. In his view, the Marxist perspective "comes closest to making sense of the multitude of activities to which government devotes its vast reservoirs of wealth, manpower, skills, and coercive powers in the United States." See his *Serving the Few: Corporate Capitalism and the Bias of Government Policy* (New York: Wiley, 1974), p. 30.

categories of people and new institutions? Or do they retard the inclusion of new elites? Do changes in governmental structure make the government more responsive to the needs of the citizenry and the needs of the times? By applying these questions to issues raised in the previous chapters, a series of propositions can be formulated about the bias of urban political change.

The Bias of Technological and Demographic Change

1. Throughout its history, American urban growth has occurred within a framework of what historian Sam Bass Warner called "privatism." Urban land traditionally has been considered a commodity for private speculation rather than a public resource. Urban growth has been considered an opportunity for a few entrepreneurs to amass wealth and for a substantial minority to enjoy "social mobility." In reality, social mobility for the masses has not resulted from a redistribution of the income; it has resulted from the growth of the total economic pie, which enabled each person to receive increasingly larger pieces of pie over the years.

2. Government subsidies of urban growth have disproportionately benefited the entrepreneurs of privatism in urban growth. The bias and consequence of these subsidies show most dramatically in the sector of transportation. Except for the earliest forms of riverboat transport, all major innovations in transportation — turnpikes, canals, railroads, highways, air travel, and the interstate highway system — have been subsidized by the federal and state governments. New transportation modes determined the locales where urbanization would occur. In the present generation, federal subsidies for suburbanization (in the form of tax incentives for home ownership, mortgage guarantees, and freeway construction) have served as an enormous prop for the construction and banking industries as well as for urban land speculators.

3. Contrary to general belief, the processes of urbanization and suburbanization have not been determined by free choice in the market place so much as they have been the result of conscious policy decisions by the institutions that control access to the housing market. These institutions are the Federal Housing Administration, the Federal Reserve Board, the banking and savings and loan industries, the construction industry, the federal and state highway planners, and the local institutions that control zoning and building permits. A given homeowner may feel that he exercises free choice in deciding to move to one particular subdivision rather than another, but all the basic

options available to him were predetermined by policy decisions made by these institutions. For the overwhelming majority of people who have migrated into suburbia since 1945, the choices were really structured between one subdivision as contrasted to others and between perhaps a half-dozen house styles within the subdivision. There was no real option to choose a planned community, a new town, a condominium apartment, a townhouse, a planned unit development, or a home in the central city. The institutions that dominate the housing market did not offer those kinds of options on a massive scale. What they offered was a proliferation of lucrative (to them) suburban subdivisions which universally featured about five or six basic housing styles. Little or no thought was given to the construction of communities rather than the construction of houses. For a substantial minority of the population (especially the poor and the racial minorities), even this limited choice was not available.

4. The geographic patterns of the contemporary metropolis are less amenable to upward social mobility than were comparable patterns in the late nineteenth-century cities. Post–World War II in-migrants do not live within easy commuting distance from the most dynamic growth areas of the metropolis as did late-nineteenth-century immigrants. The patterns of *de facto* housing segregation in the contemporary metropolis have kept the children of the poor and the racial minorities out of the best public schools and concentrated them in the most inferior inner city public schools. Because the contemporary metropolis geographically excludes minority adults from the most rapidly growing areas of job opportunities and because it excludes minority children from the best public schools, it is a definite hindrance to upward social mobility.

The Bias of Machine and Reform Politics

1. Machine and ethnic politics had a conservative bias. Except for Jews, most immigrant generations consistently voted for conservative candidates. Neither the ethnic groups (except for Jews), nor the political machines attempted to promote progressive social programs. Social mobility within either political machines or ethnic networks was limited to the leadership personnel, the elites. For the masses, social mobility came with the nation's long-term economic growth. Machine bosses gave recognition to the smaller ethnic groups by awarding a few top positions to prominent ethnics, thereby maintaining their electoral loyalty. This politics of recognition combined with lack of social pro-

grams muted class differences and made an ideological, class-based politics virtually impossible. For these reasons, machine and ethnic politics had a conservative bias.

2. There was also a liberalizing bias to machine and ethnic politics. They *did* serve as channels of social mobility for *some* lower-class immigrants. The machines *did* represent the interests of some of their ethnic constituents. The ethnics *did* create institutional channels to preserve their interests. They *did* provide *some* jobs and welfare for the needy. And they were opposed bitterly by the upper-class reformers, whose biases were overwhelmingly conservative. In these senses, ethnic and machine politics had a liberalizing bias. They broadened the political elite structure in cities.

3. Ethnic and machine politics have consistently been effectively biased against the racial minorities and unorganized ethnic groups. As blacks and other racial minorities move into urban neighborhoods, older European ethnics migrate to other neighborhoods — or to the suburbs if they can afford it. As the ethnic population declines in a big-city neighborhood, the local ethnic leadership of retailers, clergy, and politicians find their base of support diminishing. In order to protect it, they resist the entrance of the racial minorities into their neighborhoods. They have no incentive to support the integration of their neighborhoods. In this sense, the basic urban problem is not so much that the individual ethnic citizens are racist (and many are) as that the system of ethnically based politics as it functions is biased against desegregation of housing patterns.

4. Ethnic and machine politics are biased against systematic approaches to solving the urban social issues of the 1970s. The machines deal with urban problems by balancing the interests of different groups of actors. The machines are adept at forming workable compromises among competing power groups. They are not adept at systematic problem solving divorced from practical political considerations.

5. The initiators of the turn-of-the-century reform movement were biased against the European ethnics and the working and lower classes. Historical research — particularly that by Richard Hofstadter, Samuel P. Hays, and Melvin G. Holli — has demonstrated fairly consistently that reformers of city government structures were strongly supported by the upper class and by substantial elements of the downtown business community. The stated objectives of these reformers were to oust from public office the representatives of the lower classes and the ethnic minorities and to replace them with people from a higher social status.

6. Individual political reforms had a class and partisan bias. Non-

partisanship reduced voter turnout among lower-income people more than upper-income people and among Democrats more than Republicans. It helped Republican candidates more often than Democratic candidates, and it helped incumbents more than challengers. At-large elections underrepresented the racial minorities and the lower-income areas of cities. Furthermore, cities with reformed governments spent and taxed less than did cities with unreformed governments. They were also less responsive to sharp racial and socioeconomic divisions among their populations.

7. The political reforms weakened the political parties. Particularly civil service reform and more sophisticated budgeting and accounting practices made maintaining old-style patronage systems very difficult for the parties. Where the parties were unable to replace old-style patronage with more acceptable forms of material incentives, the parties atrophied. Without strong parties, however, mayors have seldom been able to exercise decisive leadership.

8. Political reformism reduced the accountability of public officials to the electorate. Because of the proliferation of special districts, suburban municipalities, and single-purpose government agencies, the governmental authority was fragmented into many different sets of hands. When combined with nonpartisan elections, fragmentation of governmental authority made it virtually impossible for voters to know which elected officials should be held responsible for given governmental acts. Furthermore, as the public bureaucracies grew, they became increasingly insulated from control by elected officials. Reformist doctrine held that policy making should be separated from policy administration. If the council members meddled too deeply in administrative matters, the bureaucrats could often fend them off by claiming that the matter was administrative rather than one of policy.

Bias in Contemporary Big-City Governance

The most significant change in urban governance in the last forty years has been the emergence of functionally organized power bases. These have been referred to as functional fiefdoms. A functional fiefdom consists of an urban agency operating in some particular sector of public affairs, its bureaucracy, its professional staff, its public employees' union, its board or commission of directors, its counterpart agencies in the state and federal government, and, finally, the private businesses, labor organizations, and interest groups which serve as a clientele for the agency.

1. Functional fiefdoms are biased against the exercise of decisive

political leadership in big cities. Since each functional fiefdom enjoys considerable autonomy in its sector of public affairs, mayors find them difficult to control. It becomes very, very difficult to coordinate the activities of various functionally specialized bureaucracies which all deal with portions of the same problem. For example, among poor families the problems of delinquency, schooling, income, and housing are interrelated. For urban governments, however, these problems are separate. Each problem is separately dealt with by separate agencies in discrete functional fiefdoms. To coordinate the activities of these four fiefdoms for a comprehensive attack on the social problems of poor families has proven virtually impossible.

2. The contemporary structure of urban government is biased against the input of the poor and the unorganized. The public bureaucracies and employees' unions have extraordinary difficulty in responding to the wants and needs of their clientele. Recent urban history is replete with examples — welfare departments that discourage potential welfare clients from applying for benefits, teachers' unions that resist the inclusion of parents and community people in the making of school policy, building code inspection departments that fail to enforce the building code. The failure of public housing and the destruction of poor neighborhoods by urban renewal and freeways are eloquent testimony to the unresponsiveness of public bureaucracies to unorganized citizens.

3. Community control has been advocated as an antidote for the biases of functional fiefdoms. In the eyes of its strongest advocates, community control purports to do for the unorganized poor in the 1970s what the labor unions did for the organizable labor force since 1933 — organize them and mobilize them to effective political action. The advocates of community control believe that current governing institutions are inherently biased against the poor, the minorities, and the unorganized. Consequently, community control is in theory a very radicalizing force. In practice, it has been fairly timid.

Bias in the Multi-centered Metropolis

Rapid suburbanization since 1945 has led to a metropolis that is multi-centered, that is, no longer centered on a single central business district. This suburbanization has led to several widespread myths about suburban homogeneity that are not supported by empirical evidence. However, considerable evidence does suggest that suburbanization has strongly reinforced the class and racial biases apparent in the functional specialization of central city government. Suburbanization also has some biases of its own that are not apparent in the central city. These biases of the multi-centered metropolis are summarized below.

1. Most of the myths about the homogeneity of suburbia as an affluent abode for the upper middle class are inaccurate. Suburbia rather than being homogeneous, has many different kinds of communities which range from very exclusive to very poor. On balance, in the older, larger metropolises of the Northeast and the Midwest, suburbanites are more affluent than their central city counterparts. In the newer and smaller metropolises, the central city residents tend to be just as affluent as the suburbanites and in many instances more so.

2. On balance the suburbanites exhibit a slight partisan bias in favor of the Republican party. Some suburbs are strongly Democratic; others are strongly Republican. Whether the suburban vote as a whole goes Republican or Democratic depends upon national trends. In Democratic years such as 1964 and 1974, the suburbs support Democratic candidates. In Republican years such as 1952, 1956, and 1972, the suburbs support Republican candidates.

3. On balance the suburbanites have no more of a conservative policy bias than do the white central city dwellers. Studies of congressional voting behavior find that the partisanship of Congressmen explains their voting behavior better than the question of whether they represent suburban or central city districts. Survey research does not find that white suburbanites are much more conservative than white central city dwellers.

4. The one consistent policy bias among suburbanites that crosses class lines and party lines is that of keeping out the racial minorities. The major devices for doing this have been informal acquiescence to an unwritten code making it difficult for realtors and homeowners to sell to minorities.

5. Local suburban politics are dominated by issues which are intricately intertwined with the policies of racial exclusion — zoning, taxes, and public education. Zoning codes and building codes in particular have been a device for making the construction of new homes expensive enough that low- and moderate-income families will be excluded from buying them. Since the racial minorities contain disproportionate numbers of low-income families, they are particularly oppressed by the suburban zoning policies.

6. The reliance of individual suburban municipalities and school districts upon their own property tax has resulted in wide disparities in property tax levels. These fiscal disparities benefit the people in high-

value suburbs. They harm people in low-value suburbs, because such people either have to suffer inferior public services (including education) or have to tax themselves at a higher rate to maintain high-quality services. This also harms those people, who, because of race or income level, are systematically excluded from the high-value suburbs.

7. In many suburbs, the costliness of relying on locally generated property tax revenues to provide services has encouraged suburban municipal governments to shift the burden for as many of these services as possible upon individual homeowners. Instead of installing public sewers, private septic systems are required. Instead of providing a public water supply, private wells are needed. Thus a situation emerges of private wealth and public penury. This benefits the more affluent people who can afford to provide their own services at the cost of keeping out the minorities and other undesirables. It works to the disadvantage of the low-income residents who can least afford to provide their own services and for whom the government provision of services constitutes a form of redistribution of the income.

8. The proliferation of suburban municipalities with their own control over zoning and the issuance of building permits has been biased against the control of suburban sprawl. This bias benefits land speculators, construction firms, real estate developers, and the owners of shopping centers. It also benefits individuals in direct proportion to their ability to purchase large-lot, single-family homes in high-value suburbs.

9. The multi-centered metropolis is biased against making public decisions and public decision makers accountable to the electorate. Because the multi-centered metropolis fragments governing authority into dozens of municipalities, school districts, special districts, and metropolitan districts, it becomes impossible for citizens to know who is responsible for what. Even when they find out who is responsible, the responsible parties normally are not vulnerable to being voted out of office.

10. Closely associated with the multi-centered metropolis's bias against accountability is its bias against individual citizen input. The Jeffersonian ideal of each citizen having an influence on his local government was supposed to be one of the advantages of suburbia. In fact, however, suburbanites exhibit much less interest in the affairs of their local governments than do central city residents in the affairs of their governments. The level of interest is measured principally by voting turnouts and the access to news media coverage of local political events. Not only are most suburbanites apathetic toward most local

political affairs, but local governments do not control the most significant political decisions. Local control exists most dramatically on questions of zoning, building permits, and public education. But the public school bureaucracies dominate public education in the suburban school districts almost as much as in the central city school districts. Even on zoning and the issuance of building permits, local citizen input is really effective only on one issue — that of zoning out the low-income residents. Most zoning and building permit decisions are made to accommodate the desires of large developers more often than they are to accommodate the desires of individual residents on the proposals being advanced by the developers.

11. The total of these biases has been against the poor and the racial minorities, who are systematically excluded from the high-value suburbs. The low-value suburbs and the central cities generally have poorer-quality public school systems than have the high-value suburbs. The poor and the minority neighborhoods also tend to be geographically far removed from the areas of the metropolis where the job and economic opportunities are growing the most rapidly. Furthermore, the lack of adequate public transportation systems hinders the access of the poor and the minorities to those job markets.

Bias in Coping with the Multi-centered Metropolis

Two general schools of thought have been identified for coping with the consequences of the multi-centered metropolis: (1) the metropolitan-governance-without-a-metropolitan-government school of thought and (2) the scrap-the-whole-system-and-start-over school of thought. These two different approaches are characterized by two entirely different patterns of bias.

1. Metropolitan governance without a metropolitan government perpetuates the existing biases of the multi-centered metropolis. The mechanisms which enable the multi-centered metropolis to exist — the special district, contracting for services via devices such as the Lakewood Plan, and intermunicipal cooperation — all enable the essential services to be provided without each suburb losing control over its zoning powers.

2. Scrapping the whole system and replacing it with a metropolitan-level, general-purpose government would theoretically reverse many of the biases of the multi-centered metropolis. Whether it does so in fact can be ascertained only by examining the results of actual attempts to create metropolitan governments. Limited forms of metropolitan gov-

ernment have occurred with city-county consolidation in Nashville, Jacksonville, and Indianapolis, and the creation of a two-tier, urban-county government in Miami. Their biases are examined below.

Bias of Strategies to Attain Metropolitan Government

1. The metropolitan governments have somewhat diminished the bias of the status quo against citizen input and accountability to the citizenry. In Indianapolis, the metropolitan reorganization plan established neighborhood councils for the purpose of increasing citizen participation. Also, the metropolitan governments have diminished the need for new special districts to provide public services. Studies in Nashville found that the residents believed that they knew which officials were responsible for their problems better under the new government than they had under the previous government. Nevertheless, evidence does not completely support the proposition. Voter turnouts in elections for metropolitan councils are typically low. And shortly after the Miami–Dade County government was created, a majority of the citizens were not even aware that it existed.

2. Metropolitan governments have begun to alleviate the fiscal disparities that are typical of metropolises. This will certainly benefit the residents of low-value suburbs and the poor and the minorities who have been excluded from the high-value suburbs.

3. Metropolitan government has a greater bias toward professional values in determining metropolitan priorities and in settling metropolitan problems than did the prereform governments. The professionalism of the city planner and the public administration specialist becomes much more institutionalized in metropolitan government than it does in suburban government or old central city government. The party politician and aldermen do not necessarily disappear under metropolitan government, but they are forced to adopt the language of the professional and to couch their objectives in the terminology of the planners. Because of this, the professional planners play a significant role in setting the agenda for issues that the metropolitan governments will confront.

4. Metropolitan governments have dealt more effectively with systems-maintenance issues such as sewer construction than they have with social-access issues such as zoning, property taxes, or public education. The most success in social issues has been made on fiscal disparities in property taxes.

5. Several urban actors think that metropolitan government will inherently be biased against them. The opposition to metropolitan gov-

ernment by suburban officials, special district officials, and the administrative officers of city and county governments suggests that metropolitan government has the capacity to counter some of the currently existing biases toward the functional fiefdoms.

6. Metropolitan government as it exists in Nashville, Jacksonville, Miami, and Indianapolis has been less biased against black communities than were the previous governments in those places. Black representation increased on the councils after metropolitanization. Black representation in appointed and executive offices increased. In some instances, such as Jacksonville, special efforts were made to improve public services in black neighborhoods as one of the highest priorities. In Indianapolis, federal program funding increased in black neighborhoods after the new government was created.

7. Despite the potential which metropolitan governments have for reversing the bias of the status quo, the opposition to them is so substantial that they are not feasible alternatives for metropolitan governance.

Bias of Incremental Change toward Metropolitan Governance

Because of the general inability to adopt metropolitan governments, city-county consolidations, two-tier county governments, or other forms of metropolitan government, other, less far-reaching means have been used to restructure metropolitan governance without at the same time creating gargantuan metropolitan governments. First of all, metropolitan planning has been extensively emphasized. Councils of government (COGs) to do the metropolitan planning have proliferated. And the A–95 review process requires federal grant applications to be reviewed by a metropolitan review agency before they can be considered by the federal agency.

1. Planning so far has had a conservative bias. Planning for highways, urban renewal, and comprehensive development has generally ignored the desires of unorganized citizens who would be affected by the plans. Furthermore, despite federal stipulations that demand citizen input on highway planning and urban renewal planning, the planning agencies have successfully avoided this citizen input.

2. Advocacy planning has been prescribed as an antidote for the conservative bias of traditional city planning. Advocacy planning challenges the traditional view of planning as a public-regarding function in which the planner is proscribed from adopting viewpoints of particular interests. The advocacy planners assert that the supposed political neutrality and public-regarding approach of traditional planners has

merely masked a conservative bias. The advocacy planners argue that public agencies should provide planners to all citizen groups that request them so that they will be able to argue effectively with the highway planners, renewal planners, and city planners who are proposing projects which they dislike.

3. Metropolitan planning has a potential liberalizing bias that was not present in traditional planning for cities, highways, and urban renewal. If successful, metropolitan planning will subordinate planning for highways and urban renewal to an overall metropolitan framework. This will reduce the insulation of these highway and renewal planners from public accountability. If metropolitan planning can affect the local control of zoning and issuance of building permits, it also will act as a curb on the subdividers and consequently will make it possible to curb some of the privatism which has dominated suburban sprawl.

4. Councils of governments (COGs) as institutions for metropolitan governance have generally been biased toward the interests of suburban governments more than toward central city governments. This was particularly illustrated by the conflict within the Cleveland COG (NOACO).

5. The need for consensus among COGs and their tendency to be organized on a constituent-unit method of representation has biased the COGs against decisive action. At best, COGs are limited instruments for attaining limited objectives. At worst, each constituent government of a COG has a virtual veto over the COGs policies.

6. The A–95 review process has functioned better on the systems-maintenance issues than it has on social issues. In fact, most grant applications reviewed by the metropolitan review agencies are given a positive comment. In extremely few instances have the metropolitan review agencies used the A–95 power to coerce suburban governments to adopt policies such as low- and moderate-income public housing that would help equalize access to middle-class life styles.

Bias of the Contemporary Federal Role in Urban Politics

The federal role in urban affairs is ambivalent. So many programs serve so many different clientele groups that the net biases are extremely difficult to sort out. Nevertheless, several tentative propositions can be stated.

1. Federal urban involvement since 1960 has made a tremendous contribution toward improving the social access of the racial minorities to middle-class life styles. This has occurred in two respects. First,

programs such as the antipoverty program, the model cities program, and others helped to create a climate that stimulated the formation of special-interest groups for the urban poor. Some examples of such groups are the Welfare Rights Organization, the community action agencies, tenants' rights organizations, and neighborhood legal services organizations. Most of these groups find a better reception in the national capital and the federal bureaucracies than they do in the state capitals and bureaucracies. Second, federal pressure for bussing to desegregate public schools, for affirmative action programs, and for nondiscriminatory housing policies have made it possible for many young, middle-class blacks to overcome discriminatory housing and employment practices they otherwise could not have overcome.

2. Despite the above, federal housing programs, renewal programs, highway programs, and antipoverty programs have not equalized the social access of the poor and the minorities to middle-class life styles.

3. Federal efforts to control suburban sprawl since the middle 1960s have been outweighed by federal programs that stimulated suburban sprawl. In particular, more federal funds have been spent on freeways and on guaranteeing FHA or VA mortgages than have been spent on metropolitan planning for controlled suburban growth.

4. Early federal grant-in-aid programs have contributed significantly to the declining accountability of urban governments to the electorate. Recent efforts such as the A–95 process and the federal regional councils would promote coordination among urban governments. Even if this were successful, however, it is not clear that the urban governments would be more accountable to the citizenry of the metropolis.

5. Despite demands that the White House articulate a national urban policy, the structure of the federal government makes the development of a feasible national urban growth policy unlikely.

6. Federal urban programs do not redistribute the income as well as federal transfer payments do. Most of the funds spent on federal programs support the salaries of middle-class people and the profits of private firms which contract with the federal government or local governments to perform services.

CONCLUSIONS

The evolution of metropolitan and urban governance in the twentieth century has shown a consistent turning away from the basic democratic principle of a government accountable to the people. The past decade saw only two innovations counter to this trend — revenue sharing, which strengthened general-purpose municipal governments, and community control, which creates a mechanism for citizen input into governmental decision making. Neither of these innovations seems likely to be powerful enough to reverse the trend. Indeed, as the federal government moves increasingly toward developing a national urban policy and subordinating its hundreds of grant-in-aid programs to the policy, the operations of urban governance might become even more insulated from accountability to the electorate.

This trend has been persistently biased against the interests of the lower classes and the racial minorities. However, it has not been biased in favor of the upper classes so much as in favor of the public bureaucracies and the private interest groups which serve as clientele for these public bureaucracies. Although this has been most apparent in the central cities, it is true in the suburbs as well.

Notes

Chapter 1

1. *Plunkitt of Tammany Hall,* recorded by William L. Riordan (New York: E. P. Dutton, 1963), pp. 11–13.
2. See Chapter 8, pp. 238–240, and see also Chapter 9, pp. 265–266. On Cleveland, see Richard A. Watson and John H. Romani, "Metropolitan Government for Metropolitan Cleveland: An Analysis of the Voting Record," *Midwest Journal of Political Science* 5, no. 4 (November 1961): 376. On Saint Louis, see Henry J. Schmandt, P. G. Steinbicker, and G. D. Wendel, *Metropolitan Reform in St. Louis* (New York: Holt, Rinehart and Winston, 1961), pp. 59ff. On Miami, see Edward Sofen, *The Miami Metropolitan Experiment* (Bloomington: Indiana University Press, 1963). On Indianapolis, see York Wilbern, "Unigov: Local Government Reorganization in Indianapolis," in Advisory Commission on Intergovernmental Relations, *Report A–41: Regional Governance: Promise and Performance: Substate Regionalism and the Federal System* (Washington, D.C.: U.S. Government Printing Office, May 1973), vol. II — Case Studies, pp. 71–72. On Jacksonville and Nashville, see Vincent L. Marando and Carl Reggie Whitley, "City County Consolidation: An Overview of Voter Response," *Urban Affairs Quarterly* 8, no. 2 (December 1972): 181–204.
3. Harold Lasswell, *Politics: Who Gets What, When, How* (New York: McGraw-Hill, 1936).
4. Students not familiar with the input-output model of political analysis might find it useful to examine one of the many systems analysis models of politics. Much of the systems analysis terminology stems from the writings of David Easton and Gabriel Almond. See David Easton, *A Systems Analysis of Political Life* (New York: Wiley, 1965), and Gabriel Almond and G. Bingham Powell, *Comparative Politics: A Developmental Approach* (Boston: Little, Brown, 1966). Some interesting attempts to concentrate on the output side of this model in order to analyze the costs and benefits of policy outputs are Thomas R. Dye, *Politics, Economics, and the Public: Policy Outcomes in the American States* (Chicago: Rand McNally, 1966), and Brett W. Hawkins, *Politics and Urban Policies* (Indianapolis: Bobbs-Merrill, 1971).
5. A discussion of urban renewal is found in Chapter 11, pp. 300–303. For a documentation of urban renewal's reducing the housing supply for the poor and the racial minorities, see John A. Weicher, *Urban Renewal: National Program for Local Problems* (Washington, D.C.: American Enterprise Institute, 1972), p. 6. For documentation of urban renewal's driving small business out of business, see Advisory Commission on Intergovernmental Relations, *Metropolitan America* (Washington, D.C.: U.S. Government Printing Office, 1966), p. 69.
6. Political change has proven to be an elusive term for political scientists to define precisely. Political change literature has primarily focused on non-Western countries which are perceived as undergoing a modernizing or a developmental process. Another focus has been the revolutionary aspects of some change. Some prominent examples of these focal points can be found in John H. Kautsky, *Political Change in Underdeveloped Countries: Nationalism and Communism* (New York: Wiley, 1962); David E. Apter, *The Politics of Modernization* (Chicago: University of Chicago Press, 1965); Leonard Binder, *Iran: Political Development in a Changing Society* (Berkeley and Los Angeles: University of California Press, 1962); Peter H. Merkl, *Political Continuity and Change* (New York: Harper & Row, 1967); and Chalmers A. Johnson, *Revolutionary Change* (Boston: Little, Brown, 1966).
7. Kenneth M. Dolbeare, *Political Change in the United States: A Framework for Analysis* (New York: McGraw-Hill, 1974), p. 7.
8. This point is made particularly by Anthony Downs, *Urban Problems and Prospects*

(Chicago: Markham Publishing Company, 1970), p. 1; and by Daniel N. Gordon, "The Bases of Urban Political Change: A Brief History of Developments and Trends," in *Social Change and Urban Politics: Readings,* ed. Daniel N. Gordon (Englewood Cliffs, N.J.: Prentice-Hall, 1973), pp. 2–21. Dolbeare, however, argues that political change is an independent process because the political system has often failed to change along with changes in the economic system. See his *Political Change in the United States,* p. 3.

9. Murray Edelman, *The Symbolic Uses of Politics* (Urbana, Ill.: The University of Illinois Press, 1964).

10. This point is made by Yasumasa Kuroda in a study of a Japanese community. See his *Reed Town, Japan: A Study in Community Power Structure and Political Change* (Honolulu: The University of Hawaii Press, 1974), pp. 7–8.

11. See Theodore Lowi, *At the Pleasure of the Mayor* (New York: The Free Press, 1964). Also see Edward C. Banfield and James Q. Wilson, *City Politics* (Cambridge, Mass.: Harvard University Press, 1963), pp. 107–110.

12. Political scientist Marilyn Gittell has described the difficulty of exercising electoral control over the New York City public school system. See her "Professionalization and Public Participation in Educational Policy Making: New York City, a Case Study," *Public Administration Review* 27, no. 3 (September 1967): 237–251. A similar point is developed by Norman I. Fainstein and Susan S. Fainstein in "The Political Evaluation of Educational Policies," in *Neighborhood Control in the 1970's,* ed. George Frederickson (New York: Chandler, 1973), pp. 195–216. See Harmon L. Zeigler, et al., *Governing American Education* (Belmont, Calif.: Duxbury Press, 1974). Also, see Chapter 5, pp. 142–143.

13. See note 5.

14. Former presidential urban affairs advisor Daniel Patrick Moynihan has argued for the articulation of a national urban policy in "Toward a National Urban Policy," *The Public Interest* 17 (Fall 1969): 3–20. Arguments that such a policy is neither desirable nor feasible can be found in Anthony Downs, *Urban Problems and Prospects* (Chicago: Markham Publishing Company, 1970), pp. 24–25; and in The Domestic Council: Committee on National Growth, *Report on National Growth, 1972* (Washington, D.C.: U.S. Government Printing Office, 1972).

15. This was the Bureau of the Budget Circular A-95.

16. Commission on Population Growth and the American Future, *Population and the American Future: The Report of the Commission on Population Growth and the American Future* (Washington, D.C.: U.S. Government Printing Office, 1972), p. 35.

17. See Michael Parenti, "Ethnic Politics and the Persistence of Ethnic Identification," *The American Political Science Review* 61 (September 1967): 717–726; and Raymond E. Wolfinger, "The Development and Persistence of Ethnic Voting," *The American Political Science Review* 59 (December 1965): 896–908.

18. The definition of politics as the allocation of values, goods, and services is adapted from David Easton, *The Political System* (New York: Knopf, 1953). The definition of politics in terms of decision making is adapted from Robert A. Dahl, *Who Governs? Democracy and Power in an American City* (New Haven, Conn.: Yale University Press, 1961), and Nelson Polsby, *Community Power and Political Theory* (New Haven, Conn.: Yale University Press, 1963).

19. This approach to defining power is analyzed extensively by Robert A. Dahl in *Modern Political Analysis,* 2nd ed. (Englewood Cliffs, N.J.: Prentice-Hall, 1970), pp. 19–25 and 32–34. Dahl asserts that power is merely an extreme form of influence in which coercion is involved. "Severe losses for non-compliance can be invoked by the power holder" (p. 32).

20. Raymond E. Wolfinger, *The Politics of Progress* (Englewood Cliffs, N.J.: Prentice-Hall, 1974), pp. 7–9.

21. See J. E. Teele and C. Mayo, "School Racial Integration: Tumult and Shame," *Journal of Social Issues* 25 (January 1969): 137–156. For editorial accounts, see "Queen of the Backlash," *Economist,* June 25, 1966, p. 1417, and "Hicksville?" *Economist,* September 30, 1967, p. 1196.

22. This viewpoint is discussed in Chapter 5, pp. 149–153. For an article on the political efficacy of the poor and the unorganized see Michael Parenti, "Power and Pluralism: A View from the Bottom," *The Journal of Politics* 32, no. 3 (August 1970): 501–532.

23. On central city business interests, see especially Edward C. Banfield and James Q. Wilson, *City Politics* (Cambridge, Mass.: Harvard University Press, 1963), pp. 261–276. On suburban business interests, see especially Charles Gilbert, *Governing the Suburbs* (Bloomington: University of Indiana Press, 1967), pp. 145ff.

24. On Detroit, see Edward C. Banfield, *Big City Politics* (New York: Random House, 1965). On Chicago, see Banfield and Wilson, *City Politics*, pp. 277–278.

25. For a background article on this practice, see *The Wall Street Journal* April 5, 1974, p. 1.

26. Historian Sam Bass Warner has asserted the importance of privatism in American urban history. See his *The Private City: Philadelphia in Three Periods of Its Growth* (Philadelphia: University of Pennsylvania Press, 1968); Warner asserts that "The tradition of privatism is . . . the most important element of our culture for understanding the development of cities" (pp. 38–39).

Chapter 2

1. The definition of urban in terms of volume, density, and heterogeneity was formulated by sociologist Louis Wirth in his article "Urbanism as a Way of Life," *The American Journal of Sociology* 44 (July 1938): 1–24. The distinction between the sociological and demographic concepts of urbanization has been made by several scholars in addition to Wirth. See especially John Friedmann, "Two Concepts of Urbanization: A Comment," *Urban Affairs Quarterly* 1, no. 4 (June 1966): 78–79.

2. United States Department of Commerce, National Bureau of Standards, FIPS Publication 8-4, *Standard Metropolitan Statistical Areas* (Washington, D.C.: U.S. Government Printing Office, 1974), pp. 3–4.

3. Peter Hall, *The World Cities* (New York: World University Library, 1971), p. 19.

4. John Friedmann and John Miller, "The Urban Field," *Journal of the American Institute of Planners* 21 (November 1965): 314.

5. Jean Gottman, *Megalopolis: The Urbanized Seaboard of the United States* (New York: The Twentieth Century Fund, 1961).

6. United States Bureau of the Census, *1970 Census of Population*, vol. I, part A, p. xiii.

7. Population of SMSAs taken from United States Bureau of the Census, *County and City Data Book: 1972* (Washington, D.C.: U.S. Government Printing Office, 1972), pp. 29–587.

8. Gottman, *Megalopolis*, chapter 1.

9. C. A. Doxiadis, *Urban Renewal and the Future of the American City* (Chicago: Public Administration Service, 1966), p. 75.

10. Kingsley Davis, "The Origin and Growth of Urbanization in the World," *The American Journal of Sociology* 60 (March 1955): 430–432.

11. The importance of transportation technology is cited by many urbanists. See especially Friedmann and Miller, "The Urban Field," and Gino Germani, "Urbanization, Social Change, and the Great Transformation," in *Modernization, Urbanization, and the Urban Crisis*, ed. Gino Germani (Boston: Little, Brown, 1973), pp. 29–30.

12. Gerald M. Capers, Jr., "Yellow Fever in Memphis in the 1870's," *Mississippi Valley Historical Review* 24, no. 4 (March 1938): 483–502.

13. United States Bureau of the Census, *A Century of Population Growth: 1790–1900* (Washington, D.C.: U.S. Government Printing Office, 1909), p. 15.

14. United States Bureau of the Census, *Historical Statistics of the United States: Colonial Times to 1957* (Washington, D.C.: U.S. Government Printing Office, 1957), p. 14. Philadelphia's 1790 population found in United States Department of Commerce and Labor, Bureau of the Census, *A Century of Population Growth: 1790–1900*, p. 11.

15. United States Bureau of the Census, *Current Population Reports*, ser. P-20, no. 249,

"Characteristics of the Population by Ethnic Origin: March 1972 and 1971" (Washington, D.C.: U.S. Government Printing Office, 1973).

16. The classic interpretation of the importance of the Western frontier to American history was made by Frederick Jackson Turner in his famous essay *The Frontier in American History* (New York: Henry Holt and Company, 1920). His argument was rejected by historian Arthur M. Schlesinger, Sr., "City in American History," *Mississippi Valley Historical Review* 27 (June 1940): 43–66, who argued that urbanization was the motive force behind the frontier movement and most of the important historical political movements. For a reformulation of the importance of the frontier in the urbanization process, see Daniel J. Elazar, *Cities of the Prairie: The Metropolitan Frontier and American Politics* (New York: Basic Books, 1970).

17. Roderick D. McKenzie, *The Metropolitan Community* (New York: McGraw-Hill, 1933), pp. 4–5.

18. See Charles N. Glaab and A. Theodore Brown, *A History of Urban America* (New York: Macmillan, 1967), pp. 113–144. For a fascinating, in-depth account of the creation of one city by the Northern Pacific Railroad see Waldo O. Kliewer, "A Railroad City: The Foundations of Billings, Montana," *Pacific Northwest Quarterly* (July 1940).

19. Sam Bass Warner, Jr., *Streetcar Suburbs: The Process of Growth in Boston, 1870–1900* (Cambridge, Mass.: Harvard University Press, 1962).

20. For a study of the impact of a subway on big-city growth, see James Leslie Davis, *The Elevated System and the Growth of Northern Chicago* (Evanston, Ill.: Northwestern University, Department of Geography, 1965).

21. See Kenneth Boulding, "The Death of the City: A Frightened Look at Post Civilization," in *The Historian and the City,* ed. Oscar Handlin and John Burchard (Cambridge, Mass.: M.I.T. Press and Harvard University Press, 1963), pp. 133–145.

22. Sam Bass Warner, Jr., documents the small-scale nature of business in Philadelphia in the late eighteenth century. *The Private City: Philadelphia in Three Periods of Its Growth* (Philadelphia: University of Pennsylvania Press, 1968), chapter 1. Oscar Handlin documents the late-nineteenth-century transition of Boston's economy from small-scale to large-scale enterprise in *Boston's Immigrants* (Cambridge, Mass.: The Belknap Press of Harvard University Press, 1941), chapter 3.

23. Chapter 1, "The Metropolitan Explosion," in Hall, *The World Cities,* contains a more complete explanation of this idea.

24. Schlesinger, "City In American History."

25. Glaab and Brown, *A History of Urban America,* pp. 293–294.

26. For a summary of this antiurban tradition, see Morton White and Lucia White, *The Intellectual Versus the City: From Thomas Jefferson to Frank Lloyd Wright* (Cambridge, Mass.: Harvard University Press, 1962).

27. On the charge of promoting segregation, see Eunice Grier and George Grier, "Equality and Beyond: Housing Segregation in the Great Society," in H. R. Mahood and Edward I. Angus, eds., *Urban Politics and Problems* (New York: Charles Scribner's Sons, 1969), pp. 300–324. On the charge of economic discrimination, see Eugene Lewis, *The Urban Political System* (Hinsdale, Ill.: The Dryden Press, 1973), pp. 221–223.

28. *Report of the National Advisory Commission on Civil Disorders* (Washington, D.C.: U.S. Government Printing Office, 1968), pp. 116–118.

29. Data on Spanish-speaking persons are taken from Bureau of the Census, *Current Population Reports,* ser. P-20, no. 250, "Persons of Spanish Origin in the United States: March 1972 and 1971" (Washington, D.C.: U.S. Government Printing Office, 1973); and from Bureau of the Census, *Current Population Reports,* ser. P-20, no. 259, "Persons of Spanish Origin in the United States."

30. Winston Moore, Charles P. Livermore, and George F. Galland, Jr., "Woodlawn: The Zone of Destruction," *The Public Interest* 30 (Winter 1973): 42. On this phenomenon, also see Ben Wattenberg, *The Real America* (Garden City, N.Y.: Doubleday, 1974), pp. 142–143.

31. The Commission on Population Growth and the American Future, *Population and the American Future: The Report of the Commission* (Washington, D.C.: U.S. Government Printing Office, 1972), p. 29.
32. United States Bureau of the Census, *Statistical Abstract: 1971*, p. 271.
33. Warner, *Private City*, pp. 38–39.
34. Bayrd Still, "Patterns of Mid-Nineteenth Century Urbanization," *Mississippi Valley Historical Review* 28 (September 1941): 187–206.
35. See David C. Ranney, *Planning and Politics in the Metropolis* (Columbus, Ohio: Merrill, 1969), especially chapter 7, "Conflict and the Planning Process: The Politics of Planning," pp. 109–138.
36. See Richard F. Hamilton, *Class and Politics in the United States* (New York: Wiley, 1972), pp. 155–180.
37. See Chapter 6, pp. 171–176.

Chapter 3

1. United States Bureau of the Census, *Twelfth Census of the United States: 1900; Volume I: Population; Part I*, p. cxxii.
2. William V. Shannon, *The American Irish* (New York: Macmillan, 1963), p. 28
3. For a history of nativist movements and their effects upon the immigrants, see John H. Higham, *Strangers in the Land* (New Brunswick, N.J.: Rutgers University Press, 1955).
4. Shannon, *The American Irish*, p. 46.
5. For a colorful history of the Know Nothing party, see Carleton Beals, *The Brass Knuckled Crusade: The Great Know Nothing Conspiracy 1820–1860* (New York: Hastings House, 1960). The decline of the party is described on pp. 252–279. The Massachusetts incident is described on pp. 227–233.
6. On lynching of Italians, see p. 65 of this book.
7. Robert Dahl, *Who Governs? Democracy and Power in an American City* (New Haven, Conn.: Yale University Press, 1966), p. 38.
8. John Tracy Ellis, *American Catholicism* (Chicago: University of Chicago Press, 1963), p. 102.
9. John Tracy Ellis, *Perspectives in American Catholicism* (Baltimore: Helicon, 1963), p. 61.
10. See Edwin Scott Gaustad, *Historical Atlas of Religions in America* (New York: Harper & Row, 1962), p. 169; and John F. Maguire, *The Irish in America* (London: Longmans, Green, 1968).
11. George Potter, *To the Golden Door: The Story of the Irish in Ireland and America* (Boston: Little, Brown, 1960), p. 359.
12. Shannon, *The American Irish*, pp. 36–37.
13. Shannon, *The American Irish*, p. 122.
14. Edward M. Levine, *The Irish and Irish Politicians: A Study of Cultural and Social Alienation* (Notre Dame: University of Notre Dame Press, 1966), p. 119.
15. Ibid.
16. Shannon, *The American Irish*, p. 116.
17. Richard J. Whalen, *The Founding Father: The Story of Joseph P. Kennedy* (New York: E. P. Dutton, 1964), chapter 1.
18. Dahl, *Who Governs?*, pp. 41–52.
19. Herbert Gans, *The Urban Villagers: Group and Class in the Life of Italian-Americans* (New York: The Free Press, 1962), p. 167.
20. Levine, *The Irish and Irish Politicians*, p. 120.
21. The identification of Irish business interests as construction, food wholesaling, real estate, and transportation comes from Shannon, *The American Irish*, p. 122.
22. Andrew M. Greeley, *Why Can't They Be Like Us? America's White Ethnic Groups* (New York: E. P. Dutton, 1971), pp. 50–51.

23. See Nathan Glazer and Daniel Patrick Moynihan, *Beyond the Melting Pot; The Negroes, Puerto Ricans, Jews, Italians, and Irish of New York* (Cambridge, Mass.: M.I.T. Press, 1963), pp. 243–250. Also see Shannon, *The American Irish,* p. 67, and Andrew Greeley, *The Catholic Experience: An Interpretation of the History of American Catholicism* (New York: Doubleday, 1967), pp. 270–271. The rationale for the statement on increasing numbers of Irish on the university faculties is taken from Andrew M. Greeley, "American Catholics — Making It or Losing It?" *The Public Interest* 28 (Summer 1972): 26–37. Greeley asserts that about a fifth of the faculty under age 30 at elite universities and colleges are Catholic (p. 28). The assumption of this author is that many of these are partially of Irish origin.

24. David Ward, "The Emergence of Central Immigrant Ghettoes in American Cities, 1840–1920," *The Annals of the American Association of Geographers* 58 (June 1968): 343–351.

25. Rudolf Glanz, *Jews and Italians: Historic Group Relations and the New Immigration 1881–1924* (New York: Shulsinger Brothers, 1970), p. 10.

26. Rudolph J. Vecoli, "Contadini in Chicago: A Critique of the Uprooted," *Journal of American History* 64 (1964): 404–417.

27. John S. MacDonald and D. Leatrice, "Urbanization, Ethnic Groups and Social Segmentation," *Social Research* 29 (Winter 1962): 435.

28. Carl Wittke, *The Irish in America* (Baton Rouge: Louisiana State University Press, 1956), p. 92.

29. Glazer and Moynihan, *Beyond the Melting Pot,* p. 204.

30. Humbert S. Nelli, *Italians in Chicago, 1880–1930: A Study of Ethnic Mobility* (New York: Oxford University Press, 1970), p. 189.

31. Ibid., p. 67

32. Lawrence Frank Pisani, *The Italian in America: A Social Study and History* (New York: Exposition Press, 1957), p. 166.

33. Dahl, *Who Governs?,* p. 38. Also, Raymond E. Wolfinger, *The Politics of Progress* (Englewood Cliffs, N.J.: Prentice-Hall, 1974), p. 30.

34. On the struggle between the Irish and Italians to control Italian wards in Boston, see William F. Whyte, *Street Corner Society: The Social Structure of an Italian Slum* (Chicago: University of Chicago Press, 1943), p. 195.

35. This is described by Samuel Lubell in *The Future of American Politics,* 3rd ed. (New York: Harper & Row, 1965), pp. 77–83.

36. Elmer E. Cornwell, Jr., in "Party Absorption of Ethnic Groups: The Case of Providence, Rhode Island," *Social Forces* 38 (March 1960): 205–211, documents a steady rise in the number of Italian ward committeemen in both the Republican and Democratic parties in Providence.

37. Lubell, *The Future of American Politics,* pp. 203, 216.

38. Ibid., pp. 79–80.

39. Theodore J. Lowi, *At the Pleasure of the Mayor* (New York: The Free Press, 1964), pp. 92, 117.

40. See Daniel P. Moynihan, " 'Bosses' and 'Reformers': A Profile of the New York Democrats," *Commentary* 31 (June 1961): 461–470.

41. See Lowi, *At the Pleasure of the Mayor,* p. 40, on New York. On Chicago, see p. 68 in Humbert S. Nelli, "John Powers and the Italians: Politics in a Chicago Ward, 1896–1921," *Journal of American History* 57 (June 1970): 67–84.

42. Nelli, "John Powers and the Italians," p. 68.

43. Greeley, *Why Can't They Be Like Us?,* pp. 87, 92.

44. Nelli, *Italians in Chicago,* p. 196.

45. Andrew M. Greeley, *That Most Distressful Nation: The Taming of the American Irish* (Chicago: Quadrangle Books, 1972), pp. 147, 152.

46. Vecoli, "Contadini in Chicago," p. 268.

47. Edward C. Banfield, *The Moral Basis of a Backward Society* (New York: The Free Press, 1958).

48. Whyte, *Street Corner Society*, pp. 208–209.
49. Glanz, *Jews and Italians*, pp. 27–28.
50. Francis A. J. Ianni, "The Mafia and the Web of Kinship," *The Public Interest* (Winter 1971), p. 88.
51. See Leonard Dinnerstein and Frederic Cople Jaher, *The Aliens: A History of Ethnic Minorities in America* (New York: Appleton-Century-Crofts, 1970), p. 216.
52. Pisani, *The Italians in America*, p. 62.
53. Andrew F. Rolle, *The Immigrant Upraised* (Norman, Okla.: University of Oklahoma Press, 1968), p. 305.
54. Pisani, *The Italians in America*, p. 65.
55. Ibid., p. 269.
56. Rolle, *The Immigrant Upraised*, p. 379.
57. Ibid., p. 269.
58. Andrew M. Greeley, "American Catholics — Making It or Losing It?" *The Public Interest* 28 (Summer 1972): 32.
59. See Russell M. Posner's two-part article "The Bank of Italy and the 1926 Campaign in California," *California Historical Society Quarterly* 37 (September 1958): 267–275, and (December 1958): 347–358; and also Russell M. Posner, "A. P. Giannini and the 1935 Campaign in California," *Historical Society of Southern California Quarterly* 39 (June 1957): 190–201. (Cited in Rolle, *The Immigrant Upraised*, p. 281).
60. Lubell, *The Future of American Politics*, p. 83.
61. The governmental viewpoint is fairly well summarized in two documents published by the President's Commission on Law Enforcement and Administration of Justice: *The Challenge of Crime in a Free Society* (Washington, D.C.: U.S. Government Printing Office, 1967), chapter 7; and the Commission's Task Force on Organized Crime, *Task Force Report: Organized Crime* (Washington, D.C.: U.S. Government Printing Office, 1967). The testimony of former Federal Bureau of Investigation director J. Edgar Hoover has been widely used in promoting the notion of the dominance of the Mafia over all organized crime in this country. See Hoover's testimony in United States Congress, Senate, Permanent Subcommittee on Investigations of the Senate Committee on Governmental Operations, *Organized Crime and Illicit Traffic in Narcotics*, 89th Cong. 1st sess. 1965, Senate Report 72. See also United States Congress, House, Appropriations Subcommittee of the House Committee on Appropriations, testimony of J. Edgar Hoover, *Hearings Before the Subcommittee of Departments of State, Justice, and Commerce, the Judiciary and Related Agencies*, 89th Cong., 2nd sess., 1966, House Report 273.
62. Among the popular exposé writings, several have dwelt heavily on the mystique of the Mafia and its supposed Sicilian origins. See Norman Lewis, *The Honored Society* (New York: Putnam, 1964); G. Schiavo, *The Truth About the Mafia* (El Paso, Texas: The Vigo Press, 1962); and Edward J. Allen, *Merchants of Menace: The Mafia* (Springfield, Ill.: Charles C. Thomas, 1962). A most spectacular book is Peter Maas, *The Valachi Papers* (New York: Putnam, 1968); the text is drawn from Maas's extended interviews with Valachi, who coined the phrase La Cosa Nostra and who supposedly was a member of that organization. A biographical account of one family in organized crime is Gay Talese, *Honor Thy Father* (New York: World Publishing, 1971). A journalistic account of selected criminal leaders is given by Ed Reid, *The Grim Reapers* (Chicago: Henry Regnery, 1969). A fascinating collection of anecdotes by an excellent investigating reporter is found in Nicholas Gage, *The Mafia Is Not an Equal Opportunity Employer* (New York: McGraw-Hill, 1971). The thoughts of a former police officer whose responsibilities dealt primarily with organized crime are found in Ralph Salerno and John S. M. Tompkins, *The Civic Confederation: Cosa Nostra and Allied Operations in Organized Crime* (Garden City, N.Y.: Doubleday, 1969).
63. Salerno and Tompkins, *The Civic Confederation*, p. 89.

64. Ibid., p. 277.
65. Richard D. Knudten, *Crime in a Complex Society* (Homewood, Ill.: Dorsey Press, 1970), p. 197.
66. Donald R. Cressey, *Theft of the Nation: The Structure and Operations of Organized Crime in America* (New York: Harper & Row, 1969), p. 21.
67. The President's Commission on Law Enforcement and Administration of Justice, *The Challenge of Crime*, p. 441.
68. Salerno and Tompkins, *The Civic Confederation*, pp. 232–235.
69. Ramsey Clark, *Crime in America* (New York: Simon & Schuster, 1970), p. 73.
70. Rolle, *The Immigrant Upraised*, p. 106.
71. Joseph S. Clark and others, *Crime in Urban Society* (New York: Dunnellen, 1970), p. 62. For an attempt to define organized crime and the difficulties in making such a definition, see Knudten, *Crime in a Complex Society*, p. 187.
72. Gordon Hawkins, "God and the Mafia," *The Public Interest* 14 (Winter 1969): 51.
73. Ianni, "The Mafia and the Web of Kinship," p. 86.
74. Ibid., p. 90.
75. See Herbert Asbury, *The Gangs of New York: An Informal History of the Underworld* (New York: Capricorn Books, 1970; originally published 1927).
76. This is noted by several writers. See Gage, *The Mafia Is Not an Equal Opportunity Employer*, p. 135; Ianni, "The Mafia and the Web of Kinship," p. 97; and Salerno and Tompkins, *The Civic Confederation*, p. 376.
77. Ianni, "The Mafia and the Web of Kinship," p. 97; Daniel Bell, *The End of Ideology: On the Exhaustion of Political Ideas in the Fifties* (Glencoe: The Free Press, 1960), pp. 128–36.
78. R. Carlson and L. Brisson, "The Web That Links San Francisco's Mayor Alioto and the Mafia," *Look* 33 (September 23, 1969): 17–21.
79. See, for example, Wolfinger's comments on the lack of influence of organized crime in New Haven politics, Wolfinger, *The Politics of Progress*, p. 75n.
80. Ianni, "The Mafia and The Web of Kinship," pp. 96–98.
81. Ibid., p. 93. Humbert Nelli makes a similar observation about Italian organization in Chicago: Nelli, *The Italians in Chicago*, p. 224.
82. Whyte, *Street Corner Society*, pp. 140–146.
83. Bell, *The End of Ideology*, p. 130.
84. Ibid., pp. 128–136.
85. Humbert S. Nelli, "Italians and Crime in Chicago: The Formative Years 1890–1920," *American Journal of Sociology* 74 (January 1969): 389.
86. Rolle, *The Immigrant Upraised*, p. 163.
87. On New Haven, see Wolfinger, *The Politics of Progress*, p. 75n. On Providence, Samuel Lubell relates the rise of John Pastore without any mention of organized crime: Lubell, *The Future of American Politics*, pp. 80–83.
88. Lubell, *The Future of American Politics*, p. 83.
89. Raymond E. Wolfinger, "The Development and Persistence of Ethnic Voting," *American Political Science Review* 59 (December 1965): 896–908.
90. Several surveys of the National Opinion Research Center (NORC) conducted at various times in the 1960s demonstrate this. Relevant examples can be found in Greeley, *Why Can't They Be Like Us?*, pp. 74, 75, 204, 207, and 208.
91. Lawrence Fuchs, *The Political Behavior of American Jews* (Glencoe, Ill.: The Free Press, 1956), p. 51.
92. Ibid., pp. 121–130.
93. On La Guardia, see Fuchs, *The Political Behavior of American Jews*, p. 158.
94. Glanz, *Jews and Italians*, pp. 31–32.
95. Ibid., p. 28.
96. Charles S. Liebmann, *The Ambivalent American Jew: Politics, Religion and Family* (Philadelphia: Jewish Publication Society of America, 1973), p. 136.
97. Glanz, *Jews and Italians*, p. 21.
98. For an interpretation of Jewish unity as motivated primarily as a reaction to anti-

Semitism, see George Friedmann, *The End of the Jewish People?*, trans. Eric Mosbacher (Garden City, N.Y.: Doubleday, 1967).

99. Fred Massarik and Alvin Chenkin, "United States National Jewish Population Study: A First Report," *American Jewish Yearbook: 1973, 74* (the American Jewish Committee, New York, and the Jewish Publication Society of America, Philadelphia, 1973), p. 295.

100. Herbert J. Gans, "Negro-Jewish Conflict in New York City: A Sociological Evaluation," *Midstream: A Monthly Jewish Review* 15, no. 3 (March 1969). Reprinted in Donald E. Gelfand and Russell D. Lee, eds., *Ethnic Conflicts and Power: A Cross-National Perspective* (New York: Wiley, 1973), pp. 218–230.

101. Liebmann, *The Ambivalent American Jew*, p. 35.

102. Ibid., p. 35.

103. Despite the large size of America's Polish population, there has been very little serious scholarly work on the American Poles or their politics. Except where otherwise noted, most of the interpretations in this book are taken from Joseph A. Wytrwal, *America's Polish Heritage: A Social History of the Poles in America* (Detroit: Endurance Press, 1961). The classic scholarly treatment of Poles in English is W. I. Thomas and Florian Znaniecki, *The Polish Peasant in Europe and America* (Boston: Richard C. Badger, 1918).

104. Oscar Handlin, *The American People in the Twentieth Century* (Cambridge, Mass.: Harvard University Press, 1954), p. 68.

105. Wytrwal, *America's Polish Heritage*, p. 256. The difficulty this creates for the aspiring Polish professional is described by Robert T. Golembiewski in the foreword to Brett W. Hawkins and Robert A. Lorinskas, eds., *The Ethnic Factor in American Politics* (Columbus, Ohio: Merrill, 1970), pp. v–x.

106. Robert A. Lorinskas, Brett W. Hawkins, and Stephen Edwards, "The Persistence of Ethnic Voting in Urban and Rural Areas: Results from the Controlled Election Method," *Social Science Quarterly* 49 (March 1969): 891–99.

107. Edward C. Banfield and James Q. Wilson, *City Politics* (New York: Vintage Books, 1963), p. 115.

108. Tammany Hall has been the subject of many fascinating studies. Among them see Seymour Mandelbaum, *Boss Tweed's New York* (New York: Wiley, 1955); Harold Zink, *City Bosses in the United States* (Durham, N.C.: Duke University Press, 1930); and Gustavus Myers, *The History of Tammany Hall* (New York: Boni and Liveright, 1917).

109. See Duane Lockard, *New England State Politics* (Princeton, N.J.: Princeton University Press, 1959).

110. V. O. Key, *Southern Politics in State and Nation* (New York: Random House, 1949).

111. John Fenton, *Midwest Politics* (New York: Holt, Rinehart and Winston, 1966).

112. On California see Bernard L. Hyink, Seyom Brown, and Ernest W. Thacker, *Politics and Government in California*, 8th ed. (New York: Thomas Y. Crowell, 1973); and Clyde E. Jacobs and Alvin D. Sokolow, *California Government: One Among Fifty* (New York: MacMillan, 1970).

113. See Frederick M. Wirt, "Alioto and the Politics of Hyperpluralism," *TRANS-action* 7, no. 6 (April 1970): 46–55.

114. In particular, see Wolfinger, "The Development and Persistence of Ethnic Voting"; Lorinskas, Hawkins, and Edwards, "The Persistence of Ethnic Voting in Urban and Rural Areas"; Gerald Pomper, "Ethnic and Group Voting in Non-partisan Municipal Elections," *Public Opinion Quarterly* 30 (Spring 1969): 79–97; and Richard A. Gabriel, "A New Theory of Ethnic Voting," *Polity* 4, no. 4 (Summer 1972): 405–428. Michael Parenti traces ethnic voting to a lack of ethnic assimilation. He argues that while ethnic acculturation took place, ethnic assimilation was much less extensive ["Ethnic Politics and the Persistence of Ethnic Identification," *The American Political Science Review* 61, no. 3 (September 1967): 717–726]. For a small collection of analytic articles on ethnic politics, see Hawkins and Lorinskas, eds., *The Ethnic Factor in American Politics*. For much less rigorous reportage on ethnic

voting, see Mark R. Levy and Michael S. Kramer, *The Ethnic Factor: How America's Minorities Decide Elections* (New York: Simon & Schuster, 1972).

115. In 1974 the Center for the Study of Democratic Institutions devoted an entire issue of its journal to this ethnic self-consciousness. See *Center Magazine* 7, no. 4 (July–August 1974).

116. See Wolfinger, "The Development and Persistence of Ethnic Voting," pp. 896–908.

117. Martin Plax, "Uncovering Ambiguities in Some Uses of the Concept of Ethnic voting," *Midwest Journal of Political Science* 15, no. 3 (August 1971): 571–582.

118. Marcus Lee Hansen, *The Immigrant in American History*, ed. Arthur M. Schlesinger (New York: Harper & Row, 1964), chapter 4.

119. See Glazer and Moynihan, *Beyond the Melting Pot*, p. 128.

120. Wolfinger, *The Politics of Progress*, p. 69.

121. See ibid., p. 70, for an elaboration of this important argument.

122. A more elaborate argument for social conflict as a conservative force can be found in Lewis Coser, *Functions of Social Conflict* (Glencoe, Ill.: The Free Press, 1964).

123. Zane L. Miller, "Boss Cox's Cincinnati: A Study in Urbanization and Politics, 1880–1914," *Journal of American History* 54 (March 1968): 823–838.

124. Melvin G. Holli, *Reform in Detroit: Hazen S. Pingree and Urban Politics* (New York: Oxford University Press, 1969), pp. 393–403.

125. For an excellent survey of black relationships with political machines in various cities, see Hanes Walton, Jr., *Black Politics: A Theoretical and Structural Analysis* (New York: J. B. Lippincott, 1972), pp. 56–69.

126. James Q. Wilson, *Negro Politics: The Search for Political Leadership* (Glencoe, Ill.: The Free Press, 1960).

127. Michael Novak, "The New Ethnicity," *Center Magazine* 7, no. 4 (July–August 1974): 18–25.

128. Martin Meyerson and Edward C. Banfield, *Politics, Planning and the Public Interest* (Glencoe, Ill.: The Free Press, 1955).

129. The focus of this book on ethnic institutional development differs from most interpretations of American ethnicity, which focus more on individuals' voting or their adaptation to the larger society than on institution building. For a summary of sociological theories of ethnic adaptation to the larger society, see Greeley, *Why Can't They Be Like Us?*, pp. 23–25. For a summary of theories of ethnic voting, see Abraham H. Miller, "Ethnicity and Political Behavior: A Review of Theories and an Attempt at Reformulation," *Western Political Quarterly* 24, no. 3 (September 1971), 483–500.

Chapter 4

1. Edwin O'Connor, *The Last Hurrah* (Boston: Little, Brown, 1956). Examples of favorable treatments of machine politics are Frank R. Kent, *The Great Game of Politics* (Garden City, N.Y.: Doubleday, 1923; rev. ed., 1930); Sonya Forthal, *Cogwheels of Democracy: A Study of the Precinct Captain* (New York: The William Frederick Press, 1946); and Harold F. Gosnell, *Machine Politics: Chicago Model* (Chicago: University of Chicago Press, 1937; 2nd ed., 1967).

2. Raymond E. Wolfinger applied the term conventional wisdom to the notion that political machines have disappeared. See his "Why Political Machines Have Not Withered Away and Other Revisionist Thoughts," *Journal of Politics* 34 (May 1972): 365–398.

3. On Chicago, Philadelphia, New Haven, and Tammany, see Wolfinger, "Why Political Machines Have Not Withered Away." On upstate New York, see James A. Riedel, "Boss and Faction," *The Annals of the American Academy of Political and Social Science* 353 (May 1964): 14–26.

4. Fred I. Greenstein, "The Changing Pattern of Urban Party Politics," *The Annals of the American Academy of Political and Social Science* 353 (May 1964): 3.

5. Theodore J. Lowi, *At the Pleasure of the Mayor* (New York: The Free Press, 1964), pp. 139–145.

6. See Edward C. Banfield, *Big City Politics* (New York: Random House, 1965). On San Francisco, see Frederick M. Wirt, "Alioto and the Politics of Hyperpluralism," *TRANS-action* 7, no. 6 (April 1970): 46–55.

7. Bernard Hennessey refers to the decline of patronage as a "received wisdom." See his "On the Study of Party Organization," in *Approaches to the Study of Party Organization*, ed. William J. Crotty, Jr. (Boston: Allyn and Bacon, 1968), p. 32.

8. Frank J. Sorauf, "Patronage and Party," *Midwest Journal of Political Science* 3 (May 1959): 115–126. Although much of the belief in the decline in patronage is apparently traced to Sorauf's article, this article itself dealt with only one rural county in Pennsylvania. The belief also appeared in many government texts which antedated Sorauf's article.

9. Greenstein, "The Changing Pattern of Urban Party Politics," pp. 7–8.

10. On state-level patronage, see Daniel P. Moynihan and James Q. Wilson, "Patronage in New York State, 1955–1959," *American Political Science Review* 58 (June 1964): 286–301. On patronage at the state level in Illinois, Indiana, and Ohio, see John H. Fenton, *Midwest Politics* (New York: Holt, Rinehart and Winston, 1966). On patronage in New England, see Duane Lockard, *New England State Politics* (Princeton, N.J.: Princeton University Press, 1959). On county-level patronage, see W. Robert Gump, "The Functions of Patronage in American Party Politics: An Empirical Reappraisal," *Midwest Journal of Political Science* 15, no. 1 (February 1971): 87–107. On urban-level patronage, see Martin Tolchin and Susan Tolchin, *To The Victor: Political Patronage From the Clubhouse to the White House* (New York: Vintage Books, 1972), chapters 2 and 4.

11. This point is made by Wolfinger in his article, "Why Political Machines Have Not Withered Away."

12. Ibid. Wolfinger argues that there never had been much centralized control, and he thus argues that this aspect of machine politics has not declined.

13. Elmer E. Cornwell, Jr., "Bosses, Machines, and Ethnic Groups," *The Annals of the American Academy of Political and Social Science* 353 (May 1964): 27–39. For a contrary argument that there was no necessary relationship between immigrant populations and the existence of machines, see Wolfinger, *The Politics of Progress* (Englewood Cliffs, N.J.: Prentice-Hall, 1974), pp. 122–130.

14. Lowi, *At the Pleasure of the Mayor*, p. 112. Emphasis added.

15. Joyce Gelb, "Blacks, Blocs and Ballots: The Relevance of Party Politics to the Negro," *Polity* 3, no. 1 (Fall 1970): 44–69.

16. Greenstein, "The Changing Pattern of Urban Party Politics."

17. *Plunkitt of Tammany Hall*, recorded by William L. Riordan (New York: E. P. Dutton, 1963), pp. 17–20.

18. Howard Penniman, *Sait's American Parties and Elections*, 5th ed. (New York: Appleton-Century-Crofts, 1952), p. 283.

19. Richard Hofstadter, *The Age of Reform: From Bryan to F.D.R.* (New York: Knopf, 1935), p. 181.

20. Edward C. Banfield and James Q. Wilson, *City Politics* (New York: Vintage Books, 1963), p. 117, argue that friendship was perhaps the most important thing that the political leaders gave to the masses.

21. Hofstadter, *The Age of Reform*, p. 181.

22. Banfield and Wilson, *City Politics*, pp. 95–96, 101–107, 110–111. Also see James Q. Wilson and Edward C. Banfield, "Public Regardingness as a Value Premise in Voting Behavior," *The American Political Science Review* 58 (December 1964): 876–887.

23. Murray S. Stedman, Jr., *Urban Politics* (Cambridge, Mass.: Winthrop Publishers, 1972), p. 123. Another textbook accepts the ethos thesis and also states that it is "far from being simply of historical interest. If 'student radical' or 'black militant' was substituted for immigrant, a statement approximating some modern views of the 'power structure' might be created. . . . The feeling that government is 'the man' or

'the system' did not pass away with the immigrant" [Eugene Lewis, *The Urban Political System* (Hinsdale, Ill.: The Dryden Press, 1973), pp. 77–78.] In addition to influencing the textbook writers, this concept of public and private regardingness also heavily influenced much empirical urban research that was conducted during the balance of the 1960s. For a review of this literature, see Timothy M. Hennessey, "Problems in Concept Formation: The Ethos Theory and the Comparative Study of Urban Politics," *Midwest Journal of Political Science* 14, no. 4 (November 1970): 537–564.

24. James Q. Wilson and Edward C. Banfield, "Political Ethos Revisited," *American Political Science Review* 65 (December 1971): 1048–1062.

25. Melvin G. Holli, *Reform in Detroit: Hazen S. Pingree and Urban Politics* (New York: Oxford University Press, 1969), pp. 393–403.

26. Joseph Lincoln Steffens, *Shame of the Cities* (New York: McClure, Phillips and Co., 1904).

27. See Jane Addams, *Twenty Years at Hull House* (New York: Macmillan, 1911).

28. Holli, *Reform in Detroit*, pp. 393–403.

29. Ibid.

30. Samuel P. Hays, "The Politics of Reform in Municipal Government in the Progressive Era," *Pacific Northwest Quarterly* 55 (October 1964): 157–166.

31. William F. Whyte, *Street Corner Society* (Chicago: University of Chicago Press, 1970), pp. 313–315.

32. Riordan, *Plunkitt of Tammany Hall*, p. 46.

33. Bruce L. Felknor, *Dirty Politics* (New York: W. W. Norton, 1966), p. 160. On the effectiveness of various kinds of fraudulent electioneering practices, see Gosnell, *Machine Politics: Chicago Model*, pp. 85–90. A detailed account of early attempts to regulate corrupt campaign practices can be found in Earl R. Sikes, *State and Federal Corrupt-Practices Legislation* (Durham, N.C.: Duke University Press, 1928).

34. See John R. Owens, Edmond Costanti, and Louis F. Weschler, *California Politics and Parties* (London: Macmillan, 1970), p. 4.

35. Banfield and Wilson make the initial distinction between centralized power in Chicago's machine-style government and fragmented power in Los Angeles's reform-style government. See their *City Politics*, pp. 101–111. This distinction has been reinforced by later commentaries. On Los Angeles see Clyde E. Jacobs and Alvin D. Sokolow, *California's Government: One Among Fifty*, 2nd ed. (New York: Macmillan, 1970), pp. 147–148; and Francis M. Carney, "The Decentralized Politics of Los Angeles," *The Annals of the American Academy of Political and Social Science* 353 (May 1964): pp. 107–122. The most extreme assessment of the centralization of power in Chicago is Mike Royko's polemical *Boss: Richard J. Daley of Chicago* (New York: E. P. Dutton, 1971).

36. Herbert Kaufman, "Emerging Conflicts in the Doctrines of Public Administration," *American Political Science Review* 50 (1956): 1057–1060.

37. Riordan, *Plunkitt of Tammany Hall*, pp. 11, 13.

38. Martin Meyerson and Edward C. Banfield, *Politics, Planning and the Public Interest: The Case of Public Housing in Chicago* (Glencoe, Ill.: The Free Press, 1955), p. 288.

39. Stedman, *Urban Politics*, p. 115.

40. Hays, "The Politics of Reform in Municipal Government in the Progressive Era."

41. For a sympathetic history of the National Municipal League, see Frank M. Stewart, *A Half Century of Municipal Reform* (Berkeley: University of California Press, 1950). For a shorter and more recent history, see Alfred Willoughby, "The Involved Citizen, A Short History of the National Municipal League: 1894–1969", a 75th Anniversary Edition of the *National Civic Review* 58 (December 1969): 519–564.

42. Robert L. Morlan, "Local Government — The Cities," in *The Fifty States and Their Local Government*, ed. James W. Fesler (New York: Knopf, 1967), pp. 469–471.

43. Ibid., p. 479. Also, for a general assessment of the city manager plan, see "Symposium on the American City Manager: An Urban Administrator in a Complex and Evolving Situation," *Public Administration Review* 31, no. 1 (January–February 1971): 6–42.

44. See Banfield and Wilson, *City Politics*, chapter 13; Robert R. Alford and Harry M. Scoble, "Political and Socioeconomic Charteristics of American Cities," in *The Municipal Yearbook: 1965* (Chicago: International City Managers Association, 1965), pp. 82–97; and John H. Kessel, "Governmental Structure and Political Environment," *American Political Science Review* 56 (1962): 615–620.

45. Gladys Kammerer, "Is the Manager a Political Leader? — Yes," *Public Management* 34 (February 1962): 26–59.

46. Ronald O. Loveridge, *City Managers in Legislative Politics* (Indianapolis: Bobbs-Merrill, 1971), p. 49.

47. George K. Floro, "Continuity in City-Manager Careers," *American Journal of Sociology* 61 (November 1955): 241.

48. George S. Blair, *American Local Government* (New York: Harper & Row, 1964), p. 213.

49. Morton Grodzins, *The American System*, ed. Daniel J. Elazar (Chicago: Rand McNally, 1966), pp. 190–194.

50. See William G. Colman, "The Role of the Federal Government in the Design and Administration of Intergovernmental Programs," *The Annals of the American Academy of Political and Social Science* 359 (1965): 28–29. Also see Roscoe Martin, *The Cities and the Federal System* (New York: Atherton Press, 1965), pp. 176–181.

51. Banfield and Wilson, *City Politics*, pp. 123–127.

52. Michael Parenti, "Ethnic Politics and the Persistence of Ethnic Identification," *American Political Science Review* 61 (September 1967): 717–726.

53. Wirt, "Alioto and the Politics of Hyperpluralism."

54. See Scott Greer, *Governing the Metropolis* (New York: Wiley, 1962), p. 70.

55. Gerald Pomper, "Ethnic and Group Voting in Non-Partisan Municipal Elections," *Public Opinion Quarterly* 30 (Spring 1969): 79–97.

56. Kessel, "Governmental Structure and Political Environment," pp. 615–620.

57. Raymond Wolfinger and John Osgood Field, "Political Ethos and the Structure of City Government," *The American Political Science Review* 60 (June 1966): 306–326. On the impact of education and Catholicism, see Terry N. Clark, "Community Structure, Decision-Making, Budget Expenditures, and Urban Renewal in 51 American Communities," *American Sociological Review* 33, no. 4 (August 1968): 576–593.

58. Robert Lane, *Political Life* (Glencoe, Ill.: The Free Press, 1959), pp. 269–271.

59. Robert H. Salisbury and Gordon Black, "Class and Party in Partisan and Nonpartisan Elections," *The American Political Science Review* 67, no. 3 (September 1963): 590.

60. Charles E. Gilbert and Christopher Clague, "Electoral Competition and Electoral Systems in Large Cities," *Journal of Politics* 24 (1962): 338–347.

61. Oliver P. Williams and Charles R. Adrian, "The Insulation of Local Politics Under the Nonpartisan Ballot," *The American Political Science Review* 53 (1959): 1052–1063. Also see Heinz Eulau, Betty H. Zisk, and Kenneth Prewitt, "Latent Partisanship in Non-partisan Elections: Effects of Political Milieu and Mobilization," in *The Electoral Process*, ed. M. Kent Jennings and L. Harmon Ziegler (Englewood Cliffs, N.J.: Prentice-Hall, 1966), p. 215.

62. Banfield and Wilson, *City Politics*, pp. 94–95.

63. Ibid., pp. 307–308.

64. Lee Sloan, "Good Government and the Politics of Race," *Social Problems* 17 (Fall 1969): 161–175.

65. Jeffrey L. Pressman, "The Preconditions for Mayoral Leadership," *The American Political Science Review* 66, no. 2 (June 1972): 511–524.

66. Howard Hamilton, "The Municipal Voter: Voting and Nonvoting in City Elections," *The American Political Science Review* 65: no. 4 (December 1971): 1135–1140.

67. Robert L. Lineberry and Edmund P. Fowler, "Reformism and Public Policies in American Cities," *The American Political Science Review* 61, no. 3 (September 1967): 701–716.

68. Clark, "Community Structure, Decision-Making, Budget Expenditures, and Urban Renewal," pp. 587–591. Clark found high correlations between reform-style government and decentralized decision-making structures. Decentralization was measured

by the number of actors involved in making key decisions and by extent of overlap
between the makers of decisions in the issue areas of urban renewal, the election of
the mayor, air pollution, and the antipoverty program. For the controversiality of
decisions and their vulnerability to disruption by community pressures, Clark used
the term *fragile*. He wrote that "for less fragile decisions, the more centralized the
decision-making structure, the lower the level of outputs" (p. 588).

69. Ibid., p. 588.
70. Scott Greer, *Governing the Metropolis* (New York: Wiley, 1962), p. 70.
71. For a discussion of special districts and a listing of sources, see Chapter 7.
72. Charles R. Adrian, "Some General Characteristics of Non-Partisan Elections," The
    American Political Science Review 46 (1952): 775.
73. Robert Wood, *Suburbia: Its People and Their Politics* (Boston: Houghton Mifflin,
    1958), p. 157.
74. Pressman, "The Preconditions for Mayoral Leadership."

Chapter 5

1. Leo F. Schnore, "The Socio-Economic Status of Cities and Suburbs," *American
   Sociological Review* 38 (1963): 122–134.
2. Frederick M. Wirt, et al., *On the City's Rim: Politics and Policy in Suburbia* (Lexington, Mass.: D. C. Heath, 1972), p. 29. Also, a study conducted by the Advisory
   Commission on Intergovernmental Relations found that in Western metropolitan
   areas, the percentage of the population earning low incomes was smaller in the
   central cities than in the suburbs [Advisory Commission on Intergovernmental Rela-
   tions, *Report A–25: Metropolitan Social and Economic Disparities: Implications for
   Intergovernmental Relations in Central Cities and Suburbs* (Washington, D.C.: U.S.
   Government Printing Office, 1965), pp. 15–16].
3. See especially Robert S. Lynd and Helen M. Lynd, *Middletown in Transition* (New
   York: Harcourt, Brace and Company, 1937); W. Lloyd Warner, et al., *Democracy in
   Jonesville* (New York: Harper & Row, 1949); August B. Hollingshead, *Elmstown's
   Youth* (New York: Wiley, 1949). A short summary and methodological critique of
   these early major works can be found in Nelson Polsby, *Community Power and
   Political Theory* (New Haven, Conn.: Yale University Press, 1963).
4. Floyd Hunter, *Community Power Structure* (Chapel Hill, N.C.: University of North
   Carolina Press, 1953).
5. Lawrence J. R. Herson, "The Lost World of Municipal Government," *The American
   Political Science Review* 51 (1957): 330–345.
6. T. J. Anton, "Power, Pluralism, and Local Politics," *Administrative Science Quar-
   terly* 7 (March 1963): 425–454.
7. Polsby, *Community Power and Political Theory*; Herbert Kaufman and Victor Jones,
   "The Mystery of Power," *Public Administration Quarterly* 14 (Summer 1954): 2–5;
   Raymond Wolfinger, "Reputation and Reality in the Study of Community Power,"
   American Sociological Review 25 (October 1960): 636–644; Robert A. Dahl, "A
   Critique of The Ruling Elite Model," *The American Political Science Review* 52
   (June 1958): 463–69.
8. In particular, this is Polsby's critique. See *Community Power and Political Theory*.
9. Robert Dahl, *Who Governs? Democracy and Power in an American City* (New
   Haven, Conn.: Yale University Press, 1966).
10. See, for example, Delbert C. Miller, "Decision-Making Cliques in Community Power
    Structures: A Comparative Study of an American and an English City," *American
    Journal of Sociology* 64 (November 1958):299–310; William H. Form and William V.
    D'Antonio, "Integration and Cleavage Among Community Influentials in Two Bor-
    der Cities," *American Sociological Review* 24 (December 1959): 804–814; Robert
    Presthus, *Men at the Top: A Study in Community Power* (New York: Oxford Uni-
    versity Press, 1964); and Robert E. Agger, Daniel Goldrich, and Bert Swanson, *The

Rulers and the Ruled: Political Power and Impotence in American Communities (New York: Wiley, 1964).

11. See, for example, Presthus, *Men at the Top*; Agger, Goldwich, and Swanson, *The Rulers and the Ruled*; Linton C. Freeman, et al., *Local Community Leadership* (Syracuse, N.Y.: University College, 1960).

12. John Walton, "Discipline, Method, and Community Power: A Note on the Sociology of Knowledge," *American Sociological Review* 31, no. 5 (October 1966): 684–689.

13. Robert S. Lynd and Helen M. Lynd, *Middletown* (New York: Harcourt, Brace and Company, 1929), and *Middletown in Transition*.

14. Lynd and Lynd, *Middletown in Transition*, p. 74.

15. Robert D. Schulze, "The Bifurcation of Power in a Satellite City," in *Community Political Systems*, ed. Morris Janowitz (New York: The Free Press, 1961).

16. Ronald J. Pellegrin and Charles H. Coates, "Absentee-Owned Corporations and Community Power Structure," *American Journal of Sociology* 61 (March 1956): 413–419. Also see comments of Daniel N. Gordon, ed., *Social Change and Urban Politics: Readings* (Englewood Cliffs, N.J.: Prentice-Hall, 1973), pp. 62–64.

17. Banfield and Wilson, *City Politics*, pp. 261–276.

18. Peter Clark, "Civic Leadership: The Symbols of Legitimacy," a paper presented at the 1960 Annual Meeting of the American Political Science Association; edited and reprinted in *Democracy in Urban America*, 2nd ed., ed. Oliver P. Williams and Charles Press (Chicago: Rand McNally, 1969), pp. 350–366.

19. Peter Bachrach and Morton S. Baratz, "The Two Faces of Power," *The American Political Science Review* 56, no. 4 (December 1962): 948.

20. On the methods of researching nondecisions see Matthew Crenson, *The Unpolitics of Air Pollution: A Study of Non-Decision-Making in the Cities* (Baltimore: Johns Hopkins Press, 1971). Raymond Wolfinger finds the concept of nondecisions so fraught with methodological problems that it is virtually unresearchable. See his "Nondecisions and the Study of Local Politics," *The American Political Science Review* 65, no. 4 (December 1971): 1063–1080. Frederick W. Frey takes a more optimistic viewpoint. See his "Comment: On Issues and Non-issues in the Study of Community Power," *The American Political Science Review* 65, no. 4 December 1971): 1081–1101.

21. For example, see Bernard Asbell, "Dick Lee Discovers How Much Is Not Enough," *New York Times Magazine*, September 3, 1967, p. 6

22. Theodore J. Lowi, *At the Pleasure of the Mayor* (New York: The Free Press, 1964). See especially chapter 7 of Lowi's book.

23. Theodore J. Lowi, "Machine Politics — Old and New," *The Public Interest* 9 (Fall 1967): 86.

24. See Roger Starr, "Power and Powerlessness in a Regional City," *The Public Interest* 16 (Summer 1969): 10.

25. Lowi, "Machine Politics — Old and New," p. 89.

26. David Rogers, *The Management of Big Cities: Interest Groups and Social Change Strategies* (Beverly Hills, Calif.: SAGE Publications, 1971), p. 117.

27. Jeffrey L. Pressman, "The Preconditions for Mayoral Leadership," *The American Political Science Review* 66, no. 2 (June 1972): 514.

28. Harold Kaplan, *Urban Renewal Politics: Slum Clearance in Newark* (New York: Columbia University Press, 1963), pp. 10–15.

29. Arnold W. Reitze, Jr., and Glenn L. Reitze, "Law: Deus Ex Machina," *Environment* 16 (June 1974): 3–5, 42. The charge was originally made by Bradford C. Snell in *American Ground Transport, A Proposal for Restructuring the Automobile, Truck, Bus, and Rail Industries*, a report to the Subcommittee on Antitrust and Monopoly of the Committee on the Judiciary, U.S. Senate, February 26, 1974.

30. For an in-depth study of this in Boston and other cities, see Alan Lupo, Frank Colcord, and Edmund P. Fowler, *Rites of Way: The Politics of Transportation in Boston and the U.S. City* (Boston: Little, Brown, 1971).

31. Marilyn Gittell, "Professionalization and Public Participation in Educational Policy

Making: New York City, A Case Study," *Public Administration Review* 27, no. 3 (September 1967): 237–251.

32. Ibid., pp. 243, 238.

33. Norman I. Fainstein and Susan S. Fainstein, "The Political Evaluation of Educational Policies," in *Neighborhood Control in the 1970's: Politics, Administration, and Citizen Participation*, ed. George Frederickson (New York: Chandler, 1973), pp. 195–216.

34. Rogers, *The Management of Big Cities*, pp. 36–37.

35. Frances Frisken, "The Metropolis and the Central City: Can One Government Unite Them?" *Urban Affairs Quarterly* 8, no. 3 (June 1973): 403.

36. Jeffrey Pressman, "Foreign Aid and Urban Aid," in *Neighborhood Control in the 1970's*, ed. George Frederickson, p. 152.

37. See David Nimmer, "St. Paul Decision Makers," a ten-article series in the *Minneapolis Star*, June 9–20, 1969, which describes five major development decisions in which the Saint Paul mayor and council are portrayed as playing supportive rather than initiating roles. This is consistent with the findings of the most scholarly treatment in print on Saint Paul planning and development, Alan Altshuler, *The City Planning Process: A Political Analysis* (Ithaca, N.Y.: Cornell University Press, 1965), pp. 17–143.

38. John F. Dillon, *Commentaries on the Law of Municipal Corporations*, 5th ed. (Boston: Little, Brown, 1911), vol. I, sec. 237.

39. Lowi, *At the Pleasure of the Mayor*, p. 225.

40. See James David Greenstone and Paul E. Peterson, "Reformers, Machines, and the War on Poverty," in *City Politics and Public Policy*, ed. James Q. Wilson (New York: Wiley, 1968), pp. 286–289.

41. J. David Greenstone, "Party Pressure on Organized Labor in Three Cities," in *The Electoral Process*, ed. M. Kent Jennings and L. Harmon Ziegler (Englewood Cliffs, N.J.: Prentice-Hall, 1966), pp. 55–80.

42. Martin E. Meyerson and Edward C. Banfield, *Politics, Planning, and the Public Interest* (Glencoe, Ill.: The Free Press, 1955), pp. 285–300.

43. Ibid.

44. See Alexander L. George, "Political Leadership and Social Change in American Cities," *Daedalus* 97, no. 4 (Fall 1968): 1194–1217; and Robert H. Salisbury, "Urban Politics: The New Convergence of Power," *The Journal of Politics* 26, no. 4 (November 1964): 775–797.

45. Pressman, "The Preconditions for Mayoral Leadership," p. 512.

46. The major sources on Lee's exercise of leadership are Dahl, *Who Governs?*, and Raymond Wolfinger, *The Politics of Progress* (Englewood Cliffs, N.J.: Prentice-Hall, 1974).

47. Norton Long, "The City as Reservation," *The Public Interest* 25 (Fall 1971): 35.

48. Allan R. Talbot, *The Mayor's Game: Richard Lee of New Haven and the Politics of Change* (New York: Harper & Row, 1967), p. 29.

49. Jewell Bellush and Murray Hausknecht, "Entrepreneurs and Urban Renewal: The New Men of Power," *Journal of the American Institute of Planners* 32, no. 5 (September 1966): 289–297.

50. See Dahl, *Who Governs?*, pp. 200–214, and Wolfinger, *The Politics of Progress*, pp. 157–202.

51. Pressman, "The Preconditions for Mayoral Leadership," pp. 512–513, 522.

52. Michael Parenti, "Power and Pluralism: A View From the Bottom," *The Journal of Politics* 32, no. 3 (August 1970): 501–532.

53. Ibid. Quotes are found on pp. 519, 521, 526, 528.

54. Ibid., p. 529

55. Michael Lipsky, *Protest in City Politics: Rent Strikes, Housing and the Power of the Poor* (Chicago: Rand McNally, 1970). See especially pp. 163–185.

56. Michael Lipsky, "Rent Strikes: Poor Man's Weapon," *TRANS-action*, February 1969, pp. 10–15.

57. Peter K. Eisinger, "The Conditions of Protest Behavior in American Cities," *The American Political Science Review* 67, no. 1 (March 1973): 11–28.

58. Jean Stinchcombe, *Reform and Reaction: City Politics in Toledo* (Belmont, Calif.: Wadsworth, 1968), pp. 147–48.

59. Harold Baron, with Harriet Stulman, Richard Rothstein, and Rennard Davis, "Black Powerlessness in Chicago," *TRANS-action* 6, no. 1 (November 1968): 27–33. Quote is from p. 33.

60. Edward C. Hayes, *Power Structure and Urban Policy: Who Rules in Oakland?* (New York: McGraw-Hill, 1972). See especially pp. 156–160, 185–200.

61. For a collection of documents and articles on the Ocean Hill–Brownsville controversy, see Maurice R. Berube and Marilyn Gittell, *Confrontation at Ocean Hill–Brownsville: The New York School Strike of 1968* (New York: Praeger, 1969). For an assessment of school decentralization on a broader scope than New York, see George R. La Nove and Bruce L. R. Smith, *The Politics of School Decentralization* (Lexington, Mass.: Lexington Books, 1973).

62. This point is argued very persuasively by Joyce Gelb in "Black Power in Electoral Politics: A Case Study and Comparative Analysis," *Polity* 6, no. 4 (Summer 1974): 500–527, and "Blacks, Blocs, and Ballots: The Relevance of Party Politics to the Negro," *Polity* 3, no. 1 (Fall 1970): 44–69.

63. See G. James Fleming, *Baltimore's Failure to Elect a Black Mayor in 1971* (Washington, D.C.: Joint Center for Political Studies, 1972).

64. Peter Bachrach and Morton S. Baratz, *Power and Poverty: Theory and Practice* (New York: Oxford University Press, 1970), p. 97.

65. See Gelb, "Blacks, Blocs, and Ballots," p. 56.

66. See Robert Blauner, "Internal Colonialism and Ghetto Revolt," *Social Problems* 16, no. 4 (Spring 1969): 393–408.

67. This is suggested by several commentaries on Chicago. Michael Novak charges that Poles and Italians are grossly underrepresented in executive positions in Chicago. He also charges that there are fewer Polish and Italian college students than there are black college students. See Michael Novak, "The New Ethnicity," *The Center Magazine* 7, no. 4 (July–August 1974): 18–25. Studs Terkel's interview with Florence Scala, a leader of the unsuccessful movement to save the Hull House neighborhood from demolition, is a graphic example of the sense of powerlessness among whites. Studs Terkel, *Division Street: America* (New York: Avon Books, 1967), pp. 29–38. On Appalachian in-migrants into the city, see Todd Gitlin and Nanci Hollander, *Uptown: Poor Whites in Chicago* (New York: Harper & Row, 1970).

68. Edward C. Banfield, *The Unheavenly City* (Boston: Little, Brown, 1970).

69. This assessment of the community action programs is adapted from Howard W. Hallman, "Federally Financed Citizen Participation," *Public Administration Review* 32 (September 1972): 421–427.

70. See Susan R. Orden, "The Impact of Community Action Programs on Private Social Service Agencies," *Social Problems* 20, no. 3 (Winter 1973): 364–381.

71. This format is adapted from Eric Nordlinger, *Decentralizing the City: A Study of Boston's Little City Halls* (Cambridge, Mass.: M.I.T. Press, 1972), p. 9. This is not the only typology of community control proposals. For a short description and critique of several others, see Mario Fantini and Marilyn Gittell, *Decentralization: Achieving Reform* (New York: Praeger, 1973), pp. 127–133.

72. Peter K. Eisinger, "Control-Sharing in the City: Some Thoughts on Decentralization and Client Representation," *American Behavioral Scientist* 15, no. 1 (September–October 1971): 36–51.

73. For some samples of this criticism see Jonathan Kozol, *Death at an Early Age: The Destruction of the Hearts and Minds of Negro Children in the Boston Public Schools* (Boston: Houghton Mifflin, 1967); Bel Kaufman, *Up the Down Staircase* (Englewood Cliffs, N.J.: Prentice-Hall, 1964); Robert Coles, *Teachers and the Children of Poverty* (Washington, D.C.: Potomac Institute, 1970); Herbert Kohl, *36 Children* (New York: New American Library, 1967).

74. Fantini and Gittell, *Decentralization: Achieving Reform*, pp. 53–55.
75. Ibid., p. 48.
76. Ibid., pp. 53–55.
77. Most of this account of decentralization in Detroit is taken from William R. Grant, "Community Control v. School Integration in Detroit," *The Public Interest* 24 (Summer 1971): 62–79.
78. Fantini and Gittel, *Decentralization: Achieving Reform*, pp. 53–55.
79. National Advisory Commission on Civil Disorders, *Commission Report*, pp. 32–33.
80. George J. Washnis, *Municipal Decentralization and Neighborhood Resources: Case Studies of Twelve Cities* (New York: Praeger, 1973). The twelve cities studied are Los Angeles, San Antonio, Kansas City (Missouri), Chicago, Norfolk, New York, Atlanta, Houston, Boston, Baltimore, Columbus and San Francisco.
81. This account of Boston's little city halls is taken from Nordlinger, *Decentralizing the City*.
82. Ibid., p. 38.
83. Milton Kotler, *Neighborhood Government* (Indianapolis: Bobbs-Merrill, 1969).
84. York Willbern, "Unigov: Local Government Reorganization in Indianapolis," in Advisory Commission on Intergovernmental Relations, *Report A–41: Regional Governance Promise and Performance: Substate Regionalism and The Federal System* (Washington, D.C.: U.S. Government Printing Office, 1973), vol. II — Case Studies, pp. 66–67.
85. For an excellent critique of the arguments for and against community control by an author who is favorable to it, see Alan A. Altshuler, *Community Control: The Black Demand for Participation in Large American Cities* (New York: Pegasus, 1970). Also see George Frederickson, ed., *Neighborhood Control in the 1970's: Politics, Administration, and Citizen Participation* (New York: Chandler, 1973).
86. Nordlinger, *Decentralizing the City*, p. 27.
87. See Joseph F. Zimmerman, *The Federated City: Community Control in Large Cities* (New York: St. Martin's Press, 1972).
88. This argument is adapted from Nordlinger, *Decentralizing the City*.
89. See Lewis Lipsitz, "A Better System of Prisons? Thoughts on Decentralization and Participation in America," in *Neighborhood Control in the 1970's*, ed. George Frederickson, pp. 46–47.
90. Victor Jones, "Representative Local Government: From Neighborhood to Region," in *Neighborhood Control in the 1970's*, ed. George Frederickson, p. 75.

Chapter 6

1. See, for example, William H. Whyte, *The Organization Man* (Garden City, N.Y.: Doubleday, 1957); David Riesman, *The Lonely Crowd* (Garden City, N.Y.: Doubleday, 1956); John Keats, *The Crack in the Picture Window* (Boston: Houghton Mifflin, 1957). For an interesting and readable critique of the antisuburban literature, see Scott Donaldson, *The Suburban Myth* (New York: Columbia University Press, 1969).
2. Leo F. Schnore, "The Social and Economic Characteristics of American Suburbs," *The Sociological Quarterly* 4, no. 2 (Spring 1963): 122–134.
3. See Chapter 7.
4. Charles R. Adrian and Charles Press, *Governing Urban America*, 4th ed. (New York: McGraw-Hill, 1972), p. 42.
5. Robert C. Wood, *Suburbia: Its People and Their Politics* (Boston: Houghton Mifflin, 1958), p. 9.
6. For one example, see James A. Maxwell, "Kentucky's Open City," *The Saturday Evening Post*, March 26, 1960, p. 22.
7. See Chapter 5, especially note 2 and the text discussion to which it is related.
8. Reported in Bennett M. Berger, *Working Class Suburbs* (Berkeley and Los Angeles:

University of California Press, 1960), p. 23. Also see William Dobriner, *Class in Suburbia* (Englewood Cliffs, N.J.: Prentice-Hall, 1963).

9. Adrian and Press, *Governing Urban America*, p. 47.

10. Wood, *Suburbia*, p. 153.

11. Murray S. Stedman, Jr., *Urban Politics* (Cambridge, Mass.: Winthrop Publishers, 1972), p. 33.

12. Adrian and Press, *Governing Urban America*, p. 46.

13. Reynolds Farley, "The Changing Distribution of Negroes Within Metropolitan Areas: The Emergence of Black Suburbs." *American Journal of Sociology* 75, no. 4 (January 1970): 524–525.

14. Harold X. Connally, "Black Movement Into the Suburbs: Suburbs Doubling Their Black Population During the 1960's," *Urban Affairs Quarterly* 9, no. 1 (September 1973): 100.

15. Frances Frisken, "The Metropolis and the Central City: Can One Government Unite Them?" *Urban Affairs Quarterly* 8, no. 3 (June 1973): 395–422. On black suburbs generally, also see Frederick M. Wirt, Benjamin Walter, Francine F. Rabinovitz, and Deborah R. Hensler, *On the City's Rim: Politics and Policy in Suburbia* (Lexington, Mass.: D. C. Heath, 1972), chapter 4.

16. See Ernest W. Burgess, "Urban Areas," in *Chicago: An Experiment in Special Research*, ed. T. V. Smith and Leonard D. White (Chicago: University of Chicago Press, 1929), pp. 113–138. Also see John C. Bollens and Henry J. Schmandt, *The Metropolis: Its People, Politics, and Economic Life*, 2nd ed. (New York: Harper & Row, 1970), pp. 48–51.

17. See Homer Hoyt, "The Structure of American Cities in the Post-War Era," *American Journal of Sociology* 48 (January 1943): 476–477.

18. See Amos Hawley, *Human Ecology* (New York: Ronald Press, 1950), pp. 268–275.

19. See John Fine, Norval Glenn, and J. Kenneth Monts, "The Residential Segregation of Occupational Groups in Central Cities and Suburbs," *Demography* 8 (February 1971): 91–101. Using census tracts as their unit of analysis and using diversity in occupation as their measures of heterogeneity, Fine and his co-workers discovered that suburban neighborhoods were very heterogeneous occupationally. In seven out of the eight SMSAs studied, they found that the suburban census tracts were more heterogeneous than the central cities. Those data refer only to occupational heterogeneity, and different results might be obtained if heterogeneity were measured in median educational levels or median income.

20. Wirt, et al., *On the City's Rim*, pp. 32–33.

21. Fred I. Greenstein and Raymond E. Wolfinger, "The Suburbs and Shifting Party Loyalties," *The Public Opinion Quarterly* 22 (Winter 1958–59): 80–82.

22. Wood, *Suburbia*, pp. 141–149.

23. Herbert Hirsch, "Suburban Voting and National Trends: A Research Note," *Western Political Quarterly* 21 (September 1968): 508–514.

24. Angus Campbell, Philip E. Converse, Warren E. Miller, and Donald E. Stokes, *The American Voter* (New York: Wiley, 1960), p. 459.

25. Benjamin Walter and Frederick M. Wirt, "The Political Consequences of Suburban Variety," *Social Science Quarterly* 52, no. 3 (December 1971): 746.

26. John C. Bollens, et al., *Metropolitan Challenge* (Dayton, Ohio: Metropolitan Community Studies, Inc., 1959).

27. Thomas R. Dye, "City-Suburban Social Distance and Public Policy," *Social Forces* 44, no. 1 (September 1965): 100–106.

28. Joseph Zikmund, II, "A Comparison of Political Attitude and Activity Patterns in Central Cities and Suburbs," *Public Opinion Quarterly* 31, no. 1 (Spring 1967): 74.

29. Oliver P. Williams, Harold Herman, Charles S. Liebman, and Thomas R. Dye, *Suburban Differences and Metropolitan Politics: A Philadelphia Story* (Philadelphia: University of Pennsylvania Press, 1965), pp. 211–220.

30. Wirt, et al., *On the City's Rim*, p. 194.

31. Wood, *Suburbia*, pp. 178–180.

32. Ibid., pp. 180–182.
33. Wirt, et al., *On the City's Rim*, p. 173.
34. United States Bureau of the Census, *City Government Finances in 1968–69* (Washington, D.C.: U.S. Government Printing Office, 1970), p. 5.
35. This is the conclusion reached by Bryan T. Downes from his study of thirty-seven suburban councils in Saint Louis County, Missouri ["Issue Conflict Factionalism and Consensus in Suburban City Councils," *Urban Affairs Quarterly* 4 (June 1969): 477–495].
36. For two examples of this criticism, see Jonathan Kozol, *Death at an Early Age: The Destruction of the Hearts and Minds of Negro Children in the Boston Public Schools* (Boston: Houghton Mifflin, 1967), or Bel Kaufman, *Up the Down Staircase* (Englewood Cliffs, N.J.: Prentice-Hall, 1964). For an analysis of suburban school system politics, see David W. Minar, "Community Basis of Conflict in School System Politics." *American Sociological Review* 31 (December 1966): 822–835.
37. Wood, *Suburbia*, p. 14.
38. Kenneth T. Jackson, "Metropolitan Government Versus Suburban Autonomy: Politics on the Crabgrass Frontier," in *Cities in American History*, ed. Kenneth T. Jackson and Stanley K. Schultz (New York: Knopf, 1972), pp. 442–462.
39. Joseph F. Zimmerman, *The Federated City: Community Control in Large Cities* (New York: St. Martin's Press, 1972), pp. 12–13. Also see David C. Perry, "The Suburb as a Model for Neighborhood Control," in *Neighborhood Control in the 1970's*, ed. George Frederickson (New York: Chandler, 1973), pp. 85–99.
40. Wood, *Suburbia*, pp. 221–224.
41. See Wilbur R. Thompson, *A Preface to Urban Economics* (Baltimore: The Johns Hopkins Press, 1965), pp. 115–120.
42. Advisory Commission on Intergovernmental Relations, *Urban America and the Federal System* (Washington, D.C.: U.S. Government Printing Office, 1969), pp. 9–10.
43. Wirt, et al., *On the City's Rim*, pp. 202–204.
44. *Serrano v. Priest*, 5 Cal. 3d 584, 487, p. 2d 1241 (1971).
45. *Minneapolis Tribune*, January 18, 1975, pp. 1–A, 6–A.
46. Wood, *Suburbia*, pp. 178–180.
47. Raymond and May Associates, *Zoning Controversies in the Suburbs: Three Case Studies* (Washington, D.C.: U.S. Government Printing Office, 1968), p. 75. Research report no. 11 prepared for the consideration of the National Commission on Urban Problems.
48. Williams, et al., *Suburban Differences and Metropolitan Policies*, p. 294.
49. Stanley Scott and John Corzine, *Special Districts in the San Francisco Bay Area: Some Problems and Issues* (Berkeley, Calif.: The Institute of Governmental Studies, 1962).
50. Richard Child Hill, "Separate and Unequal: Governmental Inequality in the Metropolis," *The American Political Science Review* 68, no. 4 (December 1974): 1557–1568.
51. Samuel Kaplan, "The Balkanization of Suburbia," *Harper's*, October 1971, p. 73.
52. Examples of this viewpoint are to be found in Norton E. Long, *The Polity* (Chicago: Rand McNally, 1962); and in Vincent Ostrom, Charles M. Tiebout, and Robert Warren, "Organizing Government in Metropolitan Areas: A Theoretical Inquiry," *The American Political Science Review* 55 (December 1961): 831–842.

Chapter 7

1. Robert C. Wood, *Suburbia: Its People and Their Politics* (Boston: Houghton Mifflin, 1958), chapter 7 and pp. 232–241. On the concept of "gargantua," see Robert C. Wood, "The New Metropolis: Green Belts, Grass Roots or Gargantua," *The American Political Science Review* 52 (March 1958): 108–122. Also see his *1400 Governments: The Political Economy of the New York Metropolitan Region* (Cambridge, Mass.: Harvard University Press, 1961).

2. Scott Greer, *The Emerging City* (New York: The Free Press, 1962), pp. 141, 149.

3. Wood, *Suburbia*, pp. 282–285.

4. Advisory Commission on Intergovernmental Relations, *Urban America and the Federal System* (Washington, D.C.: U.S. Government Printing Office, 1969), pp. 82–83.

5. See Joseph F. Zimmerman, "Substate Regional Government: Designing a New Procedure," *National Civic Review* 61, no. 6 (June 1972): 286. Zimmerman writes that "Governmental irresponsibility exists in the typical substate region encompassing two or more counties. . . . A regional government is needed now in most metropolitan areas."

6. Luther Gulick, *The Metropolitan Problem and American Ideas* (New York: Knopf, 1962), p. 24.

7. Amos H. Hawley and Basil G. Zimmer, *The Metropolitan Community: Its People and Government* (Beverly Hills, Calif.: SAGE Publications, 1970), pp. 2–3.

8. Ibid., p. 3.

9. *Reshaping Government in Metropolitan Areas* (New York: Committee for Economic Development, 1970).

10. John C. Bollens, Henry Schmandt, et al., *Exploring the Metropolitan Community* (Berkeley: University of California Press, 1961), pp. 70–71. The surgical metaphor is Bollens's and Schmandt's.

11. Hawley and Zimmer, *The Metropolitan Community*, pp. 91–92.

12. Charles R. Adrian, "Metropology: Folklore and Field Research," *Public Administration Review* 21, no. 3 (Summer 1961): 148–157.

13. Ibid., p. 150.

14. Hawley and Zimmer, *The Metropolitan Community*, pp. 91–92.

15. Vincent Ostrom and Elinor Ostrom, "Public Choice: A Different Approach to the Study of Public Administration," *Public Administration Review* 31 (March 1971): 203–216.

16. Edward C. Banfield and Morton Grodzins, *Government and Housing in Metropolitan Areas* (New York: McGraw-Hill, 1958), p. 34.

17. Daniel R. Grant, "Metro's Three Faces," *National Civic Review* 55, no. 6 (June 1966): 317–324.

18. Hawley and Zimmer, *The Metropolitan Community*, pp. 95–96.

19. Adrian, "Metropology," p. 151.

20. Norton E. Long, "The Local Community as an Ecology of Games," *American Journal of Sociology* 64 (November 1958): 251–261. Also see his *The Polity* (Chicago: Rand McNally, 1962), pp. 156–164.

21. Banfield and Grodzins, *Government and Housing*, p. 42.

22. Frances Fox Piven and Richard A. Cloward, "What Chance for Black Power?" *The New Republic* 158, no. 13 (March 30, 1968): 23. For a contrary viewpoint, see Willis Hawley, *Blacks and Metropolitan Governance: The Stakes of Reform* (Berkeley: Institute of Governmental Studies, University of California, 1972). For a review article on the question, see Dale Rogers Marshall, "Metropolitan Government: Views of Minorities," in *Minority Perspectives: The Governance of Metropolitan Regions*, ed. Lowden Wingo (Baltimore: Johns Hopkins University Press, 1972), pp. 9–30. This question is examined in Chapter 9.

23. Banfield and Grodzins, *Government and Housing*, pp. 36–38.

24. Vincent Ostrom, Charles M. Tiebout, and Robert Warren, "Organizing Government in Metropolitan Areas: A Theoretical Inquiry," *The American Political Science Review* 55 (December 1961): 838, 842.

25. On the distinction between public and private goods, see Ostrom and Ostrom, "Public Choice: A Different Approach," pp. 206–207.

26. *Serrano v. Priest*, 5 Cal. 3d 584, 487 p. 2d 1241 (1971).

27. Matthew Holden, Jr., "The Governance of the Metropolis as a Problem in Diplomacy," *Journal of Politics* 26 (August 1964): 627–647. Also see Thomas R. Dye, "Metropolitan Integration by Bargaining Among Sub-Areas," *American Behavioral Scientist* 5 (May 1962): 11.

28. Wood, *Suburbia*, p. 84.

29. Norton E. Long, "The City as Reservation," *The Public Interest* 25 (Fall 1971): 32–33. Long's analogy of the city as a reservation was actually not made in reference to the federal role in urban affairs but in reference to a different aspect of urban politics.

30. See Chapter 11, pp. 321–324. Also see Advisory Commission on Intergovernmental Relations, Report *M–47: Urban America and the Federal System: Commission Findings and Proposals* (Washington, D.C.: U.S. Government Printing Office, 1969); Council of State Governments, *State Responsibility in Urban Regional Development: A Report to the Governors' Conference* (Chicago: Council of State Governments, 1962), pp. 16–22; *Modernizing State Government* (New York: Committee for Economic Development, 1967); *Modernizing Local Government* (New York: Committee for Economic Development, 1966); and *Reshaping Government in Metropolitan Areas* (New York: Committee for Economic Development, 1970).

31. See Chapter 11, pp. 322–323. Also see Michael C. Le May, "The States and Urban Areas: A Comparative Assessment," *National Civic Review* 61, no. 11 (December 1972): 542–548.

32. Advisory Commission on Intergovernmental Relations, *Urban America and the Federal System* (Washington, D.C.: U.S. Government Printing Office, 1969), pp. 12–13.

33. Carl Dale, city planner for White Bear Lake, Minnesota. Statement at a public meeting of the White Bear Lake Planning Commission, November 1972.

34. "Tax Estimates Based on Average Market Value of Homesteads," *Citizens League News*, February 28, 1971, Minneapolis, Minnesota, pp. 2–3.

35. Metropolitan Council, *Trends in New Housing: 1969–1971; Housing Report #5, December 1972* (Saint Paul: The Metropolitan Council, December 1972).

36. Advisory Commission on Intergovernmental Relations, *Urban America and the Federal System*, pp. 9–10.

37. Wood, *Suburbia*, pp. 198–258.

38. Robert O. Wood describes Los Angeles County as a producer of services in his *Government in Metropolitan Regions: A Reappraisal of Fractionated Political Organizations* (Davis, Calif.: Institute of Governmental Affairs, University of California, 1966), pp. 92–117.

39. Richard M. Cion, "Accommodation Par Excellence: The Lakewood Plan," in *Metropolitan Politics: A Reader*, 2nd ed., ed. Michael N. Danielson (Boston: Little, Brown, 1971), pp. 224–226.

40. Ibid., p. 230.

41. Richard M. Cion, "Accommodation Par Excellence: The Lakewood Plan," pp. 230–231.

42. Advisory Commission on Intergovernmental Relations, Report *A–44: Substate Regionalism and the Federal System: The Challenge of Local Governmental Reorganization* (Washington, D.C.: U.S. Government Printing Office, 1974), vol. III, pp. 67–68.

43. See Advisory Commission on Intergovernmental Relations, Report *A–43. Substate Regionalism and the Federal System. Regional Decision Making: New Strategies for Substate Districts* (Washington, D.C.: U.S. Government Printing Office, 1973), vol. I, chapter 2, "Special Districts and Authorities," pp. 19–48, especially p. 26.

44. See ibid., pp. 21–22, for a summary of federal programs stimulating the formation of special districts. For an excellent outline of the reasons for creating special districts, see Advisory Commission on Intergovernmental Relations, Report *A–22: The Problem of Special Districts in America* (Washington, D.C.: U.S. Government Printing Office, 1964).

45. Stanley Scott and John Corzine, *Special Districts in the San Francisco Bay Area: Some Problems and Issues* (Berkeley, Calif.: The Institute of Governmental Studies, October 1962).

46. Ibid., pp. 16–18.

47. Advisory Commission on Intergovernmental Relations, Report *A–43: Regional Decision Making*, vol. I, p. 35.

48. Jameson W. Doig, *Metropolitan Transportation Politics* (New York: Columbia Uni-

versity Press, 1966), pp. 217–220. On 1973 operating expenditures, see the *National Civic Review* 62, no. 3 (March 1973): 153.

49. For a discussion of the constituent unit idea of representation on metropolitan districts, see Arthur W. Bromage, *Political Representation in Metropolitan Agencies* (Ann Arbor: University of Michigan Institute of Public Administration, 1962).

50. Advisory Commission on Intergovernmental Relations, *Report A–43: Regional Decision Making*, vol. I, p. 36.

51. Stuart A. MacCorkle, *Municipal Annexation in Texas* (Austin: Institute of Public Affairs, University of Texas, 1965), pp. 28–36.

52. Oliver P. Williams, *Metropolitan Political Analysis* (New York: The Free Press, 1971), pp. 86–93.

Chapter 8

1. Advisory Commission on Intergovernmental Relations, *Report A–44: Substate Regionalism and the Federal System. Volume III, The Challenge of Local Government* (Washington, D.C.: U.S. Government Printing Office, 1974), p. 77.

2. *Modernizing Local Government: To Secure a Balanced Federalism* (New York: Committee for Economic Development, 1966), p. 45.

3. The precise number depends upon what is counted as a consolidation attempt and what date one uses as the cutoff date. Sources are Joseph F. Zimmerman, "Metropolitan Reform in the U.S.: An Overview," *Public Administration Review* 30, no. 5 (September–October 1970): 531–543; and Advisory Commission on Intergovernmental Relations, *Factors Affecting Voter Reactions to Governmental Reorganizations in Metropolitan Areas* (Washington, D.C.: U.S. Government Printing Office, 1962), p. 71.

4. Daniel R. Grant, "Urban and Suburban Nashville: A Case Study in Metropolitanism," *The Journal of Politics* 17 (February 1965): 85. Also on the background to Nashville, see Brett W. Hawkins, *Nashville Metro: The Politics of City-County Consolidation* (Nashville, Tenn.: Vanderbilt University Press, 1966); and David A. Booth, *Metropolitics: The Nashville Consolidation* (East Lansing: Institute for Community Development and Services, Michigan State University, 1963).

5. William C. Havard, Jr., and Floyd C. Corty, *Rural-Urban Consolidation: The Merger of Governments in the Baton Rouge Area* (Baton Rouge: Louisiana State University Press, 1964), pp. 146–147.

6. Melvin B. Mogulof, *Five Metropolitan Governments* (Washington, D.C.: The Urban Institute, 1973), p. 22.

7. This point is made by R. Steven Hill and William P. Maxam in their article, "Unigov: The First Year," *National Civic Review*, June 1971, pp. 310–314, especially p. 310. Also see York Willbern, "Unigov: Local Government Reorganization in Indianapolis," in Advisory Commission on Intergovernmental Relations, *Report A–41: Substate Regionalism and the Federal System. Volume II, Regional Governance: Promise and Performance — Case Studies* (Washington, D.C.: U.S. Government Printing Office, 1973), pp. 49–51.

8. Duane Lockard, *The Politics of State and Local Government*, 2nd ed. (New York: Macmillan, 1969), p. 93. In 1974 a new Louisiana Constitution was adopted. It may end up with fewer amendments than the previous Constitution.

9. John M. De Grove, "The City of Jacksonville: Consolidation in Action," in Advisory Commission on Intergovernmental Relations, *Report A–41: Volume II, Regional Governance: Promise and Performance — Case Studies*, pp. 19–20.

10. Daniel R. Grant, "Metropolitics and Professional Political Leadership: The Case of Nashville," *Annals of the American Academy of Political and Social Science* 353 (May 1964): 78.

11. Scott Greer, *Metropolitics: A Study of Political Culture* (New York: Wiley, 1963), pp. 7–18.

12. De Grove, "The City of Jacksonville," p. 20.
13. Zimmerman, "Metropolitan Reform," p. 533.
14. Willbern, "Unigov," p. 63.
15. Robert E. McArthur, "The Metropolitan Government of Nashville and Davidson County," in Advisory Commission on Intergovernmental Relations, *Report A–41: Volume II, Regional Governance: Promise and Performance — Case Studies,* pp. 26–35, especially pp. 29–30.
16. Mogulof, *Five Metropolitan Governments,* p. 46. De Grove, "The City of Jacksonville," p. 20.
17. Willbern, "Unigov," pp. 61–62.
18. See Grant's "Metro's Three Faces."
19. Willbern, "Unigov," p. 70.
20. Grant, "Metro's Three Faces," p. 322. Also see McArthur, "The Metropolitan Government of Nashville," pp. 31–32.
21. Mogulof, *Five Metropolitan Governments,* p. 138.
22. Advisory Commission on Intergovernmental Relations, *Report M–72: Profile of County Government: An Information Report* (Washington, D.C.: U.S. Government Printing Office, 1972), p. 13. Later references to the percentage of counties using the county manager, county administrator, and county executive forms of government are also taken from this source.
23. On the weaknesses of traditional county government and proposals for reform, see Advisory Commission on Intergovernmental Relations, *Report M–61: For a More Perfect Union: County Reform* (Washington, D.C.: U.S. Government Printing Office, 1971). The discussion that follows in the text is taken principally from this source.
24. *Reshaping Government in Metropolitan Areas,* pp. 16–18.
25. Morton Grodzins, "The Federal System," in the President's Commission on National Goals, *Goals for Americans* (Englewood Cliffs, N.J.: A Spectrum Book, 1960), p. 265.
26. See Advisory Commission on Intergovernmental Relations, *Report A–44: Volume III, The Challenge of Local Government Reorganization,* p. 26.
27. *Reshaping Government in Metropolitan Areas* (New York: Committee for Economic Development, 1970), p. 45.
28. The most sophisticated attempt to date to make such apportionment of functions has been that of the Advisory Commission on Intergovernmental Relations. See its *Report A–45: Substate Regionalism and the Federal System. Volume IV, Governmental Functions and Processes: Local and Areawide* (Washington, D.C.: U.S. Government Printing Office, 1974), especially chapters IV, V, and VI.
29. Quoted in Mogulof, *Five Metropolitan Governments,* p. 64.
30. D. B. S. Paul, "Metropolitan Dade County Government: A Review of Accomplishments," from an address presented to the Local Government Law Section, American Bar Association, Miami Beach, Florida, August 8, 1965. The printed text can be found in Joseph F. Zimmerman, *Government of the Metropolis: Selected Readings* (New York: Holt, Rinehart and Winston, 1968), pp. 202–203.
31. Quoted in Edward Sofen, *The Miami Metropolitan Experiment* (Bloomington: Indiana University Press, 1963), p. 72.
32. Aileen Lotz, "Metropolitan Dade County," in Advisory Commission on Intergovernmental Relations, *Report A–41: Volume II, Regional Governance: Promise and Performance,* p. 7.
33. Oliver P. Williams, *Metropolitan Political Analysis: A Social Access Approach* (New York: The Free Press, 1971), pp. 86–93.
34. Grant, "Metro's Three Faces," p. 407.
35. See Thomas J. Wood, "Dade County Voters Reject Amendment," *National Civic Review* 61, no. 5 (May 1972): 254–255.
36. Irving G. McNayr, "A Report to the Chairman and the Members of the Board of County Commissioners," September 25, 1962. The printed text of this report can be found in Joseph F. Zimmerman, *Government of the Metropolis,* p. 199.
37. Lotz, "Metropolitan Dade County," p. 10.

38. Mogulof, *Five Metropolitan Governments*, pp. 48–49.
39. John C. Bollens and Henry J. Schmandt, *The Metropolis: Its People, Politics, and Economic Life*, 2nd ed. (New York: Harper & Row, 1970), p. 335.
40. For a positive assessment of Miami's Metro, see Lotz, "Metropolitan Dade County," p. 10. A less complimentary assessment is given in Mogulof, *Five Metropolitan Governments*, pp. 47–48, 59.
41. The following account relies heavily on *Reshaping Government in Metropolitan Areas*, pp. 70–83, and Frank Smallwood, *Metro Toronto a Decade Later* (Toronto: Bureau of Municipal Research, 1963). For another analysis of the Toronto experiment, see Harold Kaplan, *Urban Political Systems: A Functional Analysis of Metro Toronto* (New York: Columbia University Press, 1967).
42. Grant, "Metro's Three Faces," p. 403.
43. Frank Smallwood, *Metro Toronto*, pp. 31–33.
44. Lee Sloan and Robert M. French, "Black Rule in the Urban South?" *TRANS-action*, November/December 1971, pp. 29–34.
45. Advisory Commission on Intergovernmental Relations, *Report A–44: Volume III, The Challenge of Local Governmental Reorganization*, p. 102.
46. Hawkins, "Nashville Metro: The Politics of City-County Consolidation," pp. 132–133.
47. Grant, "Metro's Three Faces," p. 403.
48. Daniel R. Grant, "A Comparison of Predictions and Experiences with Nashville 'Metro,' " *Urban Affairs Quarterly* 1, no. 1 (September 1965): 34–54, especially 51–53.
49. Willbern, "Unigov," pp. 71–72.
50. Vincent L. Marando and Carl Reggie Whitley, "City-County Consolidation: An Overview of Voter Response," *Urban Affairs Quarterly* 8, no. 2 (December 1972): 181–204, especially 190.
51. Joan Carver, "Responsiveness and Consolidation: A Case Study," *Urban Affairs Quarterly* 9, no. 2 (December 1973): 246.
52. Willbern, "Unigov," p. 63.
53. De Grove, "The City of Jacksonville," p. 24.
54. Mogulof, *Five Metropolitan Governments*, p. 117.
55. De Grove, "The City of Jacksonville," p. 24.
56. See Willis Hawley, *Blacks and Metropolitan Governance: The Stakes of Reform* (Berkeley: Institute of Governmental Studies, University of California, 1972).
57. Mogulof, *Five Metropolitan Governments*, p. 119.
58. Steven P. Erie, John J. Kirlin, and Francine F. Rabinovitz, "Can Something Be Done? Propositions on the Performance of Metropolitan Institutions," in *Reform of Metropolitan Governments*, ed. Lowdon Wingo (Washington, D.C.: Resources for the Future, 1972), p. 24.
59. Ibid., p. 24.
60. Ibid.
61. Carver, "Responsiveness and Consolidation," p. 243.
62. Williams, *Metropolitan Political Analysis*, pp. 86–93.

Chapter 9

1. Robert H. Salisbury, "Interests, Parties, and Governmental Structures in St. Louis," *The Western Political Quarterly* 13, no. 2 (June 1960): 500–501.
2. Edward C. Banfield, *Big City Politics* (New York: Random House, 1965), p. 124.
3. Ibid., p. 123.
4. Ibid., p. 121.
5. Henry J. Schmandt, P. G. Steinbicker, and G. D. Wendel, *Metropolitan Reform in St. Louis* (New York: Holt, Rinehart and Winston, 1961), p. 3.

6. Scott Greer, *Metropolitics: A Study of Political Culture* (New York: Wiley, 1963), p. 38.

7. Schmandt, et al., *Metropolitan Reform in St. Louis*, p. 5.

8. Ibid., p. 14.

9. Ibid., p. 59.

10. Ibid., p. 59.

11. James A. Norton, *The Metro Experience* (Cleveland: The Press of Western Reserve University, 1963).

12. Greer, *Metropolitics*, p. 9.

13. Ibid., p. 14.

14. Estal E. Sparlin, "Cleveland Seeks New Metro Solution," *National Civic Review* 69, no. 3 (March 1960): 143.

15. Greer, *Metropolitics*, p. 16.

16. Schmandt, et al., *Metropolitan Reform in St. Louis*, p. 63.

17. Norton, *The Metro Experience*, p. 61.

18. Schmandt, et al., *Metropolitan Reform in St. Louis*, p. 64.

19. Richard A. Watson and John H. Romani, "Metropolitan Government for Metropolitan Cleveland: An Analysis of the Voting Record," *Midwest Journal of Political Science* 5, no. 4 (November 1961): 365–390.

20. Ibid., p. 376. The same point is made by Tobe Johnson in his *Metropolitan Government: A Black Analytical Perspective* (Washington, D.C.: Joint Center for Political Studies, 1972).

21. Amos H. Hawley and Basil G. Zimmer, "Resistance to Unification in a Metropolitan Community," in *Community Political Systems*, ed. Morris Janowitz (Glencoe, Ill.: The Free Press, 1961), pp. 164–167. A similar result was discovered from a survey in Dayton, Ohio; see John C. Bollens, et al., *Metropolitan Challenge* (Dayton, Ohio: Metropolitan Community Studies Inc., 1959), p. 241.

22. Brett W. Hawkins, *Nashville Metro: The Politics of City-County Consolidation* (Nashville, Tenn.: Vanderbilt University Press, 1966), pp. 110–113.

23. Edward Sofen, *The Miami Metropolitan Experiment* (Bloomington: Indiana University Press, 1963), pp. 67–68.

24. Ibid., pp. 74–75.

25. Edward C. Banfield, "The Politics of Metropolitan Organization," *Midwest Journal of Political Science* 1, no. 1 (May 1957): 77–91.

26. Sofen, *The Miami Metropolitan Experiment*, pp. 76–77.

27. Advisory Commission on Intergovernmental Relations, *Factors Affecting Voter Reactions to Government Reorganization in Metropolitan Areas* (Washington, D.C.: U.S. Government Printing Office, 1962), pp. 69–80.

28. John C. Bollens and Henry J. Schmandt, *The Metropolis: Its People, Politics, and Economic Life*, 2nd ed. (New York: Harper & Row, 1970), pp. 378, 306–307.

29. "Metropolitan Council Biennial Report, 1971–72, to the Minnesota Legislature" (Saint Paul, Minn.: The Metropolitan Council), pp. 26–43.

30. On the creation of the Metropolitan Council, see John Fischer, "The Minnesota Experiment: How to Make a Big City Fit to Live In," *Harper's* 238, no. 1427 (April 1969): 12–32. The most thorough analysis of the Twin Cities model is Stanley Baldinger, *Planning and Governing the Metropolis: The Twin Cities Experience* (New York: Praeger, 1971).

31. Melvin B. Mogulof, *Governing Metropolitan Areas* (Washington, D.C.: The Urban Institute, 1971), p. 82.

32. Baldinger, *Planning and Governing the Metropolis: The Twin Cities Experience*, pp. 120–123, 124.

33. This question is examined extensively by Thomas M. Scott in his article, "Metropolitan Government Reorganization Proposals," *Western Political Quarterly* 21, no. 2 (June 1968): 489, 498–507.

34. See especially the discussion in Chapter 7 about Charles Adrian's analysis of the attitudes of the metropolitan reformers.

35. Melvin B. Mogulof, *Five Metropolitan Governments* (Washington, D.C.: The Urban Institute, 1973), p. 139.
36. See *The Federalist Papers*, ed. Clinton Rossiter (New York: New American Library, 1961), No. 10, by James Madison, pp. 77–84.

Chapter 10

1. Oliver P. Williams, *Metropolitan Political Analysis* (New York: The Free Press, 1971), p. 93.
2. This has been noted above. For Miami, see Edward Sofen, *The Miami Metropolitan Experiment* (Bloomington: Indiana University Press, 1963). For Toronto, see Frank Smallwood, *Toronto: The Problems of Metropolitan Unity* (Toronto: Bureau of Municipal Research, 1963).
3. H. Paul Friesema, "Cities, Suburbs, and Short-Lived Models of Metropolitan Politics," in Louis H. Masotti and Jeffrey K. Hadden, eds., *The Urbanization of the Suburbs*, vol. VII of *Urban Affairs Annual Reviews* (Beverly Hills, Calif.: SAGE Publications, 1973), p. 242.
4. Ibid.
5. For a summary of the stages of planning discussed here, see Thad L. Beyle and George T. Lathrop, "Planning and Politics: On Grounds of Incompatibility?" in Thad L. Beyle and George T. Lathrop, eds., *Planning and Politics: Uneasy Partnership* (New York: Odyssey Press, 1970), pp. 3–5.
6. For a detailed discussion of the Chicago and Boston plans and their relation to the City Beautiful and the City Functional movements, see Mel Scott, *American City Planning Since 1890* (Berkeley: University of California Press, 1971), chapters 2 and 3.
7. See Alan Altshuler, "Decision-making and the Trend Toward Pluralistic Planning," in Ernest Erber, *Urban Planning in Transition* (New York: Grossman, 1970), pp. 183–186.
8. See pp. 282–283.
9. Francine Rabinovitz, *City Politics and Planning* (New York: Atherton Press, 1969), pp. 8–9.
10. Deil S. Wright, "Governmental Forms and Planning Functions: The Relation of Organizational Structures to Planning Practice," in Beyle and Lathrop, eds., *Planning and Politics: Uneasy Partnership*, pp. 68–105. esp. p. 69.
11. Rabinovitz, *City Politics and Planning*, pp. 9–11.
12. Wright, "Governmental Forms and Planning Functions," p. 73.
13. Scott, *American City Planning Since 1890*, pp. 541–547.
14. Wright, "Governmental Forms and Planning Functions," p. 87. Wright's study of 300 city planners found that two-thirds of them defined planning in physical or economic terms. Only a third defined planning in terms of what the author called people's human needs.
15. John C. Bollens and Henry J. Schmandt, *The Metropolis: Its People, Politics, and Economic Life*, 2nd ed. (New York: Harper & Row, 1970), p. 274.
16. Rabinovitz, *City Politics and Planning*, pp. 3, 132–133.
17. Scott, *American City Planning Since 1890*, pp. 507–508.
18. See Herbert Gans, *The Levittowners: Ways of Life and Politics in a New Suburban Community* (New York: Random House, 1967), especially chapters 1, "The Planners of Levittown," and 14, "Politics and Planning."
19. Ibid., pp. 386, 17, and 18.
20. See Jane Jacobs, *The Death and Life of Great American Cities* (New York: Vintage Books, 1961).
21. Wright, "Governmental Forms and Planning Functions," p. 79.
22. The New York Regional Plan of 1929 is discussed by Scott, *American City Planning Since 1890*, pp. 260–265, 447–448.

23. William H. Nash, Jr., "The Effectiveness of Metropolitan Planning," a paper presented to the Metropolitan Area Planning Council of the Commonwealth of Massachusetts, June 18, 1965. The text of a revised edition can be found in H. Wentworth Eldredge, ed., *Taming Megalopolis: Vol. II, How to Manage an Urbanized World* (Garden City, N.Y.: Doubleday, 1967), pp. 699–700.

24. Quoted in Terrance Sandalow, "Federal Grants and the Reform of State and Local Governments," in John P. Crecine, ed., *Financing the Metropolis: Public Policy in Urban Economics*, vol. IV of *Urban Affairs Annual Reviews* (Beverly Hills, Calif.: SAGE Publications, 1970), p. 182.

25. Scott, *American City Planning Since 1890*, pp. 513–518.

26. Ibid.

27. David C. Ranney, *Planning and Politics in the Metropolis* (Columbus, Ohio: Merrill, 1969), p. 104.

28. John Friedmann, "The Future of Comprehensive Urban Planning: A Critique," *Public Administration Review* 31, no. 3 (May/June 1971): 317.

29. Edward C. Banfield, "The Uses and Limitations of Metropolitan Planning in Massachusetts," a paper presented to the Metropolitan Area Planning Council of the Commonwealth of Massachusetts, June 18, 1965. The text can be found in Eldredge, ed., *Taming Megalopolis: Vol. II, How to Manage an Urbanized World*, pp. 712–714.

30. This charge is made of the Cleveland COG by Frances Frisken, "The Metropolis and the Central City: Can One Government Unite Them?" *Urban Affairs Quarterly* 8, no. 3 (June 1973): 395–422.

31. Rabinovitz, *City Politics and Planning*, p. 7.

32. Ranney, *Planning and Politics in the Metropolis*, pp. 104–107.

33. F. Stuart Chapin, Jr., *Urban Land Use Planning*, 2nd ed. (Urbana: University of Illinois Press, 1965), pp. 60–62.

34. Rabinovitz, *City Politics and Planning*, pp. 154–157.

35. Ranney, *Planning and Politics in the Metropolis*, p. 155.

36. For an excellent discussion of citizen involvement in freeway controversies, see Alan Lupo, Frank Colcord, and Edmund P. Fowler, *Rites of Way: The Politics of Transportation in Boston and the U.S. City* (Boston: Little, Brown, 1971).

37. There are many excellent descriptions of the battles over urban renewal and urban renovation. One of the most highly readable, interesting descriptions of a resident's frustrations in fighting the destruction of the old Hull House neighborhood in Chicago is contained in Studs Terkel's interview with Florence Scala in Studs Terkel, *Division Street: America* (New York: Avon Books, 1967), pp. 29–38. The battle over the expansion of the University of Chicago into the Hyde Park–Kenwood section is analyzed by Peter H. Rossi and Robert A. Dentler, *The Politics of Urban Renewal: The Chicago Findings* (New York: The Free Press, 1961).

38. Thomas M. Scott, "Suburban Governmental Structures," in Louis H. Masotti and Jeffrey K. Hadden, eds., *The Urbanization of the Suburbs*, vol. VII of *Urban Affairs Annual Reviews* (Beverly Hills, Calif.: SAGE Publications, 1973), p. 236.

39. See Paul Davidoff, "Advocacy and Pluralism in Planning," *Journal of the American Institute of Planners* 31, no. 4 (November 1965): 331–338.

40. Herbert Gans, *People and Plans: Essays on Urban Problems and Solutions* (New York: Basic Books, 1968), pp. 72–74.

41. See Lupo, Colcord, and Fowler, *Rites of Way*.

42. See Jewell Bellush and Murray Hausknecht, eds., *Urban Renewal: People, Politics and Planning* (Garden City, N.Y.: Doubleday, 1969).

43. Thad L. Beyle and George T. Lathrop, "Planning and Politics: On Grounds of Incompatibility?" p. 9.

44. Ibid.

45. Gans, *People and Plans*, pp. 72–74.

46. See Alan S. Kravitz, "Mandarinism: Planning as Handmaiden to Conservative Politics," in Beyle and Lathrop, eds., *Planning and Politics: Uneasy Partnership*, pp. 240–267. Also see Robert Goodman, *After the Planners* (New York: Simon & Schuster, 1971), pp. 171–175.

47. John W. Dyckman, "Social Planning in the American Democracy," in Ernest Erber, ed., *Urban Planning in Transition* (New York: Grossman, 1970), pp. 27–44, especially p. 28.
48. This account of the Washington Metropolitan Council of Governments is taken principally from Roscoe C. Martin, *Metropolis in Transition* (Washington, D.C.: U.S. Housing and Home Finance Agency, 1964), pp. 39–50.
49. Melvin B. Mogulof, *Governing Metropolitan Areas* (Washington, D.C.: The Urban Institute, 1971), p. 1.
50. Royce Hanson, *Metropolitan Councils of Government,* a report for the Advisory Commission on Intergovernmental Relations (Washington, D.C.: U.S. Government Printing Office, 1966), p. 27.
51. Alan Edward Bent, *Escape from Anarchy: A Strategy for Urban Survival* (Memphis, Tenn.: Memphis State University Press, 1972), p. 85.
52. Hanson, *Metropolitan Councils of Government,* p. 34.
53. Victor Jones, "Bay Area Regionalism: Institutions, Processes, and Programs," in Advisory Commission on Intergovernmental Relations, *Report A–41: Substate Regionalism and the Federal System. Regional Governance: Promise and Performance* (Washington, D.C.: U.S. Government Printing Office, 1973), pp. 75–110.
54. See Frisken, "The Metropolis and the Central City."
55. Philip W. Barnes, *Metropolitan Coalitions: A Study of Councils of Government in Texas* (Austin: Institute of Public Affairs, University of Texas, 1969), p. 67.
56. Mogulof, *Governing Metropolitan Areas,* p. 15.
57. Demonstration Cities and Metropolitan Development Act of 1966, Section 204. Quoted in Barnes, *Metropolitan Coalitions,* p. 14. However, the I.C.A. of 1968 did grant review authority for social issues.
58. Frisken, "The Metropolis and the Central City," p. 399.
59. This account of NOACA is taken from Friskin, "The Metropolis and the Central City."
60. Barnes, *Metropolitan Coalitions,* pp. 3–4.

Chapter 11

1. United States Office of Management and Budget, *Special Analyses: Budget of the United States Government, Fiscal Year 1975* (Washington, D.C.: U.S. Government Printing Office, 1974), p. 210. FY 1973 grants-in-aid equaled 23.5 percent of state and local budgets. In FY 1961 they equaled 12.6 percent.
2. Criticisms of grants-in-aid as not enabling states to establish their own priorities can be found in many textbooks on state and local government. See Thomas R. Dye, *Politics in States and Communities* (Englewood Cliffs, N.J.: Prentice-Hall, 1969), pp. 471–472; Duane Lockard, *The Politics of State and Local Government,* 2nd ed. (New York: Macmillan, 1969), pp. 36–42.
3. For critiques of the welfare system see Gilbert Y. Steiner, *The State of Welfare* (Washington, D.C.: The Brookings Institution, 1971); Frances Fox Piven and Richard A. Cloward, *Regulating the Poor: The Functions of Public Welfare* (New York: Pantheon, 1971); and Daniel Patrick Moynihan, *The Politics of a Guaranteed Income: The Nixon Administration and the Family Assistance Plan* (New York: Random House, 1973), especially chapter 2.
4. Jeanne Lowe, *Cities in a Race With Time: Progress and Poverty in America's Renewing Cities* (New York: Randon House, 1968), pp. 232–233.
5. Daniel P. Moynihan, *Maximum Feasible Misunderstanding: Community Action in the War on Poverty* (New York: The Free Press, 1969).
6. See Edward C. Banfield, "Making a New Federal Program: Model Cities, 1964–1968," in *Policy and Politics in America: Six Case Studies,* ed. Allan P. Sindler (Boston: Little, Brown, 1973), pp. 124–169.
7. Martha Derthick, *New Towns in Town: Why a Federal Program Failed* (Washington, D.C.: The Urban Institute, 1972).

8. Daniel P. Moynihan, "Toward a National Urban Policy," *The Public Interest* 17 (Fall 1969): 7.

9. James L. Sundquist, *Making Federalism Work: A Study of Program Coordination at the Community Level* (Washington, D.C.: The Brookings Institution, 1969), p. 279.

10. Ibid., pp. 3–5.

11. The most graphic analysis of problems with federal highway planning is contained in Alan Lupo, Frank Colcord, and Edmund P. Fowler, *Rites of Way: The Politics of Transportation in Boston and the U.S. City* (Boston: Little, Brown, 1971).

12. Ibid.

13. *Citizens to Preserve Overton Park, Inc.*, v. *Volpe*, 401 U.S., 402 (1971).

14. For a concise background on early public housing programs, see Jewell Bellush and Murray Hausknecht, "Urban Renewal: An Historical Overview," in Jewell Bellush and Murray Hausknecht, eds., *Urban Renewal: People, Politics and Planning* (Garden City, N.Y.: Doubleday, 1967), pp. 3–16.

15. A concise summary of the operating procedures of the public housing programs under the Public Housing Administration is provided by Roscoe C. Martin, *The Cities and the Federal System* (New York: Atherton Press, 1965), pp. 128–132.

16. Lowe, *Cities in a Race With Time*, pp. 232–233.

17. Theodore Lowi, *The End of Liberalism: Ideology, Policy and the Crisis of Public Authority* (New York: Norton, 1969), pp. 251–266.

18. Robert L. Lineberry and Ira Sharkansky, *Urban Politics and Public Policy* (New York: Harper & Row, 1971), p. 336.

19. Ibid. p. 337. On redevelopment in Newark, see Harold Kaplan, *Urban Renewal Politics* (New York: Columbia University Press, 1963).

20. Lowe, *Cities in a Race With Time*, pp. 68–72.

21. Lowi, *The End of Liberalism*, pp. 251–266.

22. See Jane Jacobs, *The Death and Life of Great American Cities* (New York: Vintage Books, 1961).

23. See, for example, Harrison Salisbury's description of the Fort Greene project in Brooklyn, *The Shook-Up Generation* (New York: Harper and Brothers, 1958), pp. 73–88.

24. For background on the Pruitt-Igoe housing project, see Nicholas J. Demerath, "St. Louis Public Housing Study Sets Off Community Development to Meet Social Needs," *Journal of Housing* 19 (October 15, 1962): 472–478. For information on the demise of Pruitt-Igoe, see Jane Holtz Kay, "Architecture" *Nation* 217 (September 24, 1973): 284–286, and G. McCue, "$57,000,000 Later: New Effort to Put Pruitt-Igoe Together Again," *Architectural Forum* 138 (May 1973): 42–45.

25. See Chester W. Hartman, "A Rejoinder: Omissions in Evaluating Relocation Effectiveness Cited," *Journal of Housing* 23, no. 2 (February 1966): 88–89. Also see Herbert Gans, "The Failure of Urban Renewal: A Critique and Some Proposals," *Commentary* April 1965, pp. 29–37.

26. Jewell Bellush and Murray Hausknecht, "Public Housing: The Contexts of Failure," in Bellush and Hausknecht, eds., *Urban Renewal*, p. 456.

27. Jewell Bellush and Murray Hausknecht, "Public Housing: It Was Meant to Fail," in Bellush and Hausknecht, eds., *Urban Renewal*, pp. 413–414.

28. Douglas M. Fox, "Federal Urban Policies Since 1945," in Douglas M. Fox, ed., *The New Urban Politics: Cities and the Federal Government* (Pacific Palisades, Calif.: Goodyear Publishing Co., 1972), pp. 96–97.

29. Implementing the principle of compensatory education, however, proved very difficult. See Jerome T. Murphy, "The Education Bureaucracies Implement Novel Policy: The Politics of Title I of ESEA, 1965–1972," in Sindler, *Policy and Politics in America* (Boston: Little, Brown, 1973), pp. 160–198. Also see Stephen K. Bailey and Edith K. Mosher, *ESEA: The Office of Education Administers a Law* (Syracuse, N.Y.: Syracuse University Press, 1968).

30. Suzanne Farkas, *Urban Lobbying* (New York: New York University Press, 1971), p. 60.

31. For a discussion of urban militant movements see Norman I. Fainstein and Susan S. Fainstein, *Urban Political Movements: The Search for Power by Minority Groups in American Cities* (Englewood Cliffs, N.J.; Prentice-Hall, 1974).
32. Sundquist, *Making Federalism Work*, pp. 3–5.
33. This account of the creation of the model cities program relies heavily on Banfield, "Making a New Federal Program," pp. 124–169.
34. Ibid., p. 125.
35. Ibid., p. 129.
36. Ibid., p. 148.
37. Sundquist, *Making Federalism Work*, pp. 117–119.
38. Marshall Kaplan, *Urban Planning in the 1960's: A Design for Irrelevancy* (New York: Praeger, 1973), pp. 110–111.
39. See Chapter 10, pp. 288, 290.
40. On multi-jurisdictional councils, see Norman Beckman, "Federal Policy for Metropolitan Governance," *National Civic Review* 63, no. 3 (March 1974): 128–132.
41. See Melvin B. Mogulof, *Federal Regional Councils: Their Current Experience and Recommendations for Further Development* (Washington, D.C.: The Urban Institute, 1970).
42. Michael Reagan, *The New Federalism* (New York: Oxford University Press, 1972), p. 84.
43. Michael N. Danielson, *Federal-Metropolitan Politics and the Commuter Crisis* (New York: Columbia University Press, 1965), p. 189.
44. Roscoe C. Martin, *The Cities and the Federal System* (New York: Atherton Press, 1965), p. 146.
45. Robert C. Wood, *The Federal Government and the Cities*, pp. 52–54.
46. Reagan, *The New Federalism*, pp. 87–88.
47. See Daniel P. Moynihan, *The Politics of a Guaranteed Income: The Nixon Administration and the Family Assistance Plan* (New York: Vintage Books, 1972).
48. Advisory Commission on Intergovernmental Relations, *State-Local Finance: Significant Features and Suggested Legislation* (Washington, D.C.: U.S. Government Printing Office, 1972), table 7, pp. 23–24.
49. Ibid., figure 3, p. 25.
50. Reagan, *The New Federalism*, pp. 130–131.
51. Ibid., pp. 130–131.
52. Norman Beckman, "Federal Policy for Metropolitan Governance," *National Civic Review* 63, no. 3 (March 1974): 128–132.
53. Ibid.; and Reagan, *The New Federalism*, pp. 130–132.
54. Moynihan, "Toward a National Urban Policy," p. 6.
55. Robert C. Wood, *The Federal Government and the Cities* (Washington, D.C.: George Washington University Press, 1961), pp. 52–54.
56. Daniel J. Elazar, *The American Partnership* (Chicago: University of Chicago Press, 1962), p. 20.
57. Morton Grodzins, "The Federal System," in the President's Commission on National Goals, *Goals for Americans* (New York: Prentice-Hall, 1960), pp. 265–282.
58. Reagan, *The New Federalism*, pp. 145–168.
59. Sundquist, *Making Federalism Work*, pp. 27–31.
60. Advisory Commission on Intergovernmental Relations, *Report M–47: Urban America and the Federal System: Commission Findings and Proposals* (Washington, D.C.: U.S. Government Printing Office, 1969).
61. *State Responsibility in Urban Regional Development: A Report to the Governors' Conference* (Chicago: Council of State Governments, 1962), pp. 16–22.
62. Douglas M. Fox, "Interest Groups in the Federal Policy Process," in Fox, *The New Urban Politics*, p. 103.
63. *Modernizing State Government* (New York: Committee for Economic Development, 1967).
64. *Modernizing Local Government* (New York: Committee for Economic Development, 1966).

65. *Reshaping Government in Metropolitan Areas* (New York: Committee for Economic Development, 1970).
66. Le May, "The States and Urban Areas," pp. 542–548.
67. Paul N. Ylvisaker, "The Growing Role of State Governments in Local Affairs," *State Government* 61 (Summer 1968): 150–156.
68. Le May, "The States and Urban Areas," pp. 542–548.
69. Harold Herman, *New York State and the Metropolitan Problem* (Philadelphia: University of Pennsylvania Press, 1963), pp. 178–188.
70. Alan Edward Bent, *Escape From Anarchy: A Strategy for Urban Survival* (Memphis, Tenn.: Memphis State University Press, 1972), p. 149. On the financial difficulties of UDC, see *New York Times*, March 16, 1975, sec. 8, p. 1.
71. Moynihan, "Toward a National Urban Policy."
72. National Advisory Commission on Civil Disorders, *Report* (Washington, D.C.: U.S. Government Printing Office, 1968), p. 1.
73. Domestic Council Committee on National Growth, *Report on National Growth, 1972* (Washington, D.C.: U.S. Government Printing Office, 1971), pp. ix–x.
74. Sundquist, *Making Federalism Work*, pp. 74–78; 81.
75. Kaplan, *Urban Planning in the 1960's*, pp. 109–118; Banfield, "Making a New Federal Program."
76. See Chapter 10, pp. 289–291. Also see Melvin B. Mogulof, *Governing Metropolitan Areas* (Washington, D.C.: The Urban Institute, 1971).
77. Mogulof, *Federal Regional Councils*.
78. Derthick, *New Towns in Town*.
79. See Stephen K. Bailey and Edith K. Mosher, *ESEA: The Office of Education Administers a Law* (Syracuse, N.Y.: Syracuse University Press, 1968); and Murphy, "The Education Bureaucracies Implement Novel Policy: The Politics of Title I of ESEA, 1965–1972."
80. *Minneapolis Tribune*, November 21, 1974, pp. 1–A and 5–A.
81. For a more elaborate discussion of this comparison of the Apollo mission with urban programs, see Anthony James Catanese, *Planners and Local Politics: Impossible Dreams*, vol. VII of SAGE Library of Social Research (Beverly Hills, Calif.: SAGE Publications, 1974), pp. 55–60.

Chapter 12

1. This position has been argued persuasively by Daniel Patrick Moynihan. See "Policy v. Programs in the '70's," *The Public Interest* 20 (Summer 1970): 90–100; and "Toward a National Urban Policy," *The Public Interest* 17 (Fall 1969): 3–20.
2. Ebenezer Howard, *Garden Cities of Tomorrow* (London: Faber and Faber, 1946; first published 1898).
3. Lloyd Rodwin, *Nations and Cities: A Comparison of Strategies for Urban Growth* (Boston: Houghton Mifflin, 1970), p. 112.
4. Rodwin, *Nations and Cities*, p. 120.
5. Ibid., p. 152.
6. Ibid., p. 153.
7. See T. W. Freeman, *The Conurbations of Great Britain* (Manchester: Manchester University Press, 1959), pp. 1–3.
8. Peter Hall, *The World Cities* (New York: McGraw-Hill, 1971), p. 31.
9. For a detailed examination of the creation of the Greater London Council, see Frank Smallwood, *Greater London: The Politics of Metropolitan Reform* (Indianapolis: Bobbs-Merrill, 1965).
10. David Gordon, "A View From the Centre: Property Survey," *The Economist* 246 (March 25, 1973): 38.
11. Rodwin, *Nations and Cities*, pp. 167–168.
12. Ibid., p. 168.
13. Hall, *The World Cities*, p. 82.

14. Ibid., p. 89.
15. Rodwin, *Nations and Cities*, p. 198.
16. Reported in *The Minneapolis Tribune*, May 27, 1973, p. 8–B.
17. Rodwin, *Nations and Cities*, p. 216.
18. The data sources for these figures on the emerging Brazilian megalopolis can be found in John J. Harrigan, "The Emerging Megalopolis in Brazil and What is Being Done About It," a paper presented to the Rocky Mountain Council for Latin American Studies, Lubbock, Texas, April 1974.
19. Irving Louis Horowitz, "Electoral Politics, Urbanization, and Social Development in Latin America," in *The Urban Explosion in Latin America*, ed. Glen H. Beyer (Ithaca, N.Y.: Cornell University Press, 1967) pp. 215–253.
20. See Rollie E. Poppino, "Brasil: novo modelo para o desenvolvimento nacional," *Revista Brasileira de Estudos Politicos* 36 (Julho 1973): 105–114.
21. On the Rio de Janeiro *favelas*, see Anthony Leeds and Elizabeth Leeds, "Brazil and the Myth of Urban Rurality: Urban Experience, Work and Values in 'Squatments' of Rio de Janeiro and Lima," in *City and Country in the Third World*, ed. Arthur J. Field (Cambridge, Mass.: Schenkman, 1970), pp. 229–285.
22. Jose Arthur Rios, "Social Transformation and Urbanization: The Case of Rio de Janeiro," Center Discussion Paper no. 24 (Milwaukee, Wis.: The University of Wisconsin-Milwaukee, Center for Latin America, December 11, 1971).
23. John J. Harrigan, "Some Racial Implications of Urban and Regional Planning in Brazil," a paper presented to the Midwest Association for Latin American Studies meeting at Terre Haute, Indiana, October 1973.
24. See John J. Harrigan, "Political Economy and the Management of Urban Development in Brazil," in *Urbanization and Inequality: The Political Economy of Urban Development in Latin American Urban Research*, vol. 5, ed. Wayne A. Cornelius and Felicity M. Trueblood (Beverly Hills, Calif: SAGE Publications, 1975).
25. Poppino, "Brasil: novo modelo para o desenvolvimento nacional," pp. 109–111.

Chapter 13

1. This distinction between the efficacy of the Apollo program and the inefficacy of urban programs is elaborated more fully by Anthony James Catanese, *Planners and Local Politics: Impossible Dreams*, vol. VII of the SAGE Library of Social Research (Beverly Hills, Calif.: SAGE Publications, 1974), pp. 55–60.
2. A more elaborate discussion of the concept of political culture can be found in Gabriel A. Almond and Sidney Verba, *The Civic Culture: Political Attitudes and Democracy in Five Nations* (Boston: Little, Brown, 1965), chapter 1, "An Approach to Political Culture." A short compendium of survey research findings on American opinions on a variety of issues over the past generation is compiled by Rita James Simon, *Public Opinion in America: 1936–1970* (Chicago: Rand McNally, 1974). The acquisition of political attitudes and the transmission of the political culture to new generations is referred to as *political socialization*. For a discussion of these processes see Kenneth P. Langton, *Political Socialization* (New York: Oxford University Press, 1969).
3. See Herman E. Daley, ed., *Toward a Steady-State Economy* (San Francisco: W. H. Freeman, 1972).
4. The Portola Institute, Inc., *The Last Whole Earth Catalog* (New York: Random House, 1971). See the catalogue's statement of purpose, p. 1.
5. United States Department of Commerce, Bureau of the Census, *Current Population Reports*, ser. P-20, no. 273, "Mobility of the Population of the United States, March 1970 to March 1974" (Washington, D.C.: U.S. Government Printing Office, December 1974), pp. 1–2.
6. Ben Wattenberg, *The Real America* (New York: Doubleday, 1974).
7. Daley, *Toward a Steady-State Economy*.

Index of Names

This is an index of names of authors and other persons mentioned in the text. Page references for subjects mentioned in the text can be found in the subject index. The letter n after the page number indicates that the reference is to a footnote or an endnote.

Aaron, Henry J., 333n
Addams, Jane, 102, 414n
Adonis, Joe, 71
Adrian, Charles, 125, 415n, 416n, 420n, 423n, 428n
Agger, Robert E., 416n
Alford, Robert R., 415n
Alger, Horatio, 85
Alioto, Joseph, 69
Allen, Edward J., 409n
Allswang, John M., 91
Almond, Gabriel, 403n, 435n
Altshuler, Alan, 168, 292, 420n, 429n
Anderson, Martin, 338
Angus, Edward I., 406n
Anton, T. J., 416n
Apter, David E., 403n
Asbury, Herbert, 410n
Asbell, Bernard, 417n

Bachrach, Peter, 14n, 167, 417n, 419n
Bailey, Harry A., 90
Bailey, Stephen, 432n, 434n
Baldinger, Stanley, 269, 428n
Banfield, Edward, 64, 88, 91, 101–102, 107n, 136, 147, 153, 199, 200, 201, 258, 280, 307, 338, 405n, 408n, 411n, 412n, 413n, 414n, 418n, 419n, 423n, 427n, 428n, 430n, 431n
Baratz, Morton S., 14n, 167, 417n, 419n
Barnes, Philip W., 292, 431n
Baron, Harold, 419n
Beals, Carleton, 407n
Beckman, Norman, 433n
Bell, Daniel, 71, 410n
Bellush, Jewell, 142n, 338, 418n, 430n, 432n
Bent, Alan Edward, 431n, 434n
Berger, Bennett, 194, 420n
Bernd, Joseph L., 126
Berube, Maurice R., 419n
Beyer, Glenn, 435n
Beyle, Thad L., 429n
Binder, Leonard, 403n
Black, Gordon, 415n

Blair, George S., 415n
Blauner, Robert, 419n
Blumberg, Leonard, 174n
Bollens, John C., 212n, 421n, 423n, 427n, 428n, 429n
Booth, David A., 425n
Bradburn, Norman M., 174n
Brisson, L., 410n
Bromage, Arthur W., 425n
Brown, A. Theodore, 44, 406n
Brown, Seyom, 411n
Bryant, R. W. G., 343n
Burchard, John, 406n
Burgess, Ernest W., 421n
Burks, David D., 8n
Byrd, Harry Flood, 83

Campbell, Alan K., 338
Campbell, Angus, 178, 421n
Canty, Donald, 174n
Capers, Gerald M., Jr., 405n
Capone, Al, 69, 72
Carlson, R., 410n
Carney, Francis M., 414n
Carver, Joan, 269, 427n
Catanese, Anthony James, 292, 434n, 435n
Cervantes, A. J., 249, 251
Chapin, F. Stuart, Jr., 430n
Chenkin, Alvin, 411n
Cion, Richard M., 222, 424n
Clague, Christopher, 415n
Clark, Joseph S., 410n
Clark, Peter, 417n
Clark, Ramsey, 68, 71n, 410n
Clark, Terry N., 123, 415n
Cleveland, Grover, 103
Cloward, Richard A., 200, 239–240n, 423n, 431n
Coates, Charles H., 417n
Colcord, Frank, 339, 417n, 430n, 432n
Coles, Robert, 419n
Colman, William, 415n
Connally, Harold X., 421n
Converse, Philip E., 421n
Cook, Fred J., 126
Cornelius, Wayne A., 435n
Cornwell, Elmer E., 59n, 81n, 408n, 413n

Corty, Floyd C., 244, 425n
Corzine, John, 422n, 424n
Coser, Lewis, 412n
Costanti, Edmond, 414n
Costello, Frank, 71
Cox, George B. "Boss," 86
Crecine, John P., 430n
Crenson, Matthew, 417n
Cressey, Donald R., 410n
Croker, Richard, 58n, 82
Crotty, William, Jr., 413n
Crump, Edward "Boss," 93
Curley, James, 25, 93

Dahl, Robert A., 14n, 134, 135–136, 139, 150, 404n, 407n, 416n
Daley, Herman E., 435n
Daley, Richard C., 58n, 109n, 118, 150, 305
Danielson, Michael N., 310, 433n
D'Antonio, William V., 416n
Davidoff, Paul, 283
Davis, James Leslie, 406n
Davis, Kingsley, 25n, 405n
Davis, Rennard, 419n
Dawson, William, 87, 118
De Grove, John M., 269, 425n
Demereth, Nicholas J., 432n
Dentler, Robert A., 430n
Derthick, Martha, 338, 431n
De Sapio, Carmine, 62–63
Diggins, John P., 62n
Dillon, John F., 418n
Dinnerstein, Leonard, 409n
Dobriner, William, 421n
Doig, Jameson W., 424n
Dolbeare, Kenneth, 7, 16n, 17, 403n, 404n
Donaldson, Scott, 194, 420n
Downes, Bryan T., 422n
Downs, Anthony, 403n, 404n
Doxiadis, C. A., 24, 405n
Dyckman, John W., 431n
Dye, Thomas R., 321n, 403n, 421n

Easton, David, 403n, 404n
Edelman, Murray, 8, 404n
Edwards, Stephen, 411n

436

Index of Subjects

9 -200